BBC:
Brainwashing Britain?

How and why the BBC controls your mind

David Sedgwick

Sandgrounder

First Printing, 2018

ISBN-978-1-9993591-0-2

Sandgrounder Publishing

To Sharon and O
for all their help and patience

Contents

PART FOUR CASE STUDIES

CONCLUSION

Acknowledgements

Nineteen Eighty-Four by George Orwell (Copyright © George Orwell, 1949) Reprinted by permission of Bill Hamilton as the Literary Executor of the Estate of the Late Sonia Brownell Orwell. © Robin Aitken, 2007, Can We Trust the BBC? Reprinted by permission of Continuum Publishing, an imprint of Bloomsbury Publishing Plc. With thanks to OUP for permission to quote from 'Brainwashing: The Science of Thought Control.' Thanks to CPS for permission to quote from 'Confessions of a Reformed BBC Producer.' Thanks to Biteback for permission to quote from 'When One Door Closes' and 'Getting Out Alive: News, Sport and Politics at the BBC.'

Thanks to the many people who have helped with the production of this book including friends and family as well as the people of Malmö, Sweden all of whom generously donated their time and patience.

There was one other thing I did feel uncomfortable about when I joined [the BBC], and still do. I've been on two courses and each time there seemed to be an attempt being made by somebody to do a job of **brainwashing**.

Tom Burns, The BBC:
Public Institution and Private World

For more than sixty years the BBC had played a leading role in **brainwashing** the middle classes. Its regime of moderation and good sense . . . had been an elaborate cover behind which it imposed an ideology of passivity and self-restraint. The BBC had defined the national culture, a swindle in which the middle classes had colluded, assuming that moderation and civic responsibility were in their own interest.

J.G. Ballard,
Millennium People

'What is our [BBC] job? Is it our job to report the news, or is it our job to **brainwash** the population?'

Robin Aitken,
Can we Trust the BBC?

Introduction

When devils will the blackest sins put on
They do suggest at first with heavenly shows

Othello, William Shakespeare

Anyone spending time on social media these days can't but help notice a growing mood of scepticism towards what is commonly known as the mainstream media, or MSM for short. The little people are frustrated. They feel cheated somehow, duped, disregarded, reviled even. The worms appear to be turning. Before the birth of the Internet the plebs took everything they heard from the MSM as the gospel truth - they had little choice. And then along came the Internet – Facebook, Twitter *et al.*

Things would never be the same again.

Britain's own lynchpin of all things mainstream, the BBC, has found itself under scrutiny like never before. 'Why should I as a licence payer,' asked a social media user of BBC News one day, 'have your biased reporting shoved down my throat?' Strong stuff: 'biased reporting' is bad enough, but to be forcibly fed this stuff? There's plenty more where that came from: 'As for the BBC,' notes a Disqus user, 'I can't bring myself to bother watching anything they broadcast now - every single thing they produce is an exercise in social engineering no matter the topic.' And then there's this: 'Keep it up BBC. Watching you dig your own grave makes better viewing than 99% of the programmes you make.' Another Disqus user summarises the situation thus:

> I never hardly watch anything from the BBC these days....it's all total drivel. Even the 'comedy' is rubbish now.....it's just not funny. And the News is always left-wing propaganda! And documentaries are usually 'historically inaccurate' being always MARXIST inspired revisionist drivel. Their costume dramas are merely an exercise in historical revisionism to promote the multi-cult Marxist dystopia.

Volumes upon volumes of books could be filled with comments such as these. 'Multi-cult Marxist dystopia . . ?' Clearly, something is not quite right here, and has not been since at least 2016 and beyond. The election of Donald Trump as US president and the UK's vote to leave the EU has, it would appear, heralded in a new age of consciousness in a hitherto docile public:

> **@Anon**
> Would we have known just how infested the BBC are with
> left wing propaganda? Brexit has been the awakening for
> many, including me.

The more it attacks the US president and the more it attempts to undermine Brexit, suspicions that have been hitherto vague began to crystallise: how does the BBC's claim to be an impartial, politically neutral broadcaster square with its continuous, at time petty and vindictive attacks on the democratically-elected president of the United States? If the broadcaster is indeed a 'national' voice representative of the country as a whole, why has it been doing everything in its power to undermine the outcome of the 2016 EU Referendum in which some 17.4 million citizens expressed a desire to leave the union?

> **@Anon**
> Brexit has exposed the BBC for what it is. Its time is up.

The mask appears to be slipping, the 'heavenly show' not quite so alluring, the proclamations not quite so convincing.

And so social media echoes to the sound of BBC bashing: *Brussels Broadcasting Corporation, British Bullshitting Corporation, Bolshevik Broadcasting Corporation*, not forgetting our own particular favourite (and inspiration for this book) *British Brainwashing Corporation*. These are just some of the more printable interpretations of the BBC acronym seen on the net. While the broadcaster has always had its critics, this is unchartered territory. Antipathy towards the corporation is visceral. 'I'm getting really fed up with the complaints and criticisms being directed at BBC News at the moment,' writes the BBC's John Simpson. 'Not so much from our usual critics . . . No – it's middle-of-the-roaders who are doing the complaining now.'[1] But it never used to be this way.

In the not too distant past Britain's national broadcaster basked in the adulation from a tame, almost naïve public. Everybody, or so it seemed, depended on the BBC. Some even adored it. In reference to its sensible, pragmatic approach to all things, Britain's post-war media playfully dubbed the corporation 'Auntie.' The name stuck. Through war and peace, Auntie remained a calm, authoritative voice even though some had started to feel uneasy with its claim to be an independent organisation, free of government interference. Reservations aside, the BBC was undoubtedly the voice of the people. By the 1950s it had carved out a niche in the British psyche so deep, so secure, that the adoption of 'Auntie' merely sealed its unique status within Britain and beyond. The question of trust would never have even occurred. Fast forward to 2018.

The calls to scrap the television licence fee grow ever louder. Accusations of bias and misconduct abound. From stories littered with inaccuracies and glaring omissions hardly a day goes by without Britain's 'national' broadcaster finding itself up to its eyeballs in yet more controversy. 'We managed to laugh our way through every crisis – and you get a lot at the BBC,' recalls former Director General Greg Dyke.[2] As we shall see in this book, the reasons for this situation run deep, much deeper than mere incompetency. Lessons can always be learnt from mistakes which are genuine. Deliberate 'errors' are another matter altogether.

The modern BBC is an entirely different animal than it was back in the 1950s when Auntie seemed to capture its essence so deftly. The modern organisation is in fact barely recognisable to its 1970s or even 1980s incarnations. Something has changed – is changing. The purpose of this book is to investigate the reasons that underpin this dramatic transformation. With its enthusiasm for all things liberal and 'progressive', to the ordinary man and woman in the street the 'national' broadcaster arguably feels ever more remote, ever more detached from their own reality than at any time in the corporation's near 100-year history.

Has the BBC become then, as some insist, the broadcasting arm of *The Guardian*, a newspaper that barely hides its contempt for the British working classes and its culture ('Down with fish and chips, the most disgusting meal on Earth') 'The Guardian isn't the BBC's favourite newspaper for nothing,' notes ex-BBC presenter Peter Sissons.[3] If this assertion is true, then the broadcaster is taking its cue from a paper that in terms of circulation lags way behind those of *The Mail* and *The Sun,* Britain's most popular daily's. Bottom line: The vast majority of UK citizens do not read *The Guardian* - presumably because they disagree with what they perceive to be its elitist, left-wing, anti-British values. In 2016, the Guardian Media Group made losses of nearly £70 million followed by a £90 million black hole in 2017.[4] For those who care to look, the writing would appear to be on the wall.

Minority views or not, the broadcaster remains a big fan. A former BBC executive confirms as much when observing that '90 per cent' of BBC staff used to 'take home' either *The Guardian* or *Independent.*[5] Later in the book we will analyse the BBC mind-set in more detail. For now it is enough to appreciate that Britain's 'national' broadcaster appears to share the worldview of a newspaper forced to beg its dwindling readership to donate funds in order for it to continue to produce 'quality' journalism that, amongst other things, snipes at working class culture and tradition.

The wisdom of a national broadcaster parroting the opinions of what is a fringe, left-wing newspaper and re-packaging them up as objective news and comment is at best a questionable strategy, suicidal at worst. Funded by a licence fee paid by people of all political denominations as well as social classes, only the blindest or most arrogant of operators would pursue a course of action guaranteed to alienate a significant majority of the UK population. Moreover, a politicised national broadcaster is the very antithesis to the public service broadcasting ethos of representation and inclusivity. Why should an audience have *The Guardian* (or Independent) minority worldview 'shoved down its throat?' Avoiding the media stranglehold of Britain's 'national' broadcaster is not that easy however. As far as influence is concerned BBC reach is simply staggering:

Television

- 8 national stations (BBC 1, BBC 2 etc.)
- 6 regional stations (N. Ireland, Scotland etc.)
- 14 local stations (BBC One London, BBC One North West etc.)
- 14 international stations (BBC America, BBC Persian etc.)

Radio

- 11 national stations (BBC Radio 1, BBC 5 Live etc.)
- 8 regional stations (BBC Radio Scotland, BBC Radio Cymru etc.)
- 50 local stations (BBC Essex, BBC Newcastle etc.)
- 130+ world capital cities receive BBC World Service

Internet

- 24 million – followers of BBC World News Twitter feed
- 38 million – followers BBC Breaking Twitter feed

Add to this BBC Asian Network, BBC Film, BBC 24 News, BBC Parliament and a multitude of online services and the scope of this organisation soon becomes apparent.

The BBC frequently leads the national debate. Its 6 'o clock and 10 o' clock news bulletins can promote a given topic to such an extent it becomes an instant talking point not only amongst suburban housewives in Surrey, but among cabinet ministers too. BBC talking points can be instantly disseminated around the world via its .co.uk and .com portals - websites regularly ranked inside the world's top 100 in terms of footfall. This is a serious level of influence.

The corporation boasts that it reaches 96% of the British public each week in some form or other and that its services are accessed 140 million times a day.[6] Not satisfied with this platform, it is plotting further expansion. As recently as 2016 the broadcaster extended its overseas reach to include services in 11 new languages including Korean, Pidgin, Yoruba and Punjabi. By 2022 the BBC claims its services will reach an estimated 500 million people worldwide.[7] 'The land grab is spear-headed by the BBC,' noted a rueful James Murdoch in his 2009 MacTaggart Lecture when discussing the theme of media expansionism, 'The scale and scope of its current activities and future ambitions is chilling.' Sooner or later the British Broadcasting Corporation will catch up with you.

And this is where it gets rather worrying. What if the British Broadcasting Corporation were to fall into the wrong hands – ideologically driven hands? That's an awful lot of power for the wrong hands to wield. Thankfully, our 'national' broadcaster operates with absolute integrity and would not dream of abusing its unique position of trust, Guardian fixation notwithstanding. 'The BBC is impartial, free and fair,' so claimed its North America reporter Jon Sopel to much hilarity once upon a time. Phew! If Mr Sopel's words do not convince, this is the corporation's own Director General:

> The BBC produces some of the nation's most loved television
> and radio and the most trusted news.[8]

Nor is this just the perception of a single, partisan BBC mandarin. Those wishing to 'Learn how the BBC is working to strengthen trust and transparency in online news,' will find comfort in the assertion that,

> Research shows ... compared to other broadcasters, newspapers
> and online sites, the BBC is seen as by far the most trusted and
> impartial news provider in the UK.[9]

'Impartial, free and fair,' 'most trusted news,' 'most loved,' 'by far the most trusted and impartial news provider in the UK' - the same memes keep cropping up, over and over again. The broadcaster clearly feels the need to convince the public. But doth not the lady – dear old Auntie – protest just a little too much? Happy, content individuals tend not to go around telling everyone how happy and content they are. It shows. We mark it in their actions and demeanour.

Brits should certainly be thankful their 'national' broadcaster is so ethical. An unscrupulous broadcaster – an ideologically driven broadcaster - could so easily infiltrate our minds. Sat on our sofas glued to the television set, evening after evening, are we not sitting ducks, prime candidates for what is colloquially known as brainwashing?

In her book *Brainwashing: The Science of Thought Control*, Kathleen Taylor offers the following enhanced definition of a term that conjures up all kinds of sinister images:

> At its heart (brainwashing) is a malignant idea ...
> it seeks to control not only how people act, but what they
> think. It arouses our deepest fears, threatening the loss of
> freedom and even identity.

Have you for a single minute considered that you could fall victim to such a phenomenon? Probably not. Have we got news for you . . .

When we watch the BBC 6 o' clock or 10 o' clock news, we assume the images that we see and the commentary that we hear is somehow accurate and truthful, untainted by subjectivity, bias or prejudice. Wrong. 'There's no such thing as "pure news," asserts Simon Jenkins:

> Everything you read in a newspaper or hear on a radio, every
> question asked and answered, is the outcome of a human
> decision to accord it priority over another item.[10]

In their analysis of mass media, Chomsky and Herman make the same point when observing that, 'The raw material of news must pass through successive filters, leaving only the cleaned residue fit to print.'[11]

Our tastes are clearly being cultivated. The question is why, by whom and to what ends? From stories asserting post-Brexit shortages in sperm and fresh sandwiches to the march of the Third Reich, mainstream news provides a daily diet of carefully processed soundbites. 'Stop watching the news' advises Morrissey in *Spent the day in bed* because, 'news contrives to frighten you,' and makes people feel 'small' and 'alone.'

But why would anybody wish to frighten us? Why would anybody wish to make us feel alone? In a thorough investigation of the dark art of mind control, Guy Arnold supplies a possible reason:

> Stress is a pre-requisite for brainwashing and the more
> anxious the subject the greater the likelihood they will be
> induced to believe what otherwise they would have dismissed
> as fancy or propaganda.[12]

Thus, cumulative exposure to stress (e.g. the news) awash with apocalyptic warnings – climate change, Nazis, Russians, Brexit, Trump, the NHS etc. – jangles the nerves to such an extent it may impair our faculty for reason and logic. Put bluntly, constant exposure softens us up; defences drop. We become that extra bit vulnerable. Anxiety usurps rationality. If there are those who would hijack our minds, there is no better way than ensuring we remain on a knife edge - nerves shot, optimism ebbing.

Yet as Arnold points out, the majority of British citizens would flatly reject the notion they could be victims of brainwashing. Brits, argues Arnold, believe such skulduggery to be the sole preserve of Johnny foreigner, presumably because he/she operates with fewer scruples than we do. Besides, this is Britain. Things like that don't happen here. It's just not cricket. However, just because we are not languishing in a bare cell somewhere deep in enemy territory does not mean we are immune, far from it. The fact that we are so certain we are *not* susceptible paradoxically may make us perfect candidates. 'Come on in. Relax. We'll start the brainwashing in just a minute,' said no brainwasher ever.

Brainwashing might not be happening in some dingy subterranean prison to a backdrop of flashlights and sleep deprivation, it might in fact be happening a little closer to home: in our lounges, kitchens and bedrooms. Imagine if you were being subjected to this psychological violation whenever you switched on the television, radio or logged onto the Internet. That would be a pretty sinister prospect in itself. But it could get even worse. The perpetrators might not necessarily be our enemies. The brainwashers might be the worst kind of foe imaginable – one that purports to be a friend, a trusted friend with 'a smiling face,' one who swears she's impartial, free and fair. While escape from the POW camp is theoretically possible, just try escaping from an entity as ubiquitous as a state broadcaster.

Undeniably, every time we consume BBC content we are exposing ourselves to its values, so it is just as well those values are so wholesome, so beyond reproach, so impartial. The BBC concluded the late Tony Benn MP, 'stands in a position of almost unique and unchallenged influence.'[13] Arguably BBC influence dwarfs even that of government. 'Shadow' government might not be that far from the reality of a potentially troubling proposition: the 'national' broadcaster wields enormous power, but unlike government is not elected and can therefore never be removed, at least not at any ballot box. We can only thank our lucky stars then that Auntie is so impartial and so scrupulously fair. We are lucky in Britain to have such an honest aunt. Many other countries are not so lucky. As long ago as the 1970s there were those in the United

States who expressed concerns regarding the growing power of television networks, influence it was feared could challenge and ultimately supersede that of government. US television networks it was argued back then:

> Are probably now beyond the check of any institution in
> our society. The President, the Congress of the United States . . .
> I think they may now be so powerful that they're beyond the
> check of anyone.[14]

If Auntie is also beyond the check of anyone, then it's a jolly good thing her ethics are so impeccable. Let's thank our lucky stars that our 'national' broadcaster is so different to its American counterparts. Funded directly by the people it serves, the BBC would never dream of emulating America's media giants who invariably provide a highly partisan view of the world to subscribers. Unlike its American counterparts the BBC is impartial. It does not have nor is it permitted to espouse political opinions.

Well, that's the theory.

'Part of my learning curve working for BBC news,' writes former presenter Peter Sissons in his memoirs, 'was discovering what a deeply political organisation it is.'[15] It appears that Mr Sissons was somewhat taken aback by the culture he encountered at Broadcasting House. The former host of the BBC's Question Time programme goes on to reveal that the corporation in fact holds 'views on everything.' Another ex-employee concurs with Sissons. Not only does Robin Aitken agree with the view that the BBC is a highly political organisation, he also suggests that the corporation exploits its position as a national institute: 'Its prestige and reputation hoodwink people into believing that in some way the BBC is 'above politics.'[16]

Hoodwink: To deceive, to swindle, to fool, to trick . . .

Could it possibly be true? Could Britain's state broadcaster really have ulterior motives – underhand ones at that? That, dear reader, is a question for you to grapple with. We are impartial in such matters. All we know is that in 2018 dissatisfaction with the state broadcaster appears to be at record levels. The purpose of this book is therefore to investigate claims that the BBC has gone native, wilfully ignoring its royal charter obligations in order to promote an ultra-progressive Guardian agenda of which it wholeheartedly approves: feminism, mass migration, The European Union, transgenderism etc. And that in doing so it subjects traditional (conservative) opinion to scorn, disdain and even hostility. From here we should be able to assess whether the broadcaster targets specific groups that do not agree with its worldview, 'wrong-thinkers' as we shall call them hereafter.

It has been suggested that one group in particular sharing some or all of the following characteristics has become the main targets of BBC attacks:

- Conservative
- Christian
- White
- Male
- Working class
- Patriot
- Pro-life
- Brexit supporter

We'll leave it to our readers to decide what, if any validity there is in such claims. Our objective, like that of our impartial counterparts at the BBC, is simply to present the facts. The rest is up to the reader.

For some readers then this book might prove to be a difficult, perhaps even traumatic journey. Think about it: imagine discovering that your dear old Auntie whose wisdom you have counted on for years – decades perhaps – and whose counsel you had sought so often, might not be quite as cuddly and reliable as you had once thought, a proposition hinted at by Neil Postman who warns,

> In the age of advanced technology, spiritual devastation is more likely to come from an enemy with a smiling face than from one whose countenance exudes suspicion and hate.[17]

From dance offs, bake offs and sing offs, the 'British' Broadcasting Corporation effortlessly draws us into its extravaganza. We not only invite the BBC into our homes, but we also invite the broadcaster into our minds. 'Tyrants of all varieties,' continues Postman, 'have always known about the value of providing the masses with amusements as a means of pacifying discontent.'

Imagine then if those yarns dear old Auntie had spun and continues to spin, and which you enjoyed so much through childhood (and adulthood) had not been so innocent or so spontaneous after all, but built upon a tissue of falsehoods. Imagine if that smiling face hid a secret: the woman who had so enthralled you – honest Aunt - had in fact been trying to deceive, mislead and trick you all these years. Think how it might feel to discover she had in fact been engaged in a sustained and cynical attempt to undermine everything you hold dear. Moreover, imagine if it transpired that your lovable old Auntie, the cuddly, smiling woman you had loved and trusted all these years, actually despised you.

Note on the text

Social media posts are used throughout the text and are reproduced in their original form. Quotes presented as @Anon are taken from various social media platforms and may therefore contain syntax, spelling and grammatical anomalies. Several quotations also retain their original US spellings.

PART ONE
CONTEXT

> We [BBC employees] were not Marxists,
> but accepted a lot of Marxist social analysis.[1]
>
> *Antony Jay*
> *Confessions of a Reformed BBC Producer*

The BBC and The Marxists

If you wish to get to the heart of an organisation, what better way than to listen to what people are saying about it? In our research into the BBC, certain words and phrases tend to crop up on a regular basis, e.g. biased, anti-British, globalist, elitist etc. And then there's another term that crops up even more regularly, one whose meaning might not be immediately evident. This from social media:

> I stopped watching BBC news 7 years ago, the same time I
> stopped paying for a licence. The rot was evident back then.
> Anybody who now pays a licence fee is directly funding 24-7 far
> left anti-British, globalist propaganda and **cultural Marxism**.

Consider too the following observations from various other social media users:

> **Cultural Marxism** is clearly out of control at the @BBC -
> the place where common sense goes to die.

> BBC is completely in thrall to **cultural Marxism**. It is what guides
> and informs all its actions. It is not in any way representative of
> us!

Is it reasonable to ask us all to pay a licence fee to fund a BBC that strives so hard to alienate so many people with its **cultural Marxism**?

#BBC is an odious propaganda channel for the Left, **cultural Marxism** at OUR expense

This from a piece entitled, 'The BBC's Cultural Marxism will trigger an American-style backlash:

What really disturbs me is that the BBC is, in every corpuscle of its corporate body, against the values of conservatism, with a small "c", which, I would argue, just happens to be the values held by millions of Britons. Thus it exercises a kind of "**cultural Marxism**" in which it tries to undermine that conservative society by turning all its values on their heads.[2]

Whatever cultural Marxism may or may not be, many people believe it plays a pivotal role within the modern BBC. In order to inform our investigation into the organisation, 'cultural Marxism' would seem as good a place as any to start. Our first step thus takes us into the territory of political ideology, to a theory that has been suggested is responsible for much of the current problems and crises facing Western Europe.

So what is cultural Marxism? Despite the terminology, it is actually a fairly simple concept to grasp. The following Urban Dictionary definition has been voted the most popular amongst its users. Cultural Marxism is:

The gradual process of destroying all traditions, languages, religions, individuality, government, family, law and order in order to re-assemble society in the future as a communist utopia. This utopia will have no notion of gender, traditions, morality, god or even family or the state.

Take a look around. Does this description accord with the world you see? Are traditions being 'destroyed?' Is the notion of gender, to take one example, being redefined, radically so? Is religion no longer the opium of the people? The best way to decide whether cultural Marxism is real or imagined is to take a good look at what is happening around you and then decide. If you believe traditions are indeed being deliberately eroded then it is a theory that may strike a chord. If you believe that western European culture is under attack on multiple fronts from a collection of –ists: multiculturalists, feminists, Islamists, atheists and any number of activists agitating against masculinity, Christianity and even white ethnicity, cultural Marxism might feel more than just a theoretical abstraction.

> **@Anon**
> The BBC evening news is becoming increasingly unwatchable.
> It's deconstructing our nation and western life more generally.
> It pursues a post-modern agenda now which is benefitting our
> enemies and destabilising Britain. It is classic Marxist strategy.
> The pace of PC accelerates.

Being the impartial and fair organisation that we know ourselves to be, we will let the reader judge whether the BBC is indeed 'deconstructing our nation.' We'll also leave you to decide whether the corporation is in fact 'destabilising Britain.' Taking a leaf out of the BBC's book, we intend to remain impartial, free and fair at all times.

False consciousness

Before we can truly begin our quest to unravel the BBC, first we must travel back to inter-war Germany, to Frankfurt where a loosely connected group of intellectuals formed what has subsequently become known as the Frankfurt School. This group of Marxist intellectuals – self declared progressives – had a mission: to change the world, well America and Europe. The rest of the world didn't particularly interest them.

In 1923, Marxist intellectuals associated with the Communist Party of Germany founded the Institute of Social Research at Frankfurt University.[3] Severely piqued that the working classes had not risen up to overthrow their capitalist masters as their guru Karl Marx had so confidently predicted, the Frankfurt group put their collective heads together to work out why the promised communist revolution had in fact not happened. There was much to ponder. Far from joining together in

16

solidarity, during the First World War and in subsequent conflicts the working classes had in fact demonstrated a very disturbing loyalty to flag, King/Queen and country. Nationalism and patriotism were alive and kicking. The intellectuals were aghast. Rather than railing against the capitalist system the Frankfurt elites swore oppressed them, the working classes it seemed, aspired through hard work and endeavour to progress within that very system, to defend it even!

Marx's economic theory, predicated upon a system of exploitation wherein the weak (workers) were ruthlessly exploited by the strong (bosses) was falling apart. There had to be oppression going on somewhere! Without victims and exploitation there could be no revolution. Marxists needed to convince people – any people – that they were being ruthlessly exploited, and that the solution lay in revolution. The Great War had however severely disappointed. Conflict over, the vast majority of people simply wished to return to their former lives.

As it stood, Marxism was all but finished, so too the long anticipated revolution. The intellectual elites had seemingly projected their neuroses upon a class who did not share its outrage, its ideology less. An explanation (and solution) was needed. Frankfurters turned their attention from economics to culture. They soon found their reason: the working classes had been tricked into believing the world they lived in and experienced was not only 'normal' and 'real' but the only sort of world possible. These credulous souls suffered from what the Marxist's came to coin as 'false consciousness' - they uncritically accepted what they read in the media, heard at church and were taught at school etc. In other words, they were victims of their culture. They just didn't know it. It all made perfect sense, at least to progressive minds. What other explanation could there possibly be to account for the masses' indifference to the Marxist's revolutionary objectives? As John Carey eloquently puts it:

> Happily gobbling down the products of the commercialised 'culture industry', the masses had developed a 'false consciousness', so that they no longer saw things as the Frankfurt theorists wished.[4]

Given that culture was responsible for creating this working class vapidity, it would obviously need to change and change radically. The idea of a stable society - imperfections accepted - horrified the Frankfurt disciples who knew that dissatisfaction was the key to their ultimate goal: power. (Western) Culture was clearly the enemy to 'progress' (Marxism).

Fleeing 1930s Germany, the Frankfurt elite arrived in America and other parts of Europe, a Trojan horse intent on wreaking havoc. In order to gain entry to the US and not arouse suspicion, the intellectuals hid their communist sympathies. With its connotations of class warfare linked to soviet ideology, those announcing themselves as 'Marxists' would have not got much further than the turnstile at Ellis Island. The émigrés had started as they meant to go on: by concealing, cheating and lying. Over time this disparate group of dreamers and malcontents would duly come to adopt much more user-friendly terms such as 'progressive.' They would even appropriate the term 'liberal' though the ideology they sort to impose on the west was anything but liberal.

As it was, the infiltrators had arrived on enemy soil. It would only be a matter of time before they achieved their goal: to turn the American dream into a nightmare. 'Work in the system,' advised Saul Alinsky, doyen of American Communists and inspiration to Democratic politicians including Barack Obama and Hilary Clinton:

> That we accept the world as it is does not in any sense weaken our desire to change it into what we believe it should be. That means working in the system.[5]

By 1934 Columbia University had become an informal headquarters. Once safely inside the evil capitalist empire they sought to bring down, the Frankfurt émigrés assumed jobs in education and government - any sphere which presented them with the influence they craved and required. With its ability to inculcate young, malleable minds the US education system naturally became a prime target. In order to spread their ideology among young impressionable minds a conduit was required that could masquerade as an intellectual discipline while at the same time disseminating the Marxist's ideology without fear of censure. In Critical Theory the dissidents found a devastating weapon.

Critical Theory

Briefly, Critical Theory is a model of social and cultural analysis that is hostile to just about every tenet of western society: Christianity, capitalism, law and order, the family, morality, loyalty, patriotism, conservatism etc. It relentlessly attacks the foundations of the west i.e. The United States and Europe while studiously ignoring the rest of the world. For example, while insisting on Euro-American culpability re slavery, it ignores the very long and ignoble history of slavery both before and since the period c. 1600-1850. In order to facilitate this attack it attempts to stratify society into opposition groups: victims and perpetrators; oppressed and oppressors; abusers and abused etc.

Indeed, in its critique of western culture and society, Critical Theory has succeeded in creating a vast range of polarised categories all of which it attempts to place in violent opposition to one another: men v women; rich v poor; black v white; able-bodied v handicapped; heterosexual v homosexual; Christian v Muslim etc. The key is sensitisation. Critical Theory relies on making people hyper sensitive to questions of race, gender, religion, sexuality etc. The aim is to create a sense of difference, thereafter alienation. When society can be fragmented into multifarious sub-groups, and from here persuaded all such groups are victims of a dominant culture, Marxists are halfway to achieving their nefarious aims. In Marxist terminology this strategy is known as divide and rule. Only by first destabilising society (divide) can Marxists hope to take control (rule). Create a problem – capitalist western society – and then offer a solution (Marxism/Communism). The Frankfurt elitists and their heirs just needed to convince these disparate groups that any woes or grievances they had were solely due to the inherent structures of western society e.g. church, school, nuclear family etc. Furthermore, individuals could now be encouraged to devolve any sense of personal responsibility, to blame an oppressive society. The seeds of victimhood were being sown that would one day blossom into grievance culture and identity politics.

If sufficient dissatisfaction and despair could be created among the populace, if it could be convinced that the current system was rotten, the way would be paved for the Marxists and their special brand of totalitarianism to take over. Easier said than done. For who but the most naïve would fall for such trickery? Surely the majority of decent, hard-working people would soon shut this dogma down? Like any other ideology, Marxism is a political construct, and as such is rarely supported by the reality of everyday life.

Undoubtedly aware of the many shortcomings of their own ideology, and in order to crush the dissent they knew must follow, the Marxists had another trick up their sleeves: political correctness. By carefully defining the limits of public discourse, by controlling exactly what ideas could or could not be articulated, Marxists could ensure the tenets of their fraudulent ideology would remain unchallenged. Opposition could now be shut down. 'Political correctness has become an intolerant creed,' so wrote Paul Dacre in *The Guardian*, 'enabling a self-appointed elite to impose its minority values on the great majority.'[6] Terms such as 'racist' and 'bigot' proved immensely successful when it came to protecting cultural Marxism from any kind of scrutiny. The march towards hopelessness – power - could continue unmolested.

In his pamphlet 'Rules for Radicals' Saul Alinsky puts the case explicitly enough. Marxists must aim to demoralise because:

> Any revolutionary change must be preceded by a passive,
> affirmative, non-challenging attitude toward change among
> the mass of our people. They must feel so frustrated, so defeated,
> so lost, so futureless in the prevailing system that they are willing
> to let go of the past and chance the future.[7]

Political correctness and later its heir 'hate speech' were calculated to do just this: turn people into a 'passive, affirmative, non-challenging' mass. Later Alinsky notes that those wishing to herald in a new system – *his* system - must be prepared to 'agitate, create disenchantment and discontent with the current values.'

Marxists stepped up their attack on 'current values.' Any individual or organisation advocating traditional values became the cultural Marxist's deadliest enemy. Politicians and political parties supporting the concept of patriotism and nationhood, the nuclear family and a moral code based on the Christian church were not only to be opposed, but viciously attacked. The drive to alienate people from those institutions which perpetuated 'false consciousness' – family, church, school - any institution that held society together had begun in earnest.

With its enthusiasm for all things radical and anti-establishment, what better place to start than at the American (and later European) university campus, homes to an endless supply of naïve young minds only too willing to help create the poisonous atmosphere dreamed of by Alinsky and his Frankfurt allies.

'We've lost our higher education'

'The indoctrination that occurs in American universities is one of the keys to the left holding and maintaining power in America,' declared US Senator Rick Santorum in 2012. 'We've lost our higher education, that was the first to go a long time ago,' the Republican presidential candidate went on to tell a crowd in Naples, Florida.[8] America was waking up, but far too late. By 2012 the infiltration had been complete for decades. American college campuses had been hotbeds of discord and unrest for some time as students, egged on by their professors, enthusiastically embraced the tenets of critical theory. A new generation of American students were thus doing exactly what the Communists wanted them to do: rejecting their own culture, tradition and antecedents.

It had however been a close call: 'Few of us (Communists) survived the Joe McCarthy holocaust of the early 1950s,' notes Alinsky in reference to what became known as 'The Red Scare' era of American politics when the senator had played a leading role in the investigation of individuals thought to have Communist/Marxist sympathies. But Alinsky and a few others *had survived . . .*'[9]

This educational rot soon spread from the US to Western Europe. The communists had correctly identified that the very tolerance that marked western liberalism out from just about every other political system in the world, from South American juntas to middle-east dictatorships, also happened to be its Achilles heel. Although it didn't know it, the west was vulnerable. A former teacher in Britain's secondary school system recalled how, according to his colleagues:

> Anyone who votes for the Conservative Party is "thick", the British Empire was "unambiguously evil" and capitalism leads to "mass inequality and misery for the vast majority of working people." The only answer was, you guessed it — the adoption of socialism, presumably led by a bunch of corduroy-wearing,

21

Little Red Book carrying school teachers. As the only right-of-centre teacher in the history department, I found lunchtimes particularly galling.[10]

Later, the same teacher, found himself 'being dismissed for holding the wrong views . . .' It is a picture familiar throughout the entire western European education system, from primary through to higher education institutes. How far and how quickly the termites had burrowed into the system:

@MichaelCrick
A teacher at the Resolution Foundation meeting said she
is a Tory but has to keep very quiet about it at her school.
"You go into the staff room, and it's like a socialist convention."

The Marxists were slowly achieving that which they had set out to do: transform the west into a world re-shaped in their own image, a world run by people like 'us' solely for the benefit of people like 'us' – a select band of elitist right-thinkers whose superior intellect naturally bestowed upon them the right to govern, lead and dominate others. It was the natural order. Though they preached equality, fraternity, brother/sisterhood and any number of utopian ideals, the aim of the cultural Marxists was and remains anything but egalitarian.

'We are not interested in the good of others,' declares a character from the totalitarian Party of Orwell's *1984*, 'we are interested solely in power.'[11] The manifestos, espousals and promises were simply the means to an end. Their messages might have been strewn with calls for tolerance, but once in power tolerance was the last thing these authoritarians had in mind. At its core Marxism is simply a way of replacing one form of bondage with another, ideological bondage in place of capitalist bondage. The working classes would simply exchange one class of masters for another.

To collapse western society, the Marxists realised they had to stir up as much discontent as they possibly could. As things stood revolution could not possibly happen. The west was too prosperous, its citizens by and large content. How to upset the applecart? In the university lecture theatre the malcontents had found their answer: infiltration of young, impressionable minds. It wasn't just aspiring revolutionaries who had swallowed the pill either, but also, as James Delingpole notes, 'that generation of long-haired students who now occupy senior positions in universities, in the judiciary, in government, in the civil service and, of course, at the BBC.'[12]

'A gradual process'

Meanwhile down at the BBC, in the shape of a new wave of trainees and fresh faced graduates, the legacy of the Frankfurt intellectuals was working its way effortlessly into the very fabric of the broadcaster's DNA. By the 1960s the corporation had begun its transformation into something more than just a producer of light entertainment television shows and erstwhile chronicler of news events: 'By the 1960s,' recalled the newly installed Director General, 'many of the old hands in the BBC who thought we were going too fast and too far were leaving. A new and younger generation was in control.'[13]

The 'national' broadcaster was morphing into an organisation very different to that which had begun back in 1922. It started to become staffed by what in modern parlance might be termed the social justice warrior, young men and women fired up by 'progressive' messages, while conspicuously lacking experience of the world outside the media bubble. Reds were embedding themselves into the BBC bed. The attack on traditional morality had begun. Not only was the corporation now pushing the barriers in terms of taste and decency, it had also taken the first steps on a journey which would ultimately transform it into the quasi-political party of modern times.

Mary Whitehouse, founder of crusading pressure group the National Viewers' and Listeners' Association, laid the blame for what she saw as a shift in morality during this decade squarely at the door of the BBC, and one man in particular:

> If anyone were to ask me who, above all, was responsible for the moral collapse which characterised the sixties and seventies, I would unhesitatingly name Sir Hugh Carleton Greene, who was Director-General of the BBC from 1960-1969. He was in command of the most powerful medium ever to affect the thinking and behaviour of people – television.[14]

Hugh Greene joined the BBC in 1940. Before becoming Director General he had supervised BBC broadcasts to Nazi Germany, Russia and Eastern Europe. Between 1950 and 1951 he was tasked with the job of building up a propaganda organisation whose aim was to attack Chinese interests in Malaya. An expert in the art of subversion, Greene liked to refer to himself as a 'psychological warrior.'

To get a flavour of an individual who did so much to reset the BBC on its current course, this summary of how he saw his role and that of the BBC which he oversaw is revealing if not a little unsettling. The following excerpts are from *The Third Floor Front*, Greene's treatise on what he regards as the BBC mission:

> The task of psychological warfare is to impose your own
> view of the situation on the enemy and then to lead the enemy
> to behave in the way you desire.

Greene's views are worth reading if only for their candour. For example, he is quite open and indeed rather proud of the BBC's role in the production and dissemination of propaganda. The admission that the good old BBC – Auntie – has long since been involved in the art of espionage, playing pivotal roles in the fight against Germany, Soviet Russia and China amongst others, may come as somewhat of a shock to those who think of it solely in terms of Blue Peter badges, The Queen Vic and ballroom tangos.

Here is Greene being typically frank about the corporation's role in the Cold War and its ultimate aim of undermining the Russian government:

> Listeners to our broadcasts can help to form a Soviet public
> opinion not unfriendly to the West . . . and thus by a gradual
> process our propaganda may effect Soviet policy. But a gradual
> process it must inevitably remain . . .

'A gradual process it must inevitably remain . . .' For those witness to BBC coverage of Russia from Brezhnev to Putin, Greene's words will no doubt strike a chilling note. Half a century after these words were written, the politically neutral BBC is still heavily engaged in an anti-

24

Russia propaganda campaign. 'It (propaganda) achieves its effects slowly and gradually,' observes Greene.

Finally, before we leave this scion of BBC-think, here's Greene's typically lofty views viz-a-viz the BBC's social responsibilities. Notice how the Director General is quite explicit about how he sees the BBC's role in shaping and influencing public opinion rather than reflecting it:

> I believe we have a duty to take account of the changes
> in society, to be ahead of public opinion rather than always
> to wait upon it.

In Greene's opinion the broadcaster should strive to be 'ahead of public opinion' – in other words no longer merely presenting but rather directing the national debate, plotting its course. The BBC had just given itself permission to get radical.

For the many millions of viewers and listeners scratching their heads over the BBC's enthusiastic support for open borders, mass migration, transgenderism, and the spread of Islam into Western Europe to name but a few issues, it is worthwhile stopping for just one moment to fully consider the full implications of Greene's comments. Rather than reflecting the world of the audience, its values and opinions, the broadcaster had decided to impose its own worldview upon them, and by doing so to assume the role of custodian. From now on Auntie knew best. The BBC had set sail in a direction that its passengers – the licence fee paying audience – had never been consulted over, and knew nothing about.

In order to achieve his aims Greene, along with his fellow anarchists and psychological warriors, were going to need every trick in the book to maintain their trajectory towards their ultimate destination. We shall return to the topic of propaganda in due course.

'The long march through the institutions'

The attack on culture however would be a hard endeavour - a war of attrition. It also had to be relentless. Over time a phrase attributed to leading Marxist theorist Antonio Gramsci, came to embody this endeavour: 'The long march through the institutions.' Uncertain provenance notwithstanding, with its acknowledgement that any attack on the institutions would be a long, hard struggle, it is a phrase that captures the essence of cultural Marxism rather adeptly. The Communists had declared war on the west only - and here is the truly genius part - the west didn't know nor would it ever. Defeating capitalism this way – through culture – would be a long, bitter struggle, but one in which the Marxists would ultimately prevail. Thanks to their rites of passage through a freshly radicalised British university campus, Marxist sympathisers had assumed a variety of roles within the British establishment, the enemy within.

In his essay 'Confessions of a Reformed BBC Producer' Antony Jay pens a candid account of his time working at the corporation during these pivotal post-war decades. Jay, who worked at the BBC from 1955 to 1964, makes some particularly illuminating comments regarding the assumptions of 'media liberals' (BBC colleagues) during this period:

> Ever since 1963, the institutions have been the villains of the
> media liberals. The police, the armed services, the courts,
> political parties, multinational corporations – when things go
> wrong, they are the usual suspects.[15]

Along with Mrs Whitehouse, Jay identifies the date of this change in prevailing attitudes within media circles to the early 1960s - the formative years of Sir Hugh Greene's tenure as BBC Director General. Bear in mind that our Frankfurt friends, ever sensitive that 'Marxist' is more often than not used pejoratively in the west, very often styled themselves 'progressives' or liberals, ever careful to conceal their true ideological allegiances.

Having firmly embedded themselves in the post-war education, welfare and social policy systems of Europe and America, the Frankfurt school had seemingly managed to indoctrinate the minds of a new generation with its subversive ideology. Over at the politically neutral BBC, under the stewardship of Greene – self-identified 'psychological warrior' and 'subversive anarchist' - the corporation was only too happy to do its bit for the Marxist cause. The focus of BBC hostility reveals Jay, 'was not individual decisions or actions by institutions; it was the institutions themselves.'[16] He continues:

But we were not just anti-Macmillan; we were anti-industry, anti-capitalism, anti-advertising, anti-selling, anti-profit, anti-patriotism, anti-monarchy, anti-Empire, anti-police, anti-armed forces, anti-bomb, anti-authority. Almost anything that made the world a freer, safer and more prosperous place, you name it, we were anti it.'[17]

Established over decades if not centuries, institutions are nothing if not resilient. In order to usher in their communist utopia sooner rather than later, Marxists and various assorted left-wing intellectuals, would need to direct their efforts towards that class whom they deemed responsible for constructing and thereafter sustaining these self-same institutions: namely, the (white) Euro-American male. Attacking the lynchpins upon which western society was founded – the engineers, lawyers, architects, administrators, builders etc. – would eventually lead to the fall of the capitalist west, or so the thinking went.

Their place at the epicentre of western socio-cultural life established for centuries, the white (heterosexual) male together with nuclear (Christian) family became Marxism's public enemy number one, the key to overthrowing the rotten capitalist west and its false consciousness. However, it would not be an easy task. The church and family were institutions that had stood solid for centuries underpinned by a strong work ethic and even stronger morality. The malcontents who now included any number of overtly and implicit left-wing groups in their ranks, as well as a fair chunk of graduates now working in the fields of social services, education and local (and national) government, had already worked out how to destabilise both church and family in one foul swoop. Decades of intense lobbying aided and abetted by political correctness, had opened up Europe and America to the phenomenon of mass migration. The intellectuals had long realised that despite their various economic disadvantages, the (white) working classes would never join in the plan to destroy their own culture and tradition. If the working classes could not be coerced, then who could?

By the 1980s the answer was clear: non-natives - people from former colonies, migrants, refugees, anyone in fact with little or no allegiance to Euro-American culture and society. The communists had their foot soldiers. Mass migration became the policy of choice among this new class of self-styled 'progressives.' Their positions of influence within various organisations from the UN through to charities and NGOs allowed them to implement a policy whereby Europe and American would be flooded by unprecedented waves of migration. All that was needed now was to sow the maximum amount of discord among the foot soldiers, teach them to resent and even to hate their hosts, and western society would soon be caught up in interminable conflict from which it couldn't possibly recover.

Certainly, in the modern era the working class would no longer be required to do the Marxist's bidding. Marxism had found a new victim class to exploit: minorities. It didn't matter what kind of minority either: ethnic, cultural, religious, sexual. Marxists had a class ripe for manipulation. The proles, plebs and working classes could now be discarded, evidence if evidence were required that Marxism never had been about inequality, justice or standing up for the disenfranchised. It had always been about just one thing: power. LGBTs, Muslims, transgenders, asylum seekers, migrants, radical feminists – whole new victim classes were created all of whom could be used to chip away at western institutions: church, family, school and that most potent symbol of western tradition, the white (heterosexual) male. The working classes could go to hell.

> I think it [BBC] has undermined seriously the respect for
> institutions in this country ... chipping away at people's
> fundamental beliefs that give their life meaning and I think
> ultimately what the BBC has been doing has been removing
> meaning from people's lives.[18]

The age of grievance and identity politics had well and truly arrived. However, the mischief makers could not achieve their aims alone. To push their radical agenda of social and racial division, they would require assistance. All that was required was an organisation whose reach was national, influence unchallenged, broadly sympathetic to the aims of the Frankfurt school and more than willing to turn traditional morality upon its head. But did such an organisation even exist, one dedicated to turning morality upon its head, one more than happy to sow seeds of doubt amongst its audience? You bet it did;

@BBC
Are you sure you don't gender-stereotype
children? #NoMoreBoysAndGirls

In its attempts to blur the distinction between the biological sexes, this
social media post is typical BBC fare. 'No More Boys and Girls' was in fact
the title of a BBC documentary which, as the title implies, attempted to
sow confusion and discord in the minds of its audience. A few more
headlines to conjure with:

The Telegraph:
'Oxbridge white blokes' like Monty Python have had their day,
says BBC comedy boss

The Sun:
Newsreading legend Sir Trevor McDonald blasts BBC for
'anti-white' hiring practices

The Telegraph:
BBC is anti-Christian and ageist, viewer survey finds

The Independent:
Doctor Who 'promotes a gay agenda', viewers complain to BBC

Lifesite:
BBC Says Communion "Tastes like cardboard, smells like hate"
in Pro-LGBT Video

Mail Online:
Furious parents slam 'damaging' BBC sex change show aimed at
six-year-olds

Turning traditional morality upon its head has always been part of
radical agendas, a way of undermining the glue which holds society
together. Sociologists use the term deviance to describe violation of
norms. Without norms society descends into chaos. Thus, BBC
enthusiasm for anything that breaks societal norms such as what it

refers to as 'gender stereotyping' can be viewed as part of a wider agenda to create just the kind of disorder required by cultural Marxism.

Post-democracy: A BBC fantasy

The Marxists had not been entirely honest about their scheme. For the beneficiaries of the revolution Alinsky and friends awaited, would in fact not be the poor, the needy or the downtrodden, but rather the intellectual elite – in other words, Alinsky and friends. Orwell describes just such a scenario in *1984*:

> And the main outlines of the world which would emerge from the prevailing chaos had long been obvious. What kind of people who would control this world had been equally obvious. The new aristocracy was made up for the most part of bureaucrats, scientists, technicians, trade-union organisers, publicity experts, sociologists, teachers, journalists and professional politicians.[19]

The birth of a 'new aristocracy' is hardly the stuff of a brave new world coalescing around notions of equality and fairness - just the opposite in fact. Orwell had seen through the charade. Many of his fellow travellers on the political left did not. On the contrary, this new world offering unlimited power in perpetuity appealed enormously. 'Intellectuals are naturally attracted by the idea of a planned society,' observes Sir Roger Scruton, 'in the belief that they will be in charge of it.'[20]

Fast forward to 2018 and following a run of populist election victories in the US and Europe, self-styled liberals – 'progressives' – as well as attempting to overturn these democratic votes, have started muttering darkly about limits to democracy. Blaming the UK's decision to leave the EU squarely on the shoulders of 'old' people and 'thickos,' certain factions of the liberal-left have floated the idea of somehow curtailing the democratic rights of this sector of society in future. It's a proposal peculiarly attractive to the authoritarian: 'At what point,' asked a presenter of BBC Newsnight on a 16 November 2018 edition of the programme, 'do you say actually democracy is not as important as the future economy and stability and prosperity of the country right now?'

Trump-supporting Red-necks and Brexit-supporting Little Englanders debarred from the democratic process! It's enough to make 'progressives' go weak at the knees. The stuff of fiction? Not quite. Intellectuals have been flirting with the idea of the post-democratic society for some time. According to an academic from the London School of Economics, the post-democratic society may just be around the corner.[21]

So, is Cultural Marxism really a thing?

According to BBC supporters cultural Marxism is yet another conspiracy theory. The European Union agrees. Wikipedia also agrees. CNN agrees. In order to disprove such theories and non-narrative messages in general, the broadcaster and its allies have invented a whole new industry to enable this end: 'fact-checking.' From the BBC's own 'Reality check' to websites such as the Democrat-supporting Snopes – a website run by anti-conservative personnel - there exists a whole raft of entities who claim to be objective fact-checkers, but who are in reality little more than left-wing political operatives. Websites like these spend their time 'debunking' conspiracy theories. But from whom do they in turn receive validation? Quis custodiet ipsos custodes?[22]

Entities not running a BBC narrative can therefore expect to be 'fact-checked' and summarily pronounced guilty by the broadcaster and its scrupulously objective allies. Independent media is invariably labelled 'alt-right' by the MSM. Faced with growing numbers of alternative media outlets, the response from the legacy media has been predictable: to slander and smear. The cynics have got some watertight arguments too: 'If cultural Marxism is a thing,' they will declare, 'how come it doesn't have its own website or an Instagram account? Explain that!' Nevertheless, such strawmen arguments are usually more than sufficient to convince those of similar political sympathies that what we have here is yet another conspiracy theory, the dastardly work of what BBC Trending is fond of calling the 'alt-right,' whatever that might be.

While there are undoubtedly some plainly silly ideas floating around out there, we at *Brainwashing Britain* prefer to keep an open mind. Today's conspiracy theory can often turn out to be tomorrow's Watergate. However, if you subscribe to the BBC – and we use 'subscribe' here not in terms of voluntary subscription (voluntary subscription? heaven forbade!) but rather in its broader sense of 'to agree' you could be forgiven for thinking conspiracy theories are merely the fantasies of deluded right-wing malcontents (left-wing conspiracy theories such as Trump-Russia 2016 US presidential collusion are never labelled as conspiracies by the BBC.)

We can be certain of one thing however: collusion between rich & powerful interests does occur. If 'conspiracy' means concealing from public view with the intent to deceive, then so-called conspiracy theories might just be more common than we might have been led to believe. So, is western culture and society under attack? Are certain ideological forces subtly, and increasingly not so subtly, attempting to undermine western culture and society? Is cultural Marxism a thing or is just one great big red herring, like the moon landings - a conspiracy theory peculiarly attractive to those of dogmatic and obsessive dispositions? If your experience tells you there is indeed a concerted effort afoot to undermine western society, then you may think cultural Marxism is very real. If, on the other hand, you feel it's just old, white men clinging onto their power, then you might scoff at the suggestion.

Paradoxically the term 'cultural Marxism' may work against BBC critics. The phrase does, after all, have a rather sinister ring about it – a contender for conspiracy theory based upon terminology alone. Rather than drawing attention to the BBC agenda, by using this phrase critics might actually be playing into the broadcaster's hands. It may be more fruitful instead to ask some simple questions. Is the BBC

- Anti-Caucasian, pro-ethnic minority?
- Anti-(white) male, pro-female?
- Anti-Christian, pro-Islamic?
- Anti-Conservative, pro-Liberal?
- Anti-traditionalism, pro-progressivism?
- Anti-populism, pro-globalism?

These are questions for you, the reader, to grapple with. Like our esteemed colleagues at the British Broadcasting Corporation, we at *Brainwashing Britain* are so impartial it actually hurts. We would therefore not wish to influence our readers one way or the other.

The Cult of the BBC

'Around the BBC there's this sort of cult that if you enter the BBC you immediately rise to a nirvana of impartiality.'[1]

I n his two-minutes hate ritual, George Orwell arguably created one of literature's most unsettling vignettes, a moment when human beings regress into spitting, snarling automatons. It's one of several episodes in which the author captures the grim essence of totalitarianism in the pages of *1984*, his novel that exposes the fraudulence that lies at the heart of extreme ideologies such as Marxism and Communism.

At certain periods during the day Party members gather for the 'two-minutes hate' rite whereby they are compelled to unload hysteria towards a figure of hate – Emmanuel Goldstein - a populist leader allegedly intent on corrupting the purity of The Party and its minions. Two minutes hate is the moment members demonstrate their loyalty to Big Brother and The Party. The atmosphere is always hostile, always febrile where, 'the sight or even thought of Goldstein produced fear and anger automatically.'[2] Two minutes hate is not just a creation of a very fertile imagination either. It is a phenomenon which is all too real. Let's take a look at a scenario not a million miles away from the one envisaged by Orwell.

'Takes an arsehole to know a shithole'

While BBC activists are not compelled to drop everything in order to scream hysterically at telescreens for two-minutes every other hour, members are still compelled to display overt signs of hostility to the BBC's own versions of Emmanuel Goldstein.

From Donald Trump and Vladimir Putin, even taking in the likes of journalists Katie Hopkins and Anne Coulter, the corporation has its very own versions of Emmanuel Goldstein. Check out the Twitter feeds of BBC employees such as football presenter Gary Lineker who, when he is not screaming abuse at Nigel Farage, UKIP and populists in general, reserves most of his vitriol for US president Donald Trump, whom he invariably labels 'a total sociopath.' Slander of democratically elected politicians - impartiality in BBC land:

> The external activities of BBC editorial staff, reporters and presenters should not undermine the public's perception of the impartiality, integrity or independence of BBC output. External activities should not bring the BBC into disrepute.[3]

BBC Editorial Guidelines

Indeed, two-minutes is not nearly enough time for the £2 million-a-year BBC activist to express the full scope of his BBC group-think inspired antipathy. 'Certainly has been an interesting 24 hours!' tweeted the US president, to which the footballer responded with:

@Gary Lineker
Oh just go away you misogynistic, racist, narcissistic, sociopath
When it comes to really shitty US Presidents, Donald Trump might just be the winningest.

Re-tweeting a BBC article to his Twitter account which showed a picture of Mr Trump next to an image of Nigel Farage brought forth some exemplary BBC group-think:

@GaryLineker
Here he is: Farage, desperate to stick his snout in his fellow pig's trough. As they say 'It takes an absolute number one c*** to know one.'

In reference to allegations that Mr Trump had labelled certain countries 'shitholes,' the BBC presenter immediately took to social media to declare that it,

Takes an arsehole to know a shithole

'Meanwhile in Hell,' observes a BBC and Observer freelance film critic, 'the venality of Trump's obscene tenure grows more grotesquely vile, foul and putrid each day.' Same sentiments, different disciple.

Two-minutes hate is engineered to keep the minions in a state of perpetual anxiety and agitation. As can be seen in these tweets, it works:

'Arsehole, c***, pig, shitty president . . .' Whereas the faithful in Orwell's novel expressed their hatred in outbursts lasting 120 seconds, 140 characters is usually more than enough for BBC activists to express theirs.

Orwell's Party

When sketching out his vision of a future society, George Orwell wished to portray the type of world that could so easily emerge should ideologues of Frankfurt persuasions ever seize power. *1984* is thus a cautionary tale. This is what happens, Orwell is saying, if power is handed over to a self-appointed elite. In the all-powerful Party he succeeded in creating a terrifying vision of what post-democracy might look like. Consisting of the elite power brokers (Inner Party members) and what can be termed its water carriers (Outer Party members) The Party accounts for approximately 15% of Oceanic society. The tripartite system in Oceanic society looks thus:

1984	BBC roles	Non BBC roles
Inner Party (2%)	Board of Governors Director General Senior executives	Senior bureaucrats/politicians global/trans-national CEOs; Senior judiciary/civil servants etc.
Outer Party (13%)	Producers Editors Presenters Correspondents	Professional classes: teachers, doctors, nurses, journalists, media/arts workers, middle management etc.
Proles (85%)	N/A	Low waged, lowly (formal) educated, unemployed, working class etc.

'Consistent with the BBC's editorial values and policies'

Browsing the corporation's advice for staff regarding social media, it would appear that far from breaking any rules, Mr Lineker and friends may in fact be observing their employer's instructions *to the letter*. BBC policy states that its presenters are, 'expected to behave appropriately when on the Internet and in ways that are consistent with the BBC's editorial values and policies.'[4] So, are the ex-footballer's views 'consistent' with the 'values' and 'policies' of his impartial, politically neutral employer? We'll leave you, the reader, to decide on that one.

Group-think on the kind of scale as witnessed in a BBC canteen, news room or Match of the Day studio is often a hallmark of a particularly sinister phenomenon, one whereby individuality has been stripped away replaced by conformity. Can there be even one other place of work in the UK where every one of its 20,000 employees subscribes to exactly the same creed? Is there another workplace in the whole country populated entirely by euro-fanatics, Trump-haters and diversity disciples? We are in the territory of the cult.

Hard and soft cults

The 1978 Jonestown massacre, in which over 900 members of a cult committed mass suicide, was the culmination of a series of events in which members had been brainwashed to such an extent they were prepared to do whatever the cult dictated – even commit suicide. The brainchild of a certain Jim Jones, The Peoples Temple Agricultural Project aka 'Jonestown' was the somewhat innocent sounding name for a scheme whose aims were anything but benign. As Taylor points out, paranoia played a crucial role in binding members of this cult together. The world was a hostile place, the cult a place of safety:

> Jones' followers worried about everything from cloning to
> sterilisation to psychosurgery; all were potential weapons in the
> hands of the racist, fascists they believed would shortly
> overwhelm America.[5]

Notice the emphasis on the diabolical aims of 'racists' and 'fascists.' Sound familiar? Jonestown was not the only cult to be obsessed with Nazis and the alt/far-right. Notice also the scare tactic: America, democracy - freedom itself - under threat from the forces of evil! It all amounts to the same thing: fear and paranoia – the bread and butter of the would-be brainwasher. As far as can be ascertained, Jones' followers genuinely believed themselves to be fighting the forces of darkness.

At this juncture it might be useful to draw a distinction between two types of cult: The hard and soft variety, where Jonestown would be an example of the former and the BBC would be an example of the latter. A 'hard' version equates to those characteristics which would readily identify a cult on the surface, its formal elements: ritual, ceremony, isolation etc. This type of cult often manifests as a total experience – its members live cheek by jowl 24 hours a day, often in self-contained locations such as the Mount Carmel Centre, headquarters to the Branch Davidian sect. Similarly, Jonestown eventually established itself in a remote part of Guyana. While members of hard cults will travel to the ends of the earth if required, some BBC staff were reportedly reluctant to relocate the 200 or so miles north from London to Salford!

Superficial differences aside, the chief feature of any cult lies in its reliance on brainwashing techniques and adherence to groupthink – soft or hard. On this level, there is not much to choose between an institution like the BBC, a soft cult, and a hard cult such as Jonestown. Examples of other soft cults would be the National Union of Teachers, the UK's university system and, increasingly, the British constabulary and judiciary.

Paradoxically, the potential for damage may be greater from soft cults. 'When communicators do not appear to be trying to influence us,' observe Pratkanis and Aronson, 'their potential to do so is increased.'[6] We already know that an enemy with 'a smiling face' can do much more damage than one whose face exudes 'suspicion and hate.' The more respectable the façade, the greater potential for harm. BBC cultists might not wear kaftans or flowers in their hair, but the all-consuming groupthink that pervades the offices, corridors and studios of Broadcasting House is essentially no different to that which controlled the Jonestown community. Clearly identifiable as a hard cult, the influence of The Peoples Temple Agricultural Project was thus relatively limited. It could be avoided. But what of the soft cult? And when that cult is embedded deep into the national consciousness, how is *it* to be avoided?

Hard and soft cults vary only by degree. Their objectives and how they go about achieving them are virtually indistinguishable. For example, all cults operate systems of reward and punishment. For a hard cult, punishment might be physical e.g. sensory deprivation or solitary confinement. Unable to be quite so brutal, punishment in a soft cult will veer more towards the psychological rather than physical. It might take the form of ostracisation, lack of promotion or excommunication - the fate that befell BBC presenter Robert Kilroy-Silk. After penning an article criticising the Arab world back in 2004, the former MP was promptly dismissed from Kilroy, his eponymous BBC topical discussion show he was hosting at the time.[7] He had defied cult group-think. Kilroy-Silk was a wrong-thinker.

A similar fate befell BBC environmental presenter David Bellamy who had the temerity to suggest that global warming – that most sacred of BBC cows – was 'poppycock.' 'From that moment, I really wasn't welcome at the BBC,' revealed the veteran broadcaster, 'They froze me out, because I don't believe in global warming. My career dried up.'[8] The message is clear enough: disobey the cult and you are finished, an outcast.

It doesn't matter whether it's a BBC2 documentary, a Radio 4 current affairs programme, website article or social media posts on Twitter, BBC types are constantly engaged in a mission to persuade you to embrace the minority worldview of the hand that feeds them. So, how do you know if you are in fact a member of a soft cult? Simple. Take a trip down the staff canteen . . .

Consider, for example, your own place of work. Likely you will encounter a diverse range of opinions in the staff canteen: colleagues may think global warming is the greatest danger of our times, the greatest scam of our times or something in between; alternatively, they might not even give a stuff about it. Take the issue of Capitalism: colleagues may view the economic system which came to define the 20th century as a benevolent or malevolent force or anything in between; alternatively they may not give a stuff about it. On the issue of the EU they may love, loathe or be entirely indifferent to the Brussels-based bureaucracy. Or they might not give a stuff. The point is that in your average staff canteen you will invariably meet people with a whole range of ideas and beliefs.

But not in the cult canteen. In the cult canteen you will encounter absolute uniformity of opinion whether the canteen happens to be in Jonestown, W1A or Salford Quays. 'Our [BBC] beliefs, recalls Antony jay, 'belonged not to the political platform but to the ecclesiastical pulpit.'[9]

When hero of *1984* Winston Smith (aka Orwell) takes a seat in the canteen at The Ministry of Truth (aka Broadcasting House) he is horrified to note the mindless conformity around him. Outer Party members (BBC editors, producers etc.) are nonsensically repeating its group-think to the point where it seems to Winston their communication no longer resembles that of humans, but the spontaneous noises made by animals. What, exactly, are these people talking about wonders Winston?

> Whatever it was, you could be certain that every word of it was pure orthodoxy, pure Ingsoc.[10] [BBC-think] . . . Winston had a curious feeling that this was not a real human being but some kind of dummy. It was not the man's brain that was speaking, it was his larynx. The stuff that was coming out of him consisted of words, but it was not speech in the true sense: it was a noise uttered in unconsciousness, like the quacking of a duck.[11]

Nor is BBC ideology confined to the canteen. Ex-BBC presenter Peter Sissons warns colleagues that in the unlikely circumstance they should manage to locate one of the few copies of the right-leaning *Daily Express* or *Daily Mail* in the BBC newsroom, discretion would be highly advisable: 'Wrap them in brown paper or a copy of The Guardian would be my advice.'[12] Having the 'wrong' opinions in the BBC newsroom or canteen is not to be recommended. Better to have the 'right' opinions even if that means quacking insensibly like a duck. Every cult exerts this sort of psychological control over its members.

'Like the quacking of a duck'
'Welcome to Germany!' joyously shouted a BBC activist at a German train station as hundreds of young male migrants filed sheepishly past. 'How do you feel?' she shrieked, the excitement in her voice palpable. Summer 2015 had seen the start of unprecedented waves of migration into Germany following Chancellor Merkel's infamous open door immigration

policy, a measure the politically neutral BBC approved of whole heartedly. Waiting for the trains to arrive, its activist was clearly thrilled. But why exactly? For many the sight of what appeared to be tens of thousands of single young males pouring into Europe was a sobering thought and one requiring a measured, rather than rapturous response.[13] No matter. The 'British' Broadcasting Corporation was ecstatic. 'Germans at Munich railway station applauding refugees arrive - great atmosphere,' excitedly tweeted the BBC's Berlin correspondent.

What about matters of social cohesion or integration? While an impartial journalist would have had much to consider, such issues would not necessarily trouble the ideologue. Indeed, circumspection or reflection were sorely absent from this particular activist. In their place was joy, pure, unadulterated joy: 'Welcome to Germany! How do you feel?' As already noted, mass migration into Europe (and America) is a bedrock of cultural Marxist strategy. Upon spying thousands upon thousands of young males arriving into Europe, the BBC activist's heart naturally skipped a beat. It is a sight that thrills cult leadership. Ergo, it is a sight that thrills the foot soldiers too.

For a representative of Britain's 'national' broadcaster to be stood at a German train station quacking in the manner of an over-excited duck might strike some as odd, but it is merely symptomatic of undying loyalty to a cult that has a zero tolerance policy towards wrong-thinkers like Robert Kilroy-Silk and David Bellamy. BBC-think is right-think.

'A path to redemption'

A striking similarity between those who called Jonestown home and those who call Broadcasting House home rests in motivation. Robin Aitken, who spent 25 years at the BBC in a variety of roles, notes that, 'The BBC sees itself as a profoundly moral enterprise, BBC people believe in the fundamental goodness of the institution.'[14]

> As Jonestown illustrates, many cult followers are idealists,
> genuinely and strongly seeking not only spiritual enlightenment
> but, also the chance to help other people. The cult is not only a
> path to redemption; it offers an opportunity to express
> goodness in a cynically hostile society.[15]

Just as Jones' followers believed they were acting for the greater good of humanity – opposing 'racists' and 'fascists,' - such is also the fervent belief of BBC cult members who see and are strongly encouraged to see enemies everywhere, especially those ubiquitous 'Nazis.' Pub, library, shop or school, the brown shirts are just waiting to unleash their ideology on an unsuspecting world. The cult becomes a means of self-actualisation, a way to project a construct of the idealised self onto the world.

> **@Anon**
> You have to understand that the people at the BBC are more evolved and better people than you- and you are lucky they can show you the correct way of thinking.

When assessing the generic outlook of Jonestown and similar groups, Taylor makes the observation that, 'cult members tend to demonise everything beyond the cult.'[16] Thus, in the eyes of the BBC, populist politicians such as Nigel Farage or Marine Le Pen and right-wing commentators such as Katie Hopkins, and even stretching out to include what the corporation contemptuously terms 'Trump's base' (63 million people) and 'Little Englander' Brexit supporters (17.4 million people) are all routinely denounced in any number of pejorative ways including 'far-right' and not forgetting the ubiquitous 'Nazi' smear.

Us (good) v them (bad) polarisation is a classic characteristic of cult psychology. Jonestown, Broadcasting House - every cult has its list of wrong-thinkers to be shunned and scorned.

Creating figures to hate, pariahs, is integral to cult psychology. In Orwell's Oceania, the Party also has its own hate figure, not one of us. This figure inspires the same revulsion that the names Trump, Le Pen or Farage etc. inspire in members of the BBC cult. As noted, in *1984*, it is not Nigel Farage rather Emmanuel Goldstein whom the cultists are compelled to hate. Goldstein is rumoured to control a subversive underground organisation called the Brotherhood whose aim is to usurp the social and political utopia established by the Party. In BBC-land, the Brotherhood translates to any offshoot of populism. But Goldstein and his Brotherhood do not exist. There is no threat. Like the BBC's ubiquitous 'far/alt-right Nazis,' the threat has been manufactured by the

Party purely to frighten the minions into submission. It works: Just the very sight of Goldstein/Trump can trigger hysteria in the Party/BBC right-thinkers:

> As usual, the face of Emmanuel Goldstein, the Enemy of the People, had flashed onto the screen. There were hisses here and there among the audience.

BBC right-thinkers/Party members understand only one thing: Goldstein/Trump is the enemy, our enemy. Their responses are just those proscribed by the BBC Executive/Inner Party: hysteria, mania, panic, anxiety. The object is to always drown out the message of the wrong-thinker/populist:

> Goldstein was delivering his usual venomous attack upon the doctrines of the Party – an attack so exaggerated and perverse that a child should have seen through it, and yet just plausible enough to fill one with an alarmed feeling that other people, less level-headed than oneself, might be taken in by it . . . he was advocating freedom of speech, freedom of the press, freedom of assembly, freedom of thought . . . [17]

Freedom of speech and thought, eternal enemies of the authoritarian, concepts to be shouted down, ridiculed and denounced as the ramblings of the extremist or BBC wrong-thinker.

'Intense peer pressure'

Fitting in with organisational culture is of course quite normal. The sooner a new employee understands what is expected of them the better for both themselves and their employer. But we are not talking here about acculturation in terms of roles and responsibilities at work. The cult wishes to dictate not so much what you do, but rather what you *think*. As Pratkanis and Aronson, note in order to achieve this end, 'intense peer pressure is applied.' Extreme psychological pressure of this sort results in, 'uniformity of opinion and behaviour in the cult, which then serves to further reinforce cult practices – if everyone is doing it, it must be right.' The excitable, not to mention bizarre behaviour of our

BBC activist in Germany becomes explicable: she is merely reinforcing cult practice. Her actions are unconscious, her behaviour automatic. The lack of reflection is part of this reinforcement process.

Psychologists have known for some time that human beings possess a powerful urge to be accepted by the group and wider society at large. But there is, of course, a world of difference between integrating into a new work environment in terms of familiarisation with procedure and being compelled to adopt a specific, highly politicised worldview by that same employer. 'In a totalist system,' notes Stein, 'only the party line is allowed, and woe betide the person who tries to float another view.'[18] Robert Kilroy-Silk would no doubt concur. Peter Sissons may sound jocular when he recalls the pressure to conform in the BBC newsroom, but his flippancy hides a sinister reality: Non-conformists - *Daily Mail* or *Daily Express* readers - can kiss goodbye to those large BBC pay-checks and quite possibly their careers too.

As cult dogma is invariably at odds with reality, the need for conformity is indeed great. Exposure to alternative ideas must be strictly censored, which is why many hard cults tend towards isolation. As far as the soft cult is concerned, existing in a milieu of intense peer pressure achieves the same objective. Either way, critical engagement is restricted.

'Views on everything'
Conforming to the BBC worldview is not an option. Signalling one's disapproval of wrong-thinkers and one's sympathy towards right-thinkers is integral to the culture of Broadcasting House. In a memoir that is as pithy as it is revealing, Peter Sissons provides some disquieting glimpses into what life is like inside the BBC temple. With regards to group-think, the former Question Time presenter makes the following comment about institutional pressure, revealing a culture that is all embracing. Totalist we might usefully call it:

> The one thing guaranteed to ruin your career prospects
> at the BBC is letting it be known that you are at odds with
> the prevailing and deep rooted BBC attitude towards Life,
> the Universe and Everything. And the BBC does have
> views on everything.[19]

If there is any feature that marks the cult out from other institutions/groups it is this requirement for absolute conformity. Those not toeing the ideological line of the BBC can expect their careers to lie in ruins. To not disdain what the BBC disdains, to not revere what the BBC reveres, to let it be known you are 'at odds' with the corporation's 'deep rooted' views marks one out as an oddity, a wrong-thinker. Disobedience viz-a-viz cult dogma always ends the same way: career suicide. Join the BBC/Party and you automatically assume its worldview:

> What opinions the masses hold, or do not hold, is looked on as a matter of indifference. They can be granted intellectual liberty because they have no intellect. In a Party member, on the other hand, not even the smallest deviation of opinion on the most unimportant subject can be tolerated.'[20]

While the working classes are at liberty to support Brexit or UKIP, members of the BBC cult have no such liberty. The cult member, on the other hand – BBC producer, editor, presenter - is required to conform to an entire worldview, which does not tolerate 'even the smallest deviation.' Despite this obvious restriction on freedom – personal and intellectual - so completely have they been absorbed into the cult, BBC types do not see any problem with this kind of authoritarianism. In his investigations into the corporation Phillip Schelsinger, Professor of Cultural Policy, Theatre, Film and Television Studies at The University of Glasgow notes that BBC staff:

> See themselves as working in a system which offers them a high measure of autonomy and are generally not cognisant of the fact that 'orientations first defined at the top of the [BBC] hierarchy' work their way downwards through a 'chain of editorial command', becoming a 'part of the taken for granted assumptions of those working in the newsrooms.'[21]

Conforming to group-think naturally leads to normalisation whereby over time cult dogma becomes accepted as obvious, apparent, plain, self-evident, what all right-thinking individuals believe.

'Orthodoxy is unconsciousness'

In their ground-breaking critique of the mass media *Manufacturing Consent*, Chomsky and Herman make a similar observation to Professor Schlesinger with regards to the unconscious normalisation of group dogma. The academics remark, not without concern, that those subjected to brainwashing techniques eventually reach a point when they have internalised the desired ideology so completely they are no longer consciously aware that the position they are supporting, arguing or emphasising is, in fact, group-think. Long having rationalised BBC dogma as the norm against which all other opinions must by definition be wrong or extreme, not for a single second does the average BBC type believe he or she is acting with anything but complete integrity.

The elite domination of the media and marginalisation of dissidents:

> ... occurs so naturally that media news people, frequently operating with complete integrity and goodwill, are able to convince themselves that they choose and interpret the news "objectively" and on the basis of professional news values.[22]

For those able to 'convince themselves' the rewards can be very significant, not least in terms of the allocation of BBC gold. Loyalty is always lavishly rewarded in any cult. People who work for soft cults like the BBC must believe they carry out their duties with absolute integrity. Such beliefs are an illusion of course, the ultimate and final victory for mind control, which in order to reach this point has had to succeed in creating a situation whereby, 'The norm is a belief that freedom prevails, which is true for those who have internalised the required values and perspectives.'[23]

Plenty of freedom then for BBC types to prosecute their duties, provided – and only provided - he or she has fully accepted the cult's dogma, a fairly significant condition by any standard. Chomsky and Herman go on to highlight how organisations like the BBC may superficially mimic the way in which a robust, objective public forum would be expected to operate. There is, however, a crucial difference. Operations like the BBC:

Do not function in the manner of the propaganda system of a totalitarian state. Rather, they permit – indeed, encourage – spirited debate, criticism, and dissent, so long as these remain faithfully within the system of presuppositions and principle that constitute an elite consensus, a system so powerful as to be internalised largely without awareness.[24]

The 'presuppositions' alluded to by Chomsky and Herman are a set of attitudes that the western mainstream media (and political) establishment brings to each and every one of its news items, all of which have been derived from an 'elite consensus.' These doctrines are none negotiable. For example, Islam is a religion of peace; American culture is vulgar; Conservatives are callous; Barack Obama is fabulous; The Israelis are villainous; Women are paid less than men etc. etc. These assumptions are numerous. They are also absolute. Put simply, for the BBC and its allies in the legacy media, debate is fine provided its parameters have been clearly agreed *prior* to starting.

For example, when it comes to discussions about former US president Barack Obama, there is an unwritten BBC pre-supposition in operation, as indeed there is for every conceivable topic under the sun. This particular BBC supposition states that criticism of the 44th US president is strictly off limits. The politically neutral broadcaster simply adores Obama. Aware of this supposition, BBC types would never dream of discussing some of Obama's more questionable policies. Rather, the debate as far as the BBC is concerned is just how fabulous was Barack Obama as US president – very fabulous or extraordinarily fabulous? 'Obama was a rare example of a leader on the left of centre who could make complex arguments more vividly accessible,' gushingly writes BBC presenter Steve Richards.[25] His farewell speech, adds Richards, was 'gloriously reflective.'

In the case of Obama's successor, Donald Trump, the BBC 'debate' is just as myopic. Just how much of a threat to world peace is Mr Trump – serious or critical? The 'debate' starts not with a discussion as to whether Trump is a threat or not, but rather with a consideration of the *extent* of the threat. The pre-supposition has kicked in: Donald Trump is a threat to world peace. Pseudo debates of this sort are very prevalent in BBC land. While Steve Richards cannot find words to adequately describe his adulation of Obama, Mr Trump is described by the same author as, 'a male chauvinist of the extreme variety.'

When Tory MP Boris Johnson compared the hijab to a post box once upon a time, the BBC was incandescent with rage. Comedian Rowan Atkinson was one of a handful of celebrities who supported Johnson's 'joke.' BBC Radio 4 did not see the funny side:

@Anon
Now R4 having a debate between someone who thinks Boris/Rowan Atkinson were wrong and someone who thinks they were wrong.

Like Mr Richards, producers of Victoria, editors of Newsnight, directors of The Andrew Marr Show etc. must all believe they are indeed taking part in 'spirited debate.' Such unconsciousness helps create an air of authenticity. Think about how often BBC activists bang the impartiality drum: *The BBC is impartial . . . Impartiality is at the heart of what we do . . . The BBC is impartial, free and fair . . .* All this while producing content which aims to undermine the Trump presidency, scupper Brexit, whip up anti-Israel antipathy and much more.

'Orthodoxy means not thinking – not needing to think,' observes Orwell in *1984*. 'Orthodoxy is unconsciousness.'[26] Contained in this sentence is a quite terrifying proposition: surrender of our critical faculty is a signifier of correct behaviour, a mark of good manners and a pre-requisite before we can be accepted into polite – orthodox – society. To think otherwise would be construed as an act of rebellion, a challenge to convention and the status quo. To think otherwise would be the sign of the wrong-thinker.

Professor Schlesinger goes on to note that BBC staff are 'a mass of conformists' who adopt, 'the model of corporate professionalism provided for them by the BBC by degrees varying from unreflecting acquiescence to the most full-blown commitment.'[27] Worryingly, nobody appears to question BBC precepts. Schlesinger appears not to have found a single voice of scepticism in the entire organisation: A cult, pure and simple, albeit one financed by the British tax payer.

What then of those brave few souls who might not have yet fully submitted to BBC group-think - the Winston Smiths of this world - where do they go? Answer: nowhere, at least not within Broadcasting House. In Oceania meanwhile it's off to room 101 for a spot of 're-education,' cultural Marxist style:

> In the media, as in other major institutions, those who do not display the requisite values and perspectives will be regarded as "irresponsible," "ideological," or otherwise aberrant, and will tend to fall by the wayside.[28]

'Falling by the wayside' is Chomsky and Herman's rather gentle euphemism that effectively means, comply or die. The BBC does not do dissent; nor for that matter did Jonestown, Waco or any other sect. Control is thus exerted and maintained. Uncritical acceptance of cult dogma is arguably the single most ubiquitous feature of cults through the ages. Even the slightest challenge to group-think will not be tolerated: 'One of the biggest offences at the BBC,' writes Peter Sissons in his memoir, 'is rocking the boat . . .'[29]

'We so rarely encountered any coherent opposing arguments'

When Orwell was sketching out his plans for *1984* he had originally intended to call his novel, 'The Last Man in Europe.' Suffocated by the ruling Party's ideology, and unable to express his own thoughts and feelings for fear of punishment, the novel's protagonist Winston Smith feels himself utterly alone in a world populated by clones and group-thinkers who look, speak and think the same – quacking ducks. To all intent and purposes he could well have been 'the last man in Europe.'

For Orwell's Oceania, built and sustained upon Party group-think, read the British Broadcasting Corporation where social occasions for young producer Antony Jay and his fellow recruits provided yet more opportunity to:

> Reinforce our views on the evils of apartheid, nuclear deterrence, capital punishment, the British Empire, big business, advertising, public relations, the royal family, the defence budget. It's a wonder we ever got home. We so rarely encountered any coherent opposing arguments that we took our group-think as the views of all right-thinking people.[30]

The process of normalisation is nearing completion when Jay and his colleagues strengthen their beliefs over dinner and drinks. For group-thinkers such as these the very suggestion that there might be an alternative opinion would seem absurd at best, seditious at worst:

> It [the BBC] was corrupt in a different way. People treated it as a fiefdom for their prejudices. They couldn't see that the nation might want something different, and that a perfectly reasonable alternative view to their own existed.[31]

In his brief spell as BBC Director General, Greg Dyke bore witness to an environment that was peculiarly conducive to group-think. The BBC 'was inbred' writes Dyke, 'which made changing its culture even more difficult.' He continues:

> BBC people tended to live their lives with other BBC people. They were their friends, their lovers, their husbands and wives. Even when they got divorced it was to go off with or marry someone else from the BBC.[32]

Inter-breeding among members is a classic aspect of cult behaviour, further allowing its ideology to consolidate and for the bonds between members to strengthen. In her extensive and illuminating investigation into what makes cults tick, Kathleen Taylor observes that members, 'often share not only their beliefs and interests, but their background and basic values too.'[33]

'What is most scary about the BBC,' comments Adam a social media user posting on Disqus, 'is the almost complete absence of any kind of dissent. What makes all these people into such supine conformists? Is it career ambition? Is it fear of isolation?'

The 'educated' disciple

What sort of person falls for the cult's tricks? Paradoxically, the more intellectual one assumes oneself to be (e.g. the 'educated' Remain in EU voter), the more susceptible to the wiles of the cult one may actually be. According to Pratkanis and Aronson, it is not the poor or the uneducated we should be concerned about, because:

Research shows that the majority of those who join cults come from middle class backgrounds, are fairly-well educated and are not seriously disturbed prior to joining. Today's cults have begun recruiting the elderly (particularly widowed women) professionals with small businesses such as dentists and lawyers and college students.[34]

'The wave of NRMs (New Religious Movements) from the late 1960s onwards has tended,' concurs David V. Barrett, 'with some exceptions, to appeal to middle-class, well-educated people.'[35] We can thus conclude that as far as the lure of the cult is concerned, the more educated people believe themselves to be – the more 'progressive' – the likelier they are to identify with the ethos of the cult and the greater the likelihood its messages will resonate.

Nor does the cult need to be in any way archetypal. As Alexandra Stein remarks, not all cults live in remote locations, chant kumbaya and worship the leader all day long. Some cults, she observes, 'may have particular beliefs in certain areas of life, yet allow autonomy in other areas.'[36] All of which brings us neatly to the BBC type.

The BBC Type

It [the BBC] is run very largely by people who do not know the working class, do not understand the working class point of view, but one seeking evidently to mould the working class.[1]

Just who are these people who believe in the righteousness of their cause to such an extent they no longer see themselves as expressing subjective opinions, but rather universal truths? What type of person thrives in the cult of the BBC? Could it be the type that prospers in the sinister ruling Party of Orwell's *1984* perhaps - the type that so readily screams abuse at mythical 'hate' figures?

> I am still not sure that the BBC is the right place for me to be – it seems to be full of spalpeens, bastards and layabouts.[2]

> Ex-BBC secretary

'A nest of lefties which promotes a progressive political agenda, and is bedevilled by political correctness,'[3] is the clichéd view of the BBC according to one ex-producer with over 20 years' service. 'Depressingly,' he continues, 'in my experience, the cliché comes uncomfortably close to the actual truth.'

> My wife comes from South Africa and her maiden name is Kruger. Our cleaning lady, who's Brazilian, is also called Kruger.[4]

> John Simpson, BBC World Affairs Editor

Is a certain type attracted to the BBC, slothful, idealistic individuals more than happy to toe the party line in exchange for a generous slice of the tax-payer funded cake? Whatever BBC employees do with their time, it does not seem to involve breaking news scoops. So what do they do all day? Work, such as it is, often comprises of sending out snarky tweets mocking Trump and Brexit or other wrong-thinkers. Before taking a look at the BBC mind-set, let's take a small diversion to a seemingly innocuous incident that nonetheless seemed to rile the organisation.

'Full of spalpeens, bastards and layabouts'

An investigation by *The Sun* newspaper in autumn 2017 which revealed BBC staff regularly fall asleep at their desks indeed brought forth a tidal wave of indignation from corporation activists. BBC Middle East correspondent Quentin Somerville immediately took to social media where he posted a photograph of himself, eyes apparently closed, sitting in what appeared to be an abandoned shack in an unknown location:

> **@sommervilletv**
> It's true @TheSun we do sleep on the job.
> Our work is a bit taxing at times. @BBCNews
> doesn't do lazy journalism. How about you?

Ouch! Soon enough, BBC activists were gleefully circulating this message. However, it appears that Mr Sommerville might have got the wrong end of the stick. *The Sun* article was based upon undercover photographs taken within BBC HQ at Broadcasting House, which clearly showed BBC employees asleep at their desks. Sommerville's staged image had presumably been taken somewhere in the Middle East, a fact that did little to prevent BBC triumphalism. We got *The Sun*!

'I'm sure people in other overnight office jobs have done the same,' retorted one BBC News producer. 'Oh yes, and if you've gone round photographing your colleagues asleep you're a weird, creepy bastard.'

'With The Sun's permission, it's finally time to sleep after my night shift,' sarcastically tweeted a BBC Radio 5 newsreader. This and others of its ilk were nothing if not eccentric retorts given that the images in *The Sun* had clearly shown BBC staff asleep *during* their shifts, not after them. The BBC Press Office waded in with, 'Even with our eyes closed, it's good to know the public trusts BBC News more than the Sun.' The 'national' broadcaster was clearly rattled.

The furore had started when a disgruntled BBC employee secretly filmed colleagues on the night-shift apparently sleeping, some of whom were wearing eye masks and one who had even brought a duvet and blanket to work! 'It's very difficult to work with someone snoring next to you,' the whistle-blower told the paper.[5] 'In a 12-hour shift I would estimate some staff do around an hour of work. You can look around and there are three or four people in a row with their feet up and soundly asleep.'

'Frank calls the BBC the best holiday camp ever,' noted a BBC secretary in her diary, 'because there is so much waste and so many people doing nothing all day.'[6] That was, however, before Twitter came along. Posting messages on the social media site can be a full-time job.

In his memoirs, former BBC executive Will Wyatt is quite open about his own habit of napping when on duty: 'I always woke up after an hour or so feeling terrible, yet rarely resisted the opportunity.' BBC sloth is not however confined to the newsroom. It appears to be endemic. 'Typists,' recalls Wyatt, 'spent most of their days, reading, chatting and knitting.'[7]

Judged by the reaction by Mr Sommerville and colleagues, with its expose of slumbering personnel, *The Sun* appeared to have hit somewhat of a BBC raw nerve. To obtain a fuller understanding of the BBC mind-set in all its superiority, we turn next to a common enough social media example.

'Watch and learn @realDonaldTrump'

Even before assuming the US presidency, Donald Trump had been a vociferous critic of his country's trade deals with various international partners, especially China:

> **@realDonaldTrump**
> We are on the losing side of almost all trade deals. Our friends and enemies have taken advantage of the U.S. for many years. Our Steel and Aluminium industries are dead. Sorry, it's time for a change! MAKE AMERICA GREAT AGAIN!

'That's really not how international trade works,' tweeted a BBC activist one fine March day in reply. Judging by his youthful looks, one could have been forgiven for assuming this BBC international trade expert had minimal experience of conducting business deals – international or otherwise. Not to worry. Cult members come in all shapes and sizes as well as ages. This publicly-funded BBC 'news channel journalist' went on to further school the billionaire businessman on the finer points of striking trade deals:

> Trade deals are not zero-sum games. There's no "winner" and
> "loser" (well, not if they are negotiated properly). The point of
> a trade deal is that both sides "win" - i.e. become more
> prosperous. Having a trade deficit with another country is not
> a sign that you have "lost"

'Not if they are negotiated properly . . .' For a man who has business interest in some 144 companies operating in 25 countries worldwide, one can only imagine Mr Trump's gratitude to this precocious BBC whiz kid for sharing his wisdom. It's not every day a business tycoon can obtain free advice from an individual whose salary is paid from a compulsory television licence fee:

> **@Anon**
> BBC intern helpfully explaining all about trade to a US billionaire
> businessman. Watch and learn @realDonaldTrump

Who but a member of the BBC could assume to enlighten a billionaire businessman with nearly half a century's worth of experience in the corporate boardroom? Laughable as these tweets are, there can be no doubting the sincerity behind them. They are in no way satirical. Brought up on the cult's anti-Trump dogma, and despite his tender years, this BBC 'online news journalist' really does believe that when it comes to the intricacies of striking international trade deals, junior knows best.

'Sure we could have done it better'

From just where does this chutzpah originate? Antony Jay vividly recalls the high esteem in which BBC types invariably held themselves:

> We saw ourselves as part of the intellectual élite, full of ideas
> about how the country should be run, and yet with no
> involvement in the process or power to do anything about it.
> We despised local government, and had no say in national
> government, and yet we were sure we could have done it better.[8]

From fresh faced interns, through Newsnight presenters up to and including Director Generals, Broadcasting House is teeming with individuals who genuinely believe they know best. As far as President Trump is concerned, there's a whole gang of BBC North America correspondents lining up to show him how it should be done. Our youthful expert on international trade deals is merely the tip of a huge talent iceberg of wealth creating entrepreneurialism and business acumen.

BBC types appear to believe wholeheartedly in their intellectual superiority. They also believe in their own infallibility. It's in the BBC DNA. They most certainly believe in BBC dogma to such an extent it is no longer viewed as dogma, but rather as truth. Our international trade 'expert' had simply been conditioned to believe that Donald Trump is always wrong, while the BBC is always right.

'We saw ourselves as clever people in a stupid world,' continues Jay, 'upright people in a corrupt world, compassionate people in a brutal world, libertarian people in an authoritarian world.' It is only with the benefit of hindsight – free of the cult – that Jay is able to see the absurdity of his younger self, his BBC self. Our intern – expert in international trade deals - merely sees himself as a 'clever' person in a 'stupid world.'

While a young producer for the BBC's Money Programme, Robin Aitken shared Jay's egotism and, with the benefit of maturity, his contrition. 'Our films attempted to undermine the right-wing economic agenda,' notes Aitken:

> It was arrogant journalism; the underlying message was that nobody in government had a clue about running an economy; our superior intellects had worked out the answers.[9]

A former executive also recalls the intransigent views that guided BBC activists. During his time as a producer on a late night BBC discussion show, Will Wyatt recalled using only contributors to publications he and his team read: the *Guardian, Observer, New Statesman* and authors 'we agreed with.' Reflecting back, Wyatt confesses that, 'we had a pretty blinkered view of the world while believing the exact opposite.'[10] BBC types believed in the cult to such an extent it made them 'blinkered' to other opinions. Blissfully unaware of their own bigotry, they thought themselves open-minded when the opposite was in fact true.

However, for every Antony Jay or Robin Aitken now cringing at his own youthful naivety and pomposity, there are hundreds if not thousands of eager young idealists willing to take their places in the cult, willing to teach an international businessman and President of the United States of America all about doing business.

Kind, compassionate types, provided . . .

Are BBC types born or made this way? Perhaps such traits are the natural development of being in an environment surrounded by so many 'clever people' – individuals 'full of ideas about how the country should be run,' and who could surely govern the United States of America – any country - so much better than any elected president or prime minister.

It's not just (certain) presidents, prime ministers and wrong-thinkers whom the impartial broadcaster despises. Imbibed with a whole range of deplorable characteristics including patriotism, common sense and Euro-scepticism, the British working class has not been the flavour of the month down at Broadcasting House for some time. Some vote UKIP. Some even support Donald Trump! Just as Orwell predicts, while hiding behind a compassionate, humanitarian mask, the ruling Party elite actually loathes the proles: 'The Party preaches a contempt for the working classes unexampled for centuries past . . . It systematically undermines the solidarity of the family.'[11]

From South Shields and Darlington to Barnsley and Merthyr Tydfil, the attitude towards non Party wrong-thinkers might indeed best be described as contempt. 'Being essentially unknowable,' writes John Carey, 'the mass acquires definition through the imposition of imagined attributes.'[12] Hence, to the average BBC type, the working class is nothing more than a racist mob, one that needs protecting from its own base instincts. The cult meanwhile is peopled by kind, compassionate humanitarians whose only wish is to make their inferiors – the proles – act and behave correctly.

'Ashamed of their own nationality'

While BBC disdain towards all things British and enthusiasm for all things non-British irritates and perplexes the ordinary man or woman in the street no end, when viewed as part of a wider ideological context this anti-British strain becomes explicable. Anti-Britishness is a political position, the natural position for those of Frankfurt persuasions, a signifier that the communicator is one of us:

> England is perhaps the only great country whose intellectuals are ashamed of their own nationality. In left-wing circles it is always felt that there is something slightly disgraceful in being an Englishman and that it is a duty to snigger at every English institution, from horse racing to suet puddings.[13]

The ultimate aim of cultural Marxism lest we forget is the dissolution of the (western European) nation state, to be replaced by a soulless, cultureless, authoritarian society much as Orwell had imagined in *1984*. As a means to an end, mass migration perfectly fits this bill. What better way to dissolve Europe – Britain – than by opening up its borders? 'The BBC is not neutral in multiculturalism; it believes in it and it promotes it,' according to a conversation reported by John Lloyd.[14]

As usual the corporation's enthusiasm for all things non-British is sharply at odds with the majority of the British population. For example, the people of Britain and Europe – its 'non-intellectuals' - consistently state their opposition to the open borders policy so beloved by the BBC.

In BBC circles disparaging British (and western European) culture and tradition is however considered a signifier of one's intellectual superiority, a tacit admission that one's sympathies align with the 'correct' side, the progressive side, the side of the cultural Marxists. Phrases like 'Little Englander' and 'little grey island' have become cornerstones of BBC-speak when referring to the UK. Our old friend Sir Hugh Greene fondly refers to England as 'this sheltered little island.'[15] On the other hand, unbridled enthusiasm for anything anti-British (or western European) is viewed with particular favourability.

That's like the National Front'

This enthusiasm for all things un-British runs deep within the BBC cult. In his essay entitled 'Self-hatred at the BBC,' John Lloyd recalls a story involving the corporation's former business editor Jeff Randall. As an individual rumoured to have right of centre leanings here was a beast as rare as he was exotic, at least within the confines of Broadcasting House.

It transpires that BBC bigwigs had decamped on an away-day. It was one of those 'blue sky' thinking events the corporate world loves so much. The BBC was asking itself some pretty big questions: *Are we out of touch with public opinion?* We'll leave our readers to guess the BBC answer to that one . . . Meanwhile:

> In a story which closed the day, Randall told of wearing
> Union Jack cufflinks to work. A producer asked him if he
> would wear them on air: Randall said he would, and was told:
> "You can't do that, that's like the National Front!"[16]

When a pair of union jack inscribed cufflinks can produce this kind of reaction from a BBC cultist - horror bordering on revulsion - is it any wonder that the idea of the BBC being or representing anything even remotely British is met with increasing derision? In many quarters the 'national' broadcaster has come to be known as 'the anti-British Broadcasting Company.'[17] 'Within the intelligentsia,' observes Orwell in Notes on Nationalism, 'a derisive and mildly hostile attitude towards Britain is more or less compulsory.' Now it takes a special kind of arrogance to not only ignore the opinion of a majority, but to also hold that majority – more precisely its core beliefs – with something verging on contempt.

During his days as a BBC executive Roger Mosey recalls an e-mail he received from Randall on the topic of the BBC's heavily biased coverage of immigration:

> Does anyone in the BBC's Policy Unit/Thought Police read
> Richard Littlejohn? They should. He reflects popular opinion far
> more accurately than the views of those whose idea of a good
> night out is reading the Indy over a vegetarian meal in a Somali
> restaurant.[18]

Randall's portrayal of the stereotypical BBC liberal makes its point well enough. Liberal sensibilities are not however shared by the majority of the UK population. Nonetheless, Liberals it is who run Britain's 'national' broadcasting corporation. To make matters worse the bulk of the corporation's £5 billion annual bounty is procured from just that class of proles of whom it so heartily disapproves. 'But sometimes – and I hope I speak without arrogance,' declares that old subversive Hugh Green, 'it is very difficult to have any respect at all for certain expressions of public opinion.'[19]

Among the many points of divergence between broadcaster and public, one stands out in particular: political correctness.

'Benevolent tyranny'

'The BBC acknowledges the political dimension of words all the time and tells us and quite firmly what we should and should not say,' so says ex-BBC presenter Edward Stourton in his investigation into the phenomenon known as political correctness.[20] This obsession with PC is yet another facet of the BBC which puts it at odds with a public many of whom do not share its wild enthusiasm for what is sometimes disparagingly called 'verbal hygiene' and even 'linguistic fascism.'

Orwell had his own word for this insidious phenomenon: Newspeak. Whether it's PC or Newspeak, the aim is always the same: control. Language is power. And no matter which moniker they go by – Marxists, Frankfurt intellectuals, Progressives, Inner/Outer Party members, BBC activists – authoritarians get a kick out of power. If it means hiding behind 'tolerance' and pretending to champion the cause of the underdog in order to achieve and hold power, then so be it.

As a tool to stymie opposition during the long march through the institutions, PC is worth its weight in gold. But there is a downside. Political correctness has become its own worst enemy. Adherents can and do take this doctrine to ludicrous lengths. Reciting a story of naming his new dog Didier Dogba in honour of Chelsea's Ivorian footballer Didier Drogba (get it?), a former host of BBC's Top Gear programme was summoned to meet a BBC executive:

> I trudged all the way over the Broadcasting House and he said, "I understand you have a new dog and you have called it Didier Dogba. It is racist."

> "I said, "It is not racist. We are all Chelsea fans in the family". He said, "Please tell me the dog is not black." I said, "It's a Scottish Terrier. Should I have called it John Terrier?"

In an article entitled, 'Out-of-step BBC urged to rethink 'PC police,' Jason Deans notes,

> A BBC executive has questioned whether the corporation should "help break the constraints of the PC police", after audience research found it is out of step with much mainstream public opinion.[21]

The BBC executive referred to is former BBC 4 Controller Richard Klein, who would appear to have taken the unusual step of breaking rank with the cult:

> By and large, people who work at the BBC think the same and it's not the way the audience thinks. That's not long term sustainable. We pride ourselves on being 'of the people' and it's pathetic. Channel 4 tends to laugh at people, the BBC ignores them.

Steeped in political correctness could it be that the BBC is becoming ever more remote from the British public who overwhelmingly repudiate this latter day manifestation of Newspeak? 'Most of our [BBC] attitudes and opinions were at odds with the majority of the audience and the electorate,' agrees Antony Jay.[22] A cynic might wonder how an organisation so clearly out of touch with public opinion could possibly have the temerity to pocket £billions from that very same public.

And so the post-1960s BBC pursues a social and political agenda best described as an acquired taste. Its sensibilities are those of the metropolitan liberal, realised by what J G Ballard calls 'benevolent tyranny.'[23] Ballard's oxymoron rather aptly captures the schizophrenic nature of a broadcaster that with programmes such as The Blue Planet, can dazzle the same audience upon whom it is intent on imposing a worldview that is as divisive as it is dangerous. For as this elite minority coerces the majority into accepting its eccentric views, tyranny indeed awaits.

Licence to print money

No discussion about the BBC can avoid the topic of money. Money is the BBC God. Like all cults, the focus on money underpins all activities to the point of obsession. 'Even before I joined [the BBC],' recalls former Director General Greg Dyke:

> I sat in a meeting discussing the likely licence fee settlement and was struck by how everyone just wanted as big an increase as possible.[1]

Currently it receives around £5 billion per annum, of which about £4 billion derives from the British public. An eye watering twenty percent of its entire income (£1 billion) is spent on staff salaries![2] To put these figures into perspective, £5 billion is more than the total GDP of countries such as Swaziland, Montenegro, Guyana, Liberia and many others. Unsurprisingly, the corporation clings to its licence fee, tenaciously resisting all calls to modernise a funding model devised back in the 1920s.

Let's begin with a situation that if we wished to be polite we might call an anomaly, and if we wished to be rude we might call daylight robbery: the television licence fee. Imagine the following scenario: each week you read a number of publications: *What's on TV, Autosport, Cosmopolitan* etc. At the end of the week you receive a bill from your newsagent on which you notice an item you did not order and you do not read: *The Guardian*. Puzzled, you seek out your newsagent to ask why you have been charged for a newspaper you do not read.

'I don't want the Guardian, thanks,' you inform him.

'Right. So do you still want to receive the other titles?'

'Yes, of course!' What the Devil is he talking about you wonder. You did not mention anything about cancelling any other titles.

'Ah. But if you don't order the Guardian, you can't read any of these other titles. Sorry.'

'But I don't read the Guardian! I don't want the bloody Guardian!'

'No Guardian, no other papers or magazines. Sorry.'

And just to add insult to injury just imagine the weekly cheque you are about to write out to the newsagent goes not to your preferred reading choices who must survive on advertising alone, but straight into the pockets of *The Guardian*! What would you say? Probably you'd be fairly annoyed. Why should you have to subscribe to a left-wing newspaper you *don't want* in order to receive magazines and newspapers you *do want*? That would just be outrageous, right?

Yet in 2018 that's exactly the position faced by increasing numbers of people. Only it's not *The Guardian* they are being forced to buy, it's the BBC. If you don't wish to subscribe to the BBC you have no choice. If you don't watch BBC, but do watch ITV, Channel 5, Dave, Yesterday and the umpteen other Freeview channels you still pay the BBC. The reason for this bizarre situation is due to the way the broadcaster has been allowed to exploit its pre-eminent position.

When the television licence fee was introduced it covered just a single channel – BBC 1 and later, BBC 2. With the arrival of ITV and Channel 4, the crafty broadcaster ensured commercial television would also be included under its licence fee remit. Thus, as the number of television channels has exploded in the UK since 2000, the broadcaster has lobbied government to retain the system devised in the 1920s which treated the BBC as a monopoly, a highly privileged monopoly at that. What this means is that irrespective of whether you use BBC services or not, you still pay for them. Consider the case of Sky. Having paid your subscription, but before you can watch Premiership football, NCIS Los Angeles or The Blacklist, first you have to pay the BBC. Imagine shopping only at Asda, Aldi and Lidl but having to pay Tesco for the privilege!

Furthermore, many people in the UK nowadays choose to watch their TV online. Television consumption models are changing only nobody appears to have informed the BBC. Take for example EU nationals. Polish, Romanian and Bulgarian citizens while working in the UK often prefer to watch television from their own countries. Laptops, tablets, I-pads, mobile telephones, accessing content from abroad has never been easier. But there's a snag. If you wish to catch up on the news from Warsaw or Sofia first you pay the BBC. As to why you are legally obliged to pay a third party – the BBC – in order to watch a foreign broadcast on the World Wide Web on a personal device in the privacy of your own home has never been satisfactorily explained.

Witnessing ever more commercial rivals enter the television fray, the BBC knew that its monopoly would soon enough come under threat. In order to ensure the public kept paying it billions of pounds per year irrespective of whether they watched the BBC or not, the devious broadcaster succeeded in ensuring that the television licence was extended to cover ALL television services in the UK, not just BBC. As the age of the Internet dawned, the broadcaster ensured its licence remit extended to now include all live (and recorded) broadcasts in the UK.

Only watch Freeview? Only watch the news in Polish via Internet live streaming? You pay the BBC. You neither need nor want the BBC? Tough, because you've got it. If that isn't bad enough, there's a particularly vicious sting in the tail: should you decide that there is no reason at all to pay the BBC £150 per annum on top of your Sky and Internet subscriptions and you decide to boycott the television tax, you might find yourself in very hot water.

'Gasps from the audience'
Those opting out of the BBC television tax scheme can look forward, sooner or later, to meeting TV Licencing, the company that the BBC pays to do the dirty work of cash collecting. By using a third party to collect its licence fee money, the broadcaster is able to distance itself from a process that often gets ugly. Complaints of high pressure selling techniques are common. A *Daily Mail* undercover investigation revealed TV Licencing agents had applied just such techniques on a war veteran with dementia and a desperate young mother in a women's refuge.

> **@Anon**
> The BBC currently TAXES us for PC propaganda. TV Licensing
> is a BBC company disguised by name to distance @BBC from
> the unhappy business of collecting money with menaces

'We will drive you as hard as we can to get as much as we can out of you because we're greedy,' a TV Licencing boss told an undercover reporter. TV Licencing's 'heavy handed' tactics had already been discussed in parliament as long ago as 2007 when Conservative MP Gary Streeter's early day motion criticising 'intimidating' tactics had been supported by 60 fellow MPs.

Having reviewed video evidence, Damien Collins MP said, 'It's very concerning. This is being done in the BBC's name.'[3] Not for the first time in its history, the corporation feigned surprise.

Non-payers, a significant proportion of whom are young, single mothers can face fines and even imprisonment - the fate that befell some ninety unfortunate individuals in 2015, mostly women. Suspected non-payers consistently claim they are subjected to harassment and even threats from TV Licencing agents, who operate on a commission basis the aim of which is to ensure the conviction of ever more licence non-payers. In 2016 over 100,000 women, the majority of whom pleaded not guilty, were successfully prosecuted for licence evasion – 70% of total cases.[4]

@Anon
I was threatened with 7 days in prison . . . I was a single parent on income support I couldn't afford the fine and the JP told me pay up or face 7 days in jail.

@Anon
I had a 70 year old patient with a weak heart this week who had a very dangerous panic attack, caused by a threatening letter from the TV Licensing authority because he was £5.50 behind with his license payments

TV Licencing indeed targets the poorest and most vulnerable in society. Those unable to pay – the unemployed, the working poor – can expect to find themselves inundated with letters whose tone could be best described as menacing. The television tax is a flat charge and as such hugely disadvantages the poor. But that's ok. Because according to the corporation, poor people watch more television than the rich: 'While the licence fee does constitute a higher proportion of lower households' expenditure,' admits James Heath, a BBC Director of Policy, 'these households also consume more BBC TV than richer households.'[5]

@Anon
RS is asked about women in the criminal justice system. Gasps from the audience as he reveals that there are currently seven women in prison for failing to pay their TV licence
@TheHowardLeague

'A nationally representative survey'

Heath goes onto to suggest that the British public actually quite likes paying the TV tax! In fact, according to the research he quotes people are keener than ever to pay the BBC ever more money: 'A nationally representative survey of 1,015 UK adults by Ipsos MORI,' writes the BBC executive, 'shows that public support for the licence fee has grown over the last 10 years.'

The polling company – Ipsos MORI – is regularly commissioned by the BBC and has an exceedingly happy knack of providing the broadcaster with precisely the results it so badly wants to hear. Heath continues:

> Our most recent research suggests willingness to pay the licence fee is high, with 7 out of 10 people prepared to pay the current level of the licence fee at £145.50 or more.

All of which might strike as somewhat odd the 250,000-plus signatories to a petition on 38 Degrees.org calling for the abolition of the licence fee. Heath's claims are certainly not supported by a plethora of independent research. In 2014, *The Times* reported the results of a YouGov poll, remarking that, '39 per cent believe that the £145.50 fee is good value for money — but precisely the same number say that it is not.'[6]

Such overwhelming enthusiasm for the television tax might also come as somewhat of a surprise to those members of the British public who took part in an ICM poll for *The Sunday Telegraph* in 2013 which found 70% of people wanted to abolish altogether or cut the cost of the television licence: 'More than half the public think the television licence fee should be scrapped,' reported *The Telegraph*, 'and the BBC forced to find new ways to fund itself.'[7] That this research was *not* commissioned by the BBC and *not* carried out by Ipsos MORI may or may not be significant. A firm of independent analysts - Whitehouse Consultancy Media - commissioned this particular research.

'The BBC is a world renowned institution of which I am a keen supporter,' said Chris Whitehead, Whitehouse's Chairman, 'and it is alarming that its support-base has been allowed to erode to this low level.'

'Put public trust at risk'

Where does all that tax-payer cash go? While the BBC spends plenty of money on programmes, it also spends a disproportionate amount on salaries. BBC activists are paid way above any comparable rates; several hundred are paid six-figure salaries. And these already more than generous salaries just keep getting bigger. In 2018 some 500 activists were awarded a 25% pay rise while a further 123 staff members received 50% raises.[8]

Between 2005 and 2013, the corporation awarded severance payments of £369 million of tax-payer money to outgoing staff . . . [9] 'The BBC has too often breached its own already generous policies on severance payments,' reported the National Audit Office in 2013 after decades of eye-popping pay-offs to senior staff. This was a massive rebuke for the BBC. The audit concluded that in a culture where excess and greed were the norm, BBC senior managers had been effectively helping themselves to public money. Never was this culture more apparent in 2011 when the corporation awarded Mark Byford £949,000 of tax payer's money as severance payment. Byford took the cash, 'because they gave it me . . .'[10] This extraordinary payment had been authorised by his good friend, Mark Thompson, the BBC's Director General at the time who had allegedly ensured Byford received the maximum possible and more. This followed severance payments to The Chief Operating Officer (£666,400) and a Departmental Director (£600,000) amongst a glut of enormous pay-offs that same year. The National Audit report also found evidence of 'unusual' payments made to third parties. Overall, the review concluded, that:

> The BBC has breached its own policies on severance too often
> and without good reason, exceeded contractual entitlements and
> put public trust at risk.

Such a damming report might have finally stymied excesses of BBC pay-offs, but it could not prevent the corporation from exploiting tax payer money in a different way. Typically, it simply shrugged off the report's many criticisms.

Soon enough it was business as usual down at Broadcasting House. While the majority of Britain's public services workers were facing pay freezes in 2017 and had for some years, the BBC was awarding over 1,800 staff pay rises of 10%.[11] Nor could the broadcaster be prevented from finding ways to inflate the salaries of its already generously compensated senior staff. In 2018 *The Times* reported that, 'the broadcaster regularly breaks its own pay guidelines in order to increase the wages of high-earning staff.'

Remarking that 1,500 BBC employees actually received salaries over and above the maximum stipulated for their pay grade, the paper went on to observe that, 'salary top-ups are particularly common in the highest two grades.'[12] Top-ups, gigantic severance payments for old pals, multi-million pound salaries, bonuses and pension schemes, all financed by the British tax payer, many of whom live a hand-to-mouth existence on social security handouts, some of whom are incarcerated for refusing to pay the TV licence fee.

So just how much do BBC staff actually earn? It has been a question much discussed, but one with which the publicly-funded broadcaster had steadfastly refused to co-operate. Until 2017 . . .

'A poacher's charter'

After months of pressure, on Wednesday 19 of July 2017 the BBC was finally forced to release a list that contained salary details of all BBC staff paid over £150,000 per year. Naturally the corporation fiercely resisted the move. For an organisation rich in the rhetoric of equality long suspected revelations of grossly inflated salaries could only add more egg to the broadcaster's face. For example, before leaving the BBC in 2010 chat show host Jonathan Ross had reputedly been paid a staggering total of £18 million over three years! Naturally the BBC defended the salary level. It was the right amount for someone of Ross's 'talent.' And it was the 'market' not the BBC which dictated the presenter's worth. After 13 years on the BBC pay roll, Ross signed up for ITV for a paltry £1.5 million per year. Little wonder that speculation about BBC salaries intensified. The corporation dug its heels in.

Director General Tony Hall told Sky News, to no avail, that such a move would equate to a 'poacher's charter,' the inference being that salaries revealed, rival broadcasters would be in a position to lure 'talent' away from the BBC with vastly improved remuneration offers, such had happened with Ross . . . A total of 214 BBC employees were finally revealed to earn over £150,000 per year! The average UK salary in 2016/17 was £26,500. Hardly surprising that Hall and his colleagues had resisted the call for transparency so doggedly:

The BBC £150k + club[13]	No of employees
£500,000 +	7
£450,000 – 499,000	3
£400,000 – 449,000	6
£350,000 – 399,000	7
£300,000 – 349,000	10
£250,000 – 299,000	12
£200,000 – 249,000	38
£150,000 – 199,000	131

Fig. 1

While some unfortunate (mostly female) individuals languished in prison unable or unwilling to pay the television licence fee, huge numbers of BBC employees were collecting super-sized salaries courtesy from that same TV tax. By way of comparison we list average salaries for selected UK job according to Payscale.com:

Average UK salaries	
Head teacher	£68,261
Doctor (G.P)	£50,664
Police officer	£30,571
Qualified Teacher	£27,890
Registered Nurse	£23,468
Journalist	£23,152
Admin. Assistant	£16,652

Fig. 2

Although it had long been suspected that the publicly-funded BBC payed its so-called talent more than generously, the extent to which this was true shocked many. In an era where the financial situation facing public sector workers had been much in discussion, the incredible yearly salaries paid to the likes of Chris Evans (£2.2 - £2.5 million) and football pundit Gary Lineker (£1.8 - £2 million) seemed nothing short of obscene.

'A Poacher's Charter . . .'		
BBC's top paid 'talent'	**Employer July 2017**	**Employer July 2018**
Chris Evans[14] (£2.2 – 2.5m)	BBC	BBC
Gary Lineker (£1.8 – 2.0m)	BBC	BBC
Graham Norton (£850 – £899k)	BBC	BBC
Jeremy Vine (£700 – £749k)	BBC	BBC
John Humphrys (£600 – £649k)	BBC	BBC
Huw Edwards (£550 - £599k)	BBC	BBC
Steve Wright (£500 - £549k)	BBC	BBC
Claudia Winkelman (£450- £499k)	BBC	BBC
Matt Baker (£450 - £499k)	BBC	BBC
Alex Jones (£400 - £449k)	BBC	BBC
Nicky Campbell (£400 - £449k)	BBC	BBC
Stephen Nolan (£400 - £449k)	BBC	BBC
Andrew Marr (£400 - £449k)	BBC	BBC
Alan Shearer (£400 - £449k)	BBC	BBC

To put these astronomical figures into perspective, Evans' salary was *15 times greater than* that paid to the British Prime Minister! If that wasn't bad enough, over 200 BBC members of staff earned more than Theresa

May's prime ministerial salary of £142,000 per annum. 'Obscene,' 'gross,' and 'disgusting,' were just some of the comments heard as the BBC was slammed by the public and media alike, although as ever, the left-wing media gave the corporation a much easier ride than its counterparts on the right.

'All in all, it made for a deeply uncomfortable day for the BBC and its top presenters,' wrote *The Guardian*, 'just as the government, and its cheerleaders in the anti-Beeb right-wing press, had intended.'[15] Anti-beeb Right-wing Press? But isn't the BBC, according to some, a right-wing organisation? Moreover, having long been one of the most vocal critics of the gender pay gap, the revelation that its female 'talent' was paid considerably less than male counterparts left a very embarrassed, though predictably less than contrite BBC. Lineker's £1.8 - £2 million salary was almost *ten times* greater than the salary of fellow sports presenter Clare Balding (£150,000 - £199,000). Meanwhile, host of Radio 4's Today programme John Humphry's huge salary of between £600,000 - £650,000, compared particularly unfavourably with that of the veteran broadcaster's female co-host Sarah Montague, whose own salary did not even make the £150,000 cut off point!

Despite this sordid state of affairs, the BBC went on the attack. In the light of such shocking revelations, one or two half-hearted acknowledgements followed and a few platitudes were heard in which the corporation begrudgingly admitted that it 'had to do better' in terms of parity in pay. Overall, however, the BBC was fundamentally correct while its many critics were fundamentally wrong. It should not have surprised anyone then when the BBC Press Office began drawing attention to a piece of research by none other than . . . Ipsos MORI which declared that:

@BBCPressOffice
Nearly 4 in 5 UK adults think that the BBC should be able
to try to get the highest quality presenters, actors and
reporters - even if it means paying similar to what other
broadcasters pay.

Did 4 in 5 UK adults really approve of these huge BBC salaries? If so, then why, just days before the disclosure, had the BBC warned its staff about a potential public backlash? Did not a substantial majority of Brits (80%) approve of these astronomical salaries? According to the same polling company more people support the payment of huge BBC salaries than support the monarchy (76%) or think the NHS is one of the biggest problems facing the UK (61%). And yet...

'In terms of support for talent included in the [salary] disclosures,' so went a BBC statement, 'we have an established way of dealing with such things.' The BBC was seemingly getting ready to protect its 'talent,' but from what – messages of solidarity? Congratulations? Overwhelming public support notwithstanding, it seems the corporation was taking the threat of a public backlash very seriously. Some of its top 'talent' were even offered enhanced security if required. Two million-pounds-a-year football presenter Gary Lineker was just one of many BBC staff preparing for an onslaught that Ipsos MORI research strongly suggested wasn't coming: 'Happy BBC salary day,' tweeted the Match of the Day presenter, 'I blame my agent and the other TV channels that pay more. Now where did I put my tin helmet.' Despite 80% support – a massive vote of public confidence – the ex-England footballer was sufficiently worried about reaction from the same public to reach for his 'tin helmet.' As to which TV channels 'pay more' the Match of the Day presenter did not say – ITV perchance?

'The corporation's bosses are braced for attacks on presenters and other high paid 'talent' when the list of stars earning £150,000 or more is made public,' reported *The Telegraph*, adding that:

> A BBC source said: "People are extremely worried about safety, not only for themselves but also their families. There is a worry they will receive a torrent of abuse online."[16]

But according to Ipsos MORI 4 out of 5 Brits *supported* BBC salary rates - well didn't they?

'Ipsos MORI for the BBC'

So, did 80% of the British public really think that the BBC should be paying its employees anything up to £2.5 million per year, and that over 200 BBC staff should be paid more than the British Prime Minister? A closer inspection of the BBC Press Office tweet's (very, very) small print reveals that the 'research' was indeed carried out by 'Ipsos MORI for the BBC.' In other words the BBC itself had commissioned and paid for the research. Crucially then, this was not a piece of independent research free of any partisan interest. Exactly how then did Ipsos MORI manage to establish that 80% of the British public had no problems paying BBC employees large chunks of licence fee money – their money? Here's the question the 1,032 respondents were asked to agree or disagree with:

> Getting the highest quality presenters, actors, actresses, directors and news reporters is competitive as these people are in demand from many broadcasters. If it means paying similar to what other broadcasters pay, what do you think the BBC should do?[17]

Note that respondents are told that securing the services of such people is 'competitive' and that such people 'are in demand from many broadcasters.' Note also that no actual figures are mentioned in terms of salary levels: 'paying similar to what other broadcasters pay.' But exactly how much do 'other broadcasters' pay their staff, £50k? £100k? £200k? £2.5 million? While guessing a ballpark salary figure for teachers or nurses may be possible, reaching a figure – any figure - for broadcasting salaries would be nigh on impossible. The lack of benchmarking is apparent – purposely so.

Most glaringly of all, the BBC is of course not at all like 'other broadcasters.' Perhaps most significantly, it receives £4 billion pounds from the compulsory licence fee every year. Comparing salary levels between a tax-payer funded non-commercial broadcaster and commercial rivals seems therefore next to useless. For example, teachers in the comprehensive system are paid much less than counterparts in the private sector. NHS surgeons are paid less than those in private practice and so on.

The survey is already exerting subtle pressure. gently steering respondents towards the outcomes desired by ISPOS Mori and the organisation paying them to conduct the 'research,' the BBC. The statement could however have been worded in any number of ways:

> It is right the BBC pays presenters like Chris Evans & Gary Lineker circa £2 million per year.

Worded this way, it is highly debatable whether '4 out of 5' people would have agreed with this particular statement. 'The Great BBC survey' indeed found the precise *opposite* to Ipsos MORI, that almost 80% of the British public strongly disagreed with paying BBC employees exorbitant salaries:

It is right the BBC pays presenters like Chris Evans & Gary Lineker circa £2 million per year.[18]				
Strongly agree	Agree	Neutral	Disagree	Strongly disagree
7 %	3%	2%	10%	78%

The Twickenham effect

The late essayist Christopher Hitchens it was who, as ever, succinctly summed up the essence of an industry that is worth tens of millions of pounds a year: 'The first thing to notice, surely, is that these voyages into the ocean of the public mind are chartered and commissioned by wealthy and powerful organisations, who do not waste their money satisfying mere curiosity.'[19]

Put simply, professional polling companies such as Ipsos MORI deliver the results their clients want. The Twickenham effect denotes how organisations like Ipsos MORI carry out their research within carefully selected demographic groups among whom they can predict, with a high degree of certainty, will deliver the desired answers. In the case of the BBC research will invariably be conducted in affluent areas, the habitat of professionals and graduates likely to have liberal views and be supportive of the European Union, areas just like . . . Twickenham. Working class areas can similarly be excluded. Middle class metropolitan liberals sympathetic to left wing causes will do just fine. This way, Ipsos MORI can obtain the 'correct' results for its client, the BBC, who can then go on to claim 80% of the British public support paying its employees enormous salaries from licence fee money.

'The great majority of the public say that they want the BBC to try to have the best talent on its programmes,' wrote Director General Tony Hall in the BBC's General Review of 2017, adding, 'If we are to give the public what they want, then we have to pay for those great presenters and stars. The public agree.' Hall's next claim had a rather familiar ring about it:

> New research shows that four out of five members of the public think that the BBC should be able to try to get the highest quality presenters, actors and reporters for its programmes and services -even if it means paying similar amounts to other broadcasters.[20]

Not according to the huge public backlash that followed the BBC announcement. Nor according to research carried out by *The Telegraph* in the immediate aftermath of the pay revelations which found 60% of respondents disagreeing with the statement, 'Do you think big BBC stars' salaries are justified?'[21]

A 'Right-wing' broadcaster

As preposterous as it might seem to anyone watching, reading or listening to BBC content on a regular basis, there are those who maintain the corporation is right-wing - a mouthpiece, so they insist, for the Conservative party or even UKIP no less!. OK, the fact that many of these critics' political sympathies lie over to the left of the political spectrum may help to explain this bizarre accusation. And yes, they are talking about the *same* organisation that adored Tony Blair and New Labour (still does) and despised Mrs Thatcher and her Tory administration (still does).

The more sophisticated reader will appreciate that the BBC is in fact many things to many people. Above all else it is an integral part of the British establishment. From its shockingly biased coverage of the General Strike back in 1926 through Suez and including the 2016 European Union Referendum, the BBC has been a dependable and steadfast ally of the British government upon whom it relies for the continuation of its royal charter, which in turn legitimises its annual collection of some £4 billion from British tax payers. It's all a question of priorities.

Money makes the BBC world go round. It pays for exorbitant salaries. It pays for eye-popping expense claims. It pays also for mouth-watering pension entitlements. In BBC land money can even trump political allegiance, albeit temporarily. This is because the government of the day has the power to seriously diminish or even cut off altogether the BBC's lavish funding derived from the TV licence fee. It just so happens that more often than not the government of the day happens to be Tory. Hence, the broadcaster is forced to tolerate conservatives. In an ideal world such as was witnessed from 1997-2010, when a Labour government held sway, the BBC had cause for a double celebration: firstly and most importantly its preferred political party had power; secondly, under Labour administrations royal charter renewal is never in any doubt whatsoever.

Under Tory administrations however the BBC's approach becomes one of pragmatism: wise not to bite the hand that feeds you, *too hard*. Strangely, even when they effectively hold the BBC's purse strings and could reasonably appoint an independent enquiry into its activities, conservatives do nothing. The average Tory seems to have become resigned to BBC treatment:

> It is a recurring feature of the Tories' dealings with the BBC
> that they have often quietly accepted blatantly unfair treatment:
> a sort of Stockholm Syndrome response where they end up
> fawning over their tormentors.[1]

Besides, provided the modern Tory party continues to pursue 'progressive' rather than conservative policies, the BBC can be guaranteed not to be too harsh on the party and its people. The name of the boat – Tory or Labour – is in many ways immaterial. What matters is the direction of travel. And as of 2018 the 'Conservative' party are drifting in a direction of which the BBC heartily approves: leftwards.

'The BBC,' observes Robin Aitken, 'is a profoundly influential opponent of nearly everything social and political conservatives believe.'[2] This antipathy towards the political right manifests throughout BBC content, and has done since at least the 1960s. So when Panorama produced a documentary in 1984 accusing certain Tory MPs of having links with the far right, perhaps it should have surprised no one. The programme's premise was easily debunked. 'Maggie's Militant Tendencies' had been a textbook case of sloppy programme making which had started with its far-right premise and worked backwards until the 'evidence' fitted accordingly. For example, the programme accused one Tory MP of attending a far-right rally in Italy, when he had in fact been in attendance at a rally for railway enthusiasts! In response, the broadcaster claimed to have made an error. All in all, 17 other similar 'errors' were catalogued in the programme. Naturally, the BBC denied any wrongdoing. In the ensuing High Court battle which followed the broadcaster was successfully sued for substantial damages, but not before it had squandered millions of pounds of tax payer money. 'The plan discussed [by BBC top brass] was to keep the libel case going through the courts as long as possible,' notes Jean Seaton, 'partly on the grounds that the BBC could outspend the MPs as the legal costs mounted.'[3]

Though it eventually lost the court case after it was revealed its far-right premise was based on nothing more substantial than scurrilous gossip, contrite the BBC was not. On the surface it seemed like one BBC hatchet job too far. Surely action would have to be taken. Mrs Thatcher knew all too well the deleterious effect the BBC was having upon public life. And yet save for a little sabre-rattling nothing of substance happened. When it could and should have taken decisive action, the Thatcher administration did what all Tories do, roll over. Veering between mildly derisive to overtly antagonistic, the corporation continues to treat figures on the political right with something less than impartiality.

'Massive left-wing bias at the BBC'

'Always funny watching rabid lefties going into meltdown over suggestions to defund the "right-wing" BBC,' writes a social media user. True enough, calls to reform or ditch the television licence fee have invariably come from true conservatives, although since his emergence followers of Jeremy Corbyn have joined the throng. It would seem that anything less than worshipfulness of the Labour leader is deemed by his supporters to be an act of political sabotage by a once dependable BBC. 'In my BBC days,' recalls Antony Jay, 'the Labour politicians always felt (quite rightly) that the BBC was on their side.'[4]

Jay's sentiments are consistently echoed by those who have worked on the inside of Broadcasting House. As far back as 1934 the BBC's first Director General Lord Reith expressed himself relieved with the appointment of John Coatman as News Editor as, 'an offset to the left-wing influence of which we have so much.'[5] For those on the inside, the BBC's political sympathies are not in doubt, nor have they ever been. The Tory party's first-ever Head of Broadcasting from 1947, John Profumo, remarked how he, 'wanted to keep an eye on left-wing bias at the BBC.'[6]

In an article entitled, 'What is the loneliest job in Britain: being a Tory at the BBC.' Robin Aitken puts the 'right-wing' BBC myth firmly to bed:

> For three decades I was that rare breed - a Conservative at the BBC. In my time working on programmes such as Today and Breakfast News I couldn't have formed a cricket team from Tory sympathisers.[7]

Regarding his time working on the BBC's flagship financial programme, Aitken notes that, 'The Money Programme staff were a typical BBC lot . . . They were also, almost without exception, men and women of the centre-left.'[8]

We have already come across Jeff Randal. The ex-*Sunday Telegraph* and *The Sunday Times* journalist joined the BBC in 2001 as its first Business Editor. He lasted just four years in post. 'Randal had found himself,' states John Lloyd, 'a man of centre-right views, regarded "as an extremist" at the BBC.'[9]

Evidence of Auntie's left-wing sympathies appears to be overwhelming. We have already heard from Peter Sissons, who cautions BBC personnel to hide their copies of right-leaning newspapers like *The Daily Mail* inside a copy of the left-wing *Guardian*. Interviewed in 2010, then Director General Mark Thompson made some particularly illuminating comments regarding his organisation's political bias. The title of the article – 'There was massive left-wing bias at the BBC' – merely confirms what the likes of Reith, Profumo, Jay, Aitken, Sissons and others have already intimated. Interestingly, in the interview Thompson was trying to suggest that this 'problem' no longer existed, that left-wing bias was a thing of the past:

> It [the BBC] is like the New Statesman, which used to be various shades of soft and hard left and is now more technocratic. We're like that, too. We have an honourable tradition of journalists from the right [working for us].[10]

Comparing the BBC to the left-wing New Statesman is revealing enough in itself, but what really gives the game away is the suggestion that the presence of right-wing journalists at the BBC is some kind of 'honourable tradition' - akin to having an occasional mufti day at work. It's the sort of sentiment made by someone who believes by allowing a conservative to work in the inner sanctum of the corporation he is making a concession, a great one at that.

Keeping tabs on BBC political bias is not for the faint-hearted. Boasting 20,000 activists pumping out a constant stream of propaganda across a huge media platform, it's a task that requires significant resources, not to mention time. The few independent studies (not BBC funded) that have been attempted invariably find significant bias, particularly in terms of left-wing/pro-EU sympathies. For example, a 5-year analysis of the BBC's Panorama programme found 'consistent left-wing bias,' in both its selection and presentation of a range of topics. Panorama, the study concluded, was anti-free market and pro-regulation; anti-business and pro-increased public spending. The study also concluded that the programme was anti-United States, exhibiting what it described as 'naked anti-Bush bias.'[11] Overall, the study concluded that, 'left of centre messages are privileged and right of centre messages are ignored, side-lined and sometimes even ridiculed.'

Keen support of the US Left-wing Democrat party extending to something verging on adulation for Barack Obama, and corresponding antipathy to a long line of Republican presidents from the Bushes through to Donald Trump, and the case for the BBC's supposed right-wing bias gets ever shakier. Throw in its even more fanatical promotion of mass migration, open borders, transgenderism, LGBT issues, The European Union and Islam to name but a few, and suggestions of right-wing bias become farcical.

Besides, under the recent leadership of Liberals such as David Cameron and Theresa May, the modern Conservative Party is arguably less right-wing than at any point in its 200-year history. If this is the case, Mark Thompson's observation that the modern BBC leans neither Left nor Right, is more technocrat and less partisan of yore, starts to make *some* sense. It might also help to explain the erroneous assumption that the BBC is 'right-wing.' Amongst other things, this simplistic assertion fails to recognise the growing incongruity between the modern Conservative Party and actual conservatism as a political belief system. Witness, for example, the corporation's antics in the run up to the European Referendum of 2016 and its subsequent flip flopping between support for Theresa May's Conservatives and Jeremy Corbyn's Labour Party. When Labour appeared to be edging towards support for article 50 and Brexit, BBC ardour cooled considerably. Equally, when the Tory government appeared to be executing an outrageous policy U-turn from a party committed to delivering Brexit to one which seemed determined to undermine it, BBC support similarly adjusted from red to blue. The BBC position was clear enough: support whichever of Britain's two main parties appeared to endorse its own pro-EU, anti-Brexit stance. Party politics mattered not. Provided Labour or Tory supported the BBC's position on Brexit, the broadcaster was more than happy to throw its weight behind that party, irrespective of any ideological affinity.

That BBC policies are finding common ground with successive Tory administrations is due solely to a fundamental change in the direction of travel of the Conservative Party, *not* the broadcaster.

The Farage Fallacy

'Nigel Farage is always on Question Time! That proves the BBC is right-wing!' A much-heard complaint from those of a left-wing disposition and apparent proof of the BBC's right-wing sympathies, is the supposed ubiquity of Nigel Farage as a BBC guest – especially on Question Time, a political discussion programme. Giving so much air-time to a right-wing politician is indisputable evidence, so the argument goes, of the BBC's fondness for all things on the right of the political spectrum. Why else would Mr Farage be given so much air time?

However, such complaints fail to take BBC chicanery into account. Inviting a politician onto a panel show in which he or she is a lone voice – often pitted against two, three or even four opposing unified voices – is lost on peddlers of the Farage fallacy.

'FFS, Farage on bbc again!' complained one Twitter user after the politician had featured on a Newsnight story about crime in Sweden. 'FFS, it was a 10 second clip from LBC which was used to try and discredit Farage, you left-wing loon,' replied another user. Indeed, the Newsnight segment had used a clip from LBC radio in which the ex-UKIP leader had claimed Sweden to be the rape capital of Europe. This clip was followed by Swedish politicians rubbishing Farage's claim. As transparent as this tactic had been, the less sophisticated social media users had clearly fallen for it: 'Farage is always on the BBC!'

Also lost on such people is the question of audience. As we shall see, BBC studio audiences don't materialise out of thin air. They are specially selected. In the case of an appearance by Nigel Farage it can be guaranteed the audience will consist of a large majority of left-wing voices. Added to an 'impartial' BBC host, panellists who disagree with anything and everything he says, a specially selected anti-Farage studio audience and the supposed ubiquity of the ex-UKIP leader on BBC Question Time might just become explicable. Politicians such as Nigel

Farage enter a BBC den, one that while it may look as if it is providing a platform, has in fact been specifically designed to portray him and his politics as marginal, isolated and, above all else, extreme. No resounding applause for Nigel? Why, that's because 'nobody' agrees with him. It's a BBC trick as old as the hills. Although putting a sinner in the medieval stocks might be some people's idea of promotion, those with a more sophisticated appreciation of media practice will no doubt grasp the rationale.

Research from *The Guardian* in 2015 however paints a somewhat more nuanced picture.[12] Taking their starting point as the 2010 General Election, the newspaper checked which politicians had appeared most on Question Time in the interim period:

13 Appearances	
Caroline Flint	Labour
11 Appearances	
Nigel Farage	UKIP
Douglas Alexander	Labour
Diane Abbott	Labour
Ken Clarke	Conservative
Grant Shapps	Conservative

Fig. 3

Caroline Flint is always on Question Time! That proves the BBC is left-wing! Diane Abbott is always on Question Time! That also proves the BBC is left-wing! When viewed in context, Nigel Farage appears on BBC Question Time neither less nor more than other prominent UK politicians. So, why the complaints? The reason is simple enough: provided the corporation is playing to type – supporting liberal-left causes, guests and policies - there will not be a peep out of Labour supporters long since brought up on content heavily tilted towards their cause. However, the moment the same critics perceive the left-wing bias has been counteracted or reduced even slightly, the protests begin: 'Nigel Farage is always on Question Time!'

Consider the composition of the Question Time panel following the vote to leave the European Union in 2016, a period when Mr Farage might have been expected to have figured even more prominently on QT than ever before. Our analysis of 37 editions between the June 2016 vote and June 2017, found just a single panel appearance for Farage compared to the 5 of Emily Thornberry, Labour's Shadow Foreign Secretary. Emily Thornberry is always on Question Time! And what of Joanne Cherry and Leanne Wood of the SNP and Plaid Cymru respectively, each with 3 appearances? Nigel Farage is always on Question Time! Music to the BBC's ears. The louder the accusations of right-wing bias, the more it can freely roll out that most durable of BBC proverbs: 'We get accused of bias from both the left and the right.'

It's always worth remembering at any junction, but especially at this one, the much-quoted words of BBC stalwart Andrew Marr when describing the make-up of the modern corporation: 'The BBC is not impartial or neutral. It's a publicly funded urban organisation with an abnormally large number of young people, ethnic minorities and gay people.'[13] The young, the gay and ethnic minorities – right-wingers to the very core . . .

It's not just Andrew Marr however who throws a particularly large spanner in the BBC right-wing claim. If you really want to know about an organisation ask the people who have worked there. As noted, some of the BBC's most distinguished personnel including two former Director Generals have remarked about the corporation's inherent left-wing bias: From Lord Reith in the 1920-30s, Antony Jay (1950-60s), Will Wyatt (1960-90s) Robin Aitken (1970-2000s), Peter Sissons (1980-2000s) Jeff Randall (2000s) and Mark Thompson during the 1980-2000s – all have agreed that the BBC is institutionally left-wing in orientation. The chapter on Narratives will develop this observation further.

'Complaints from both sides'

With that well-rehearsed BBC proverb ringing in our ears, let's take a small diversion in order to consider a hypothetical situation. Imagine a football match between City and United. In one match all the decisions go the way of City. United fans are not happy. The ref, they reckon, might well have been wearing a City shirt.

Bias! Scream United fans. The ref was biased!

'It's true City got all the decisions today,' announces an FA spokesman with only a hint of smugness. 'But United got all the decisions in their earlier match. City got a biased ref but so too did United.' A pause. A wide grin comes over the spokesman's face. He's done this many, many times before:

'We reckon that shows we're getting it just about right...'

Or imagine the Mayor who takes bribes from each of two criminal gangs vying for control of the town's drugs trade. In his defence, when his case comes to court, the Mayor proudly announces that he takes bribes from both sides – he's not fussy – indisputable proof he claims of his impartiality and thus evidence of suitability to hold public office.

It doesn't matter how big the avalanche of criticism it receives regarding political bias, the BBC always comes back with its tried and tested defence: *We get complaints from both sides*. From the Director General down to the bellboy, when required the entire BBC workforce can pull this proverb out of the holster quicker than Jesse James.

Atypicality in action

Human beings are creatures of habit. We cherish stability. When routines are established anything that breaks that routine tends to stand out. New colleague started at your place of work? We notice. Next door neighbour gone and bought themselves a new car? We notice. Had a new haircut? We notice. Things tend to catch our attention when they *change*, not when they remain *the same*. By contrast the status quo is largely taken for granted:

@Andrew_Adonis
I'm writing to Lord Hall, the BBC DG to suggest that Andrew Neil no longer be a BBC politics presenter because of his pro-Brexit bias

When it appeared on Twitter, the above tweet from a prominent Labour politician raised more than a few eyebrows. A staunch EU supporter, Adonis was not happy. In fact he was rather angry. It appears that a BBC presenter had done something out of character: he had failed to prosecute the pro-EU agenda of the corporation during a TV interview. Adonis immediately cried foul. Used to and wholly approving of the BBC's fervent EU bias – 'normal' procedure - the Labour peer had duly reacted to what was a change in BBC routine of seismic proportions.

Viewers familiar with The Daily Politics Show or This Week will know Andrew Neil as a political interviewer who does not pull any punches. Not good enough for Adonis. In his view, adopting an equivocal attitude to the EU did not demonstrate impartiality, but rather equated to a serious breach of his own pro-EU expectations.

Mr Adonis, note, does not intend writing to the Director General regarding the pro-EU bias displayed by a legion of BBC political presenters from Andrew Marr, Emily Maitlis, Kirsty Wark and including light entertainment personalities such as Gary Lineker and Graham Norton. Institutional pro-EU bias seems just fine with the Labour peer.

Nor did Mr Adonis seem duly disturbed regarding the corporation's adoption of language devised by pro-EU factions, and consistently used by its news and current affairs activists, e.g. 'hard Brexit,' 'Brexit rebel,' 'crashing out of the EU,' 'people's vote,' etc. The broadcaster's brazen use of pro-Remain rhetoric appears not to disturb Mr Adonis in the slightest.

Only 95% pro-EU? Not good enough, indicative of pro-Brexit bias. As far as the BBC is concerned, it cannot get enough of Mr Adonis' laments. It just goes to prove, 'We get complaints from both sides . . .'

CNN and BBC: Soulmates in impartiality

From Rock n' Roll to Rap, from The Simpsons to The Sopranos, it is often suggested that whatever trends and fashions begin in the US eventually arrive upon UK shores. Where the US leads the UK follows. Broadcasting appears to be no different, at least in terms of partisan political broadcasting where a network called CNN is one of the leading players.

Like the BBC, the American cable giant is a ubiquitous presence in the US, its rolling news an inescapable reality of airports and public spaces all over America. Like Britain's crafty state broadcaster, thanks to the vagaries of US cable subscription, it is nigh on impossible to avoid the Atlanta-based network. When it comes to the production and dissemination of the elite consensus, nobody holds a candle to CNN.

> **@Anon**
> BBC is going way of CNN. They are activists promoting globalist propaganda. They are no longer "real news" sources.

'The most trusted name in news.' CNN's slogan has a familiar ring to it. Like its ideological British cousin, in matters political this omnipresent television network claims to be impartial. The links between the two organisations are indeed well established with the BBC regularly quoting from and using the network as a source for a proportion of its American output and vice versa. CNN's hysterical coverage of the Trump presidency lurching to ever darker places, the bonds between the two channels become ever stronger.

United in impartiality and trust, the two organisations have much in common. While critics of CNN variously label it the *Counterfeit News Network, the Clinton News Network* or *the Communist News Network*, we have already noted the various interpretations of the BBC acronym. The similarities between the two broadcasters are striking indeed. Just as its London counterpart has been dogged by a catalogue of controversies in recent years, CNN has also been involved in its fair share of scandals. From cutting guests off mid-sentence not on 'narrative' to allegedly staging fake interviews and protests, the network has come in for an avalanche of criticism in recent years.

Take the G20 summit held in Hamburg in July 2017. While thousands of riot police fought running battles with mobs setting fire to the German port's streets and looting its shops, CNN were reporting that 'an eclectic and international mix of demonstrators peacefully flooded the streets.'[1] In fact, almost 500 police officers received injuries during the riots. 'The violence against police has reached a whole new level,' a Hamburg police spokesman said.[2] Such was the level of violence, days after the summit had ended, Hamburg's Mayor publicly apologised to the city's residents for the disturbances.

For many British viewers CNN first came to prominence after President Trump had famously branded the network 'fake news,' in the aftermath of his ascension to the US presidency in 2016. Stung by such criticism of its fellow anti-Trump travellers, the BBC naturally sprung to the defence of its American ally discrediting the president's 'fake' news CNN accusation at every possible turn. 'Trump's endless onslaughts on respected outlets, which include CNN and the BBC,' asserted a BBC presenter, 'are a reflection of his sense of fragility.'[3]

No, insist the corporation, CNN is (like themselves) impartial purveyors of news, and as such above reproach. In labelling their broadcasting soulmates as 'fake' Donald Trump on the other hand was little more than an unhinged demagogue. Not every organisation however was jumping to the defence of CNN a la BBC. When reflecting upon how, in the distant past CNN had once been a byword for objectivity, *The Washington Times* noted, not without regret that:

> Those days are long gone. Watch any 10 minutes of CNN, and
> now you'll see nothing more than a nonstop — and often
> vicious — diatribe against President Trump.[4]

Despite its history of set-ups, cut-offs and staged interviews, Britain's own impartial media giant stands by its equally impartial friends in Atlanta. As far as the BBC is concerned, CNN is scrupulously fair in its coverage of the news. Not however according to a team from Harvard who took the not inconsiderable trouble to analyse US media coverage of Donald Trump's first 100 days in office.[5] Among the outlets analysed along with CNN were several other favourite anti-Trump BBC sources including *The New York Times* and *The Washington Post.*

The researchers scrutinised the output of all three organisations in terms of whether they presented the US president in a negative or positive light. Here's what they found:

	Negative %	Positive %
CNN	93	7
New York Times	87	13
Washington Post	83	17

Fig. 4

The BBC might have thought CNN to be impartial, but the researchers begged to differ concluding that, 'Trump's coverage during his first 100 days set a new standard for negativity.' Further analysis by the Media Research Centre revealed that 96 of CNN's guests interviewed over a 24 hour period had been Trump critics, with just 7 guests supportive of the president.[6]

By any standards we care to choose CNN is evidently not an impartial news network, anything but. In the light of this damning evidence *The Washington Times* sums the network up thus:

> CNN has become a far-left network that harangues the right and praises the left, almost nonstop[7]

The impartial CNN and the equally impartial BBC, birds of a feather.

'A CNN poll in December'
In an interview for BBC Radio 4 on 30 December 2017, *Correspondents Look Ahead*, BBC presenter James Naughtie offered this insight into the supposed unpopularity of US president Donald Trump, citing none other than 93% Trump-negative CNN as his source:

> His rating at the end of one year in office is lower than the ratings, on equivalent poll findings since the '50s, than any other President in our lifetimes. I mean, a CNN poll in December had him at 35%. Obama at the same time was at 75%.[8]

Was Donald Trump really so unpopular? It all depends on where you go to get your news:

@DRUDGE
Rasmussen Poll shows Trump at 46% APPROVE this morning with 53% DISAPPROVE. What about Obama at same exact date first year in presidency?? 46% APPROVE, 53% DISAPPROVE.

Political commentator and former consultant to President Clinton, Dick Morris knows a CNN-inspired poll when he sees one:

The reality is that the electorate — as opposed to the random sample of voters and non-voters that the media is using – largely applaud the job Trump is doing . . .'[9]

Naughtie had simply selected the poll that best fitted the impartial broadcaster's anti-Trump narrative – a poll by CNN . . . 'Donald Trump might be more popular than you think,' noted Politico in an article that examined the tendency for Trump's opponents to skewer the results of polls.[10] James Naughtie didn't seem to think so.

Creating a Liberal-left echo chamber
Is the BBC guilty of adopting tunnel vision? During his decade long sojourn with the broadcaster, Antony Jay appeared to think so. According to Jay, BBC types like himself engaged only with media that reflected their own prejudices;

We (BBC employees) were great consumers of media, where reality was filtered and organised for us by people like ourselves.[11]

In December 2017, the same month of the CNN poll, the 'national' broadcaster was positively swooning over an interview conducted by Prince Harry with that most favourite of BBC faves, Barack Obama. When the ex-president spoke about the dangers that he foresaw in the Internet, the broadcaster's ears pricked up:

One of the dangers of the internet is that people can have entirely different realities. They can be cocooned in information that reinforces their current biases.[12]

Could this be the first step in a battle to censor and control the Internet so there could be no 'different realities' to those preferred by Barack Obama and his number one fan club, the neutral BBC? 'The former president expressed concern about a future where facts are discarded, noted the BBC, 'and people only read and listen to things that reinforce their own views.'

'Why do you lie CNN?'

'Nancy Sinatra is not happy,' so went a CNN tweet of January 2017, 'Trump will use her father's song at inauguration,' to which Ms. Sinatra replied, 'That's not true. I never said that. Why do you lie CNN? For the American network it was just another day at the office, misrepresenting, hustling and 'misspeaking' generally.

Despite Ms Sinatra's firm denial and an avalanche of criticism, two years after tweeting what was a blatant lie, CNN has not deleted this false claim. Little wonder that reference to the Atlanta organisation is often accompanied with the sobriquet 'Fake News.' Notwithstanding CNN's reputation for playing fast and loose with the truth, the BBC habitually refer to the network as 'respected.'

Obama was right to be concerned. Insulating individuals from conflicting opinions, echo chambers are a common enough feature of modern life. It goes without saying of course that Obama's 'facts' equate to whatever supports the Democrat political agenda. The former US president is not a fan of Fox News or Breitbart. He is however likely to 'reinforce' his own views by watching and listening to the likes of CNN, MSNBC (or even the BBC) and by reading the highly partisan *Washington Post* or *New York Times*. He would not be the only one:

BBC Silicon Valley Reporter:
In 2018 I'm going to have pay for the New York Times,
aren't I? I've seen "you've reached your limit" more than
I've seen my own family.

'Could we be missing out if we only mix with people "just like us?"[13] It's a question that appears to occupy the BBC no end. However, when the broadcaster says 'we' what it actually means of course is 'they' – BBC wrong-thinkers and members of the despised tribes who ought to pay more attention to right-thinkers. Reinforcing your views via the BBC however is a different matter entirely.

'Cocooned in information that reinforces their current biases'

'Often, we seek out, process and retain information that confirms our views,' continues the BBC article, 'while discarding information that disagrees with our opinions.' Is it true? Do 'we' accept that which accords with our views, rejecting that which does not? It sounds like a sure fire recipe for disaster.

Figure 5 is an analysis of the Twitter activity of five BBC American correspondents during an 8-week period in 2017. The data refers to the number of tweets and re-tweets that referenced or linked to personnel working for or associated with three Liberal and three Conservative-leaning US media outlets including the three analysed in the Harvard research – CNN, New York Times (NYT) Washington Post (WP). These outlets are balanced with Fox News, New York Post (NYP) and Washington Times (WT) outlets which are generally considered to have conservative leanings.

BBC bias towards the US Liberal-left media is overwhelming, though hardly surprising. But that is not the end of the story by any means. If the analysis were extended to include left-wing supporting outlets such as Politico, Buzzfeed and MSNBC, that astonishing figure of 92% would rise even higher. Social media aids the construction of echo chambers like nothing else. On the evidence of this worrying data, Obama is dead right to express concern about a future where 'facts are discarded and people only read and listen to things that reinforce their own views.'

	Liberal-left			Cons-right		
	CNN	NYT	WP	Fox	NYP	WT
K.Ghattas	3	10	10	0	1	0
J.Sopel	10	4	4	3	0	0
A.Zurcher	32	17	39	11	0	0
K.Kay	48	45	48	6	5	0
L.Trevelyan	6	9	23	2	0	0
Sub total	99	85	124	22	6	0
Total	**308 (92%)**			**28 (8%)**		

Fig 5.

So, the next time you read, watch or listen to a BBC activist reporting on America – especially on the Trump presidency – it might be worth bearing in mind their fondness for three US media outlets in particular, each of which has been proven to be anything but fair, balanced or impartial in their coverage of the Trump administration, just the opposite in fact.

'Funded by the BBC Trust . . .'

To end this section we present something that caused great hilarity in the *Brainwashing Britain* office. In 2013 the left-wing New Statesman printed an article with the intriguing title, 'Hard Evidence: How biased is the BBC?' Eureka! This sounded like it might be worth a read . . . Before we get too excited, the lead academic who undertook this research states that he and colleagues at Cardiff University completed a major content analysis of BBC coverage, which was 'funded by the BBC Trust . . .' [14]

Sure enough the research disproved everything you knew – or *thought* you knew about the BBC. A couple of gems in a paper crammed full of goodies:

So what about the accusation that the BBC is pro-EU? Again the evidence points in the opposite direction.

So the evidence from the research is clear. The BBC tends to reproduce a Conservative, Eurosceptic, pro-business version of the world, not a left-wing, anti-business agenda.'[15]

It really is true: the BBC is right-wing! We know this to be true because a BBC financed academic tells us so. Case closed.

PART TWO
NARRATIVE

Life, if you looked about you, bore no resemblance not only
to the lies that streamed out of the telescreens, but even to the
ideals the Party was trying to achieve.[1]

George Orwell
1984

Right and Wrong Think

The following social media posts from a 'BBC Script Editor,' make for interesting reading. While browsing through these unpleasant effusions think back to our discussion of cults and the requirement for conformity. To those familiar with the BBC's 'deeply political' worldview, the content of these messages – encased in orthodox BBC group-think - may come as no surprise, even if the manner of expression might:

On Israeli PM, Benjamin Nethanyahu:
Hey arsehole why did you murder #Razan?

On outgoing Daily Mail editor, Paul Dacre:
Lot of love for Dacre on here tonight. So there should be.
He's earned it. The cunt,

On the NHS:
Make no mistake: the Tories WANT the NHS to be
under-funded, under-resourced & under-staffed - it makes it
easier to privatise

On President Assad's visit to Syria:
Fuck off, please, and don't come back. You absolute animal.

On a pro-EU march:
Nothing will stop me marching for the EU - least of all a bunch of sunburnt meatheads[2]

On President Trump/Russia:
Trump wants Russia back in the G7. Could he be any more of a Kremlin puppet? If Russia wants back in, they should get the fuck out of Ukraine first

All in all a pretty stringent set of views we think you'll agree. And all tweeted from an account sporting the legend, 'BBC Script Editor.'[3] He is not alone. A producer of BBC Radio 4's You and Yours programme took to social media one day to vent his fury upon the 17.4 million Brits who had voted for Brexit, very much against the wishes of the impartial, free and fair cult to which he belongs:

> If you know Brexit is likely to be a disaster, if your atavistic
> anger scrambles your brain as you reach for a response to
> the Rees-Moggs of this world or their smiling idiot sucubuses
> [sic] or to florid faced little Englanders in the question time
> audience . . .

The targets here are fairly standard BBC wrong-thinkers: pro-Brexit Conservative MP Jacob Rees-Mogg and Brexit voting Brits who had been blinded by what the BBC right-thinker labels their 'atavistic anger' - a jibe at Brits who value their culture and traditions and who, much to BBC fury, are proving remarkably resistant to the broadcaster's 'progressive' globalist agenda. Thus, these are just the type of people any self-respecting cultural Marxist has been trained to abhor. The reference to 'florid faced' is yet another example of BBC antipathy towards the white, working classes whose ruddy, healthy complexions genuinely appears to disgust BBC types.

So, are these obnoxious views typical down at Broadcasting House? If we cared to, having extrapolated these messages, we could follow the BBC lead and hold them up to be representative of the corporation as a whole as it invariably does for UKIP or other members of the despised tribes. With its ability to distort and misrepresent, extrapolation is a favourite BBC tactic. We could so easily exploit it in this instance. But we won't. Because that wouldn't be particularly impartial nor would it be especially ethical . . .

'Us' and 'them'

In BBC land there are 'us' and people like us - Guardian readers and assorted 'progressives' (Inner and Outer Party members of *1984*). And then there's everybody else – *1984*'s proles. Before we go any further, let's take a look at how BBC types view themselves in relation to non-BBC types:

The BBC Personality Cult	
We (right-thinkers) are:	**They (wrong-thinkers) are:**
Intellectual	Dim-witted
Tolerant	Prejudiced
Cultured	Philistine
Open-minded	Small-minded
Cosmopolitan	Parochial
Visionary	Reactionary
Compassionate	Unkind
Progressive	Regressive
Refined	Vulgar
Rational	Unthinking

Fig. 6

'Like-minded groups of individuals'

We have already made some remarks about how cult members become almost fanatical in their devotion to its dogma. We have also suggested that the British Broadcasting Corporation expects – demands - from its members a similar if not greater level of compliance. The objective is uniformity of thought aka group-think.

It has further been suggested that cults of any description, soft or hard, tend to project a view of the world that is both polarised and idealised: the cult versus the world wherein the cult is 'good' and the world beyond is 'bad.' The reason is simple enough: in its valiant struggle against bigotry, tyranny and ignorance and its equally admirable aim to change the world into a better place, cult/Party/state broadcaster finds itself engaged in the eternal struggle between good and evil. In order to achieve its aims, the group must marshal its troops behind a litany of simple messages which simultaneously consolidate loyalty to the in-group and hostility to the outsider.

In her book *Brainwashing: The Science of Thought Control*, Kathleen Taylor observes that a generic feature of cults is:

> Simplistic, dualistic thinking like that noted by Robert Lifton in Communist ideology (good/evil, believer/heretic, saved/damned) and a tendency towards utopian thinking.[4]

In BBC land this 'tendency towards utopian thinking' manifests itself in what its activists themselves openly call their 'narratives:' This is Evan Davis, host of BBC Newsnight:

> Like-minded groups of individuals share a narrative about many things, as indeed does much of the media: that the French economy is sclerotic, that America's lack of gun control is mad, that a prime minister is inept, that Russia is evil and so on.[5]

Perhaps most alarming is not merely the fact that organisations like the BBC hold such beliefs in the first place – premised largely upon stereotypes, prejudice and generalisations - but rather that these beliefs are enduring; they rarely, if ever change. For example, should Donald Trump's administration ever manage to eradicate world poverty, cancer and AIDS, the BBC view of him would not change one iota. The impartial broadcaster would still loathe the US president. Its view is rigid, inflexible, immutable. MSM media narratives rarely change, nor are they intended to.

'When journalists go to report on a story,' remarks Davis' Newsnight colleague Gabriel Gatehouse, 'we strive for accuracy and balance, but we often also go in search of a narrative.'[6] This is the closest it gets to the BBC admitting that rather than arriving at a story with a blank piece of paper, its activists arrive with the story already written. Clearly, when it comes to the BBC what is *excluded* is arguably just as important – more so – than what is included. Contradictory testament will always be excluded from BBC narratives where possible. 'That America is bad and Israel evil,' Robin Aitken remarks, 'are two of the assumptions that just can't be questioned.' Thus we are presented with the very epitome of thinking that is simplistic and dualistic. It matters not what America or Israel do. As far as the BBC is concerned, until the day these countries come round to the BBC world-view – the correct view – they will always remain 'bad' or 'evil.'

Ultimately, BBC narratives serve a purpose: to promote certain (political) ideas while diminishing and/or denigrating others. When you switch on the television to watch the BBC Six or Ten o' clock news be assured you are not receiving the actual news, you are receiving a version that has been formulated in accordance with the appropriate BBC narrative. The message received by a BBC audience is precisely that which promotes the broadcaster's worldview. As we shall see, the state broadcaster has a narrative for every occasion; from French politics to fracking, from the question of private gun ownership to the emotive subject of abortion, the BBC really does have 'views on everything.'

'Our despairing narrative'

When working for BBC Scotland Aitken recalls another BBC narrative which, despite a plethora of contrary evidence, it insisted on propagating ad infinitum. According to the broadcaster, Scotland was forever on the point of economic collapse:

> Our despairing narrative portrayed a Scottish dystopia – a stricken land brought to its knees by an uncaring government of greedy southrons. In fact the country was undergoing a painful industrial revolution, Our chosen narrative could have argued that a country with oil, electronics and banking as economic mainstays had cause for optimism. But as BBC journalists our predominant focus was on declining industries and lost employment.[7]

'The despised tribes'

It's not just America, Israel or Russia whom the BBC portrays in the same old negative way. In 'Can We Trust the BBC?' Robin Aitken proposes a list of groups which he labels 'the despised tribes' and whom he suggests are particularly hated within the corridors of Broadcasting House. These 'tribes' include: Orangemen, whites in Africa, Israel's Likud Party, Italy's Northern League, France's Front National Party, American Christian fundamentalists, conservative Roman Catholics and UKIP amongst others.

We could add numerous other political groups to this list such as Viktor Orban's Fidesz Party in Hungary, Alternative fur Deutschland in Germany and the Swedish Democrats. Donald Trump supporters in the US and Brexit voters in the United Kingdom could also be included. And with ordinary citizens across Europe – mothers, fathers, grandparents – being added to the BBC's 'far/alt-right' category, the list of wrong-thinkers grows larger by the day.

Writing for *The Spectator*, Rod Liddle identifies several majority groups whose views the BBC considers to be 'antediluvian' and 'beyond the pale.' Included in these groups he lists those who think there are only two genders (56%) and those who do not identify as feminist (93%) etc. According to Liddle, the BBC attitude towards such groups is not *how do we respect their opinions* but rather, 'what can we do to make these morons change their minds?' He continues, 'Those views quoted above are simply wrong, so far as the BBC is concerned, and there's an end to it, even when those views are in a clear majority.'[8]

'Diversity includes everyone,' according to the BBC's intriguingly entitled Head of Diversity, Inclusion and Succession. 'The BBC belongs to everyone in the UK whatever their background so everyone at the BBC has a responsibility to ensure that we represent, and are representative of, the public we serve.'[9] That the BBC 'belongs' to everyone will be welcome if not surprising news to any number of despised tribes from UKIP voters to the 'morons' who desire Scottish independence and Brexit.

In order to propagate this narrative, BBC Scotland activists cynically ignored that which contradicted their pre-conceived story of Scottish doom and gloom. In order to keep the population in a state of anxiety, fear and anger, the propagandists selected and edited; they *excluded*. For here was a classic narrative of the oppressed (Scotland) and the oppressor (England). As such this was an opportunity far too good to be missed by any self-respecting cultural Marxist intent on sowing discord. 'In the six years I worked there,' adds Aitken, 'the BBC Scotland view of the world was deeply misleading.'

It's not just Scotland that the broadcaster presents through a distorted prism. Take the topic of America. The BBC is innately hostile to Americanism and what it deems to be the brash brand of capitalism it exports around the world. It is even more hostile to the various manifestations that Christianity sometimes takes in the States. And it is extremely hostile towards gun ownership and the pro-Life movement. Thus, it arguably despises God-fearing Americans perhaps more than any other tribe on earth. In BBC-land Americanism equates to vulgarity. It is this wholly ideologically driven view of America that the broadcaster invariably exposes to its audiences. Scotland, America: different countries, same approach: partial, one-sided, disingenuous and deliberately misleading.

We can therefore conclude that BBC narratives have little or nothing to do with news, but are rather vehicles for promoting its own worldview, a view as we have seen that encodes the policies of a powerful, global establishment. A BBC narrative is simply a rendition. It presents a single view of the world. Although this playbook may work in the short term, it's a strategy guaranteed to implode sooner or later. Are people really ignorant of how the broadcaster goes about its work? Although it might come as a surprise to BBC types, a significant number of people appear to be woke regarding BBC machinations, are not quite as stupid as Broadcasting House appears to assume.

When people were asked to judge how fairly and accurately it reports on certain topics the results were revealing.[10] Respondents appeared to somewhat trust the BBC in matters equine and meteorological, but as far as matters political are concerned trust is noticeably lower - considerably so:

Which word(s) best describes your level of trust in the BBC to report fairly and accurately on the following topics:					
	V High %	High %	Neutral %	Low %	V Low %
Trump Presidency	2	3	5	13	77
Israel-Palestine	1	3	13	24	58
Brexit	0	1	3	10	84
The Grand National	20	21	51	0	6
Weather	18	21	44	7	9

Fig. 7

Black and white: The BBC worldview

BBC narratives are characterised first and foremost by polarisation – good v bad, and not without reason. Presenting just two sides of any argument and then pressuring and manipulating people to pick a side – your side – is one of the cultural Marxist's most potent weapons. Debating the ground between polar opposites can mean only one thing: arrival at a more nuanced appreciation of the topic in hand - anathema to Comrade Alinsky and his Frankfurt allies for whom rational discussion can only lead to one place: rejection. Political Machiavellians have long since appreciated this reality. Thus, the objective is always to railroad, to obviate. BBC narratives are designed to bypass debate, to simplify and above all else to polarise.

For example, when it comes to the topic of mass migration Britain's politically neutral broadcaster deliberately presents the issue as a polarisation between good people who support mass migration (open border right-thinkers) and anti-migration bad people (closed border wrong-thinkers). Yet for the majority of people the immigration debate is much more complex than a question of racial identity. Nonetheless, it suits the broadcaster to polarise the debate in this way. Those resistant to its multi-cultural mantra will be invariably presented in the most negative way possible, usually compared to neo-Nazis and labelled as 'far-right' extremists. Instructing fellow cultural Marxists to always strive to polarise any debate between Us (good) and them (bad), in

'Rules for Radicals,' Alinsky illustrates his point by quoting from scripture: 'He that is not with me is against me.' (Luke 11:23)

Ultimately BBC narratives enable the broadcaster to side-step complexity. They enable it to batter down dissent. They enable it to hustle, railroad and manipulate. They enable it to accuse and brand. Most importantly of all, narratives enable the BBC to reduce complex issues to the level of the superficial whereby Scotland is a country forever exploited by the cruel, indifferent forces south of the border, and where Israel is a country forever abusing the rights of Palestinians. There is no grey area, just good v evil. Pick a side.

In keeping with the simplistic, dualistic thinking of the cult, here's a selection of just a few BBC narratives from an almost inexhaustible supply. Virtually all BBC content is based upon deliberate polarisation:

Very, very good	Very, very bad
Democrats	Republicans
• Barack Obama	• Ronald Reagan
• Hilary Clinton	• George Bush
• Elizabeth Warren	• Donald Trump
Liberal-Left	Cons-Right
• Tony Blair	• Margaret Thatcher
• Gordon Brown	• Ian Duncan Smith
• Sadiq Khan	• John Redwood
Europhiles	Euro-sceptics
• Anna Soubry	• Boris Johnson
• Chuka Umunna	• Jacob Rees-Mogg
• Vince Cable	• Nigel Farage
Globalists	Nationalists
• Angela Merkel	• Vladimir Putin
• Emmanuel Macron	• Viktor Orban
• Jean Claude Juncker	• Matteo Salvini

Fig. 8

BBC narratives do not just cover politics. The broadcaster's good v bad polarisation covers just about every conceivable topic. A particularly revealing narrative involves people in the public eye. From Hollywood A-listers through to JK Rowling and Lily Allen, provided they concur fully with BBC group-think, the broadcaster will happily portray these celebrities in a positive light. Provided the likes of George Clooney, Angeline Jolie and friends are promoting open borders, mass migration, gun control and pro-choice policies etc. they will receive nothing but love from the BBC. Right-think is rewarded, wrong-think punished. This way the broadcaster, along with its mainstream allies, is able to control the boundaries of public debate; or more precisely on behalf of rich, powerful interest groups the BBC hierarchy is able to control what its employees present as news and how they present it.

Outside of politics BBC wrong-thinkers are strikingly thin on the ground. There are a dearth of public figures daring to challenge BBC group-think. The reason is fairly simple: the BBC smear machine. In the traditions of bullies since time immemorial, the threat of retribution from the 'national' broadcaster ensures that celebrities with 'wrong' opinions keep them to themselves. By far the biggest category of all is the broadcaster's socio-cultural and political narratives of which we present just a few examples:

Very, very good	Very, very bad
Mass migration	Moderate migration
Palestine	Israel
State education	Private education
Islam	Christianity
Urban	Rural
Homosexual	Heterosexual
Pro-choice	Pro-life
Anti-guns	Pro-guns
Antifa	Pegida
Rohingya Muslims	White S. African farmers

Fig. 9

BBC narratives also extend to media organisations of course. In keeping with the Marxist playbook, there is never any grey area. Left-liberal media is good; right-Conservative media bad:

Very, very good	Very, very bad
CNN	Fox News
Buzzfeed	Russia Today
New York Times	Breitbart
The Guardian	The Sun

Fig. 10

BBC narratives perfectly encapsulate the broadcaster's 'progressive' world-view in all its simplistic, polarised glory. Entities that agree with BBC-think are very, very good; those who disagree are very, very bad. Those on the 'good' side can be treated with sympathy, reverence and respect; those on the 'bad' side with disapproval, contempt and scorn. BBC 'Goodies' are invariably fawned over (e.g. Merkel, J K Rowling etc.) and issued with free passes for transgressions, while baddies (e.g. Salvini, Putin) are excoriated. BBC goodies are always innocent, BBC baddies always guilty. Such is the framework by which BBC activists produce 'news' and comment.

A number of BBC narratives are not polarised: e.g. The NHS is failing; The police are institutionally racist; Climate change is one of the biggest disasters facing mankind; Katie Hopkins is a horrible bigot; The gender pay gap is real; in his support for Donald Trump, Kanye West is mentally unstable etc.

Master and sub narratives
Should a BBC activist wish to create a piece of propaganda he or she first checks the appropriate BBC master narrative, although the vast majority are of course already deeply ingrained.

Take for example a story concerning Melania Trump. The BBC activist immediately knows the appropriate master narrative: *Donald Trump is very, very bad*; Ergo, *Melania Trump is very, very bad*. Now all that is required is a suitably negative angle, or sub-narrative: A favourite

BBC anti-Melania Trump sub-narrative concerns reactions to the First Lady on Twitter. BBC sub-narratives invariably highlight how Mrs Trump is 'mocked' online. The golden rule is that they remain subordinate to the master narrative. Just try finding a positive BBC story about the US First Lady, one not dripping with snark and dislike.

BBC activists follow these narratives instinctively. Indeed, so automatic are their reactions, the average Panorama or Newsnight editor is highly unlikely to be even mildly aware of what is their own unconscious behaviour. This slavish devotion to right-think manifests itself in Orwell's Oceania, where:

> A Party member is not only required to have the right opinions, but the right instincts. Many of the beliefs and attitudes demanded of him are never plainly stated . . . if he is a person naturally orthodox (in Newspeak a good thinker) he will in all circumstances know, without taking thought, what is the true belief or the desirable emotion.[11]

Thus the BBC/Party right-thinker knows instinctively what opinions are 'correct' and which are 'incorrect.' Formulating a suitable sub-narrative in keeping with these edicts is the task of the propagandist. Whichever way they arrive at their final piece, the result is always the same: a partial news story, one tailored not to reality but wholly to the demands of master narratives already planned and formulated. Let's look at a few of the corporation's favourite master narratives.

Caucasians are very, very bad

Racism is when someone is discriminated against (singled out) because of their race, the colour of their skin, their nationality, their accent or first language, or their ethnic or national origin. Racism is a hate crime, and is illegal.

BBC Advice

One of the BBC's most ubiquitous narratives involves Caucasians – specifically white European and American Caucasians. This, recall, is the demographic targeted by cultural Marxism, especially any individuals who happen to be male, Conservative and Christian - bedrocks each and every one of western, capitalist society. On the subject of racism, here's just a few BBC headlines where the subjects appear to have been 'singled out' because of 'the colour of their skin:'

Do these twenty-nine white men run America?

Inside the mind of white America

Elderly white men block change at FA

bbc.co.uk

Whipping up racial tension is somewhat of a BBC speciality. Cultural Marxism never relents, never lets up. Nobody – individual or institution - is immune from its attacks, no target considered off limits:

@BBCTalkback
Why are the Royal Family so "white", given that UK society is so ethnically-diverse these days?

When western society is divided – into white and non-white, men and women etc. – only then can it be conquered. Thus, wherever there are cultural Marxists to be found there will be attempts to divide society into black and white, Christian and Muslim, gay and straight, oppressors and oppressed etc.

Just as Hugh Greene noted, propaganda works cumulatively. It must be consistent and therefore it must, absolutely must - be persistent.

The BBC's anti-white messages are indeed ubiquitous, from its news website 'trying to explain arranged marriages to white people,' even through to BBC local radio, one of whose presenters asked his phone-in audience to consider the following question one day:

> 'Do you think it's true that white people don't do enough for the elderly in this country?'[1]

Which was followed up by another question of a similar vein: 'So what do you think of white people who put elderly relatives in a care home?' For all those 'white' people caring for relatives elderly or otherwise, one can only imagine how offensive these generalisations must have sounded. Racial attacks like these are the modus operandi of the cultural Marxist. Here's the presenter of the show responding to a caller who mentioned that her mother happened to live 75 miles away:

> Let me ask this question very directly to everybody who is
> **white** listening to my programme: if you had an elderly
> neighbour for example, would you look out for them? Would
> you pop round and make sure they'd had something for dinner?
> Would you keep an eye on them? Or do you think it's true that
> white people are becoming increasingly selfish, self-centred . . .

The BBC presenter presumably was not aware of the UK's Good Neighbour awards, or the numerous Good Neighbour schemes that operate up and down the country, staffed by volunteers who help the elderly in their homes, some of who are even rumoured to have 'white' skin.

> If someone discriminates against you because of your race,
> the colour of your skin or where you're from, that's racism.
> And racism is a crime.

bbc.co.uk

Having duly noted the BBC's definition of racism, the following job advertisements which appeared on its networks might puzzle some:

@BBCNewsbeat
BBC Newsbeat is looking for a Trainee Multi-Media Journalist.
This is a @_CreativeAccess scheme for people from a black,
Asian or non-white ethnic minority background. Know anyone
who'd be suitable? Share with them!

bbc.co.uk/careers:
We want experienced, senior TV professionals who are disabled
or from black, Asian and minority ethnic backgrounds to get an
all-access understanding of commissioning at the BBC

'A dying breed'

Not content with ensuring that opportunities to join the cult increasingly
exclude 'white' people, the BBC is taking pains to shape its existing
cohort in line with its 'progressive' agenda. When BBC producer Jon
Holmes was axed from Radio 4's The Now Show in September 2016, it
appeared to be just the latest move by the broadcaster aimed at reducing
the number of white faces within the corporation. A saddened and
bewildered Holmes took to social media:

@jonholmes1
Sad to announce I've been axed from @BBCNowShow
as 'we want to recast with more women and diversity.'
Tsk. And I didn't even punch a producer

Holmes who had worked on the show since 1997 was told his fate in a
telephone call with a female BBC producer. He was not the only one to
have fallen foul of BBC policy. In a Mail Online article, Holmes related,
'how one woman presenter was given a job only later to be told 'we can't
have you, because you are too white and middle class.'[2]

The drive to target the white male appears to be well under way
at Broadcasting House and has been for some time. In autumn 2018 a
BBC executive announced that the era of what he termed white men
'explaining stuff' on the BBC had come to an end: 'There's a mode of
programming that involves a presenter, usually white, middle-aged and
male, announced the BBC executive, 'standing on a hill and telling you
like it is'. We all recognise the era of that has passed.[3]

The envisaged marginalisation and even extinction of the white male appears never to be far away from the BBC mind. Indeed, the thought seems to set the BBC pulse racing. We turn next to a story that appeared on its news website and which featured two narratives beloved by the corporation: *Nigel Farage and the white male are very, very bad.*

The image that appeared on the UK politics page of the BBC's news website on 20th September 2017 appeared innocent enough – an image which spliced together portraits of three men who happen to share the Christian name, Nigel.[4] The article itself had been written in response to data released by the Office of National Statistics regarding changing fashions in baby names. As ever with the BBC it wasn't quite as simple as that. The BBC's spin was, well, pure BBC. Nigel? Out of the thousands of names they could have written about the BBC had chosen Nigel . . . Accompanying the image of the three Nigels – ex-racing driver Nigel Mansell, musician Nigel Kennedy and politician Nigel Farage – was a caption: 'the last of a dying breed?'

It transpires that the name Nigel is not as popular as it once was. For the BBC this could only mean one thing: 'It now seems there was no surge in people wanting to name their baby after Nigel Farage,' joyously read the BBC article. But had parents ever been in the habit of naming their children after Mr Farage as the BBC was implying? Not according to official data recording the number of babies christened Nigel over the decades:

Number of UK babies named Nigel at birth						
1950	1963	1970	1980	1990	2000	2010
1,943	5,529	2,469	413	125	25	18

Fig. 11 Source: Wikipedia

By the time Mr Farage became leader of UKIP in 2006, the name Nigel had long been out of fashion, which makes the BBC claim that parents who choose the name do so in honour of the politician rather difficult if not impossible to substantiate. Nonetheless, the broadcaster couldn't resist linking this trend to the ex-UKIP leader and by doing so suggesting that it somehow represented a reliable gauge of the politician's popularity. Nigel joined a list that included given names such as Gary,

Clive, Barry, Maurice and Norman which have all fallen out of fashion over the past few decades. Nonetheless, Britain's impartial broadcaster had eyes for one name only – Nigel.

Three days after the BBC propaganda piece appeared, Mr Farage achieved 1 million Twitter followers, a remarkable milestone making him the third most followed UK politician on the social media site behind David Cameron and Jeremy Corbyn with 1.8 and 1.5 million followers respectively.

But the BBC were not quite finished bating Mr Farage yet. In another article entitled, 'Could this Willenhall baby be the last Nigel?' the corporation could hardly hide its glee when reporting that: 'The name (Nigel), according to latest figures, is on the brink of extinction in England and Wales, with fewer than three Nigels born in 2016.'[5] It even managed to track down the father of the Wildenhall baby to demand why he had chosen Nigel as a name for his child: 'Despite its unpopularity, dad Kieran Ball had his heart set on the name.' Tracking down parents in an attempt to shame them for choosing the name Nigel for their child – an appropriate use of tax-payer money by any standards.

Do you get the BBC message? It is rather subtle, but for those who missed it allow us to explain: *Nobody cares for white males that much. In the BBC's touchy-feely multi-cultural Britain, the likes of Nigel Farage are a dying breed, and (hopefully) won't be around much longer.* Oh so subliminal. Oh so very BBC.

Wot, no diversity?

Using three middle-aged white males to represent what it termed a 'dying breed' was a nothing if not an eccentric way to frame a story that had nothing to do with actual 'breeds' – dying or otherwise - but had everything to do with changing fashions in baby names. How exactly can a name be a 'breed?' Is Charlotte a breed? Oliver? Abdul? The Oxford Dictionary.com defines breed as, 'A stock of animals or plants within a species having a distinctive appearance and typically having been developed by deliberate selection.'

While Christian or given names clearly do not fulfil the criteria for a breed, the white male could so easily. The BBC seems to think so. It also appears to believe the 'breed' is (hopefully) dying out . . . What then of that most sacred of BBC cows, diversity? Wasn't this image of a trio of middle-aged white men together with gleeful 'dying breed' headline, well, a little too white? As one of the UK's most famous holders of the name, boxing legend Nigel Benn would have had every reason to complain about an article sorely lacking in its representation of multi-cultural Britain. The former boxing legend is one of Britain's best known sportsmen. After a career which included becoming a Commonwealth and World champion at middle and super-middleweight, in 2013 Benn was inducted into the World Boxing Council Hall of Fame.

Could the inclusion of Mr Benn in the image – a black male – have rather scuppered the BBC's subliminal message i.e. that the white male is a 'dying breed?' Surely not! For that sort of stunt would have been the work of a petty, vindictive and malevolent operator. Deliberately omitting Mr Benn from its montage of Nigels would have been the work of a particularly unscrupulous broadcaster, one seemingly intent on maintaining the cultural Marxist attack on the white male. As if Britain's scrupulously fair broadcaster would stoop so low . . .

'Shame on you BBC'
In 2015, BBC Three aired a documentary intriguingly entitled 'Britain's Biggest Sexists.' As absurd as the premise sounds, the broadcaster was seemingly intent on compiling some sort of nationwide chart based upon sexism.

So who would make the BBC shortlist? And more to the point – based upon what criteria? Rappers perhaps, the lyrics of whose songs routinely refer to women as 'bitches' and whose videos often sexualise young black women? Or maybe those communities wherein the male - husbands, father, brothers and uncles - insist it is their right to exercise authority over women in accordance with religious doctrine?[6]

And what about those organisations where sexual misconduct had been allowed to go unchecked? What about the BBC itself, an organisation which according to *The Independent* was, 'facing multiple investigations after being accused of "silencing" gender discrimination and harassment victims through its use of non-disclosure agreements.'[7] As for the title of 'Britain's Biggest Sexists' the BBC was faced with an embarrassment of riches. So who would the BBC select for its shortlist? Why, the straight white male of course:

- Students
- Andy Grey (footballer) and Richard Keys (broadcaster)
- Company bosses
- Pick-up artists

For an organisation that promotes multi-culturalism with something like the zeal of the Spanish inquisition, its shortlist of 'sexists' was hideously lacking in diversity. Britain's 'biggest sexists' were, from top to tail, a single colour: white. The BBC's multi-cultural Britain had suddenly and inexplicably become very, very white.

In the case of Andy Gray and Richard Keys – 'disgusting turds' in the words of the programme – the former football commentators had committed the heinous crime, once upon a time, of making a joke about women's supposed (mis) understanding of the offside rule, a crime for which both men had been pilloried and had eventually lost their jobs. Having watched 'Britain's Biggest Sexists' and duly noting the one dimensional focus of its critique, one social media commentator summed up the programme as:

> A disgusting, man hating campaign at its finest. All the pick-up artists they show were white men, despite all the female and plentiful non-white male 'pick up artists' they only show the white guys. Now I'm not white myself but even I can see the pure hatred and bias towards this group of our society and no one seems to say a word about it. as if it does not exist, as if it isn't happening. Shame on you BBC.

Donald Trump is very, very bad

Another day, yet another anti-Donald Trump headline from the impartial, free and fair, politically neutral, publicly-funded 'national' broadcaster. Since announcing his intentions to run for US president in 2015, the BBC's anti-Trump narrative has become ever more bellicose threatening at times to spin out of control:

> 'Europe hates Trump. Does it matter?'
>
> BBC Magazine

In terms of sheer weight the BBC's anti-Donald Trump narrative beats all-comers. Rarely a day goes by without it producing another anti-Trump piece of 'journalism.' While the BBC is clearly not too keen on the US president, many appear to support the American billionaire:

> **@Anon**
> My friends in Switzerland tell me the crowds to see
> @RealDonaldTrump were huge. I am half British as well
> as American and I love the guy. Here in Eastern Europe
> where I live they ALL love him. The 'everybody in Europe
> hates Trump' rumour is as fake as news gets.

'As fake as news gets'

Europe hates Trump? As far as generalisations go they really don't come much bigger than that. Perhaps what the politically neutral broadcaster had intended to say was, dependent perhaps on the amount of BBC content they consume, a proportion of left-wing western Europeans may indeed hate the US president.

Of all the people and organisations it despises – and there are many - the BBC reserves especial disdain for one individual in particular: Donald Trump. The maverick businessman represents a real threat to the elites whose interests the BBC so faithfully and unreservedly represent. His opposition to open borders, mass migration and subsequent disenfranchisement of America's blue collar workers puts him very much on the wrong side of the BBC and its 'progressive' allies. Throw in the fact that he's a (rich) white, heterosexual male – Christian too! – and BBC antipathy becomes ever more explicable. Anti-Trump propaganda has become a BBC signature dish. Every single one of its 20,000 + activists genuinely loathes the US president. The cult has its own Emmanuel Goldstein – a figure to hate:

A BBC Radio 4 Producer:
Perhaps it's because I work in the media, but Trump's #FakeNewsAwards bullshit angers me even more than his other bullshit.

An individual who 'very proudly works for the BBC':
Sorry, I said the word "president" when I meant to say "lying sack of slime."

'I'm prejudiced against people who voted for Trump,' announces British actress Miriam Margoyles, at the outset of her BBC documentary, 'Miriam's Big American Adventure.'[1] Days later on the corporation's late night political programme This Week, after hearing a defence of Mr Trump from the journalist James Delingpole, presenter Andrew Neil muses, 'that's a point of view we don't often hear on here.'[2]

Soon after this revelation the end credits of BBC's Newsnight programme whisk the viewer off to a field somewhere in Norway. 'Now a new theory has emerged online,' announces presenter Evan Davis, 'that Norway is in fact helping Mr Trump to maintain his very closely guarded cover up. Judge for yourself. Good night.' The VT focuses on some clumps of grass in said field. Apparently this is all a big BBC joke. It seems Davis and his BBC paymasters are comparing the clumps of grass in the Norwegian field to President Trump's supposed toupee. How droll. And so it goes on and on and on . . .

The broadcaster appears not to care too much at all for America's forty-fifth president. A selection of typical BBC Trump headlines:

Museum offers Trump a toilet

Did President Trump forget the words to the national anthem?

Quiz: Could you pass Donald Trump's brain test?

A porn star scandal Trump can't shake

Can we tell if Donald Trump has a high IQ?

Nor is BBC antipathy confined to Mr Trump himself. As far as the scrupulously fair BBC is concerned any member of the Trump family is game for its scorn, ridicule and general ill-will. Indeed, its anti-Trump narrative is arguably the finest example of BBC impartiality you will find anywhere on its immense media platform. Let's take a brief look how the tax-payer funded broadcaster invariably presents not only Mr Trump himself, but the president's closest family.

Has Melania Trump 'liked' a tweet mocking her marriage?[3]
BBC conjecture as to whether Melania Trump had liked a tweet which referenced her marriage sent the broadcaster into a frenzy in May 2017. And no, this was not an article from a salacious tabloid pushing cheap, tacky gossip. It was the BBC.

> We should be honest and open about what we don't know
> and avoid unfounded speculation.[4]

bbc.co.uk

Had the First Lady actually liked the tweet in question? The BBC was positively salivating. Wouldn't it be just fantastic if Mr and Mrs Trump had marital problems? The BBC crossed its impartial fingers.

'Seems the only wall @RealDonaldTrump has built,' read the original tweet, 'is the one between him and @FLOTUS Melania Trump.' Given that this salacious tweet was the work of an anonymous anti-Trump Twitter user any broadcaster worth its salt would have dismissed it as quickly as it took to press the 'delete' button, right? Wrong. The 'national' broadcaster couldn't wait to join the feeding frenzy. Despite the original tweeter confessing that the account which liked his tweet was very likely not that of Mrs Trump, the BBC was not going to let this non-story drop without wringing out every ounce of ill-will possible. Judged by the tone of its article, it would appear that Britain's state broadcaster has intimate knowledge of the Trump's marriage. How else could it have made statements such as the following, which purport to know how Melania feels towards both her private role as wife and public role as First Lady?

> The former model was being forced into a role she did not want, by a husband she potentially wasn't overly fond of.

According to the BBC, Melania Trump is not 'overly fond' of her husband – news to the Trumps no doubt. And there you have BBC 'news' – cheap, tacky speculation contrived to upset, insult and offend. The article continues in much the same vein until, mercifully, it ends. Did Melania Trump 'like' the original tweet? Oh how the BBC would love to know; how it would love to think the Trump's marriage is on the rocks:

> It will remain a mystery for now. Attempts to get the White House to comment on the "like" by US media have so far yielded no results.

> Either way, those watching the Trumps' marriage closely will no doubt use this as further proof all is not well between the First Couple.

It is unclear whether the BBC includes itself among 'those watching the Trumps' marriage closely.' 'Did Melania Trump swat away her husband?' breathlessly speculated the broadcaster when it spotted what it hoped was Mrs Trump momentarily brushing off her husband's hand on a visit to Israel. And so it goes on and on and on: 'Overheard in the office,' tweeted an 'award winning producer and reporter for BBC Newsnight,' 'Trump's more affectionate to Macron than he is to his own wife . . .'

'We report to the highest of standards of fairness'

The Fake News Media,' so tweeted president Trump one day, 'has been so unfair, and vicious to my wife and our great First Lady, Melania.' Intent on damaging the Trumps any which way it can, no sooner had Mr Trump been sworn in as US president than the 'national' broadcaster began its obsession with the former model. Here's a flavour of the type of article BBC activists immediately began penning about Mrs Trump:

Melania Trump mocked for 'positive social media' speech

Melania 'upstaged' by Korean pop star

Melania Trump book donation snubbed by US librarian

'Snubbed', 'upstaged,' 'mocked.' If you were wondering whether all these BBC stories were anything more than a petty, vindictive and rather spiteful campaign against America's First Family, then rest assured you would have been way off the mark. The BBC's Head of News Gathering affirmed as much:

> **@jonathancmunro**
> @BBCNews is 1 of the most respected news brands in the world. We report to the highest of standards of fairness whether we're inside @WhiteHouse or not.

Judged by a selection of his social media posts, a BBC Syria and Middle East activist certainly appeared to bear Mrs Trump something bordering on ill-will. Regarding the Trump's marriage the activist was only too happy to share his expertise, apparent in his choice of hashtag, #sadnessinhereyes, from a post accompanied by a picture of Mrs Trump. He even appeared to know all about Melania's motivations for marrying her husband:

> When all you wanted was a Sugar Daddy and now you are the First Lady of the United States of America.
> #sadnessinhereyes

The BBC activist wasn't finished there. Next, he moved onto the First Lady's Twitter profile, supplying yet more inimitable analysis:

> Melania Trump has the creepiest Twitter cover photo.
> And why is her name IN CAPITALS?!

A 'Senior Writer/Producer at BBC Trending weighed in with an impartial gem of her own. The following social media message was accompanied by a quartet of pictures featuring Mrs Trump in various guises: 'I think she's trying her best.'

'Ivanka Trump, looking at people and nodding'

Whilst the BBC gleefully reports how Melania Trump is routinely 'snubbed' and its activists inform their social media followers about her supposed marital problems, it is her husband who receives the lion's share of the broadcaster's 'fairness.' A couple of gems from its Senior North American correspondent:

> Of course Trump is a Michael Jordan fan. Most of his
> views on the world were cemented in place by the end
> of the 1980s

> Of course this argument only works if you believe the
> American people would never elect an unstable simpleton
> as president[5]

To be fair to the broadcaster its disdain is not just limited to Mr and Mrs Trump. Its antipathy extends to every member of the Trump family: Eric, Donald jnr and even 10-year old Barron Trump. Britain's 'national' broadcaster appears to be not overly fond of the entire First Family. For once, it truly can claim to be impartial. So, when Mr Trump's daughter, Ivanka tweeted one day about tax cuts she posted a short clip of herself on White House duties, attending yet another engagement meeting officials and members of the public:

> We're working to make tax cuts & the expanded Child
> Tax Credit a reality for American families. The time is now!

The BBC North America activist reposted Ms. Trump's tweet, adding his own comment for good measure:

> Ivanka Trump, looking at people and nodding

'I guess one can only pity an individual who rises each day to solely bitch, snipe & hate on anyone called Trump,' wrote one social media user in response. 'Sad.' Imagine you are an impartial state broadcaster. Who, in your impartiality, fairness and neutrality would you choose to cover the Trump White House? Would you choose an objective, non-partisan professional or a paid up Obama-admiring Democrat who exhibits a pathological hatred to not only Mr Trump but his family too? Would you employ a hater of all things Trump to report fairly and impartially about Mr Trump?

'Snark makes the speaker feel a strength they know deep down they do not possess,' observes Ryan Holliday. 'It shields their insecurity and makes the writer feel that they are in control.'[6]

'Utterly ridiculous: Trump wiretap claims'

@realDonaldTrump
Terrible. Just found out that Obama had my "wires tapped" in Trump Tower just before the victory. Nothing found. This is McCarthyism!

When Donald Trump tweeted his suspicions that Trump Tower – campaign HQ during his successful 2016 presidential run – might have been wiretapped by the Obama administration, the impartial broadcaster flew into a blind rage:

'Utterly ridiculous'

Trump 'wiretap' claims . . .

Stories duly began pumping out of Broadcasting House, all of which had just one aim: to discredit Mr Trump's claim. The corporation scoffed. It mocked. It scorned.

The 'national' broadcaster couldn't wait to pour scorn on the billionaire politician's claim: 'Trump wiretap claims: President has these paranoid conspiracy theories', so went the headline of one story on its news website. Moreover, the President's claim had been 'rejected' by just about every sane person on the planet, at least according to the BBC. Within 24 hours, the Ministry of Truth had produced over 40 separate stories all of which trashed Trump's wiretapping claim. The scrupulously fair BBC was on a roll: Trump's claim was 'utterly ridiculous;' it was 'nonsense.'

> Trump stands by unverified wiretap claim

> Newsday: UK Spy Agency Rejects Trump Wiretap Claims

> Claims GCHQ wiretapped Trump 'nonsense' - NSA's Ledgett

> Trump wiretap claims: 'President has these paranoid conspiracy theories'

> The World Tonight: 'No evidence' Obama ordered wiretap on Trump - FBI chief

> The Newsroom: Trump's Wiretapping Claims Rejected

But what exactly had happened to journalism? After all, here was the president of the United States openly claiming that his predecessor had plotted to undermine/overthrow himself and his administration – incredible, unprecedented and, moreover, criminal . . . If ever there had been a time for objective, quality journalism now was that time. Not however in BBC-land. Unable to suspend its Trump antipathy for even a moment, rather than suspending disbelief the way journalists are want, rather than investigating, the impartial, free and fair broadcaster bypassed objectivity and scepticism altogether going straight into attack - a vicious, scornful attack.

'No ifs or buts'
Sure enough, BBC activists were soon queueing up to do their bit in this propaganda exercise. As far as the open-minded hacktivists were concerned, Mr Trump's claim was the paranoid delusion of a diseased mind. As ever it all came down to those good old BBC narratives: *Barack Obama is very, very good; Donald Trump is very, very bad.* Simple:

> **@awzurcher**
> Every support pillar under Trump's wiretapping claim is crumbling

@BBCJonSopel
FBI director torpedoes the @POTUS tweet claim that
@BarackObama hacked Trump Tower. No ifs or buts.

Endless wiretapping stories duly appeared on the BBC news website, all spinning the same line: Trump's claim is bonkers.

While the BBC merely scoffed at Mr Trump's wiretapping claims, real journalists were actually taking the trouble to investigate an assertion that if found to be true, might lead to the impeachment of Barack Obama and a coterie of high-ranking officials from the former president's administration. Much to the BBC's embarrassment the truth soon started to emerge. The Obama administration *had* been spying on the Trump campaign. Egg all over its face, the broadcaster managed just a single story about the biggest political scandal to hit America since Watergate:

'FBI wiretapped Trump campaign chief Paul Manafort – reports.' Just a single story. Just a few brief, paragraphs reluctantly confirming that Mr Trump had in fact been right all along. Over forty stories attacking, ridiculing and scorning the US president against a single, solitary story (reluctantly) vindicating him. Balance, BBC style.

'Every support pillar under Trump's wiretap claim is crumbling'
The truth will out according to the old adage. As ever, when it comes to wrong-thinkers the BBC's denouncement had been premature:

The Telegraph
Former Trump campaign chairman Paul Manafort 'wiretapped before and after election.'

Reuters
Trump campaign adviser was wiretapped under secret court orders: CNN

RT.com
Trump was right!' Twitter goes wild after CNN admits FBI wiretapped Trump aide Manafort

The Hill
It looks like Obama did spy on Trump

Washington Times
Obama spied on Trump's campaign. Where's the outrage?

Fox News
Trump is right -- He and his campaign were victims of a political attack by the Justice Department and FBI

But, but . . . Stormy Daniels
'Let's be clear,' wrote Larry O' Connor in *The Washington Times*, 'The DOJ and FBI, under Barack Obama, investigated and spied on the Trump presidential campaign complete with wiretaps, informants and moles. They also concealed the activities from congressional oversight for months.'[7] As an unprecedented political scandal brewed in America through Winter 2017 and into Spring 2018, over in BBC land it was, well, business as usual. Activists were doing everything to deflect away from Obamagate or Spygate as it was starting to become known. BBC coverage continued to obsess over an obscure ex-porn actress who had allegedly had an affair with Mr Trump in the distant past:

> Does Trump lawyer's 'hush payment to Stormy Daniels break law?

> Stormy Daniels warns Trump on SNL 'storm's a coming baby'

> Stormy Daniels and Trump: The conflicting statements

Meanwhile, independent journalists of whom the BBC habitually refer to as 'fake,' 'alt-right,' or other slurs, were doing what real journalists do - busily investigating this sensational claim.

@Anon
While fake news BBC pump out endless Stormy Daniels crap, real journalism is taking place, the kind fake news BBC hacks can only dream of.

It was indeed business as usual for the impartial broadcaster, fiercely protecting the interests of the privileged elites. Such was the seriousness of this claim, BBC activists could smell only too well to where it might lead: the exoneration of Trump and the indictment of Obama – a scenario that could not possibly be allowed to happen, so diversion it was: Stormy Daniels, Stormy Daniels, Stormy Daniels . . .

Orthodoxy is unconsciousness.

'It's absolutely amazing how President Trump knows and speaks the truth weeks or months before it comes out,' wrote one social media user. 'The pattern is predictable. POTUS says "Trump Tower was wiretapped." The Goebbels Media all attack him as paranoid and a liar. Things start to leak out. Eventually the full truth of the matter comes out. The Goebbels Media tries to quibble but eventually prints a retraction on page 34 on their web site with no link to the home page. Then they move onto the next attack.'

Brexit is very, very bad

'The BBC is very balanced in its EU coverage. Every pro-European voice is balanced by an anti-Brexit voice.' (Anon)

The early hours of the morning of 24 June, 2016 witnessed a funereal gloom descend upon Broadcasting House. In tones usually reserved for the death of a monarch, at 4.39 am, a shaken and clearly choked David Dimbleby solemnly announced that the UK had voted to leave the European Union. The BBC's dreams and ambitions had, it seemed, been dashed to pieces. The long march through the institutions had been halted, even if temporarily. So too had generous amounts of funding courtesy of the EU. Reality took a while to settle in. Accepting that the BBC worldview had been rejected – decisively so – was a bitter pill to swallow for inhabitants of the temple. BBC mourning began almost immediately. In the days that followed, it was reported that the BBC's Director General:

> Went round the London dinner circuit wailing that BBC balance had "lost us the election". It had given too much credibility to leave. I disagree. The BBC may have "lost" the election, but it was not during the campaign – rather through its years of brazen pro-EU bias.[1]

Grief soon gave way to pragmatism. Less than 24 hours after the historic vote the BBC began a propaganda campaign the aim of which was to cynically reverse the decision to leave the European Union.

Indeed, the broadcaster became notorious for its 'despite Brexit' catchphrase, a piece of linguistic deception used to explain away any positive post-referendum economic news: Soaring manufacturing sector? Despite Brexit. Increasing employment figures? Despite Brexit. Conversely, any negative post-referendum economic news was invariably 'because of Brexit . . .' For example, in August 2018 BBC Northern Ireland Business News reported that, 'Almost half of NI firms postponed or cancelled investment plans due to Brexit.' Similarly BBC Somerset reported on a, 'Bin crew shortage 'due to Brexit and nuclear build.' And so on and so forth.

'You found one!'

The corporation's anti-Brexit bias pops up everywhere, not just on political output. This is The Archer's, Radio 4's long-running soap opera set in a rural English community:[2]

Oliver:	How's the soft-fruit business? I heard there'd been some unpleasantness aimed at the pickers
Adam:	Yes unfortunately. There are one or two people who seem to think the Brexit thing has given them a licence to abuse foreigners
Oliver:	Terrible isn't it?
Adam:	I'm sure it's just a few bored kids
Oliver:	We were foreigners in Italy but our neighbours couldn't have been more welcoming

Italians 'welcoming,' Brits hostile. Stereotypes well and truly confirmed. Where is the evidence that Italians are more welcoming than Brits? There isn't any of course, but it suits the BBC anti-Brexit narrative to invent such a crude stereotype.

The real problem however is not so much this type of unrefined pigeonholing, which is bad enough, but the apparent unawareness of BBC cultists who mindlessly propagate such tropes. During an October 2017 edition of Question Time from Portsmouth, the following question was posed: 'Should Mark Carney and the BBC admit Brexit will happen, and get behind Britain instead of deprecating our nation and continually weakening our bargaining stance?' One of the panel members happened to be Tory MP Jacob Rees-Mogg, who we shall be hearing much more about later in this book. Attempting to answer the question, Mr Rees-Mogg found himself under attack from the programme's host, David Dimbleby:

JRM:	The BBC, dear Old Auntie. How many times have we heard in spite of Brexit? In spite of Brexit a

record three million jobs have been created, since 2010. In spite of Brexit unemployment is at its lowest level since 1975. In spite of Brexit England defeated the West indies at Lords (laughter)

D D: (Interrupting) I'm sorry can you actually specify an occasion when you've heard that – you say that, but can you . . . Have you got a quotation?

JRM: I've got some other quotations . . .

D D: (interrupting) No, have you got a quotation saying in spite of Brexit?

JRM: Well you just have to listen to the news . . .

D D: (interrupting) Well that's a generalisation. Have you got a specific . . .

JRM: (interrupting) I think anyone who has listened to the news recently has heard the in spite of Brexit terminology

D D: (Incredulous) ARE YOU SURE?

JRM: And I think the audience knows that (audience agreement)

D D: Are you sure? (more audience agreement)

JRM: Yes, the audience seems to agree

D D: (Pointing) Shaking their heads there. You found one!

We have already drawn attention to passivity in cult members, the requirement to uncritically accept dogma. The question arises: does David Dimbleby genuinely believe what he is saying here – that the BBC does not repeat its 'despite Brexit' mantra at the drop of a hat, or does he actually know but chooses to feign ignorance as required? Is unconsciousness indeed orthodoxy as Orwell suggested?

'Have you got a quotation saying in spite of Brexit?'
Just a small selection of headlines from the BBC News website:

BBC Scotland:
UK cities bid to be European Capital of Culture - *despite* Brexit
Food and drink sector confident *despite* Brexit vote, BoS survey finds

BBC Northern Ireland:
Quinn Industrial Holdings 'positive *despite* Brexit'
Head of Invest NI: *Despite* Brexit economy is 'thriving'
Dale Farm's £20m investment to go ahead *despite* Brexit

BBC Technology:
Despite Brexit, the UK is adopting the GDPR in its own Data Protection Bill

BBC UK Politics:
UK construction rises *despite* Brexit vote

BBC Arts and Entertainment:
UK cities vie to be European Capital of Culture 2023 *despite* Brexit

BBC Business:
Davos 2017: UK bosses optimistic *despite* Brexit fears
Ryanair raises passenger growth forecast *despite* Brexit
Siemens promises UK investment *despite* Brexit warning
Jaguar Land Rover confident *despite* Brexit
Obama: special relationship remains *despite* Brexit

BBC Hampshire and Isle of Wight News:
New Forest EU business grants continue *despite* Brexit vote

Lurid anti-Brexit headlines continue to pour out of the BBC: 'Fears grow across the Atlantic over Brexit fallout,' or 'UK warned on cost of 'hard Brexit.' The warnings are always dire, the consequences even direr.

Indeed, the politically neutral broadcaster seems to relish its pivotal role in what has become known as Project Fear. When it comes to stoking up fear and anxiety the broadcaster could, for once, truly claim to be world class.

Project Fear is actually no different from Project anti-Trump or Project anti-white male. Each project relies upon disengenuity and is achieved using the same box of BBC propaganda tricks. Pro-EU bias has become so overwhelming in fact that critics have started speaking of the Brussels Broadcasting Corporation.[3]

When a BBC writer blamed Brexit voters for the delay in Dr Who getting its first female doctor, BBC bias threatened to descend into farce.[4] No matter how outlandish the claim, provided it was of an anti-Brexit nature the impartial broadcaster was only too happy to give it oxygen. Brexit became a subject ripe for the BBC tactic of omission. Anxious to prove that the vote to leave the EU had been a catastrophic mistake, the BBC simply ensured the majority of positive post-Referendum economic news never made it to any BBC platform and those that did make it were invariably qualified by its 'despite Brexit' tag.

@Jefferson_MFG
Once again @BBCNews features a negative UK manufacturing story yet fails to report on all the new factory openings & 1000's of jobs created

YouGov polls feature prominently on the BBC news website. However a YouGov poll of December 2017 put the broadcaster in a tricky position. Research carried out in the period leading up to Christmas revealed significant changes in how the UK viewed the decision to leave the EU:

@NCPoliticsUK
At this point would you prefer Britain remains in or leaves The European Union?

Prefer that Britain stays in the EU	39
Prefer that Britain leaves the EU	48
Don't know	13

While Remain in EU saw support crash from 44% to 39%, support for Leave EU increased representing a 9% margin in favour of Leave, the highest margin recorded since the 2016 vote. Predictably, the results of this YouGov poll failed to spark BBC interest, although just a day later it did report a YouGov poll in which 37% of people thought London's railways had got worse . . .

'It's harming Britain!'

Dating back to 1895, The Proms is an eight-week season of classical music concerts held predominantly at London's Royal Albert Hall. The season culminates with the Last Night of the Proms an event traditionally covered by BBC radio and television, which comprises performances of some of Britain's most renowned classical pieces such as 'Rule Britannia,' 'Jerusalem' and 'I Vow to thee my Country.' Infused with these stirring classics and the traditional waving of union jack flags, the Last Night of the Proms is an unashamedly patriotic affair.

Audience surprise and discomfort can be imagined in the 2017 Proms when conductor Daniel Barenboim used the platform to launch into a scathing attack on Brexit which went on for seven minutes. Broadcast live on BBC television and radio, Barenboim delivered a pitch perfect BBC narrative, bristling with anti-Brexit allusion. 'Isolationist tendencies and nationalism in its very narrow sense is something that is very dangerous,' lectured Barenboim from his lofty position atop of the conductor's podium. Forty-eight hours before the conductor's extraordinary antics, pianist Igor Levit had unexpectedly performed the EU anthem, Beethoven's Ode to Joy as an encore, a decision the BBC defended as an 'artistic choice.'

Conservative politicians were quick to condemn what they perceived to be unprecedented politicking of a national celebration. 'The BBC will happily go along with anything that supports the Remain cause,'[5] Andrew Bridgen MP for Leicester told *The Sun* newspaper, voicing the thoughts of many. 'The BBC must be neutral,' said fellow Conservative Andrew Rosindell, taking a similarly dim view of the broadcaster's latest attempt to undermine Brexit, 'if it's not, that is wrong and can't continue. It's harming Britain.'

BBC Europhile sympathies had been evident as long ago as 1969 when the BBC's then director of music William Glock had floated the idea of dropping some of the stirring British anthems that had characterised the Last Night since its inception, in order to make the event, 'attractive to 40 million viewers in Europe.'

It wasn't just Conservative MPs who were left reeling by the BBC's audacity. Renowned classical musical writer Norman Lebrecht was one of many pundits left disappointed by events at The Proms: 'Using the Proms as a political platform risks damaging a national treasure,' cautioned the author of 'The Complete Companion to 20th Century Music,' before adding, 'this was a very bad night for the reputation of the BBC Proms.'[6]

The BBC and fake news

> Even in the 80's I was becoming suspicious of the true motives of
> the BBC. They seemed to favour the IRA over Brits and they
> seemed to disapprove of our regaining the Falklands. But in the
> past five years their bias has increased dramatically and has now
> penetrated just about every aspect of their output, from news to
> drama and through to documentaries. The majority of their
> programmes are unwatchable, overwhelmed by political
> propaganda. Clearly they believe their mission is to campaign
> relentlessly for the leftist world view and to stifle any other view.
> They suppress, they distort, they mislead and they lie. They are
> the biggest purveyors of fake news in the world.

Anon

Before we go on to tackle the subject of propaganda it seems appropriate to consider the related topic of fake news. Are MSM 'errors' calculated attempts to mislead or merely innocent mistakes? Let's begin with a typical morsel of #bbcfakenews, the type that is casually dropped into its content all day long.

When Darren Osborne rammed a van into a crowd of people outside London's Finsbury Park mosque in June 2017, tragedy ensued. One man died and several others were injured. The attack had been deliberate. It was the latest such incident in 2017 that had also included deadly attacks at Westminster (4 dead), Manchester (22 dead) and London Bridge (8 dead). Yet compared to the somewhat modest BBC coverage allocated to these numerically deadlier atrocities, Osborne received virtually 24-hour coverage from Britain's impartial 'national' broadcaster. Day in day out, the case featured on every one of its main news channels. There was no escaping the name 'Darren Osborne.'

Continuing with its round-the-clock coverage, BBC News at One reported the latest developments in Osborne's trial: 'The prosecution say that Darren Osborne became obsessed also with events in Rochdale,' announced Daniel Sandford, 'where Muslim men were accused of abusing young women.'[1]

This innocent sounding statement contained not one, but *two* deliberate pieces of fake news:

1 – The men in question had, in fact, been *convicted* of the crimes in question.

2 – They had been convicted of abusing young *girls* – some as young as 13.

How could Britain's 'national' broadcaster – replete with 20,000 activists – make such a basic 'error?' For an organisation which prides itself on excellence and has resources and networks unrivalled in media, the British Broadcasting Corporation sure makes a heck of a lot of 'errors . . .'

'Inadvertent alterations'

It's not just in recent times that the broadcaster has been dropping bloomers. The British Broadcasting Corporation has form. Next up, yet another example of fake news, this time from the 1980s.

> **@Anon**
> BBC was raised on fake news. Personally seen actions – photographed them. Read the reports being sent in for BBC and it blew my mind. The truth was far, far away from the reports most often

Summer 1984 witnessed a bitter struggle between coal miners and Mrs Thatcher's Conservative government. The miner's strike has divided the country. Both sides having dug their heels in, the situation was becoming hostile. In June 1984 police arrived at the Orgreave coking plant, South Yorkshire where miners were picketing. Battle lines were drawn. Tempers began to fray. That evening BBC News viewers watched a sequence which showed a miner throwing a missile followed by a police charge. The miners had clearly provoked the police. Subsequently they got what they deserved: a beating. Public sympathy, hitherto behind the miner's cause, could well have changed following this incident. There was just one tiny problem . . .

The incident had not happened in the way portrayed by the BBC. The police had in fact charged the miners first; the missile had been thrown *in response* to police aggression. Writing in 2015, David Conn sets out how the BBC report unfolded:

> The BBC showed miners throwing stones and other missiles at
> the police, followed by mounted officers charging into them,
> and then officers chasing miners, some clearly being hit over the
> head with truncheons.[2]

In order to weaken the miners' cause, the BBC had edited the footage in such a way as to suggest the pickets had been the aggressors when in reality the 6,000 strong police convoy had arrived looking to make an example of the strikers. Discussing an IPCC (Independent Police Complaints Commission) investigation of 2012, Conn notes that:

> The report says the BBC had indeed reversed footage in its news
> broadcast that night, an accusation the BBC has never officially
> accepted.

In 1991 South Yorkshire police paid almost £500,000 to 39 miners in respect of amongst other things, assault and wrongful arrest. However, It took several years for the BBC to admit to having changed the sequence of events that June afternoon, and when it finally did, predictably it claimed that the sequence of events had been 'inadvertently' altered in 'the haste of putting the news together.'[3] Notwithstanding, as late as 2014, the BBC had found a CNN-style excuse to explain away its actions: the broadcaster had not tried to mislead anyone, any discrepancies in coverage had occurred because of a failure, 'to record some of the violence due to a camera error.'[4]

Careless 'errors' like this have been occurring since the BBC started to broadcast in the 1920s. And they're *still* happening. 'The government,' noted the BBC's first Director General, 'know they can trust us not to be really impartial.'[5]

In his 2015 memoir, ex-BBC executive Roger Mosey recalls a particularly invidious example of BBC chicanery. When the broadcaster decided to file a report about immigration in the UK it solicited opinion from the general public within a certain town. To nobody's surprise, the one white respondent featured waxed lyrical about the benefits of immigration. In his position as editor, Mosey says he was unconvinced. Was such a glowing endorsement really representative of white voices generally? Mosey wanted to know. It turns out the majority of white people questioned had not expressed enthusiasm for the effects that immigration was having on their locality. The reporter had cynically dropped all critical views from the final edit, a situation Mosey says produced, 'an unacceptably sanitised piece of reporting.'[6] Fake news – decades before the term had even been invented.

'The projector is able to avoid the unpleasantness in themselves'

The BBC is on a quest and has been for some time – and we are not necessarily thinking of its daily campaign to unseat the democratically elected president of the United States, nor are we necessarily thinking of its campaign to subvert the outcome of the largest democratic vote in British history, the 2016 European Referendum vote. The quest we actually have in mind is combating fake news. And who better to tackle this dark art than the Grand Masters themselves? Want to know how to protect your home from burglary? Ask a burglar . . .

Approximately how much BBC content do you think is fake news? [7]				
All	Most	Some	Little	None
8%	48%	36%	5%	3%

Fig. 11

Fake news! Fake news! It's everywhere, in schools and colleges, pubs and clubs, boats, trains and planes. If you listen to the BBC, Fake News is the greatest threat to mankind, after global warming (or should that be cooling?). Writing for *Intercept*, Glenn Greenwald recognises hypocrisy when he sees it. 'The most important fact to realise about this new term,' notes Greenwald, 'those who most loudly denounce Fake News are typically those most aggressively disseminating it.'[8]

As every good Marxist knows, if you accuse your enemies of committing your own sins, you assume a position that often proves virtually impossible to subsequently challenge: 'Accuse the other side of that which you are guilty.' Goebbels' may or may not have said this phrase at the 1934 Nuremberg rally, but it's an idea so duplicitous it sits rather well in his hands. In psychological terms adopting a position of supreme self-righteousness, calling out the perceived sins of others in the manner of religious zealotry, can often be attributed to subliminal feelings of guilt. Such behaviour can sometimes be a cry for help or even, in certain circumstances, a tacit confession. According to Psychological Dictionary.org, projection is a defence mechanism wherein, 'unenviable or unpleasant traits, impulses or ideas are attributed to another. In this way, the projector is able to avoid the unpleasantness in themselves.'

The BBC versus Fake News! Does this mean the BBC intends to put its house in order at last? Not quite. Fake news is not a BBC problem rather it's everybody *else's* problem. The BBC has its own house in order thank-you very much. We know this is to be true, because it tells us so, over and over again:

> The BBC is recognised by audiences in the UK and around the world as a provider of news that you can trust. Our website, like our TV and radio services, strives for journalism that is accurate, impartial, independent and fair.[9]

Not according to a survey conducted by One Poll between November and December 2017, which found 1 in 6 people (17%) said they trusted the BBC.[10] A social media poll of 2018 returned a similar result:

I'm American and I want to know . . . Does British public trust the BBC? This isn't a political question.

Trust BBC News	16%
Don't trust BC News	84%

18,308 votes – Final result

The BBC is thus going into battle not against itself, but rather against all those pesky news sites – largely Internet based and largely conservative in outlook – who invariably do not agree with its narratives.

'An incentive to inflate the threat'
Yet for a majority of people, so-called fake news is not quite the problem the BBC would make out. As strange as it may sound, the plebs are more

than capable of filtering Internet content for themselves, engaging with that which rings true, disregarding that which does not. Who but an authoritarian would suggest that a single political view is 'correct,' and that other, alternative views must therefore be 'incorrect?' Who but an authoritarian would suggest that 'incorrect' views require censorship?

Fake news, as Attkisson points out, is in fact the obsession of a mainstream media no longer able to control the news cycle as it did prior to the Internet explosion. 'Fake news' is the BBC response to being scrutinised. It is the scream of a toddler who must now share its toys with others. It is the scream of the bully, the monopolist, the brat. It is a ploy, the ultimate aim of which, is to censor organisations and individuals daring to challenge mainstream media narratives:

> It isn't the public that's clamouring for content to be filtered, censored or otherwise "curated." The push is coming from corporate, political, news, and special interests who want to dominate the narrative and crush information that's contrary.[11]

Along with its mainstream allies, Britain's devious 'national' broadcaster is simply attempting to create a crisis where none exists. This way it can provide a 'solution' – more censorship of wrong-think. 'Nobody knows how big a problem fake news is,' asserts the corporation's news website, 'and many of those who talk about it have an incentive to inflate the threat.'[12]

That people gravitate towards media that reflects their own views, experiences and aspirations is not a novel idea. That those same people will be inclined to believe the editorial line in that same media is hardly the stuff of revelation. Using data, statistics and testimony to advantage private and political agendas is the oldest trick in the book. 'Fake news' is as old as the media. No, the BBC insists, Fake News is a modern plague, a real and present danger. Be afraid, be very afraid.

Who can be trusted to combat this threat to western democracy? Self-appointed 'fact-checkers' such as - the 'independent,' BBC-approved Snopes for instance and other right-thinking organisations, a chilling prospect for anyone of even a mildly libertarian persuasion. In the mind of the liberal supremacist commoners do not flock to alternative news and media portals because their arguments are superior or because they simply resonate better with experience, but rather because such media possess *inferior* arguments etc. That's because people are basically stupid. If you can't see the superiority of the liberal worldview, you must be deficient in some way. Either that or you have been deceived by dastardly populists. 'It is all too easy to condemn as stupid anyone who supports populist politicians or appears unperturbed by their falsehoods,'[13] writes an impartial BBC Newsnight presenter.

> **@AMRCtraining**
> The @BBCNews are reporting a drop in #apprentice
> figures since the levy May-June. @AMRCtraining can
> report that we have just had a record breaking intake
> in September! #sheffieldssuper #Engineering

Having created the problem (fake news) and also the solution (social media censorship) the BBC can then ensure conflicting narratives never see the light of day again. Back to the 1950s we go, the BBC heyday, when everybody not only watched and listened to Auntie, but believed everything she said; back to a time when the population had no way to challenge the proclamations from the state broadcaster. Happy days.

'Irresponsible scare stories put out by the BBC'

As an example of wilful fake news we turn to Money Box, a long-running financial affairs programme which airs on BBC Radio 4. First, a little in the way of context. In 2016, once Theresa May's Conservative government granted the BBC yet another extension to its Royal Charter ensuring the corporation would receive somewhere in the region of £45 billion from British taxpayers over the next decade, the 'national' broadcaster, vaguely tolerant of May's party until that point, immediately turned upon the Conservatives with a vengeance.

Boris Johnson, Michael Gove, Priti Patel, the BBC went after a host of Tory MPs, hoping to oust them from their cabinet positions. The fact that they all just happened to be Brexiteers was surely just coincidence. In the case of Patel it worked. After relentless BBC pressure, the Secretary of State for International Development resigned her post. When it finally dawned on the BBC that former Remainer Mrs May herself was actually promising to deliver Brexit too, the corporation turned its hostility onto the Prime Minister. Until this point the neutral broadcaster had been hoping that May would thwart Brexit in the same way Corbyn's Labour party had been promising.

Ever mindful however that the May government could radically alter the terms of the royal charter, in the lead up to 2016 the activists at Broadcasting House had softened their tone towards the Tories and Conservatives in general. Wafer thin as this strategy had been, it worked. The Tories duly renewed the BBC's charter. Kerching! The champagne corks popped long into the night at W1A.

For true conservatives it was a depressing state of affairs. The party had had it in its power to seriously upset the BBC cash cow had they had a mind to. Unfortunately, the majority just wanted a quiet life. They certainly did not want to find themselves the target of BBC smear campaigns. The white flag was duly hoisted from Conservative Central office, as is always the case. The BBC had its billion pound bounty.

Little wonder that the more credulous mistook the BBC's ambiguous attitude towards the Tories in and around the EU vote as evidence of right-wing bias. It wasn't. It was merely the BBC ensuring it got what it wanted: another decade of tax payer's cash. Like a faithless, calculating lover, once it had got what it wanted the BBC treated May's Tories with customary contempt. Natural antipathy towards conservatives aside, there was an even greater need to sack the Tories from number 10: Brexit. Mrs May and co were showing worrying signs of respecting the outcome of the EU Referendum. The impartial broadcaster could not allow that to happen.

'Who puts a turkey on the table?'

One of the BBC's favourite attack weapons became something called Universal Credits – a government welfare policy much derided by the Labour party. Introduced in 2013, the aim of Universal Credits was to reform a chaotic benefits system that involved a bewildering number of agencies and associated bureaucracy. The aim was to make a single, monthly payment thereby simplifying the system for claimants as well as reducing administration costs. As with all major reforms the initiative had plenty of teething problems.

By late 2017, the BBC had joined the Labour party in lambasting the scheme almost on a daily basis. Getting Jeremy Corbyn's anti-Brexit

Labour party into 10 Downing Street had become somewhat of a Holy
Grail for the politically neutral BBC who, 18 months after the vote to
leave the European Union, had still not given up hope of thwarting the
result.

It was hardly surprising then when BBC Radio 4's Money Box
programme reported on Universal Credits in November 2017.
Undermining Mrs May's government was now a BBC priority. Christmas
fast approaching and tens of thousands of families in the UK reliant on
this monthly 'top-up,' it would be a particularly inopportune time for
these essential payments to be placed in jeopardy, but that is exactly
what BBC Radio 4 Money Box presenter Paul Lewis told shocked
listeners to the programme would happen. Indeed, the presenter had
already taken to social media to disseminate his message:

> **@paullewismoney**
> On @BBCr4today shortly about 100,000 universal credit
> claimants in weekly paid work who will get no benefit this
> Xmas

The BBC news website weighed in with a scare story of its own,
'Universal credit: 'Thousands' without Christmas payments.' 'Thousands
of people on universal credit will not receive a payment at Christmas,'[14]
warned the article going on to allocate space a-plenty to an individual
who corroborated the corporation's latest despairing narrative. 'So close
to Christmas,' asserted the BBC interviewee, 'anybody who will need to
make a claim won't receive any money this side of Christmas.' Then the
article really hit its emotional blackmailing stride:

> So [there is] concern there about how do they buy toys? How
> do they feed themselves? How do they [pay for] gas, electric,
> and who puts a turkey on the table?

'Simplistic assertions . . . re-tweeted uncritically'
In his book *The Rise of the Outsiders,* BBC Radio 4 host Steve Richards
cautions that, 'Twitter can distort the reporting of politics, allowing
outsiders to reach large audiences with simplistic assertions that are re-
tweeted uncritically by like-minded followers.'[15]

One hundred thousand people without money at Xmas! No benefits! No money! No turkey on the table! No Xmas cheer! 'Simplistic assertions' and some more. Panic duly ensued. Lewis' tweet spread quickly around social media, re-tweeted by 1,000s of 'like-minded followers:'

> **@Anon**
> Astonishing expose of Govt incompetence by Paul Lewis.
> Universal Credit claimants in v. low paid weekly work will get
> no benefit at Xmas

Anger, frustration and fear spreading amongst those likely to be affected by this appalling news - the 'evil' Tory plan as exclusively reported by BBC Radio 4 - a backlash against Mrs May's administration began: 'Seasons greetings from your caring compassionate Conservative party,' wrote one social media user, 'New Universal credit claimants 'will get no money before Christmas.' Anger was starting to brew. 'Imagine having to wait for universal credit all over Xmas,' wrote another. 'I feel sorry for people that are going to suffer this Xmas because of this evil govt.'

Soon enough this irresponsible piece of fake news – calculated to whip up anger and resentment against the Tory government – had gone viral. As far as fake news goes, this BBC Radio 4 example surely plumbed new depths. On November 25, in an effort to quell the anxiety whipped up by the BBC, the Department for Work and Pensions were forced to clarify the situation:

> **@dwppressoffice**
> @MoneyBox corrects its misleading #UniversalCredit
> story. No one on UC who's paid weekly will see a drop in
> total income in any assessment period. UC payments adjust
> to people's earnings so they get a stable income each month
> including over Christmas.

For reasons best known to itself, BBC Radio 4 had either not bothered to check this vital piece of information with the DWP first, or had deliberately decided to omit it from their broadcast and social media interactions.

'Fake news was put out on our national broadcaster'

Such was the panic that ensued following this piece of BBC fake news, towards the end of November the subject was even discussed in the Houses of Parliament when a backbench MP (BB) addressed The Chief Secretary to the Treasury, Elizabeth Truss MP:

> B B: Would my right honourable friend like to comment on the irresponsible scare stories put out by the BBC first on Radio 4, then on BBC Breakfast Time, on its website and across all its media platforms that up to 100,000 people on in-work Universal Credit would receive no benefits over the Christmas Period?
>
> Cries of shame! shame!
>
> L T: Well I think it's disgraceful that fake news was put out on our national broadcaster when Universal Credit is actually helping people get into work and earn extra money. And I think it's particularly poor that some of the lowest income people in our society have been unnecessarily worried . . .

Given the amount of distress it had caused, the apology by Money Box's Paul Lewis when it eventually came was as unduly trivial as it was short: 'Apologies to anyone on Universal Credit who was in any way unnecessarily alarmed.' Former Work and Pensions Secretary Iain Duncan Smith, who created Universal Credit, was left distinctly unimpressed: 'This apology is a small and inadequate correction. Having given the department no proper opportunity to rebut the false item, the item then ran on all their news headlines without correction.'

> Imagine how headache-free a life as @TheSun journalist must be, where you don't have to fact-check, just file nonsense.
>
> Senior Reporter, BBC Stories

For our next example of fake news we turn once more to that BBC favourite, Donald Trump – who else?

140

'Let's fight fake news!'

In July 2017 Mr Trump visited Poland to a media scrum and rapturous applause. CNN and the BBC could only watch in horror as the arrival of the US president on Polish soil triggered huge enthusiasm among the people packing into the streets of the capital city. Poland seemed to love Trump. Such a scenario certainly did not fit with the BBC's pre-written anti-Trump master narrative, not forgetting its sweeping generalisations ('Europe hates Trump'). What possible angle then would the pair of impeccably impartial news organisations take?

Soon footage appeared on social media of the moment US and Polish presidents met, a few seconds of footage which seemed to depict the wife of the Polish president snubbing Mr Trump's hand in preference for that of his wife, First Lady Melania Trump. Moments later the dignitary – Mrs Duda - duly shook Mr Trump's hand, an interaction purposely edited out of the footage in order to suggest that the American president had indeed been snubbed. He had not.

Looked at from another angle it was clear that Melania had simply been stood in Mrs Duda's eye-line. Furthermore, in shaking Mrs Trump's hand before that of her husband's, Mrs Duda had simply been observing Polish custom - not that such context mattered to either the BBC or CNN who eagerly spread the edited clip around their various media platforms. Why let truth get in the way of a story that fits your narrative? *Poland snubs Trump! Trump is very, very unpopular and nobody likes him – in fact Europe 'hates him . . .'*

It probably came as no surprise to find the impartial BBC seizing upon what was an utterly innocuous incident. The broadcaster had sensed an irresistible opportunity to further its anti-Trump narrative, and so duly spread the incident throughout its vast media platform. Thus the 24 million or so followers of the BBC World Twitter found this message popping up on their feeds:

@BBCWorld
The moment President Trump is left hanging after
trying to shake hands with the Polish president's wife.

Reading this tweet it is entirely possibly to conclude that Mr Trump did not shake hands with the president's wife at all, that he was completely snubbed. He wasn't. But that's just precisely what the BBC wanted its believers to think.

Concerned that media outlets such as CNN and the BBC were attempting to create a diplomatic incident that had never actually occurred, the President of Poland immediately took to Twitter where he took a thinly-veiled swipe at the fake news twins and the rest of their mainstream news cronies:

> **@AndrzejDuda**
> Contrary to some surprising reports my wife did
> shake hands with Mrs and Mr Trump @POTUS after a
> great visit. Let's FIGHT FAKE NEWS.

They might have just been called out by the president of Poland, but Atlanta and London weren't finished yet, not by a long chalk. As the US president spoke to packed Warsaw crowds waving stars n' stripes flags, the BBC's American cousins were doing a more than passable impression of a fake news organisation when reporting that, 'Conservative Polish politicians bus in adoring crowds for Trump speech.'

Like any major capital city, access to central Warsaw – especially on the occasion of a visit by a US President – is virtually impossible via private vehicle. Thus, the residents of the Polish capital use buses and trains, just like in any other major European city. The 'adoring' crowds had simply caught the bus to town, the quickest and most economical way to travel to the city. Meanwhile, the equally impartial BBC Newsnight programme chose to cover the historic visit to Poland by interviewing two rabid anti-Trump critics, a Liberal New York academic and a journalist from left-wing publication Politico.[16.] Joined in their Trump loathing by the BBC's impartial left-wing host James O'Brien, this was, in football parlance, a thrashing: Anti-Trump 3 Pro-Trump 0. Balance and impartiality, BBC style.

The Manchester march against hate

It was a warm evening in Manchester on 22 May 2017 as throngs of excited people – the vast majority of them children and teenagers – attended a pop concert at the city's Manchester Arena. The gig finished just before 10.30pm. As it threaded its way out of the venue to where parents waited, a terrorist lay in wait for the happy and carefree audience. What happened next shocked the world. Twenty-three people died (including the perpetrator), the youngest of whom was an eight-year old girl. The blast injured another 119 people, 23 of them critically. Less than two weeks later 8 people died and another 48 were injured in a terrorist attack that took place in and around London Bridge.

It soon emerged that both attacks had been carried out by Islamic terrorists. Given that various authorities had been aware of the activities of at least some of the attackers involved, the level of public anger and frustration rose to understandably high levels. If one or more of these fanatics had indeed been on the radar then why had they been allowed to carry out their crimes with seeming impunity?

Worried by the backlash that would surely follow from the BBC *et al* if they had apprehended the terrorists in advance of their deeds, UK security and intelligence services had been obliged to be reactive rather than proactive. Public outrage increased. It did not take an expert in intelligence to realise that those whose job is the protection of the public faced some formidable obstacles in the pursuit of that duty, namely the Liberal media establishment.

Politicians of all persuasions were soon lining up to utter the usual platitudes: the terrorists would not 'divide us' etc. Predictably the responses were as mealy mouthed as they were disingenuous. The ineffectual political response to these outrages was perhaps best summed up by Andy Burnham, Mayor of Manchester, who urged people to carry on as if nothing had happened on that horrific evening, remarks that seemed particularly crass given the horrific and unprecedented nature of the attack.

How then to respond in such circumstances? Carry on as normal until the next attack as per the advice of Burnham? The public mood hardened. When faced with the sheer ineptitude of Andy Burnham and friends it should perhaps come as no surprise that direct action becomes ever more likely. Thus, on Sunday 11 June 2017 a march – 'UK against hate' - took place in the streets of Manchester. Sikhs, Hindus, and ex-Muslims joined members of the LGBT community and high profile anti-Islamists such as Tommy Robinson in a peaceful march through the same streets that just weeks' earlier had born witness to the carnage of the Manchester Arena. People from all walks of life joined the march.

'On route to M'cester to crack some EDL skulls'

Let's see how the BBC reported the march, a multi-faith march and one containing a large number of concerned parents, grandparents and just ordinary people dismayed by the response of British authorities. Here is the tweet sent out by the Manchester-based BBC North West Tonight and which was subsequently deleted:

> **@BBCNWT**
> Estimated about 700 English Defence League protestors marching through Manchester city centre. Anti-racist counter demonstration being held.

Firstly, and perhaps most egregiously, as many eyewitness testimonies pointed out, this was not an English Defence League march. Among the estimated 3-4,000 (not 700) protestors were BAME (Black, Asian and minority ethnic) speakers such as David Ramos together with representatives from a wide range of faith groups which included Sikh Awareness Society leader Mohan Singh and ex-Muslims such as Shazia Hobbs and Mohammad Fiaz, a Christian convert from Islam.

Secondly, while the BBC were more than ready to demonise the protestors, as 'EDL' note the sympathetic description of violent Antifa thugs as 'anti-racist,' some of whom were fast approaching Manchester, and who, it seemed, were taking this BBC North West Tonight tweet at its word:

> **@Anon**
> On route to M'cester to crack some EDL skulls
> 700 fascists in town #antifa

The BBC's erroneous 'EDL' assumption seems to have been based solely on the presence at the march of Mr Robinson, an individual the corporation habitually insist on referring to as the 'ex-EDL leader' despite him having long since left the organisation. Whatever it might or might not have achieved, BBC North West Tonight's tweet had certainly helped to inflame the minds of some individuals.

There was just one problem: it was fake news. This was not, as BBC North West announced, an EDL march. In the aftermath of the tweet, eye witnesses and others immediately took to social media to call out the BBC's tactics and correct its false reporting. Within minutes of posting, the tweet had accumulated well over 1,500 replies. For the majority of its tweets, @BBCNWT struggles to reach double digits in replies:

Replying to @BBCNews

➢ The anti-racists threw bottles at the gay, black and ethnic marchers what actually happened. No far right were there.

➢ Reporting the truth isn't part of their agenda

➢ This is absolute propaganda.

Soon enough BBC North West Tonight's fake news was being called out. Although it's a tactic the BBC has used ad infinitum over the years, the advent of social media had allowed the public - perhaps for the very first time - to challenge this blatant lie. 'I'm a 52 year old mother of a 20 year old,' wrote one user. 'Never marched in my life & many people I met had felt equally compelled to show solidarity.' This is the testament of another first time marcher:

> I was there today. I am just a mum. A mum who could have spent this Sunday as I have countless others, making Sunday dinner, making sure homework is done, ironing uniforms. But what good is an ironed uniform to a son that gets blown up? Was I scared? Yes, I went alone. Did I deserve to be spat at and have Nazi screamed in my face? No! I am not a racist far from it. I'm just a mum, but a mum who's kids deserve to grow up in peace. I won't be as scared next time.

Is it any wonder that the BBC is amongst one of the strongest of voices lobbying for Internet censorship? Social media posts like those above not only destroy its cherished and wholly false narratives but also help to erode the corporation's reputation as a trusted, impartial source of news.

Somewhat tellingly, having been called out, the BBC response was not to issue a retraction or indeed to apologise to the mothers, fathers, brothers and sisters the smears against whom had led to abuse from its favourite spitting and snarling Antifa thugs. The tweet was simply deleted. It disappeared. Just like that. No apology. No admission. Unfortunately for the BBC plenty of Twitter users obtained a screenshot of the tweet pre-empting what would be a rather clumsy attempt to airbrush it from history. Had this tweet been yet another one of those BBC 'errors' (despite emanating from the very place the march was taking place – central Manchester) surely the correct and proper course of action would have been to issue a public apology?

To BBC weather watchers the 'EDL' tweet was an all too familiar trick: smear big, apologise (but *only* if caught) small. This time the apology had not been small; it had been non-existent. It is just this type of behaviour that appears to be eroding trust in the corporation:

Do you believe that the BBC offers a fair and even balance in their news reporting?

Yes	10%
No	86%
Don't know	4%

16,964 votes – Final result

When popular radio presenter Jon Gaunt asked listeners to his Talk2MeRadio show whether or not the BBC were 'purveyors of fake news' the response was unequivocal. Ninety percent of listeners agreed that the BBC were indeed 'purveyors of fake news.' It's a fairly typical response. When quizzed about BBC trust and honesty, it is very unusual for more than 10% of social media users to express confidence in the broadcaster.

Although the BBC's North West regional office had been called out on its lies, and had been subsequently forced to delete the offensive tweet, the national BBC website had no such compunction. The EDL narrative is a particular favourite at Broadcasting House, used over and over again to inflame opinion and of course justify the 'skull cracking' behaviour that it invariably foments.

Fake news fail? Triple down . . .

With BBC North West having just experienced an epic fail with its cynical attempt to frame the Manchester march as 'EDL' one might have expected BBC national news to exhibit restraint. Not a jot. Unable to resist framing the march as EDL, the BBC simply repeated comments made by the left-wing Mayor of Manchester, Andy Burnham, he of the 'carry on as normal' advice to terrorist attacks, and who was also attempting to promote the same narrative.

The 'national' broadcaster seized upon comments made by Burnham, which had now shifted from the actual EDL to 'EDL-types' – or, as we have noted, just concerned families.

> Mr Burnham tweeted: @gmpolice are stretched to limit & in middle of on-going investigation. These EDL-types who came today need to have a look at themselves.
>
> 'To those saying they weren't EDL - I honestly don't care. They still need to take a long, hard look at themselves. @gmpolice deserve better.'
>
> Former English Defence League (EDL) leader Tommy Robinson was a speaker at the event. He initially said protesters would "walk in silence through the city to honour the dead".[17]

The BBC had managed to get its EDL slur in not once, not twice, but three times – tripling down, let's call it. Despite the overwhelming evidence already noted, simply by selecting elements that fitted its narrative and amplifying those elements (Burnham's comments) the broadcaster had managed to imply that the march had had, in fact, *everything* to do with the EDL. Not content with repeating this smear notice how the report attempts to suggest there never had been any intention to 'walk in silence,' a claim that would no doubt surprise the thousands of parents and children who attempted to do just that prior to the arrival of the BBC North West Tonight-inspired Antifa 'skull crackers.'

Andy Burnham didn't particularly 'care' about veracity, nor it seemed did an impartial, free and fair broadcaster determined to pursue its EDL narrative at any cost.

'Fake news is not a problem that is going to disappear soon,'[18] writes BBC media editor and ex-*Independent* journalist Amol Rajan. How very true. As the BBC North West Tonight's Manchester EDL tweet and subsequent BBC national coverage proved – fake news is indeed not going to disappear anytime soon.

'Rolls eyes'

As every good Communist knows, brainwashing works particularly well upon young minds. Exposed to propaganda from a tender age, those indoctrinated often carry forward ideas into adulthood where they can prove stubbornly resistant to alternative messages. 'Marxists have had considerable success in deliberately propagating Marxism through the Russian education system,' note Hutchinson and Young, 'Like the Nazis they have shown how generations of children can be effectively indoctrinated provided the entire resources of the state's schools are used for that purpose.'[19] What better way to indoctrinate the minds of the young than by actually turning up at schools and colleges, taking advantage of pupils' vulnerability and naivety?

> **@BBCNews (UK)**
> BBC to help students identify 'fake news' Kamal Ahmed
> and Tina Daheley are among BBC journalists who will take
> part in events targeted at pupils.

In late 2017 the BBC announced it was planning to visit 1,000 schools and colleges to help students identify 'fake news.' Orwell's junior anti-sex league, Nazi youth, The Communist Youth League of China, the objective is always the same: the infiltration of young minds, to exert total control, to brainwash. Catch 'em young is a tactic straight from the playbook of some of history's worst regimes. The BBC was planning to visit schools in order to give pupils, 'the equipment they need to distinguish between what's true and what's false.'

The news that Britain's 'national' broadcaster was planning to help students identify fake news was greeted by a mixture of hilarity and incredulity by social media users. Here's just a tiny smattering of the replies this BBC announcement garnered:

Replying to @BBCNews

➢ The BBC are going to "brainwash" students how to spot fake news, are they going to get them to watch BBC news on a loop?

➢ If anyone needs help identifying fake news its BBC journalists. Perhaps students could help THEM.

➢ Ironic to say the least

➢ Hey students watch @BBCNews it will help you identify fake news

➢ @BBCNews couldn't identify fake news if it bit them in the face

➢ So they only get to view your leftie socialist views and not a healthy left right balance

➢ By broadcasting it every day?

➢ Headline news, "Wolf employed to guard sheep"

➢ *Rolls eyes*

PART THREE
PROPAGANDA

The BBC is, and has long been, the
most refined propaganda service in the world.[1]

John Pilger
Filmmaker, journalist

Ministry of Truth

In order that the British Broadcasting Corporation can prosecute its agenda, so that it can present information according to the demands of the 'elite consensus,' it diligently composes stories that promote one of the many pre-written narratives we encountered in part two. We use the verb 'compose' deliberately to highlight the fact that BBC content is very carefully crafted, and we are not necessarily thinking in terms of basic journalistic practice such as proof-reading. We are thinking about ethics. While a truly objective journalist can and should report with fidelity and impartiality, those following a blueprint have no such liberty and yet they must somehow convince themselves that integrity is at the heart of their activities. Orwell had a name for this outrageous act of self-deception: double-think.

When a BBC activist creates his/her latest piece calculated to demonise Israel or undermine Brexit they do so in the belief they are acting with the utmost integrity for double-think, according to Orwell, 'is the act of holding, simultaneously, two opposite, individually exclusive ideas or opinions and believing in both simultaneously and absolutely.'

If you have wondered how the BBC can claim to be impartial, free and fair while behaving in precisely the opposite manner i.e. biased, prejudiced and unfairly – wonder no more. Thanks to double-think squaring the circle becomes kid's play:

I am an impartial, objective journalist who nevertheless:

- Misrepresents views which contradict the BBC worldview
- Smears entities that disagree with the BBC worldview
- Selects and edits material specifically to support the BBC worldview
- Amplifies whatever supports BBC narratives
- Suppresses whatever contradicts BBC narratives
- Applies different standards depending on whether individuals or organisations share the BBC worldview

Thus, the BBC activist can freely compose sneering anti-Melania Trump hit pieces while believing his or her actions are in full accordance with the principles of impartial journalism. Not for a single moment however would the activist believe themselves to be complicit. That's the beauty of doublethink: 'To deny the existence of objective reality,' explains Orwell, 'and all the while to take account of the reality which one denies.'[2] Probably there are some members of the cult who know exactly what they are doing: *Ok, so I twist the truth, mislead and attempt to inflame, but only because of the threat of the Nazis, populists and the Alt-right. In fact, I have to act this way – it's imperative I do. Humanity itself is at stake. Ultimately, I am doing the right thing.*

Either way, the circle has been squared. Fully immersed in cult psychology, narratives synthesised, Ministry of Truth activists are free to engage in a behaviour whose end product is pure propaganda.

Lessons from history

When we think about propaganda likely we imagine war, specifically WWI and WWII. Propaganda arguably came of age during these conflicts. Both sides certainly exploited traditional journalism as well as the new mediums of radio and cinema in order to manipulate popular opinion.

In the US, initial reluctance to join what was perceived to be a distant war in Europe was overcome by the efforts of a special propaganda unit commissioned by President Woodrow Wilson's administration. The unit's brief was simple: prick the American conscience. Copywriters and artists duly got to work. Amongst other things they aimed to stir up feelings of patriotism as well as fear, whatever was required to win over the American people. The United States went into overdrive, producing propaganda on a staggering scale. Messages were always stark: America, freedom was under threat! The enemy threatened the American way of life! One infamous poster depicted a fearsome Nazi helmet-wearing gorilla, carrying a bloodied club in one hand, a distressed woman in its other: 'Destroy This Mad Brute,' implored the copy, 'Enlist!'

Propaganda clearly works on many levels, chiefly emotional. The idea is to sway, to influence, to affect change. In order to do this it must avoid being rational. After all, if war propaganda showed the true horror of war in all its gory and bloody violence then the effort would be seriously weakened if not completely wrecked. An image of a disabled veteran unable to tie his own shoelaces is hardly likely to help enlistment. Wounds, death, amputations – the realities of war are therefore purposely omitted. Propaganda can thus be said to be the effort to change opinions, attitudes and behaviours based upon information which is partial, incomplete or as is often the case, wholly fallacious. Whilst advertising may also fulfil these criteria to a certain extent, the aim of propaganda is to effect change in the political rather than commercial sphere.

When it comes to the principles of propaganda, who better than the masters themselves to provide instruction? In *Mein Kampf,* Adolf Hitler makes an observation that will ring true for anyone who has experienced even cursory BBC coverage of Brexit or the election of Donald Trump as US president:

> All effective propaganda must be limited to a very few points and must harp on these slogans until the last member of the public understands what you want him to understand by your slogans.[3]

Brexit will be a disaster! Brexit will destroy the UK economy! Brexit is bad! Brexit will make the UK poorer! Propaganda is a battering ram. It can and does batter people into submission. These observations are repeated by Josef Goebbels, the Nazi Party's Minister for Popular Enlightenment and

Propaganda, who notes that, 'The rank and file are usually much more primitive than we imagine.' Often regarded as the master of the dark art, Goebbels goes on to observe:

> Propaganda must therefore always be essentially simple and repetitious. In the long run only he will achieve basic results in influencing public opinion who is able to reduce problems to the simplest terms and who has the courage to keep forever repeating them . . . [4]

Goebbels also notes that the bigger the lie, the more likely people are to believe it. Thus when the BBC claims to be impartial, despite the evidence of their own eyes, some people will readily believe this assertion. This is because acceptance often requires less effort than rejection. The Nazi propaganda guru understood human nature well: People are lazy. It is easier to accept information that confirms existing beliefs rather than taking the considerable effort required to research, check and investigate. Not only this, but the human ego is fragile. Who amongst us would acknowledge to being fooled?

Drawing on the combined thoughts of these undoubted masters both Nazi and US, propaganda principles can be summarised thus:

- Keep it simple – avoid abstraction
- Appeal to emotions
- Repeat key idea to point of saturation
- Present only one side of the argument
- Continuously attack opponents
- Pick out one particular enemy for special vilification

Exposed on a daily basis to a continuous stream of BBC narratives, it takes a particularly robust character to resist the cumulative effect of these messages. Repetition makes a concept familiar. The more familiar a concept, the more likely we are to accept its premises. The Mere Exposure Effect is what psychologists label the human instinct to prefer the familiar over the unfamiliar in the absence of reason or logic. In repetition, the propagandist creates the feeling of familiarity. For example, Trump and Putin, Putin and Trump - the BBC ensures its audience hears this link virtually every day until their supposed relationship is no longer in doubt.

There is a final, crucial element that can be added to our principles of propaganda: the source of the propaganda must be credible, or at least *thought* to be credible. If you want the population to believe your spin it is absolutely imperative that the source is trusted. While government is invariably viewed with suspicion who could doubt the sincerity of an organisation that produces The Archers, covers the Oxford-Cambridge boat race and reports the shipping forecast every evening on Radio 4? 'The fact that we humans often use the credibility of a communicator to guide us in the rejection or acceptance of a message,' warn Pratkanis and Aronson, 'opens the door once again for mindless propaganda.'[5] Beware who you trust.

@Anon
The difference between Nazi state propaganda and BBC is
that the Nazis didn't make its population pay for it under
pain of imprisonment.

In order to influence its audience the Broadcaster relies upon a whole range of techniques which we can label as propaganda tactics. Often this can be a simple matter of language choice. Whether a BBC activist chooses to describe a crowd of marchers as 'rioters' or 'protestors' will depend entirely upon political affiliation. Right-wing marchers will be labelled 'rioters' or as is usually the case 'far right,' while left-wing marchers will invariably be 'protestors' or 'anti-fascists.' By the selection of just a single word, the broadcaster can influence how several million people perceive or 'read' a situation.

For example, when a Kashmiri athlete became embroiled in a visa row upon entering the United States to participate in the 2017 world snowshoe championship held at New York, Britain's 'national' broadcaster was incensed: 'Kashmir Muslim athlete denied US visa due to 'current policy.'' After the athlete in question had been arrested on charges of sexual molestation of a 12 year girl during his US sojourn, the BBC headline had subtly altered: 'Indian athlete held over sex abuse in US.' As to why the broadcaster decided to change 'Muslim' to 'Indian' in its headlines we leave for the reader to hypothesise. The point to make is that the change in focus had been *deliberate*. The BBC was attempting to manipulate how its audience reacted to both stories. Tricks like these are ubiquitous across the BBC. Consider the phrasing of the following headline:

> Three Palestinians killed after deadly stabbing in Jerusalem
> bbc.co.uk

Scanning this headline might lead the reader to assume that three Palestinians had been stabbed to death in Jerusalem, presumably by Israelis. This is precisely what the broadcaster hopes it audience will assume. It would no doubt come as a surprise to the casual reader to discover that the Palestinians of the BBC headline had, in fact, just stabbed to death a 23-year old female Israeli border security officer. In the aftermath of the murder, Israeli security forces had shot and killed the terrorists responsible. After sustained pressure, the BBC's original deliberately misleading headline magically became:

> Israeli policewoman stabbed to death in Jerusalem[6]
> bbc.co.uk

Notice how the change in focus radically affects how the incident is understood. Until being called out by various people including Donald Trump Junior, the impartial, free and fair broadcaster had hoped to manipulate sympathy towards three 'innocent' Palestinians, more victims of Israeli brutality.

@DonaldTrumpJr
So nice of the @BBC to take down their ridiculous tweet from this morn. If they didn't flagrantly mislead they wouldn't have to be called out.

Nor is this disturbing example of political bias unique. 'We have to stay impartial,' concedes BBC Middle East activist Jeremy Bowen, 'but I have a little more latitude to take the audience a bit by the hand and take them in what I believe to be the direction towards understanding.'[7] Language is power. Words shape the way we interact with the world.

'Acceptable premises'

As to the reasons why a broadcaster that professes to be impartial should operate in ways which harmonise so perfectly with explicit propaganda tactics, it's over to Chomsky and Herman once more. According to the academics the mass media, 'Defends the economic, social and political agenda of privileged groups.' They continue:

> The media serve this purpose in many ways: through selection of topics, distribution of concerns, framing of issues, filtering of information, emphasis and tone, and by keeping debate within the bounds of acceptable premises.[8]

'Selection,' 'distribution,' 'framing,' 'filtering,' 'emphasis,' 'tone' - Just a few of what can be labelled BBC propaganda tactics. By using these tools, the broadcaster ensures its audience is presented with a highly selective view of the world, a view that is wholly cognisant with the interests of powerful groups.

These tools allow the broadcaster to present debate in what Chomsky and Hermann term 'within the bounds of acceptable premises.' To understand what they mean by this phrase, take the thorny issue of mass migration. The movement of people from very poor to rich countries undoubtedly benefits corporations – local and multi-national - who can readily exploit this vast pool of cheap labour, while avoiding troublesome issues such as worker's rights: working hours, pension rights, holiday entitlement etc. From slum landlords right through to globalist corporations, mass migration makes the rich richer. However, influx of cheap and pliable labour forces has the opposite effect on the indigenous working poor: it makes them poorer.

The way it frames and filters the immigration debate together with how it chooses to emphasise certain issues (e.g. 'desperate' children) and minimise others (e.g. crime), the 'British' Broadcasting Corporation presents this contentious topic in an overwhelmingly positive light. Furthermore, critics of mass migration are routinely attacked and often demonised. If Chomsky and Herman are correct this is because the BBC is acting for and on behalf of society's 'privileged groups,' i.e. those of the corporate and multi-national variety who benefit most from a cheap pool of compliant labour. It is most certainly not acting for and on behalf of the working poor whose opposition to mass migration manifests in voting for anti-migration political parties such as UKIP in the UK and Front National in France, both of whom the impartial broadcaster attacks, derides and smears with varying levels of ferocity. For the BBC the 'acceptable premise' in the mass migration debate is very simple: mass migration is good, opponents are bad.

By exploiting the opportunities offered by propaganda the broadcaster is able to thus present a highly partisan view of the world to its audience. Recourse to propaganda allows BBC activists to produce ideologically-saturated content while simultaneously claiming to be disinterested, neutral observers. Propaganda is the key. Unable to directly voice its stringent views due to its royal charter obligations, Britain's 'national' broadcaster falls back on techniques that have proved so devastatingly successful in the quest to control minds. From choice of language, choice of images through to tone of voice, BBC propaganda involves a bewildering array of techniques, some more subtle than others that when taken together, add up to a powerful, extremely persuasive opinion former and moderator.

1984: A BBC blueprint?

Before we look at examples of BBC propaganda in detail it may be illuminating to develop the parallels already alluded to between Orwell's infamous Ministry of Truth and the organisation upon which it was based, the BBC.

Between 1941 and 1943 Orwell worked as a producer for the BBC's Eastern Service, a department charged with creating propaganda aimed at a predominantly Indian audience. When it became clear that his efforts had been largely in vain – only a tiny minority of the target audience were listening to the broadcasts – Orwell resigned his post. In the years that followed the author would frequently draw upon his experiences working at the BBC in his writing.

His dystopian masterpiece *1984* has often been described as prophetic. Aware of the human tendency toward authoritarianism to an almost hyper-sensitive extent, Orwell wrote his novel to serve as a warning of what could happen if a tiny band of elitists such as the Frankfurt school (or ideological descendants) ever managed to get its hands on the levers of power. Theirs being a wholly fraudulent ideology,

Orwell was only too aware of the extreme methods such a regime would require in order to maintain its power and what this would involve, namely fear and tyranny. The ex-BBC producer also knew something else. Thanks to his experiences at the corporation, Orwell knew that in order to keep the population in a state of constant anxiety – a prerequisite for control - propaganda was the key.

Set in a post-democratic society – eerily similar to the kind envisaged by the Frankfurt mob and comrade Alinsky – *1984* portrays a world controlled by just these sorts of ideologues. Aided by a vast communication and media network this collection of totalitarians impose a rigid, oppressive system of group-think upon the populace, the aim of which is to strip the people of their individuality and ultimately their humanity. Citizens live in a 24-hour surveillance society enforced by the sinister Thought Police. The numerically greater proles (the working class) meanwhile consume a daily diet of cheap, salacious and above all else undemanding entertainment produced by the Party. Think: Cash in the Attic, Strictly Come Dancing, Mrs Brown's Boys etc. The proles are thus diverted from the political milieu.

Meanwhile Party propaganda is everywhere. Its slogans are displayed in public places: War is Peace! Freedom is Slavery! (The BBC is impartial . . .) Lies become truth and vice versa. Oceanians are bombarded with the most blatant falsehoods: 'We've kind of got to tell a lie,' observes a BBC script writer. 'We'll go back into history and there will be black people where, historically, there wouldn't have been, and we won't dwell on that.'[9] In order to maintain the precepts of this fraudulent society, a misinformation campaign as vast as it is devious is required. For example, when chocolate rations are decreased from 30 to 20 grams, the Ministry broadcasts that rations have actually been *increased* to 20 grams! A lie, an outrageous, bald falsehood, but while The Ministry of Truth holds sway, one that can never be disproven.

'In the end they believe their own propaganda'

The Ministry of Truth is a vast, unfathomable department charged with pumping out Party propaganda pertaining to so much more than just chocolate rations. In common with its compatriots at the BBC, the Party of Orwell's Oceania also has a propensity toward making exaggerated claims regarding its relationship with 'truth.' Both organisations – real and fictional – share the same obsessive desire to convince people of their honesty and integrity, something that should be all too apparent in their deeds. The greater the deceit, the more urgent the need to convince otherwise.

Orwell's Ministry of Truth is the embodiment of a society so far immersed in self-deception it can no longer distinguish between fact and fiction. The Ministry of 'Truth' (Broadcasting House) is in fact, a place where the most egregious lies are told, where the most outrageous deceptions are spun, a place where the most sinister falsehoods are born. Orwell's time at the BBC had not been *entirely* wasted . . . Compare Malcolm Muggeridge's description of the BBC with the author's fictional Ministry of Truth which follows, both dating from the 1940s:

> The BBC came to pass silently, invisibly, like a coral reef, cells busily multiplying until it was a vast structure, a conglomerate of studios, offices and passages along which many passed to and fro; a society with its kings and lords and commons, its laws and its dossiers and revenues and easily suppressed resurrections.[10]

> The Ministry of Truth contained, it was said, three thousand rooms above ground level, and corresponding ramifications below. Scattered about London there were just three other buildings of similar appearance and size.[11]

The Ministry of Truth aka Broadcasting House is a propaganda machine par excellence. It is a place dedicated to diversion and subversion: the diversion of attention and the subversion of truth. Orwell's description paints a picture of endeavour on an epic scale. The Ministry of Truth is a temple to deception:

> Beyond, above, below were other swarms of workers engaged in an unimaginable multitude of jobs. There were the huge printing shops with their sub-editors, their typography experts and their elaborately equipped studios for the faking of photographs. There was the tele-programmes section with its engineers, its producers and its teams of actors chosen for their skill in imitating voices.[12]

159

The raison d'être of the Ministry is not to reflect, but rather to *create* reality. In order to achieve this aim it has developed into a vast, technically advanced operation which churns out a daily production of films, reports and announcements whose aim is to keep the proles in a state of semi-stupor, dazzled by ballroom sequins and blue planets. Anaesthetised on their sofas, the working class can be subdued, placated. Consider this part of the BBC's Mission statement taken from its royal charter:

> The Mission of the BBC is to act in the public interest, serving all audiences through the provision of impartial, high-quality and distinctive output and services which **inform, educate** and **entertain**.

However where it promises to inform The Ministry of Truth misleads; where it promises to educate it indoctrinates; where it promises to entertain it stultifies. In *Manufacturing Consent*, Chomsky and Herman provide a much more expansive explanation of the BBC's 'mission:'

> It is their [the mass media] function to **amuse, entertain** and **inform**, and to inculcate individuals with the values, beliefs, and codes of behaviour that will integrate them into the institutional structures of the larger society. In a world of concentrated wealth and major conflicts of class interest, to fulfil this role requires systematic propaganda.[13]

As society is run by a privileged elite acting entirely for and after its own interests 'systematic propaganda' is necessary in order to convince the proles to adopt appropriate attitudes and beliefs that will serve these wealthy and powerful groups. Propaganda recycled and repeated facilitates this process. 'Preparation or carefully doctored propaganda to familiarise people with a new concept,' notes Arnold, 'is a necessary introduction to an acceptance of any brainwashing activity.'[14]

Critics would suggest this is precisely what BBC content is tailored to do: convince the masses how they ought to think, feel and react to the world around them in accordance with the wishes of the elite. An unethical broadcaster would do this not by faithfully reporting, but by *distorting* its content accordingly. It has no choice. For to report faithfully would invariably not encode the objectives of the elite, as its wealth and power is attained and sustained at the expense of the weak, the poor and the vulnerable.

As an approach to journalism this is a profound departure from a discipline that above all else strives not to pre-judge, one that reaches conclusions at *the end* of the journalistic process not *before* that process has even begun. 'The trouble with those who engage in such activities,' Arnold reminds us, 'is that in the end they believe their own propaganda.'[15] Just ask any BBC activist from foot soldiers to the big beasts such as John Simpson or Kirsty Wark if he or she believes they are complicit in producing propaganda. You can probably guess how they would react.

'The communicator must appear unbiased and trustworthy'
It is no accident that The British Broadcasting Corporation is forever telling its audience how trustworthy it is. As Shakespeare demonstrated so artfully with 'honest' Iago, outward appearances can and often do mask malign intentions. In *1984* Big Brother - patient, benign and temperate - is actually sucking the life out of the citizenry as it listens to the mighty one's calm, authoritative and inspirational tones. Gaining public trust is vital:

> The BBC is recognised by audiences in the UK and around the world as a provider of news that you can trust. Our website, like our TV and radio services, strives for journalism that is accurate, impartial, independent and fair.[16]

If you wish your propaganda to be successful, best distance yourself from government, which is precisely what the BBC takes considerable pains to do. 'The propagandist finds it important not to appear to be a propagandist,' observe Pratkanis and Aronson. 'In order to be successful, the communicator must appear unbiased and trustworthy.'[17]

The final word on this brief discussion into what is essentially wilful deception must go to the grand master himself: 'Propaganda,' warns Goebbels, 'becomes ineffective the moment we become aware of it.'[18]

The BBC box of tricks

The BBC has a whole arsenal of propaganda techniques which it deploys to further its agenda, analysis of which would take up several volumes alone. Thus in the section that follows we content ourselves with analysis of just a selection of its various ruses:

- Make 'em laugh: BBC 'comedy'
- Make em tremble: The fear factor
- Focus: delay, pivot, juxtaposition
- Health-checks
- Bias by omission
- The BBC smear machine
- Misrepresentation
- Amplification and suppression

Make 'em laugh: BBC 'comedy'

Amongst the many weapons in its armoury, comedy is a particularly powerful technique that enables the BBC to secrete its values into the public arena. Humour can be a devastatingly effective tool as the BBC knows so well. 'The most potent weapons known to mankind,' notes comrade Alinsky, 'are satire and ridicule.'[1]

There is certainly much more to BBC 'comedy' than meets the eye. When we giggle at the butt of a BBC joke we are not only laughing at a particular foible, we are being encouraged to subtly reject the target in much broader terms. Objects of BBC comedy are invariably wrong-thinkers. Moreover, by consistently mocking these individuals the broadcaster can imply there is a consensus against these targets. The objective is to portray wrong-thinkers as isolated, friendless and eccentric. Canned laughter, unsympathetic hosts and studio audiences specially selected for their potential antagonism further help to create this illusion.

The BBC's comedy crucible can indeed be a cruel and lonely place, especially for the wrong-thinker. Meanwhile right-thinkers are spared this public humiliation, the modern equivalent of being put in the medieval stocks. Transgressors are not pelted with rotten fruit and veg, but rather with insults and slurs. Underpinning the apparent frivolity of Have I Got News for You, Mock the Week *et al*, is something insidious: the BBC is pulling the strings, controlling what the public comes to accept as reasonable and unreasonable opinions, conditioning its responses: brainwashing. As a shared experience humour can be a powerful tool of the propagandist; after all, who amongst us does not wish to 'get' the joke. Those who don't get the joke cannot claim to be cool. They are not part of the 'in' crowd.

The BBC thus exerts huge social pressure on its audience. Everybody is laughing – or appears to be – shouldn't you? Come that ubiquitous canned laughter it is all too easy to be swept along on this tide of hilarity, especially for younger audience members for whom social acceptance is such a crucial stage of their psychosocial development. The younger the audience the greater the need to be perceived as a member of the majority, as a BBC right-thinker. For those not joining in social isolation may await.

The Spiral of Silence Theory

Elisabeth Noelle-Neumann, a German political scientist, presented her Spiral of Silence Theory in 1974. This theory introduces the concept of 'social isolation' whereby the behaviour of individuals is regulated in accordance with the norms of society's dominant groups. Briefly, 'Isolation pressure' is exerted on those whose behaviour (and opinions) is met with disapproval e.g. frowning, turning away or even 'unfriending.' In order to avoid being shunned people fall silent and conceal the behaviours etc. they perceive will be frowned upon.

Those people meanwhile who feel their behaviours and opinions meet with public support are apt to become more confident and louder. A vicious circle ensues, The Spiral of Silence. Right-thinkers become louder, wrong-thinkers become quieter. The majority of people are unaware just how much their behaviour is regulated by public opinion, or more exactly what is *perceived* to be public opinion and will self-censure according to these perceptions. Thus, by promoting certain ideas over others organisations within the mass media can, and do, exert tremendous control over both public and private spheres.

Public shaming is a favourite BBC trick that ensures the behaviours and opinions of dominant groups are reinforced. This trick is especially effective when used on individuals in the public eye. Make a favourable comment about a BBC wrong-thinker e.g. retweet a Twitter post from Nigel Farage and the person involved could easily find themselves named and shamed by the 'national' broadcaster. The threat of social isolation which may follow is a powerful deterrent. If you want to remain in the broadcaster's good books then whatever you do, do not attend a fundraising dinner for a member of one of the BBC's despised tribes:

> Michael Gove apologises for attending Ian Paisley dinner
> bbc.co.uk

Should you happen to interact with a BBC wrong-thinker the broadcaster will ensure your apology will be prominently featured on its media platform as a deterrent for others. Look what happens when a BBC wrong-thinker re-tweets a double-plus BBC wrong-thinker:

Ian Paisley sorry for retweeting Katie Hopkins comment
bbc.co.uk

Social isolation is the kiss of death for those in the public arena. Certainly, those hoping to have a long and successful career in their chosen fields would be best advised to choose their contacts very carefully - in line with BBC policy - or face the consequences. Exploiting the psychology behind the Spiral of Silence Theory is just one of many ways the impartial broadcaster maintains control over the public forum while normalising the minority elite consensus.

'Impossible to avoid joining in'

There is a moment in *1984* which is not too far removed from the kind of response the BBC is hoping to elicit from audiences of its 'comedy.' It occurs during the two minutes hate ritual. The appearance of Emmanuel Goldstein on the ubiquitous telescreens sparks hysteria among the Oceanic population. 'In a lucid moment,' the anti-hero of Orwell's harrowing tale is horrified to note that he too is also taking part in the hysteria: 'The horrible thing about the Two Minutes Hate was not that one was obliged to act a part, but that it was impossible to avoid joining in.'[2] Winston's reactions, unwitting and spontaneous, are just the sorts of involuntary behaviour that occur when groups conform under threat of sanctions or even worse perhaps, estrangement from the in-group. Joining in with the crowd is an integral part of ensuring self-preservation, a way of signalling one's submission to Party ideology.

In Oceania everybody screams at the telescreens because everybody else is doing just that. Psychologists have long understood the dynamics of crowd behaviour. They have also known about its dangers:

> Historically, because large groups of people have been able to effect dramatic and sudden social change, in a manner that bypasses established due process, they have also provoked controversy.[3]

Given that manipulating crowds – audiences – can 'effect dramatic and sudden social change,' it is little wonder the BBC ruthlessly exploits the comedy genre. From a purely pragmatic viewpoint, comedy has few equals when it comes to setting and controlling an agenda. The dynamics of BBC 'comedy' work on the principle of group psychology: If you are not with us, then surely you are against us: Marxism 101.

'Spotted: a right-wing comedian on the BBC!' Rod Liddle's article for *The Spectator* magazine might have been light-hearted enough, but the former BBC editor's message was clear enough: BBC 'comedy,' like its news and drama is skewered to reflect and legitimise a specific worldview. Having recovered from the shock, Liddle reflects on his own sense of euphoria at this rare sight: 'Why should I be grateful to the BBC for allowing one single representative of majority opinion on air?' These musings lead the journalist to raise a truly disturbing point: 'And so we end up being grateful,' continues Liddle, 'when someone who speaks for the majority – or at least a very large minority – actually gets airtime.'[4] By dictating what passes for socially acceptable, what its audience should or should not ridicule, the BBC is half-way to taking full control of our malleable minds.

'Horrifying reactionary values'

How does the BBC treat a straight, white, privately educated male? How does it treat a straight, white, privately educated male who also happens to be a pro-life Conservative? And if the person in questions just happens to be a Christian and Eurosceptic too?

A monologue attacking conservative MP Jacob Rees-Mogg, complete with copious amounts of canned laughter appeared on an edition of BBC2's The Mash Report, a 'comedy' show aimed at the 16-35 age group. Here are some of the 'highlights:'

> He (Jacob Rees-Mogg) consistently votes against gay rights, women's reproductive rights, human rights and equality. He's an absolute rotter isn't he? Rees-Mogg attributes many of his opinions to his Catholic faith . . .

> He opposes same sex marriage. He also opposes abortion even in cases of rape and incest . . . He voted to block unaccompanied child refugees in Calais from finding safety in the UK. Rees-Mogg would have absolutely hated Jesus. He was an immigrant who could walk on water.

The pro-life old Etonian is unapologetic about his views - when people hold terrible views that can ruin people's lives, the last thing you want is an apology. Jacob Rees-Mogg stated in an interview "I am what I am." Echoing the voices of gay people across the world whose rights he sought to curtail.

So the question is, was Jacob Rees-Mogg born this way?"[5]

Did you spot those BBC narratives? *Catholicism is very, very bad; Abortion is very, very good; Private education is very, very bad; Migrants are very, very good; Immigration control is very, very bad etc.*

But surely the piece de la resistance is the final part of this 'comedy' monologue in which this representative of the pro-Islamic BBC goes on to accuse the Conservative politician of wishing to turn the clock back, 'to a golden age where women were second class citizens (and) homosexuality was illegal . . .' Now that really is funny, albeit inadvertently.

'An absolute rotter' . . . a 'meek-sceptic' . . . 'pro-life Old Etonian' . . someone who holds 'terrible views' . . . was he (Rees-Mogg) 'born this way?' . . . 'horrifying reactionary values' . . . 'Rees-Mogg would have absolutely hated Jesus' . . . Do you get the feeling the broadcaster doesn't care much for Mr Rees-Mogg? The MP seems to embody just about everything the non-judgemental BBC despises. Not only is he a product of the English public school system, he's also a conservative! It gets even worse: He's Catholic, and as such is also pro-life. And if all that wasn't bad enough, Mr Rees-Mogg advocates a sensible and manageable system of immigration into the UK! Oh and he's also a Brexiteer - in BBC land, 'terrible views' each and every one. And get this – according to the BBC 'comedian' he's also 'unapologetic' about his wrong-think!

What a 'rotter.'

Politicians have reason to fear the satirist and rightly so. Why then does The Mash Report and BBC programmes of its ilk reserve their scorn and ridicule solely for the likes of Boris Johnson, Michael Gove, Nigel Farage and of course Jacob Rees-Mogg - straight, white, male conservative politicians who also happen to be Euro-sceptics? Is it just coincidence? After all, if ever there was a subject for satire, then calamitous Labour MP Diane Abbott could have few equals. We will not however find a single BBC programme mocking or exposing the many shortcomings of this black, female, EU-supporting, prominent Labour party front-bencher, calamities notwithstanding. As far as the BBC is concerned, Diane Abbott is not a suitable topic for satire.

Look at it this way: if Jacob Rees Mogg MP is a suitable target for BBC mockery, then so too should be Diane Abbott MP. She isn't. He is.

'Shut up and die'

Having portrayed Mr Rees-Mogg as some kind of devil incarnate to an impressionable BBC 'comedy' audience, how might this character assassination play out in the real world? Take a man with 'terrible views,' subject him to sustained attacks across an enormous media platform and who knows where this might lead – to retribution perhaps?

> **Daniel Hannan:**
> A Leftist mob ambushes Mogg on his doorstep, shouting at his young children: "Your daddy's a totally horrible person, lots of people hate your daddy". What is happening to this country, for the love of God?

From the moment he assumed a role as a leading Brexiteer, Britain's virulently pro-EU 'national' broadcaster launched a sustained and scathing attack on the MP for North East Somerset. BBC vilification of Mr Rees-Mogg as witnessed on The Mash Report has been a consistent theme of its post-Brexit coverage of Brexit supporting public figures. Mr Rees-Mogg has not been its only target. The broadcaster has also attempted to stir up antipathy towards Boris Johnson, another prominent Brexit-supporting, privately-educated, straight white Conservative politician.

In August of 2018, the BBC's anti Rees-Mogg smear campaign appeared to have paid off. While away on a family holiday thugs vandalised the politician's family home and his wife's car. Graffiti scrawled on the vehicle included, "shut up and die," and "shithead." Messages daubed on the MP's home included "posh scum." The word "twat" was scrawled on the MP's garden in which the vandals had sinisterly constructed a wooden cross hung with condoms, a reference presumably to the MP's pro-life views so scorned by BBC 'comedians.'

The thugs had also left a dildo-covered condom on the bonnet of Mrs Rees-Mogg's Land Rover.

Now you might think an elected member of the British parliament targeted in this way - and thanks to the BBC - a prominent member at that ('a thoroughly modern bigot') would be pretty newsworthy. Alas, not Auntie. The impartial broadcaster appeared none too keen to report what was not only a horrific attack on an innocent family, but an assault on free speech and democracy. The story *did* appear on its news website. But it wasn't on the Home page, nor was it on the UK page. It eventually turned up buried on the Somerset page of the BBC's regional news section far, far away from prying eyes. Nothing to see here. Meanwhile, BBC main headlines on its Home page on this day included: 'My dad wore the same socks for four days,' and 'What we learned from the Love Island reunion,' amongst others . . .

Make 'em cry: The Fear Factor

It is no coincidence that in *1984* the citizens of Oceania live in a perpetual state of anxiety. Paranoia reigns. Spies are everywhere. Saying – thinking – the wrong thoughts incurs treatment of the most brutal type. If Orwell's imagined super-continent is not at war with Eurasia, then it's at war with Eastasia and vice versa. War is Peace say the Party slogans. Enemies are everywhere - in the war zones of Asia and beyond. Enemies intent on destroying the Party lurk even closer to home in Oceania where, 'even thought of Goldstein produced fear and anger automatically.'[1] For those who haunt the corridors of Broadcasting House, the merest thought of Emmanuel Goldstein (Trump, Farage etc.) can also invoke apprehension, panic and dread.

Project Fear was the rather apt name given to the very strenuous efforts that went into persuading the British people to vote to remain a member of the EU in the run-up to the 2016 Referendum. As fanatical supporters of the political bloc, experts in stoking up fear and anxiety not forgetting its unsurpassed expertise in the production and dissemination of propaganda, Britain's 'national' broadcaster naturally played a prominent role in this effort: 'Is Brexit a disaster in waiting for Northern Ireland? asked BBC Question Time.' 'No fresh sandwiches after Brexit' BBC Newsnight told its audience. And so it went on and on and on. Phantoms, spectres, menaces; as every propagandist worth his or her salt knows, fear is always the key.

Once again the corporation is hoping to exploit the psychology of the crowd. In his study of crowds, French psychologist Gustav Le Bon wrote extensively about the tendency for people to flock together and thereafter to follow the leader. Blindly following others is fraught with danger not least when panic can usurp logic and lead to mob violence etc. 'In particular Le Bon believed in the essential conservatism of crowds and their fear of change,' observes David Welch. 'A fearful, disoriented crowd – or nation – could therefore easily be manipulated.'[2] Le Bon's ideas are particularly useful to propagandists who are typically looking to exert control over large swathes of people.

Overwhelmed by anxious feelings, we are more likely to override rationality or logic. We are more likely to turn to the manipulator, to uncritically accept his or her diagnosis and accept too their solutions.

What better way to stoke fear than to create a bogeyman – an Emmanuel Goldstein - around whom these fears can coalesce? Donald Trump, Nigel Farage, Boris Johnson, Tommy Robinson, Viktor Orban, Steve Bannon - the list goes on.

And the politically correct broadcaster has a whole retinue of not just bogeymen, but bogey*women* too: Marine Le Pen, Katie Hopkins, Ivanka Trump etc. How then does it create these figures of hate? Whether it's Le Pen, Wilders or Orban, the BBC's portrayal is always the same: it rests entirely upon hyperbole. Britain's 'national' broadcaster notes one ex-employee, 'turned George Bush into a clownish hate figure for the British people . . . there's no way the British people will ever feel respect for, or get to know George Bush. The BBC has made sure that won't happen.'[3] This process of crude distortion, of incessant exaggeration allied with misrepresentation leads ultimately to caricature and with it a feeling that targets are somehow sub-human, other, alien. The result is yet more polarisation: us (right-thinkers) v them (wrong-thinkers). 'One serious consequence,' of this polarisation note Pratkanis and Aronson is that, 'out-group members are dehumanised: they are represented in our mind by a simple, often derogatory label.'[4]

By far the broadcaster's most popular derogatory label is 'far-right.' With its association to fascism, political violence and Nazism it's one that the BBC uses liberally and indiscriminately to demonise wrong-thinkers. Derogatory labels such as these help accentuate the gulf between us and them, the good and the bad:

> The creation of an evil out-group serves the dual purpose of making members feel good about belonging to their own group ("I'm glad I'm not like them") and increasing their fears about leaving and not supporting their own group ("I don't want to be like them; I can't let them take over the world").[5]

Nazis, Nazis everywhere . . .

> If we're not careful, the Union Flag / St. George's Cross will become a modern-day swastika.
> BBC Script Editor

The BBC maintains an impressive daily production line of Nazi and Neo-Nazi themed stories. No matter how tentative the link the merest whiff of Nazi, neo- or otherwise, will bring the BBC bloodhounds from wide and far. Hardly a day goes by without the corporation producing yet another Nazi-themed story. Oddly, stories warning of the dangers of Stalinism, Marxism and Communism are rather thin on the ground. Here's just a small selection of headlines directly referencing Nazis which appeared on the BBC news website in January 2018:

> Holocaust Memorial Day: A **Nazi** in the family

> Cornwall Council candidate sorry for **Nazi** uniform posts

> Ethan Stables trial: Landlady's 'fear over **neo-Nazi** pub plot'

> Jersey woman who hid Jewish friend from **Nazis** honoured

> Far-right Austria minister's **'Nazi** language' causes anger

> Pub's **'Nazi**-themed' German night Facebook posts banned

> Self-proclaimed **Nazi** guilty of stirring up racial hatred

> **Neo-Nazi** case: Two men plead not guilty to terror charges

> Bobsledding in a World War Two **Nazi** war bunker

As revealing as these headlines are, they tell only half the story. There are in fact many more stories that deal with Nazi-related themes. In the same month visitors to the BBC website would have also come across stories with the following headlines: 'In spite of Hitler, I'm here to talk at my grandson's school,' or 'Naked Auschwitz demonstrators who killed sheep convicted,' or 'The Tattooist of Auschwitz - and his secret love.' And so on and so forth.

In a column for *Unherd*, Douglas Murray wonders what next for the growing number of self-identifying Nazi hunters whipped up into a frenzy by the BBC's unceasing hysteria:

What are these 'anti-Nazis' going to do to find their Nazis? Where will they look? For after all, where can Nazis be found in modern Britain? They are not in the phone book. Nor do they appear to openly congregate in public areas. Given this fact, do our anti-Nazis not find themselves in a conundrum? Do they not, perhaps, find themselves in the situation of a hound with no foxes to chase?[6]

This is pretty much what happened at a much-hyped white nationalist rally in the town of Charlottesville in 2018, one year after the infamous riots in the same town. The mythical Nazi army of BBC prophecy singularly failed to materialise:

@Anon
Looks like #UniteTheRight2 is comprised of a few dozen
dudes who marched down the street and dispersed while
the far left protestors who arrived thinking they would fight a
non-existent Nazi army raised havoc and attacked the cops

While Mr Murray and the more rationale may scoff at the transparency of such indoctrination techniques, crude as they are, it is entirely probable that just the mere mention of the names Gert Wilders or Marine Le Pen is enough to conjure up visions of brown shirts, Nuremberg rallies and even Nazi death camps in the minds of BBC types and true believers - conditioning that Pavlov himself would have been justly proud.

The BBC's 'far/alt-right' category just keeps getting bigger. Not only does it include concerned grandparents marching against terrorism in Manchester, London and elsewhere, it also appears to extend to those concerned about the growing number of cases of child sexual exploitation in the UK: 'Why is the alt-right so obsessed with paedophilia?' asked a BBC Trending producer once upon a time.

So according to BBC Trending, unease over paedophilia is no longer a concern of decent citizens, but an obsession of the alt-right and neo-Nazis. We'll leave the reader to speculate why this should be . . .

Focus

Whenever we consume BBC content, we do so from a highly specific viewpoint at the exclusion of all other angles. Here we will explore three ways in which the BBC ensures its audience encounters a story only through its own prism: pivot, juxtaposition, and diversion.

The pivot

Occasionally the broadcaster is forced to report on stories it would very much prefer its audiences did not see or hear. When four young African-Americans were convicted of torturing a mentally-disabled white man in Chicago in 2016 and live-streaming their acts on Facebook, outrage was palpable. Chicago police described the prolonged attack as 'sickening.' Given the ferocity of the attack and the victim's disability this was a story that aroused international condemnation. All of which presented a real dilemma for the BBC. As watchers of the violence perpetrated upon white farmers can testify black attacking white is most certainly not part of the cultural Marxist agenda. Much as it wanted to the broadcaster could not ignore this particular story.

Should the broadcaster wish to deflect attention it has a number of methods. Usually it simply ignores the event. News the public does not see or hear effectively means the event did not happen. Omission is a BBC favourite. Failing this, it will opt to minimise events. However, such was the level of violence involved in this case minimisation was not possible. Instead, the broadcaster opted for the pivot. A disabled, vulnerable white man might have been horrifically tortured by a gang of black youths, but the BBC was very anxious that its reader's concerns should not linger too long on these gruesome details, and it certainly did not want its readers to consider the racial implications.

Here's how the neutral broadcaster chose to end its report into the sustained and horrific torture of a disabled white man:

> The incident has provoked a strong reaction on Twitter,
> especially among the alt-right - the fringe group whose members
> celebrated US President-elect Trump's election win with Nazi
> salutes.[1]

Bizarrely, we've ended up at a completely different location from where we started. Why would prolonged torture of a disabled man provoke outrage 'especially among the alt-right?' And why focus on what the broadcaster itself admits is a 'fringe' group? Outrage to this incident was worldwide. Do you see what the devious broadcaster did here with its focus? Instead of dwelling on the implications of this horrendous crime, we find ourselves at the 'alt-right,' Donald Trump and of course that perennial BBC favourite, Nazis . . .

Juxtaposition

When President Trump decided to donate $1 million from his personal fortune to help the victims of Hurricane Harvey in August 2017, the gesture made headline news around the world:

Trump to donate $1 million to Texas recovery - CNNPolitics
Aug 31, 2017 · President Donald Trump will donate $1 million of his fortune to recovery efforts in Texas, though the White House says he hasn't determined which group or ...
https://www.cnn.com/2017/08/31/politics/trump-donation-harvey...

Trump Pledges $1 Million Donation to Harvey's Victims – The
Aug 31, 2017 · WASHINGTON — President Trump has pledged to donate $1 million from his personal fortune to storm victims in Texas and Louisiana. "He would like to join ...
https://www.nytimes.com/2017/08/31/us/trump-harvey-donation.html

Here's Where Trump Donated his $1 Million For Harvey Relief
President Donald Trump and the first lady, Melania, personally donated $1 million to Hurricane Harvey relief efforts, the White House said Wednesday.
https://www.nbcnews.com/politics/white-house/here-s-where-trump-d...

Fig. 12

Even Mr Trump's fiercest critics took time off to recognise this gesture. Even the 87% and 83% negative anti-Trump *New York Times* and *Washington Post* conceded the president's compassion at what was a very difficult time for the United States. However, there was one organisation that just could not bring itself to acknowledge this act of generosity. The gesture might have been making headline news around the world, but on the BBC news website it was only good enough for a single sentence buried deep within an article imaginatively entitled 'Texas governor says Houston recovery a 'multi-year project.'

Imagine you are a BBC activist. You notice that Mr Trump is the subject of praise around the world. You check your master narrative: *Trump is very, very bad.* How then do you turn a positive into a negative? Here's how you do it via the BBC news website:

> The White House also said Mr Trump would donate **$1m** of his own money to the relief effort.

> Dell Technologies CEO Michael Dell and his wife, Susan, have also pledged to donate **$36m** to launch a Rebuild Texas Fund with the aim of raising more than $100m for recovery efforts.

> The couple, both Texas natives, said on Friday they plan to donate **$18m** immediately to launch the fund through their eponymous foundation.[2]

Do you see what the BBC did here? By searching for and finding news of a much larger donation than Mr Trump's, the BBC activist had achieved his or her target, producing an anti-Trump sub-narrative: *Donald Trump is very, very mean.* BBC narratives invariably lack subtlety.

It didn't end there. While the article went on to extensively quote Texas Governor Greg Abbot's thoughts on Hurricane Harvey, the broadcaster selected its quotes with the utmost care. Here's the part of Mr Abbot's press conference that *did not* make it onto any BBC news platform:

> I am so proud of the way the President and the Vice President and their entire cabinet have stood up, stood strong and

supported the people of Texas. I have never seen a President and Vice President or cabinet who have responded as swiftly and as effectively to people in need.

Business as usual then for Britain's state broadcaster: Omission of key quotes by Governor Abbot praising Mr Trump and his administration, and deliberate juxtaposition of Mr Trump's donation with that of another donor in order to undermine the president. A typical day's work down at the impartial, free and fair 'national' broadcaster.

And so the BBC had yet another anti-Trump sub-narrative to add to its burgeoning collection. Turning a positive into a negative in just a couple of paragraphs. Haters gonna hate.

Diversion

Who but the BBC could turn the horrific death of an innocent young girl into anti-Trump invective? As incredible at it sounds, that is just what the impartial broadcaster did on 1 December 2017 in an article bizarrely entitled, 'Kate Steinle: Trump outrage over murder case acquittal.'

Yup, it's all about Trump's 'outrage.'

On a July afternoon in 2015, San Francisco resident Kathryn Steinle had been accompanying her father on a day trip to the city's popular Embarcadero waterfront. Without warning, Kate was shot in the back. The terrified young woman collapsed into her father's arms pleading for him to save her life. Two hours later she died in hospital. The leisure pier upon where she had been shot was just yards from her home.

It later transpired that her murderer had been deported from the US on no fewer than five previous occasions, and at the time of the shooting was on probation. San Francisco's status as a sanctuary city was blamed by many for Kate's murder as was United States' immigration policy. In the aftermath of the killing pressure mounted for legislation to ensure the tragic chain of events that lead to the murder could never occur again. As of 2018 'Kate's Law' is still hoped for and anticipated.

The decision to find her killer not guilty of murder or manslaughter caused uproar. Kate's killer was ultimately charged with illegal possession of a firearm. The BBC angle was eccentric to say the least. For this was the kind of story that would, under normal circumstances, prove irresistible to BBC activists: a young woman murdered by a thuggish male with a gun! A holy Trinity of BBC activism. Not only this, but here was a young woman and family who had been badly failed by the criminal justice system. Stand by for BBC outrage, oodles and oodles of outrage. Americans! Men! Guns!

Only not on this occasion. Poor Kate Steinle might have been brutally slain, a young woman with the rest of her life ahead of her, but BBC activists didn't seem too fussed at all. There was no indignation, no laments, no sorrow, no epithets. We didn't hear anything about a life cut short, one full of promise etc. etc. Nor was there any attempt to manipulate the emotions of its audience against men and more specifically men who use guns.

The reason for this unusual display of BBC reticence was simple: Kate's killer was Mexican – an illegal Mexican migrant. Had a God-fearing Republican pulled the trigger that would have been a different matter altogether. *(Illegal) migrants are very, very good* . . .Besides, there was another BBC narrative at play here. In the aftermath of a killing that had shocked America, Donald Trump had mentioned Kate's case on several occasions.

For reasons best known to itself the BBC decided this story was not actually about the tragic and unlawful killing of a young woman by an illegal migrant, but rather about Donald Trump's 'outrage:' President Trump described the verdict as "disgraceful,' read the BBC website:

"No wonder the people of our country are so angry with illegal immigration," he said in a pre-dawn tweet on Friday.[3]

While the BBC report is conspicuously lacking in any form of tribute to Miss Steinle and sympathy is certainly in short supply, generous coverage *is* granted to the explanation of the killer's actions. It was all a mistake. He hadn't meant to fire three shots, let alone kill somebody etc. The BBC became very anxious that its readers should sympathise not with the victim, but with the perpetrator.

So who was Kate Steinle? What kind of woman was she? By what mechanisms had the US immigration system so catastrophically failed her? There were many questions hanging in the air. The BBC however did not seem interested in any of them. Something else had caught its attention - something much more useful than journalistic enquiry. It took the broadcaster no time at all to arrive at one of its favourite destinations, Donald Trump:

> Overnight, white supremacists left candles and messages
> saying "build the wall" on the pier, NBC News reported.

'White supremacists' linked to Donald Trump's wall. Who but an impartial, free and fair publicly-funded broadcaster could resist temptation like that? (For the record NBC is a virulently anti-Trump television network).

So how did the impartial national broadcaster choose to end its report into the tragic death of Kate Steinle? With a meditation about the futility of her death – indignation at such a futile waste of life? With a tribute from family and friends as is appropriate on these occasions? No. This was not about Kate Steinle. For the BBC this was all about one man:

> He described the death of Ms Steinle as 'a senseless and totally
> preventable violent act committed by an illegal immigrant'.

> In June, Mr Trump announced a plan called "Kate's law" – named
> for Ms Steinle - which he said would increase penalties for
> deportees who re-enter the US.

> Defence lawyer Francisco Ugarte said after the verdict that the
> case had been used to 'foment hate.'

And of course the final word in this story brings us back once again to a favourite BBC narrative, 'hate.' Well, at least it wasn't the Nazis . . .

Health checks

Atrick the BBC never tires of playing is offering up health checks. It's a tactic that does not go unnoticed. 'It is always the same,' responded a social media user. 'Left wing commentators introduced as "experts", non-left wing ones introduced as the nearest thing to Hitler.' Far from glowing introductions for some guests, free passes for others. What exactly is the crafty broadcaster up to here?

> **@Anon**
> Quite extraordinary introduction on @BBCr4today - leftist
> think tank IPPR introduced as just a think tank, whereas the
> IEA introduced as a "right wing free market think tank"

During the course of its activism, the BBC often uses and refers to numerous third parties – pundits, representatives, witnesses etc. Depending on the extent to which entities agree or disagree with the BBC worldview will dictate whether or not they are issued with a BBC health-check. What is a health-check? Put simply, it's a warning, a signal to the audience regarding how seriously (or not) it is supposed to take the views or opinions of the person or organisation in question. In other words, by its decision to provide a 'warning' (or not) the broadcaster is subtly attempting to influence its audience's judgements.

The neutral broadcaster has a fairly standard way of issuing its health checks: those on the liberal-left end of the political spectrum typically do not receive health checks, while the opposite is true for individuals or organisations with known sympathies towards conservatism. The political right will invariably be identified as such. This phenomenon of issuing free passes to political friends and allies while singling out enemies is a ubiquitous feature of BBC content.

For example, when BBC Question Time visited Guildford in October 2018 among the five panellists were Brexit-supporting Tory MP James Cleverley and anti-Brexit Labour MP Keir Starmer. A fervent supporter of the EU, the Labour politician has been somewhat of a darling of the anti-Brexit movement in the UK since the 2016 vote. Here's how presenter David Dimbleby introduced both politicians at the start of the programme:

And with me tonight the deputy chairman of the conservative party and elected as an MP in 2015 and a **staunch Brexiteer**, James Cleverley, Keir Starmer, lawyer, former director of public prosecutions and now Labour's shadow Brexit secretary . . .[1]

A health-check for Cleverley, a free pass for Starmer – BBC balance. The reason for the disparity is simple: By adding warnings to right of centre figures only, the BBC is attempting to portray Liberal (left-wing) views as normal - so normal they do not require flagging up. Conservative opinion on the other hand is highlighted thus making it seem to be going against the grain of 'normal' BBC-think. Leftism thus becomes accepted as a default position.

Glossary of BBC Health-checks	
anti-fascist *counter-protestor* *fact-checker* *independent* *respected* *moderate*	Any entity that agrees with BBC's globalist agenda of open borders and mass migration and/or is hostile to conservatism or populism etc.
controversial *conspiracy theorist* *hardliner* *divisive* *extremist* *far-right* *Islamophobe* *populist*	Any entity that disagrees with BBC's globalist agenda of open borders and mass migration and/or is sympathetic to conservatism or populism etc.

Fig. 13

A tale of two political commentators

To get an idea of the treatment meted out to left and right-wing political figures take a look at the following BBC introductions of left-wing commentator Owen Jones and right-wing US commentator Ann Coulter. The BBC news website regularly mentions both these figures. However, whereas Jones is invariably introduced in terms of professional standing (writer/journalist) by the same token Coulter is almost uniformly tagged in terms of her political alliance (conservative). As of 2018 Ms Coulter has written 13 books many of which have appeared in the New York Times' Best Seller List. *Godless: The Church of Liberalism* debuted at number one on the list in 2006. In our analysis the BBC news website introduces her as 'author' on just 4 occasions. While Jones is rarely identified by his left-wing political allegiance, Ms. Coulter is almost guaranteed to be labelled 'conservative,' 'right-wing' or 'Republican':

		Mentions on bbc.co.uk
Owen Jones	'Left-wing, Labour' etc.	8 / 56
Ann Coulter	'Conservative, right-wing' etc.	51 / 63

Fig. 14

In our analysis, Jones' political allegiance is rarely mentioned. His left-wing affiliations are mentioned just 14% of the time by the BBC news website. Compare this to Ms Coulter whose Republican/Conservative affiliations are mentioned over 80% of the time by the same website. The broadcaster is also apt to introduce Coulter by an array of less than complimentary phrases such as a 'conservative firebrand,' 'a massive/fervent Trump supporter' or an 'ultra/provocative/staunch conservative.' And there's also our own alliterative favourite, 'controversial conservative columnist.' More imaginative titles include 'Queen of right wing extreme,' and 'the leggy siren of the Republican right.'

Jones meanwhile is referred to as 'Momentum supporter' (once) as well as 'activist' and 'campaigner.' Indeed, rather than having a political health check of any sort Jones is just as likely to be labelled as plain old 'Owen Jones' without any introduction whatsoever. *The Guardian* writer certainly does not enjoy the level of modification allocated to his American counterpart. Modifiers such as 'controversial' or 'provocative' are never used by the BBC when introducing him, but for many this is exactly what he is - controversial and provocative.

'Sorry, there are no results for left-wing CNN'

BBC bias is not only apparent in the way it describes individuals, but in how it describes organisations. A quick search on the BBC news website for rival US cable channels CNN and Fox News returns some interesting results. Searching for 'right-wing Fox News' yields results a-plenty: 'Right-wing Fox News,' 'Right-wing news outlet,' 'Right-wing TV network Fox News,' 'The right-wing Fox news broadcaster,' etc.

By contrast, searching for 'left-wing CNN' on the BBC news website does not yield very much. In fact there are no results in the BBC news database for this particular phrase. The Atlanta-based network, often referred to by social media users as 'fake news' is never health-checked by the BBC, but is often described in glowing terms e.g. 'one of the most respected networks in US television history.'[2]

'Repressive tolerance'

> We are far more likely to give a favourable hearing to a slanderous assertion about a politician we hate than one we love.[3]

> Evan Davis, BBC presenter

Provided an organisation (or individual) fully agrees with the BBC world view it will be subjected to hardly any health-checks whatsoever. Moreover, provided they attack Conservatives, Republicans, Populists etc. the politically neutral 'national' broadcaster will even indulge in a spot of PR for them, using words such as 'respected' to bolster credibility. Legitimisation is the aim.

If this all sounds hugely partisan in favour of left-wing groups and prejudiced against right-wing entities, that's because it is. It's meant to be. In his 1965 essay 'Repressive tolerance.' Herbert Marcuse, a leading Marxist academic and prominent member of the Frankfurt School, explains what he means by the phrase 'liberating tolerance:'

> Liberating tolerance, then, would mean intolerance against movements from the Right and toleration of movements from the Left... Not 'equal' but more representation of the Left would be equalization of the prevailing inequality.

Thus in health-checking the political Right but not the political Left, the BBC is merely playing its part in the glorious struggle which begins and ends with the long march through the institutions.

For example, when Nigel Farage stood down from politics following the 2016 EU referendum, the broadcaster seized upon the opportunity to produce a spiteful 'comedy' about the former UKIP leader entitled 'Nigel Farage Gets His Life Back.' However, when BBC favourite Tony Blair retired from UK politics it decided not to produce a similar piece of satire. 'Tony Blair makes a mint,' did not air on the BBC and never will. Yet as far as divisive politicians go you'd have to travel far and wide to find a politician quite as reviled as the former Labour prime minister. The BBC will never introduce Mr Blair as 'controversial' 'divisive' or any of the other health-checks it reserves for figures on the political right. Liberating tolerance - or, 'impartiality' as it's known down at The Ministry of Truth.

Notwithstanding their fraudulence Marcuse's theories were greeted with wild enthusiasm by certain strands of the political and media establishment as explained by Encyclopedia.com:

> As liberalism and leftism made common cause in the historical crucible of the late 1960s and the 1970s, the Marcusian approach to tolerance insinuated itself into even ostensibly mainstream or "pure" liberal thinking as well as into the governing rules and practices of institutions, such as universities, under liberal-left control.

Despite the spuriousness of Marcuse's ideas organisations like the BBC had all the justification they now needed: the political Left and Right could be treated entirely differently. A bitter parody of a Nigel Farage did not require a similar attack on a Tony Blair. It was just the latest duplicity sanctioned by cultural Marxism.

For example, when left-wing activist and BBC favourite Brendan Cox was exposed as an alleged serial sexual abuser in early 2018, the reaction of Britain's left wing media could be described as muted at best, indifferent at worst. Cox was one of their own. As a left-wing political activist the BBC had long sought his anti-Brexit and anti-Trump views. When they did eventually report on Cox the BBC and its MSM allies sought not to exploit his misdemeanours, but rather to explain them away. *The Labour party supporter was sorry, had seen the error of his ways, was on a 'journey' etc.* Yet this was the same BBC that had excoriated (and continues to do so) President Trump for lewd comments ('grab the pussy') made in the past – *comments* not actions. Cox by contrast had admitted to grabbing a female co-worker by the throat and sexually threatening her. But that was OK. Marcuse said so.

Hypocrisy, double standards, it no longer mattered. Entirely different standards can nowadays be applied to political allies and enemies. Chomsky and Herman talk of 'worthy and unworthy victims,' a distinction drawn by the liberal mainstream media, and which seeks to elicit sympathy only for those victims whose politics coincide with those of MSM heavyweights such as CNN and the BBC. It all adds up to the same thing: when it comes down to questions of morality and legality, for organisations like the BBC it's a question of political affiliation. Coverage and editorial attitude towards perpetrators (and victims) is dictated purely according to political sympathies.

Provided it agrees with the BBC worldview, the corporation will go out its way to present right-thinkers in a positive way even indulging in a spot of public relations as it is apt to do with the Trump-hating US blog Buzzfeed.

Buzzfeed: 'The "respected" news site'
When Donald Trump floated his infamous idea of a temporary ban on Muslim immigration into the US late in 2015, Britain's state broadcaster went ballistic. The BBC kicked off with a typically lurid headline on the front page of its news website:

> 'Racist', 'fascist', 'utterly repellent': What the world said about Donald Trump[4]

Notice how the BBC headline tells us what the 'world' said about Mr Trump. When the BBC say 'world' what it actually means is a select group of Liberal-left establishment figures who share the same worldview as the politically neutral broadcaster and whose 'outrage' it promotes throughout its vast media platform. In a long, simmering article the BBC raged against Mr Trump's proposal. The fury of the politically neutral broadcaster was a sight to behold. It directed the full force of its tax-payer funded artillery in Mr Trump's direction. Right at the very end of what had been a furious and elongated BBC tirade a few voices that supported the ban were introduced. It was as if the broadcaster had suddenly remembered its royal charter obligation:

'Some people must think it was the right thing to say, right?' Thus, the article ended with a typically superficial attempt at 'balance' and a less than subtle attempt at sarcasm.

As ever, BBC 'balance' consisted of masses of anti-Trump opinion against a tiny minority of supportive voices. And of course those pro-Trump voices all carried the usual BBC health warnings: Thus Ann Coulter is described as a 'right-wing pundit.' Rush Limbaugh is a 'conservative talk radio host' who along with 'a cadre of conservative talk radio hosts defended Mr Trump.'

Attempting to portray majority opinion as minority opinion is one of the oldest BBC tricks. By the same token, the broadcaster routinely attempts to portray minority views – BBC opinion – as majority consensus. Trump's 'Muslim ban' might have been causing BBC types to froth at the mouth, but such was not the response outside the temple. 'From time to time it (liberal media)' observes Antony Jay, 'finds an issue that strikes a chord with the broad mass of the nation, but in most respects it is wildly unrepresentative of national opinion.'[5]

So much for the BBC's 'world.' What about the real world, the one that exists outside the Liberal media bubble – what do ordinary people think about Mr Trump's policy? If you took the BBC article at face value you might well have believed that what the BBC dubbed 'Trump's Muslim Ban' was deeply unpopular, supported only by a tiny smattering of crackpots - 'right-wing pundits' and 'conservative talk show hosts.'

Not quite. According to research conducted by Chatham House the majority of Europeans seem to think Mr Trump's words were absolutely 'the right thing to say:'

Most Europeans want immigration ban from Muslim-majority countries, poll reveals[6]

The study, conducted by Chatham House, had been conducted before then presidential candidate Trump had raised his so-called Muslim immigration ban, the parameters of which had been set by the Obama administration – a fact consistently ignored by the BBC. *The Independent* reported that, 'An average of 55 per cent of people across the 10 European countries surveyed wanted to stop all future immigration from mainly Muslim countries.'[7] In fact, the majority of people surveyed seemed to agree not with Britain's raging, frothing state broadcaster, but with the US president on this issue. But surely, surely, surely 'Some people must think it was the right thing to say, right?' There must be one or two people out there who agree with Mr Trump's insanity, right?

Just 55% of Europeans. . .

Meanwhile a Rasmussen poll found 57% of Americans supported a temporary travel ban, while 33% opposed the proposal.[8] A poll for Reuters found 48% of Americans in favour with 41% opposing.[9] A survey conducted in Australia found 49% of respondents in favour of banning immigration from Muslim countries.[10] But surely, surely 'some people must think it was the right thing to say, right?' To put the icing on a classic piece of BBC impartiality, the article returns to the Buzzfeed editor. No health-checks however for pro-Clinton, Democrat supporting Buzzfeed. On the contrary:

> Buzzfeed's editor-in-chief issued a memo to all staff to clear
> up a style point about referring to Mr Trump, authorising the
> respected news site's journalists to call the Republican
> frontrunner a liar and a racist.[11]

Note the use of 'respected' here to describe Buzzfeed – a tactic used purely to convince BBC readers that the website's opinion of Mr Trump - 'racist,' 'fascist,' and 'utterly repellent' - carries weight. So precisely how trusted is the BBC's 'respected' news site. This trusted:

Pew Research
Liberals Trust CNN, Conservatives Trust Fox News, and No One Trusts BuzzFeed[12]

Anti-Trump invective to one side, what then could possibly explain why Buzzfeed is considered so 'respected' down at Broadcasting House - ideological empathy maybe?

Buzzfeed Canada
Would you like to write for @BuzzFeed? WELL YOU CAN. @BuzzFeedCanada would particularly like to hear from you if you are not white and not male.

Buzzfeed headline
37 Things White People Need To Stop Ruining In 2018[13]

Buzzfeed reporter
KILL a straight white man on your way to work tomorrow.

Buzzfeed also just happened to be the organisation infamous for printing the discredited 'piss-gate' dossier, a tissue of slurs even passed on by Trump-hating CNN. While printing 35 pages of what it strongly suspected to be unverified lies and smears about the US President might make Buzzfeed News 'respected' in some people's eyes, many others begged to differ. 'You just published fake news,' MSBNC host Chuck Todd told Buzzfeed's editor-in-chief Ben Smith who, in the aftermath of his decision to publish the 'piss-gate' dossier was desperately trying to justify his actions. Writing in *The New York Post*, John Podohertz summarised the situation thus:

> At a moment when journalists are up in arms about "fake news," what BuzzFeed has done here is take fake news to a new level. Its editor, Ben Smith, acknowledges "there is serious reason to doubt the allegations."[14]

Buzzfeed – the 'respected' news organisation . . .

Bias by omission

'The BBC was very good at creating an atmosphere where not only did you avoid certain topics, but you didn't even think at a conscious level that you were avoiding them.'[1]

When it comes to shaping the news agenda omission is one of the broadcaster's most enduring tactics. Omission entails nothing more complicated than holding back stories and information that do not fit into the broadcaster's pre-written narratives. The corporation filters out those stories that do not fit its narratives on a daily basis.

For example, when Goldberg Sachs boss Lloyd Blankfein confessed that Brexit had not damaged the economy in the way prophesied by the pro-EU lobby headed by the BBC it meant a serious setback for anti-Brexit factions, who had been hoping and praying for the worst possible economic news. *Brexit is very, very bad*: In fact, according to the BBC, Brexit was supposed to wreck the British economy and worse. 'I would have thought there would have been a worse outcome by now,'[2] Blankfein told Politico in Spring 2018. It was a statement that seriously contradicted Brexit doom and gloom. Predictably, while Blankfein's previous Brexit pessimism had been duly and faithfully reported by the broadcaster his latest comments failed to make it onto any BBC platform . . .

It's not just Brexit revelations that don't make it onto the BBC. When an Iraqi over stayer threatened to 'kill all the English' during a church service in County Durham, the impartial broadcaster was nowhere to be seen. Bursting into the middle of a sermon the 29-yeard old began swearing and shouting at the congregation. 'I will f****** kill you and all the English bastards,' the man threatened.[3]

This was one example of a racially aggravated attack – a real hate crime – that the BBC had no interest in whatsoever. While bursting into a church threatening to kill the 'English bastards' inside does not merit a single sentence or mention, imagine if the positions were reversed: an English hooligan bursting into a Mosque threatening to 'kill all the Muslims.' Just imagine that copious BBC outrage. Reports of racist graffiti usually fill the pages of BBC news: 'Mosque in Cumbernauld sprayed with racist graffiti;' 'Mosque sprayed with racist graffiti;' 'Racist graffiti sprayed on Leicester house.' And so on. The broadcaster is however not always so concerned about such cowardly acts. It all depends.

But in August 2017 there was one story of racist graffiti that managed to slip past the eagle-eyed corporation. 'No whites allowed after 8pm' read a message scrawled on a wall in the Alum Rock district of Birmingham. Had 17 August not been such a busy news day the BBC would no doubt have covered this disturbing story. It just so happened that there were far more pressing issues to cover on this summer's day: Jewellery recovery ('Woman finds long lost ring on carrot in her garden') new cartoon characters ('Marvel's first Nigerian superhero revealed') and faux pas tales to make you chuckle ('Irish waitress makes PM wait after failing to recognise him').

Clearly, when reporting news the BBC appears to operate quite different standards depending on to what extent events fit with its pre-written narratives; while certain stories are quietly dropped, others are plastered all over its media platforms. Let's have a more detailed look at how the broadcaster uses the tactic of omission to shape what becomes 'news.'

When a group of 'Asian' males viciously attacked a traffic warden in autumn 2018 the BBC response was nothing short of indifference. A guy got kicked. Big deal. The incident was relegated to the Birmingham and Black Country page of its news website: 'Man charged after traffic warden stamped on in Alum Rock,' went the underwhelming BBC headline. Nothing to see here. Reading that headline you might assume there had been some kind of altercation – a road rage incident perhaps - that had ended with a motorist assaulting a traffic official. Nothing could have been further from the truth.

As ever, the impartial, free and fair broadcaster had omitted to mention some pretty important facts:

- The traffic warden was white
- He was attacked by a gang of five males
- Perpetrators took turns to stamp on the victim's head
- The attack was sustained, lasting several minutes

Predictably, on this occasion the scrupulously fair broadcaster made no attempt to play up the racial angle. No 'hate' crime here whatsoever. Yet footage of the attack reveals a quite shocking level of violence of the sort associated with the very 'hate' of which the BBC ordinarily can't get enough.

We've asked our readers to use their imagination on several occasions in this book already, and now do so once again. Imagine then if a gang of white males had attacked a traffic officer identifying as BME. Imagine the extent of all that BBC outrage: Hate crime! Racists! Nazis! White supremacists! BBC audiences would never have heard the end of this unprovoked 'hate' crime. It's that old Marxist trick once more, repressive tolerance.

A tale of two BBC stories

For a textbook example of how the BBC omits that which it does not want its audience to see, we turn to the US and a fairly standard example of BBC chicanery.

The news that Hilary Clinton had been implicated in the rigging of the Democrat party presidential nominations of 2016 was one of the biggest US news stories for decades. The former First Lady had indeed ensured that it was her name that went forward as her party's nomination for the US presidential race later that year rather than that of rival Bernie Sanders. Long hinted at by political insiders, in November 2017 the truth finally emerged: Clinton had indeed conspired to steal the nomination from Mr Sanders. After high ranking Democrat operative Donna Brazile spilled the beans, Mrs Clinton had no other option but to confess to this shocking act of political sabotage. It was an act of unprecedented magnitude never before witnessed in American political history.

Here then was an absolutely huge story. Not surprisingly the affair painted an entirely new picture of Mrs Clinton, a candidate who had spoken and preached at length on the world stage about honesty, integrity and American values. At the very least that rhetoric now sounded hollow. Downplaying this sensational story the mainstream media went into damage limitation mode. Mrs Clinton was, after all, the candidate of the Left – *their* candidate.

Over at Broadcasting House the confusion can only be imagined. The impartial broadcaster had backed Mrs Clinton 100% for the US presidency. Under normal circumstances a story contradicting the BBC narrative (*Clinton is very, very good*) can be omitted. But these were not normal circumstances – far from it. The broadcaster had to cover this story, but how?

Let's imagine for a moment that Donald Trump had confessed to stealing the Republican party nomination. Imagine if you will all that BBC hysteria: 'Trump Stole Republican nomination! Trump: the illegitimate President!' How the BBC would have milked those headlines for all their worth. Days, weeks – months of lurid headlines would have followed. Its activists would have been tweeting all day and night. BBC news programmes would have lead with the story and devoted copious amounts of air-time to it. Trump-hating figures such as Maggie Haberman of *The New York Times* would have been allocated oceans of oxygen to denounce the 'illegitimate President' on Newsnight, Marr, Today, the 6 and 10 'o clock news and as many other BBC platforms as possible. BBC North America activists would have been invoking comparisons to Darth Vader, Hitler and Satan himself. The impartial, free and fair broadcaster would have gone into meltdown. In a word, the BBC response would have been epic. But this was not Donald Trump. It was Hilary Clinton. As a right-thinker fully in tune with BBC-think the broadcaster had neither time nor interest in Clinton's stupendous transgression. Time for a little bit of that liberating tolerance.

Hilary Clinton: The art of burying bad news

Readers to the BBC's News website on 3 November 2017 would have encountered several stories this cool autumnal day. The headlines included stories about allegations of sexual misconduct of a Hollywood actor and Labour MP. Browsers would also have noted a story entitled 'Parachute husband hid money problems' and an equally intriguing story 'How I threw away a modern work of art.' But just where was that huge humdinger of a story about Mrs Clinton?

While Mrs Clinton was absent from the BBC front page, Mr Trump was not. In its wisdom, the impartial broadcaster had decided to splash yet another anti-Trump piece on its front page. Thus, instead of reading about Clinton's dishonourable behaviour readers were treated to a long and rambling piece entitled, 'The time when America stopped being great' – not a news story, but an opinion piece dripping with standard BBC anti-Trump sentiment.[4] Meanwhile the real blockbuster story was quietly buried away in a place where the BBC hoped no-one would see it.

For those determined souls clicking through the BBC website the story finally emerged on the US/Canada page. This was one particular story the BBC did *not want* its audience to engage with. But it so badly wanted its readers to click on the anti-Donald Trump opinion piece and so it promoted that 'story' at every opportunity. While the Clinton story did not even warrant an image, the Trump hit piece was accompanied by a large image of ex-Republican president Ronald Reagan superimposed behind Mr Trump.

BBC coverage: 3 November 2017

Let's take a look how the BBC news website covered these two stories on 3 November 2017, though we use the term 'story' advisedly. 'Unless there is a foundation of fact and evidence,' warns the BBC's Richard Sambrook, 'then perspectives, opinion and comment are worthless. That's why in newspapers the news pages come first and the comment pages in the middle.'[5]

BBC news website	Anti-Trump BBC opinion	Democrat race rigged
BBC News	Yes	-
Headline?	Yes	-
+ image?	Yes	-
BBC News > World	Yes	-
Headline?	Yes	-
+ image?	Yes	-
BBC News >World >US/Canada	Yes	Yes
Headline?	Yes	-
+ image?	Yes	-

Fig. 15

'The time when America stopped being great,' is not actually a news story. As noted, it's a somewhat muddled and inflammatory anti-Trump opinion piece by the BBC New York correspondent. As to why an opinion piece should occupy (prominent) space on a publicly-funded national news website is a matter for the BBC. We think you know the impartial answer to that one already. The second item is an actual news story, a gigantic one at that: 'Elizabeth Warren agrees Democratic race 'rigged' for Clinton.'

That final paragraph pivot trick, again

When the BBC finally gets around to reporting the Clinton story it comes as no surprise to find the manner in which it decides to conclude its report into this staggering story of political treachery: the final paragraph pivot trick. By deliberately switching focus at the end of the article the BBC hopes to limit damage to its ally and deflect attention onto another BBC target/wrong-thinker. What better demonstration of impartiality could there be than to pivot the focus away from Clinton's breath-taking wrong-doings onto someone else entirely:

> Mr Trump is himself under scrutiny in a Justice Department investigation into whether his campaign aides colluded with Russians in an effort to sway last year's election.[6]

In a story purportedly about Clinton's culpability the impartial broadcaster closes with Trump and, of course, Russia . . . Repetition, repetition, repetition. The art of brainwashing.

Sometimes omission involves holding back a story until it tallies with a BBC narrative. Next we turn to an example where the neutral broadcaster deliberately held back a huge story right until the moment it could spin it to fit with one of its most cherished pre-written narratives.

Billionaire author falsely smears US President

Remember the above headline from the BBC? Probably not, because it never actually appeared on any BBC platform. But this is exactly what happened in Summer of 2017. The only problem was the sequence of events leading to what should have been a huge story did not fit any BBC narrative: *JK Rowling: very, very good; Donald Trump: very, very bad.*

When BBC darling and arguably the world's most famous author J K Rowling went on a Twitter rant against President Trump in July of 2017, the 'national' broadcaster found itself not for the first time in a tricky spot. The strength of BBC admiration for the Labour-supporting Harry Potter author is matched only by the impartial broadcaster's loathing for the forty-fifth US President. The corporation simply can't get enough of J K Rowling and now she was slagging off Donald Trump! And when Rowling tweets the BBC are never far behind. Steeped in BBC right-think the broadcaster simply adores Rowling tweets.

A BBC darling attacking a BBC villain? Good v Evil! Irresistible ...

Yet the broadcaster was showing uncharacteristic restrain. Twenty-four hours after the author's extraordinary attack, and not a single word or article could be seen or heard on any BBC platform. Meanwhile social media had gone into meltdown. Clearly something was not quite right here. The BBC was holding back. But why? Surely, this fitted every possible criteria for news?

The explanation was simple enough. On this occasion it was the children's author who had been the aggressor, falsely smearing President Trump in a series of eight tweets sent out from her Twitter account on 28 July. 'World famous author 'slams' Trump!' The broadcaster likes nothing more than to encourage celebrity-endorsed anti-Trump messages, the more vocal the better. Under ordinary circumstances the BBC would have been chomping on the bit to gleefully spread this story around its various media platforms. Only not this time.

'A Monster of narcissism'

Having seen a clip of the US president supposedly ignoring the outstretched hand of a handicapped child during a public engagement, the billionaire children's author immediately took to Twitter where she unleashed a frenzied attack on the president. 'How stunning and how horrible, that Trump cannot bring himself to shake the hand of a small boy who only wanted to touch the President,' tweeted Rowling to her 11 million followers. 'Trump' she went on to tweet is a 'monster of narcissism.' If that was not bad enough another tweet came flying off the press: 'Now he pretends not to see a child in a wheelchair,' she told her followers, 'as though frightened he might catch his condition.' Some very serious not to mention slanderous accusations which caused a social media storm.

Yet still no word from the BBC. Had the state broadcaster departed on vacation this 28th of July? As news of Rowling's blistering attack spread around social media, the 'British' Broadcasting Corporation remained strangely deaf to the furore. The Queen of Twitter v The President of the USA – a box office dream! Meanwhile, over at Broadcasting House, crickets . . .

The reason for BBC reticence was simple enough. Soon after Rowling's astonishing outburst footage emerged of Mr Trump not only shaking the hand of the boy in question, but also kneeling down to speak to the youngster. The original footage had simply been edited in such a way as to reflect badly on the billionaire politician, to dupe people like Rowling into confirming their visceral hatred of the American President.

As the story spread around the world the BBC remained resolutely quiet: *J. K. Rowling is very, very good; Donald Trump is very, very bad.* How could this story possibly fit into any of its pre-written narratives? It couldn't. By the end of the evening of 28th July and with Rowling coming under a firestorm of criticism for comments that were as ill-judged as they were spiteful, there was not a single mention of the story on any BBC platform. Yet here was quite a story: a billionaire author followed by millions with influence to match had publicly smeared the president of the United States of America! Newsworthy? Surely worth at least a few lines . . .

For an organisation that supposedly takes fake news so seriously – and what could be more serious than a world famous celebrity spreading fake news about a US president? - the BBC was conspicuous only by its absence. Suddenly, fake news didn't matter. Covering this story would have meant a) portraying Trump as a victim of a vicious smear and b) portraying Rowling as the perpetrator of that smear. Unthinkable. As the original video of the president greeting the young boy surfaced there was no chance that the BBC could spin this one in Rowling's favour, not without seriously damaging its credibility.

Along with its fellow left-wing travellers from *The Guardian* to Channel 4 news, the BBC did not carry a single word about Rowling's extraordinary behaviour – potential defamation of the US president lest we forget. In the face of sustained criticism Rowling obstinately refused to delete her dishonest tweets. BBC silence remained deafening. Could anything possibly persuade the 'national' broadcaster to cover this story about one of its favourites? How about a plea from the mother of the little boy, who had this to say to the children's author: 'Trump didn't snub my son & Monty wasn't even trying to shake his hand - 1) he's 3 and hand shaking is not his thing and 2) he was showing off his newly acquired secret service patch.'

Here then were all the ingredients of a great story, but *still* the BBC remained resolute in its avoidance. Do certain individuals – right-thinkers, people like us - receive a free pass from the impartial BBC? When, under an avalanche of unrelenting criticism, Rowling eventually decided to make an 'apology' on August 1 – three days *after* her original tirade - the BBC suddenly became interested. 'To that boy or his family, I apologise unreservedly,' tweeted Rowling, 'These tweets will remain, but I will delete the previous ones on the subject.' Not exactly the most gracious apology ever seen or heard and not even a single word of apology to the US President, the target of her original smears, but enough for the BBC to suddenly wake up.

Thus, no sooner had Rowling tweeted her 'apology,' and now finally able to spin a story in line with its pro-Rowling sympathies, the BBC news website announced that, 'JK Rowling apologises over Trump disabled boy tweets.'[7] Prior to this development as far as the BBC had been concerned the story never existed.

Rowling never did apologise to the President for her lies and for deliberately misleading her 11 million-plus Twitter followers. No matter, the BBC had a headline that portrayed the author favourably. Knowing that the real facts would invariably show Rowling in a negative light, in their long-awaited though very brief article, the BBC predictably attempted to downplay actual events. Though video footage clearly showed Mr Trump's extended interaction with the boy the BBC chose a nothing if not eccentric way to report this crucial element of the story:

> Mr Trump is said to have shaken the boy's hand as the president entered the room.

Notice the deliberate use of the passive voice here: 'is said to have shaken.' Is it a rumour? Did Mr Trump shake the little boy's hand or not? The BBC isn't too sure. While millions of social media users managed to see the footage, it appeared that Britain's leading media organisation replete with cutting edge technology and over 20,000 personnel was among a tiny minority who had not . . .

197

A tale of two marches

Omission is by far the BBC and MSM's most favoured propaganda tactic, and with good reason. If a story is not in the news then for millions of people it does not exist. News is not an objective reality. It is simply a collection of items selected by the propagandist to further specific objectives. The public see and hear only that which society's powerful forces wish them to see or hear.

BBC activists were out in full force to follow the 'Tories Out' march of 1 July 2017 in London. Indeed, the march even made it onto Saturday night television when the corporation included a report as part of its evening news bulletin. This was one march the BBC was determined would receive maximum coverage, publicity that Labour apparatchiks could only have dreamed. Organised jointly by Momentum, trade unions and various left-wing fringe elements its anti-Tory message was foreseeable enough. Predictably, the BBC was there every inch of the way reporting on what was essentially a non-event. 'This is the left,' breathlessly announced its correspondent from the edge of the march, 'flexing its muscle in the aftermath of a very positive election result under Jeremy Corbyn.' Admiration was palpable.

While a by-product of public marches is the creation of as much noise and disruption as possible, the real objective is to pile pressure onto the target – in this case Theresa May's Conservative government. Wherever there is a march, whether its Trump or Tory bashing, the BBC will never be far behind. Cultural Marxists love nothing more than to march, figuratively and literally. Unless . . .

Just one week before the 'Tories Out' event another large public march had taken place. Attended by an estimated 10,000 people the football lads' alliance 'March Against Terrorism' had passed silently through the very same London streets just seven days earlier. Marching under a banner of 'United against extremism' the football march was organised to protest the recent Westminster, Manchester and London Bridge terror attacks in which a total of 28 people had been killed. Marchers gathered at St. Paul's Cathedral from where they walked in silence to London Bridge to lay wreathes in honour of the victims.

In stark contrast to the generous coverage of the 'Tories Out' march, the 'March Against Terrorism' received no coverage whatsoever on the BBC. Some marches it appears are more equal than others.

'If no established news organisation is running it, it's not real'

Nothing at all on the BBC? Not to worry, 'Adopt journalistic reflexes: check different sources for a story online,' advises the BBC's Washington correspondent writing for *Marie Clare*. 'If no established news organisation is running it, it's not real.'[8]

The BBC and left-wing media not 'running it', attended by 10,000 protesters, 'The March Against Terrorism' was apparently 'not real.' In response to numerous complaints the BBC issued a standard reply in which it explained its decision to omit the March Against Terrorism from its entire news network:

> On Saturday 24th June our main news focus in terms of coverage and resources was the plight of thousands of people evacuated from tower blocks in Camden in North Lodon [sic] overnight the night before.

> Many marches and protests take place in cities around the UK, particularly at the weekends, and we do often cover some of them, but by no means all.

With the BBC's meagre resources deployed entirely on the Grenfell Tower fire story, its news coverage for Saturday 24th June was understandably curtailed, manifest in the following analysis of news coverage of BBC Radio 4's three main news and current affairs programmes. While the broadcaster was far too busy to cover trifling affairs such as a protest of several thousand people in central London, it did manage to cover Yemeni cholera epidemics and Mozambique loan scandals (Fig. 16).

Some social media users were seemingly unconvinced by the BBC's response. The march had passed off peacefully. 'Why no coverage?' asked a social media use, 'it's orderly and peaceful. A punch-up would have made it "Right Wing" and your camera crews would have been there like a shot.'

While tens of thousands of protestors marching in central London against terrorism does not capture the BBC's imagination, a handful of protesters in a Lincolnshire field protesting drones most likely will ('Anti-drone protest at RAF Waddington') Likewise, when Katie

Hopkins turned up in Lewes to promote a recently published book the BBC were duly on hand to report 'dozens' of people demonstrating:

@bbcsoutheast
Dozens of people are demonstrating against the controversial columnist @KTHopkins who is giving a talk in #Lewes tonight.

BBC Radio 4 news coverage (24 June 2016)	Today	PM	Midnight News
Grenfell Tower fire	•	•	•
Corbyn at Glastonbury	•	•	•
Landslide in China	•	•	•
British Lions rugby tour	•		•
Women's cricket world cup	•		•
Liverpool armed forces day	•	•	•
Church of England donations		•	•
Europcar overcharges clients		•	•
Houses of Parliament cyber attack		•	•
Andrea Leadsom urges patriotism	•		
Martina Cole releases new novel	•		
EastEnders producer leaves show	•		
Mozambique loans scandal			•
Walsall stabbing			•
UK robotics convention	•		
World's longest sniper kill	•		
UK fishing rights post Brexit	•		
Yemen cholera epidemic			•
Colombia releases Dutch hostages			•
The battle for Mosul		•	
Body of Scottish priest found			•
London March Against Terror			

Fig. 16

'For the good of diversity'

It has already been suggested that the BBC treats wrong and right-thinkers quite differently, as noted with J K Rowling. Duplicitous behaviour like this raises a disturbing question: just how far is the broadcaster prepared to go to cover for right-thinkers? 'If a journalist hides the truth,' observe Wikileaks, 'they are no longer journalists; they are partners in the crime they are hiding.'[9] Worth bearing this observation in mind during our next story.

In summer 2017 a certain female Labour MP wrote an open letter to *The Sun* newspaper criticising what she called numerous 'Islamophobic' articles the paper had printed over the years.[10] Over one hundred MPs signed the letter in support. Over 500 did not. In 2016 the same woman had been temporarily suspended from the Labour party following a Facebook comment which was adjudged to have been anti-Semitic. The MP later apologised to the House of Commons for the 'upset and hurt' her words had caused to the Jewish community. Upon election to Parliament, the newly elected MP had worn a headscarf and sworn her oath on the Quran. Less than twelve months after her apology the same Labour politician was back in the news again – but not *all* news.

Days after her letter had been delivered, the MP took to Twitter where she came across a tweet supposedly composed by a left-wing journalist. Referencing the infamous grooming scandal in the Yorkshire town of Rotherham the tweet read:

> Those abused girls in Rotherham and elsewhere just need to shut their mouths. For the good of diversity

Incredibly, the MP not only 'liked' the tweet, but also re-tweeted it to her Twitter followers! It seemed unbelievable. Just days before, she had criticised Sarah Champion MP for speaking out about grooming gangs in her Rotherham constituency. Having attacked her fellow Labour MP for unmasking the racial and cultural identity of these gangs, her actions looked even more unfathomable - sinister even. Thousands of young girls had been viciously abused because of the very thing the politician seemed to be advocating: silence. The MP deleted her social media interactions some minutes later. But the damage had been done. Twitter never forgets. Although it transpired that the original tweet had been sent from a parody account, this fact hardly excused these actions. As a storm began a spokesman for the MP claimed she had made a 'mistake.' However, as many people were quick to point out her actions had required not just one, but three 'mistakes:'

1 – to click 'like,'
2 – to click 're-tweet'
3 – to confirm the re-tweet

In other words, this could hardly be excused as a slip of the finger. In the light of testimony from grooming gang survivors the MP's actions were even more alarming. A 13-year old victim called 'Emma' told listeners to LBC radio how authorities had reacted when she had attempted to report the names of those who had sexually abused her:

> As soon as I said the names, I was made to feel as though
> I was racist and I was the one who had the problem.
> I knew I wasn't racist, but that was used as a way to
> silence me.[11]

As the Labour leadership remained obdurately silent calls grew for the MP to be disciplined. A petition on Change.org soon gathered over 50,000 signatures urging Labour leader Jeremy Corbyn to sack the MP in question. Their pleas fell on deaf ears. Corbyn and Labour did not even acknowledge the seriousness of this matter, let alone take any action.

While right-leaning media organisations such as *The Sun, The Daily Mail* and *The Daily Express* rightly reported on the story, the left-wing media circus went eerily silent. *The Guardian, The Independent* and Channel 4 news all avoided covering this highly disturbing story. Similarly, while it had eagerly covered the same politician's criticism of Champion and her letter just days' earlier, there was not a word about her subsequent Twitter interactions on the entire BBC network, public outcry notwithstanding. BBC Trending, which ordinarily just loves to expose faux pas on Twitter, was notable only by its absence.

BBC editors had faced a tricky question: Could the MP's social media actions be positively spun in any way whatsoever? Could they be defended in any way? Answer: No, they could not. Solution? Ignore. Omit. Imagine a scenario in which members of UKIP had been sexually grooming underage Muslim girls. Imagine also that Nigel Farage went on to like and re-tweet a social media post instructing the victims to keep their mouths shut. Allow yourself to imagine the scope of BBC hysteria: weeks and weeks of coverage: national and local news; Newsnight, Question Time, Today, Any Questions etc.

> The crisis of trust in media is largely the fault of journalists, who have made a habit of missing big stories, and who still fail to speak for many of the disenfranchised and alienated.[12]

Amol Rajan, BBC Media Editor

August 16: A tale of ~~two~~ one deleted tweet

While deleted tweets seeming to endorse the sexual abuse and subsequent silencing of young white girls did not catch the BBC's attention, there was one Twitter deletion on August 16 that *did* manage to rouse its interest:

> Trump tweets cartoon of train hitting CNN reporter
> bbc.co.uk

'Fake News Can't Stop The Trump Train,' so read the message written across the top of an image showing a locomotive train hitting a cartoon figure upon whom a CNN logo had been superimposed. 'The tweet was deleted 30 minutes after being posted at 07.00 New York time,' the BBC helpfully informed its readers.

'One mark of a smear outfit is that it zeroes in on its enemies but gladly overlooks the same behaviour of its friends,' notes Attkisson.'[13] The BBC's meagre resources perpetually over-stretched, it couldn't possibly cover *two* Twitter deletion stories on the same day! The MP's re-tweet would simply have to wait. Or better still be omitted altogether.

> White House officials told NBC the train image - captioned "Fake news can't stop the Trump Train" - had been "inadvertently posted" and when "noticed it was immediately deleted". In another presumably unintentional retweet, the US president shared - and then also deleted - a post by someone who said of him: "He's a fascist, so not unusual."[14]

Which of these stories, dear reader, in your role as an impartial state-funded journalist would you consider real news this day of 16 August? A story about an elected member of the British parliament engaging in what can only be described as highly disturbing behaviour, or a snippet about 'someone' who had called the American president a 'fascist?' Young girls sexually abused on an industrial scale or a hateful social media comment posted by a troll? Pick a story.

Donald Trump Jnr "likes" a social media post

Sometimes liking a social media post meets with BBC disapproval. It all depends on who is doing the liking: 'Lauren Hogg, who survived the recent shooting at a school in Florida,' writes the BBC news website, 'called on the first lady to "have a convo" with her stepson Donald Trump Jr. who liked social media posts accusing Lauren's brother David of being an FBI stooge.[15]

When re-tweeting IS very, very bad . . .
While the BBC steadfastly refused to report on the actions of a Labour Member of Parliament, it did however manage to report on some alleged 'anti-Muslim' re-tweets. 'A Conservative councillor reported the BBC website 'has been suspended by his party over allegations he shared anti-Muslim tweets.'

Demonstrating its famed impartiality for all to see the BBC fell on this particular story of Twitter re-tweets like a pack of hungry wolves. What had the local Conservative councillor done exactly? Re-tweeted a story about the migrant crime wave in Europe and added a comment:

> Mr Potts, who represents Knowle, also asked is "anybody surprised?" while retweeting negative stories about immigrants on Twitter.

Without any discernible irony the BBC report on Mr Potts' tweeting activity goes on to quote the comments of a Tory council leader which, as might be expected, are censorious. But that's not all the official – Bob Sleigh - says in the BBC article:

Mr Sleigh said retweeting suggested people were associated with the views expressed . . ."[16]

Let's unpick the BBC 'logic' behind its promotion of this story. In BBC-land re-tweeting a message invariably suggests approval. Just ask Bob Sleigh. The broadcaster was rather anxious that its readers should receive Mr Sleigh's thoughts on this matter, presumably because they helped to clinch his colleague's guilt. In sharing the original post the hapless Tory councillor must have therefore agreed with its sentiments i.e. its 'negative' take on immigrants. Why else would he have shared it on social media?

Clearly, in BBC-land sharing social media posts equates to agreement. If re-tweeting does indeed indicate 'people were associated with the views expressed,' then what this implies about the motivations of certain Labour MPs we leave to you, the reader, to conclude. Perhaps this revelation explains why the corporation so resolutely failed to report a single word about the MP's social media interactions. Repressive tolerance. Free passes for right-thinkers, call it what you will, it all adds up to one and the same thing: duplicity.

BBC balance: 125 to 1

The lifeless body of Alan Kurdi was washed up on a Greek beach in 2015. In Sweden, Ebba Åkerlund was on her way home from school when she was caught up in the Stockholm terror attack of April 2017. While the death of the young Syrian boy was seized upon by the globalist mainstream media, the same media virtually ignored the young Swedish girl's death.

Here's the number of stories on the BBC news website as of September 2018 in which the victim is either mentioned or is the focus of the main story:

Total number of stories on bbc.co.uk

Alan Kurdi	Ebba Åkerlund
125	1

Agenda? We'll leave it to the reader to speculate as to the reasons for this spectacular disparity . . .

Misrepresentation

The BBC influences the public debate in a myriad of ways, some clunkier than others. For instance, when a BBC News Channel 5pm bulletin in April 2017 introduced a studio guest as a 'community nurse from London' the audience might have been forgiven for believing the guest was just that – a nurse who had been asked to relate her experience of working in the NHS. But that was only half the story at best.

As the guest launched into an anti-Tory tirade suspicions began to grow – rightly as it turns out. For the 'community nurse' just happened to be a member of the Labour party, whose journalism had appeared on the 'revolutionary socialist website,' *Counterfire*, and in the communist *Morning Star*. It later transpired the 'community nurse' was a staunch Jeremy Corbyn supporter and had addressed several left-wing rallies in the past. The BBC's studio guest currently ripping into the NHS policies of the Tory government was, in fact, a left-wing political activist. By happy coincidence her views on the NHS coincided perfectly with those of the BBC. The broadcaster had obviously 'forgotten' to inform its audience of its guest's stringent political alliances. It happens.

These kinds of tricks are fairly commonplace within the BBC. 'I was able to use bias in my reports by giving less time to one than the other (side)' revealed former BBC eastern region chief political reporter and current Labour MP Clive Lewis. 'I reported on both but . . .was able to project my own particular political positions on things in a very subtle way.'[1] Like the 'community nurse,' Mr Lewis' political views just so happen to coincide entirely with those of the politically neutral broadcaster.

People not like us: wrong-thinkers

While people 'like us' will be sneaked onto mainstream news programmes or be allowed to project their own political opinions (and those of their employer) into the public forum disguised as impartial reporting, BBC treatment of wrong-thinkers is not quite as accommodating.

When Professor Karol Tarnowski was interviewed for a BBC documentary about the Catholic church the result shocked the academic.

By careful editing, the programme makers – BBC Panorama – had contrived to entirely misrepresent him: 'It is intellectually dishonest to trim statements to suit a thesis already decided a priori, from above,' an incandescent professor told *The Catholic Herald*. 'Since the BBC has acted so unfairly towards me I feel I have an obligation to forewarn all those with whom it may seek co-operation in the future.'[2] The professor's contributions had largely not fitted the BBC narrative: *Christianity (and Catholicism) are very, very bad*. In order to make his comments fit, Panorama had edited out any positive comments while retaining the few negative comments he had made about Catholicism.

Tarnowski is not the only one to experience this ubiquitous BBC tactic. This was the reaction of a prominent Leave EU campaigner whose interview had been similarly 'cleansed . . .'

> **@Anon**
> That's the last interview I'll give @BBC. All my arguments highlighting how UK goldplates EU woman's equality laws were cut out.

Speakers whose interviews do not support the BBC narrative invariably find themselves surplus to requirement, their contributions discarded. When Tory MP John Redwood refused to co-operate with a BBC Radio 4 attempt to undermine Theresa May's Brexit negotiating position, the broadcaster attempted to cajole him into agreeing with the BBC position. 'They continued to try to get me to disagree, ' (with the prime minister's position) related Redwood on the Comment Central website. 'I explained again that their thesis that the Leave supporting MPs disagreed with the PM and were "rebels" was simply untrue.' Unable to persuade him to agree with its BBC 'thesis' the interview was quickly dropped.

Similarly, when a pro-Brexit businessman was interviewed by the BBC his opinions, which strongly contradicted those of the broadcaster, were simply omitted from the final cut of the programme:

> A couple of hours ago I let you know I had been interviewed for BBC World at One where I gave a robust defence of "No Deal" from a business perspective, but the BBC decided not to play my interview and only broadcast the views of a Remain businessman

Should your point of view not support the BBC worldview expect it be chopped and shaped, watered down, reduced to those soundbites the broadcaster can use to prosecute its own agenda, or if not, omitted altogether.

Misrepresentation can take many forms. It might be deliberately attributing words or opinions to people who have never said such things; it might take the form of editing interviews in such a way so the speaker appears supportive or critical of a favoured BBC narrative. In the example that follows it took the form of wilfully ignoring the substance of a major US news story.

'Trump lied to Comey'

When FBI director James Comey testified before the US Senate Intelligence Committee in June 2017, the results were not exactly what the impartial BBC had been hoping for. The investigation into alleged Russian interference in the 2016 US presidential election ongoing, and with the politically neutral broadcaster daily promoting ever more lurid Trump-Russia propaganda, Broadcasting House activists were hoping and praying that Comey would somehow implicate president Trump with the dastardly Putin and his evil Russian empire. The broadcaster smelt blood.

Alas, it was not to be. Once Comey had testified BBC anticipation soon turned to anti-climax. The former FBI Director effectively cleared Mr Trump of any involvement with Russia. Furthermore, he went on to confirm that the president had never even been under investigation in the first place! *The Washington Examiner* summed up events thus: 'MSNBC's Chris Matthews conceded that there is no case for collusion.'[3] The reference to Matthews was deliberate. MSNBC are one of several virulently anti-Trump US media networks all of whom were, in the light of Comey's testimony, having to concede defeat - albeit grudgingly.

All of which represented a significant headache for a now very, very deflated BBC. How on earth could its activists spin this one? Day after day, week after week, month after month, the neutral broadcaster had been going to unprecedented lengths to promote the Trump-Russia conspiracy theory. Yet here was a story that could not possibly fit with the BBC master narrative: *Trump is very, very bad* and one of its most favourite anti-Trump sub-narratives: *Trump is a Russian plant.*

The BBC task was not an easy one: how to report the facts of the Comey testimony but also inflict maximum damage on Mr Trump? Simple – misrepresent what had happened. As news broke of Comey's testimony it was 2017 General Election night in the UK. While a panel of pundits pored over the night's events in the BBC studio, at the bottom of the television screen a loop informed viewers of the latest election losses and gains. But this was not the only news BBC viewers received:

> Trump lied to Comey ... Trump lied to Comey ... Trump lied to Comey

Round and round the message went on the BBC loop. Repetition, favourite tactic of Herrs Goebbels and Hitler. In the light of Comey's revelations this was a nothing if not an eccentric summary of the congressional hearing. Given that the hearing had been specifically convened to investigate alleged Russian collusion, a headline to the effect that none had been found might naturally have been expected, But no: Trump lied to Comey ... Trump lied to Comey ... Trump lied to Comey.

So what of Russian collusion and Mr Trump's alleged puppet-master Vlad Putin, and the two men's plot to steal the 2016 US election? Not a lot actually, in fact nothing at all. BBC amnesia had set in with alacrity. Somewhere between Washington and BBC land, all that stuff – Russia and Putin – had got lost. Now that it led to a dead end the impartial broadcaster had had enough of Russia, for now. It had a brand new angle.

During his testimony the former FBI Director had described what he felt were unfounded criticisms aimed at his stewardship from the Trump team. 'The administration chose to defame me,' claimed Mr Comey, 'and more importantly the FBI by saying the organization was in disarray . . . those were lies.'[4] The BBC "lie" had merely been an observation that Comey's management of the FBI fell short of required standards, a claim that had also been made on numerous occasions by the Democrats. In the OIG report of June 2017 Comey was described as 'insubordinate & incompetent.' His competence had in fact long been a point of convergence between both Democrats and Republicans.[5]

Trump's "lie" therefore had been to state that the FBI under Comey had been 'in disarray.' Naturally, Mr Comey disagreed with that assessment. But what precisely did this difference of opinion regarding the competence of James Comey's leadership and management skills have to do with the congressional hearing into alleged Russian collusion and Mr Trump's supposed culpability? Answer: nothing.

Its favourite anti-Trump sub-narrative now seriously derailed, the BBC simply ignored the outcome of the congressional hearing. The broadcaster replaced it with a non-story. The hearing which had just cleared Mr Trump of any impropriety suddenly became all about James Comey's hurt feelings. Viewers reading the BBC summary – 'Trump lied to Comey' – could have been forgiven for believing that Mr Trump had committed some sort of gross offence linked to Russian collusion, and had tried to cover himself by lying to the FBI boss, which is of course precisely what the impartial, free and fair broadcaster wished its audience to think.

Nothing but nothing stops a BBC narrative, not the testimony of the FBI and certainly not inconvenient facts or the truth. Trump lied to Comey . . . Trump lied to Comey . . . Trump lied to Comey . . . BBC propaganda looped on and on into the night manipulating anybody who had not taken the trouble to check out the details of the hearing for themselves.

Staying with the US president our next example of misrepresentation entails a quite shocking case in which the broadcaster attempted to mislead by deliberately misreporting the US' president's actual words.

'An 'Honest mistake'
When President Trump addressed the UN General Assembly on 25 September 2018 naturally the speech was widely reported around the world. Remarks about the Iranian regime featured prominently in the speech. The president spoke about taking sanctions against Iran, promising that 'more will follow.' Nothing remotely contentious here unless of course the goal is to misrepresent the US president:

> **@BBC News (world)**
> Donald Trump tells UN General Assembly "war will follow"
> after his decision to re-impose sanctions on Iran, who he
> accuses of 'slaughter in Syria and Yemen'.

War will follow? Yes, BBC News World had actually reported the president's words in just this way. But was it true? Had the president of the United States of America really threatened Iran with war? The clues were everywhere. Having just heard the declaration of what could easily be the start of World War III the reactions of UN delegates were rather underwhelming: there weren't any reactions. No alarm or shock anywhere to be seen. Odd. After all, it's not every day a US president threatens war, especially during a speech to the United Nations! But no, not even a raised eyebrow to be seen amongst the 100s of delegates.

Meanwhile 23 million BBC News followers were understandably sent into a panic by the BBC tweet. 'UN is not the right podium to unleash threat of war,' wrote one BBC follower. 'He wants war. The "incident" that will secure another 4 year reign,' asserted another. 'Can't wait for World War III,' added yet another. People were clearly spooked.

Although the BBC communication had the effect of terrifying some, many others were not so easily duped. Perusing the transcript of the speech turns up no mention of the phrase reported by the BBC. What the transcript does provide is both the context and actual words spoken by the president. Accessing the transcript - available on the White House website - would have taken an ethical journalist just a matter of seconds:

> The United States has launched a campaign of economic pressure to deny the regime the funds it needs to advance its bloody agenda. Last month, we began re-imposing hard-hitting nuclear sanctions that had been lifted under the Iran deal.
>
> Additional sanctions will resume November 5th, and **more will follow**. And we're working with countries that import Iranian crude oil to cut their purchases substantially.[6]

As noted, transposing the words 'war will follow' makes absolutely no sense. The topic of sanctions against Iran is already clearly established.

'Only a matter of time before your bias gets people killed'
The context of the president's words could not have been clearer, which might just explain why panic had not broken out amongst UN delegates.

Perhaps this explains the vicious social media backlash against the BBC which soon followed:

> Stories like this are seriously dangerous, changing his words could start a war

> Zero standards. If you're listening to tone/context & listening to his WORDS, there's no way you even get close to 'war . . .' What does it say about YOU that you'll look for ANYTHING in order to run a negative report on the President.

> The lies being spread here are staggering. This is actual dangerous fake news which could have massive geopolitical implications, for real. It's only a matter of time before your bias gets people killed, if it hasn't already happened.

Having been called out on social media, the BBC was forced to issue a clarification in which it claimed to have 'misheard' the president's words: 'It looks like we misheard the President. It was our bad and we've issued a clarification.' However, not all social media users were convinced. Amongst the numerous people and agencies listening to the president's speech only one had 'misheard' him: the BBC . . .

> You knew exactly what you were doing

> Not good enough. You purposely lied

> Our bad? What are you 12 years old?

@BBCNews (World)
Clarification: @realDonaldTrump's actual words appear to be 'more will follow.' #honestmistake

Appear to be? It certainly appeared that BBC News (World) had not bothered to check its misconceptions with the White House official transcript. Surely the broadcaster would immediately delete its 'honest mistake?' Not quite. For reasons not entirely clear the alarming message was allowed to stand for almost 24 hours where it could be seen by potentially millions of people. The scrupulously fair broadcaster seemed in no hurry at all to delete its mendacious tweet. Another social media roasting duly followed:

> ➢ Delete the tweet then rather than leaving it hoping it incites reactions by people missing your 'clarification.'

> ➢ It's probably safer for the world to just delete this tweet

> ➢ Just delete your tweet and then write a new tweet apologising for it. It's what normal people do. Obviously you have an agenda.

> ➢ In case you're curious, the fact that you're leaving "war" up and then tacking on a cutesy "clarification" instead of deleting your LIE . . . is what we're talking about when we call you FAKE NEWS

Amplification and Suppression

Sometimes there is no escaping a BBC story. Take the example of the Grenfell Tower fire. With its villains (Tory administration) and victims (largely immigrant occupants) this was a story the broadcaster was determined to milk for all it was worth. Coverage went on 24/7. Summer 2017 and Houdini himself could not have escaped the BBC's incessant Grenfell narrative. Other stories such as the horrific grooming scandal which occurred in Telford, by contrast hardly troubled the BBC radar.

> **@Anon**
> The BBC does not simply present news, it exercises its own agenda of PC and Virtue Signalling - trying to influence our views. It majors on certain topics and blocks others

Depending how closely they match BBC narratives stories are either promoted or stifled within the broadcaster's network. For example, in the run up to the Iraq war the broadcaster naturally represented the elite interests that were pushing for conflict with Saddam Hussein's regime. Voices of opposition such as Tony Benn and George Galloway, 'Were all but drowned out in the vast amount of air-time devoted to the warmongering deceptions of Tony Blair, Donald Rumsfeld and Jack Straw.'[1]

In other words the BBC was strictly regulating the amount of exposure it allocated to the two sides of the debate. The pro-war argument was thus made with minimal resistance. Public opinion, overwhelmingly against war at the outset, could be slowly changed in accordance with the wishes of the 'war-mongers' of Washington and London. It worked. Thanks in no small part to the BBC, consent was ultimately manufactured for one of the greatest foreign policy disasters of recent times.

In line with the objectives of the elite consensus the BBC duly ensured eloquent anti-war voices were kept off the air, as indeed it has done with Brexit. Pursuing control over Iraq's natural resources, the global elite had already decided a long time ago that Saddam Hussein had to go. By controlling what the public sees, hears and reads, Britain's 'national' broadcaster helps global interests achieve their goals. In treating stories this way, the broadcaster achieves two essential propaganda aims:

1 – Make small stories big

2 – Make big stories small

Having succeeded in minimising stories, the BBC can then go on to print claims such as the following: 'If mainstream media isn't reporting it, the likelihood is that it's out on a limb somewhere.'[2] Effectively, the BBC has the power to create a news environment which is wholly artificial, amplifying that which agrees with its worldview, suppressing that which does not. Ensuring stories that reflect the BBC worldview receive maximum exposure - we refer to here as amplification. Omitting or minimising those stories that do not agree with the BBC worldview we refer to as suppression.

What everyone thinks
Amplifying stories that promote the minority BBC worldview is just one part of a propaganda exercise that attempts to convince us that the BBC's opinions represent what the rest of Britain – the world – thinks. Astro-turfing is one of the broadcaster's go-to psychological tactics. It's a trick as old as the hills. As a device that can literally create reality propagandists adore it. Sometimes it pops up in the movies.

The 2016 American Civil War drama *The Free State of Jones* tells the true story of a revolt which happened in Mississippi. In one particularly tense scene the film's hero decides to protect the inhabitants of an isolated ranch from marauding troops. In the best interests of suspense there is of course a problem: a mother and her three very young daughters live on the ranch. How can they be expected to defend it from professional soldiers? The hero has a plan.

When the soldiers arrive they can hardly contain their disbelief, or their amusement. Guns cocked, hero, mother and three daughters - barely old enough to walk - prepare to defend their home, a motley crew. Are they serious? This is going to be a walkover. But wait . . . The villains' smiles turn to frowns. For pointing out of every window in the ranch are yet more guns, a mini battalion just waiting to unleash hell. Underestimate the enemy at your peril! The troops make a tactical withdrawal promising to return. Our hero has saved the day. The soldiers have fallen for one of the oldest tricks in the book. They've been astro-turfed.

According to *The Guardian* astro-turfing is, 'the attempt to create an impression of widespread grassroots support for a policy, individual, or product, where little such support exists.'[3] In other words astro-turfing is a form of deception.

For organisations like the BBC astro-turfing is heaven sent. How many times have you encountered a BBC report quoting the outrage or condemnation of a tiny, select group of the usual suspects: a spokesperson for left-wing charities and NGOs (Refugee Action, Greenpeace); a Trump-hating Hollywood celebrity; obscure pro-EU bureaucrat, all of whose views are presented as being representative of a majority. These types of right-thinkers are forever popping up on BBC programmes or being quoted on its website. By promoting the opinions of such people and the organisations they represent the corporation is deliberately trying to mislead its audience, hoping to sway them, to make them believe those views are much more popular than they are in reality – what everyone thinks.

Astro-turfing is just one of many ways the broadcaster attempts to exert control over what its audience thinks, reacts and ultimately how it behaves. In this section we will analyse just a few of these tactics.

'Genuine question – who the hell is James Chapman?'

Ever heard of James Chapman? Neither had we, not until that is the BBC started to splash his somewhat eccentric opinions all over its various platforms one day in August 2017. How do you go about gaining generous BBC exposure? Just repeat a favourite BBC narrative: *Brexit is very, very bad.*

Fair to say that not many people outside the Westminster bubble had ever heard of a certain James Chapman before the BBC took a keen interest him. The former advisor to Brexit secretary David Davis MP quit politics in June 2016 for a career in public relations. A staunch ally of arch-remainer and chief architect of Project Fear, George Osborne, for a brief moment in the miserable summer of 2017 Mr Chapman became a BBC darling. Twelve months into his new career the tweets began. Chapman hated Brexit. His tweets soon alerted the BBC.

In next to no time Chapmen was on Radio 4 where he duly declared that Brexit would be a 'calamity' for the UK. James Chapman PR guru was suddenly everywhere. The BBC could not get enough of him. The anti-Brexit tweets of this hitherto obscure PR man and fanatical Europhile were promoted all over the BBC's platforms, 'Let's be honest,' said Chapman, 'if we had an effective electoral law leading Brexiteers would now be in jail.'[4]

Jail? Was Chapman being serious? Even more revealing these tweets were presented by the BBC not ironically or even with mild mockery. The lack of outraged voices lining up to 'slam' these 'controversial' opinions were notable only by their absence. That familiar superior tone so prevalent when the BBC disapproves was also not in evidence. As strange as it may sound the BBC appeared to be treating Chapman's fringe opinions with absolute sincerity. 'Genuine Question,' asked one social media user, 'who the hell is James Chapman?'

Meanwhile, real news ...

While busily amplifying the fringe views of a single hard-core Euro fanatic, on the very same day – August 11 - the BBC chose *not* to report on a piece of ground-breaking research conducted by Oxford University and The London School of Economics, which questioned over 3,000 respondents about a range of Brexit issues including single market membership, freedom of movement and the much-discussed Brexit 'divorce' bill. Much to the dismay of the BBC the research found that two–thirds of voters supported a so-called 'hard' Brexit. Not unsurprisingly this significant piece of research – the largest and most detailed of its kind since the referendum – failed to appear on any BBC platform.

Discussing the findings Professor Sarah Hobolt of the LSE said: 'Overall, this means that there is on aggregate higher levels of support for outcomes that resemble the 'hard Brexit' position put forward by the government.'

'The findings will disappoint politicians and campaign groups hoping to mitigate or even stall Brexit,' wrote Buzzfeed, the organisation responsible for breaking the story and one, as we have seen, the BBC usually has lots of time for. 'They reveal that while Leave voters remain united behind a hard – or even no-deal – exit, Remainers are much more divided.'[5] Such was the disappointment of one 'campaign' group it decided to ignore the story completely. This joint effort between two of the UK's most esteemed institutions failed to make it onto any BBC platform, radio, TV or online. Meanwhile the ravings of one James Chapman, 'democrat' were splashed all over the BBC universe.

'Flaccid dumplings'

James Chapman was allocated BBC space purely because his anti-Brexit views matched so perfectly those of Britain's state broadcaster. Courting the BBC is easy when you know how. All you need to do is agree with its narratives. Fame – often fleeting – is sure to follow. When a US journalist wrote a withering review of a visit to Trump Tower Bar and Grill shortly after Donald Trump's US election victory, despite the triviality of such an event the BBC just couldn't wait to jump on board. Sure enough, the review was featured on BBC Newsbeat under the headline, 'Donald Trump, 'flaccid dumplings' and the short-fingered feud.'

Never ones to pass up a chance to have a dig at the US president, the BBC was positively salivating. A negative review of a Trump restaurant was an opportunity not to be missed. The quote chosen by the BBC to splash all over its article in the form of a sub-heading was predictably spiteful:

Could be the worst restaurant in America[6]

Has impartiality ever flown so high? At this juncture an objective observer might have asked themselves a couple of crucial questions: who was the writer of this 'review' and for what purpose(s) was he/she writing? Alas no information on the writer was forthcoming.

The BBC was however more than happy to reproduce the review's content, revelling in its lurid prose which described the Szechuan dumplings as 'flaccid gray . . . with flaccid, gray innards'. The steak meanwhile was 'slumped to the side over the potatoes like a dead body inside a T-boned minivan.' The burger was described as a 'sad little meat thing . . . hiding its shame under a slice of melted orange cheese.' The writer concluded her invective thus: 'It was slop: as soon as I got home, I brushed my teeth twice and curled up in bed until the nausea passed.'

As reviews go they don't come any more subjective than this. Nonetheless, Britain's scrupulously fair broadcaster was more than willing to give a platform for what can only be described as a tirade.

'Vulnerable to exaggerations and lies'

Let's fill in some of the context that the BBC, in its wisdom, 'forgot' to include in its article. Firstly, the review appeared in *Vanity Fair* - a virulently anti-Trump Liberal publication which spends a worrying amount of time stalking the US president. Secondly, the writer of the piece and erstwhile restaurant critic Tina Nguyen is a regular columnist for the same anti-Trump magazine. Any alarm bells ringing? For a flavour of her work here are the headlines of just a few of her many articles written about Donald Trump:

> Donald Trump is already using his presidency to enrich his business

> How Donald Trump bullied his own Trump tower tenants

> Who will lie to the press for Trump next?

The list goes on and on and on. Alarms bells ringing now? They ought to be. Nguyen's contempt for the US president is clear enough. What chance then of an objective, balanced critique of his restaurant? Could an individual whose antipathy towards Trump verges on the psychotic really be trusted to produce a balanced review? Had they not taken the trouble to check Nguyen's 'credentials' out for themselves, readers of the BBC article could have been forgiven for believing that Trump Bar and Grill is the dining experience from hell, its food the stuff of nightmares - which is of course precisely what the BBC hoped its readers would think.

Prejudices of a *Vanity Fair* hack journalist aside, if the broadcaster had been at all interested in representing Trump Bar and Grill fairly there was a much more trustworthy source of information it could have consulted. Had it wanted to check whether Nguyen's experience was indeed a true reflection of the quality on offer at Trump Bar and Grill, the BBC knew exactly where to turn as BBC Newsnight's Evan Davis remarks:

Tourists everywhere know they are vulnerable to exaggerations and lies, and they take requisite precautions as a result . . . they check Trip Advisor . . .[7]

Let's take Mr Davis' advice then. After all, the last thing we would want is to be misled by 'exaggeration and lies . . .' Let's do as he recommends, take a look at Trip Advisor:[8]

Trump Tower Bar and Grill

257 Reviews | #2,010 of 9,005 Restaurants in New York City | Certificate of Excellence | ££ - £££ | Midtown | American, Bar

---

Who then should we trust – a *Vanity Fair* writer who maligns Trump on a daily basis or a stack of objective views posted on the one of the world's leading review sites for a restaurant awarded a Certificate of Excellence? The impartial broadcaster opted for the former. The BBC article goes on to express itself puzzled as to the reason for Trump's criticism of *Vanity Fair:*

> He didn't explain why he's so angry with the magazine and its editor Graydon Carter.
>
> But maybe, just maybe, it has something to do with a review of the Trump Grill restaurant that appeared in the magazine.

Or maybe, just maybe it has something to do with lousy journalism? Or maybe, just maybe, it has something to do with wrongful and wilful misrepresentation?

The BBC smear machine

I f you wished to call someone a rude name but the position you held precluded you from doing so, how might you get around this tiresome situation? Imagine for example you wanted to label Mr X as a 'bastard.' You really, really loathe Mr X. But there's a fly in the ointment: you are a publicly-funded broadcaster charged with producing impartial content. How do you circumvent this proviso?

Easy. Get someone else to do it for you: smear by proxy.

In a speech made at Chatham House in March 2018, former Prime Minister John Major launched a scathing attack on Theresa May's Brexit strategy. Naturally, the BBC was all over the speech. As might be expected Major's words were soon amplified all over its various platforms. There is little that gives the impartial, free and fair broadcaster more pleasure than a spot of Brexit bashing. On that evening's edition of Newsnight the corporation excelled itself. The BBC's news and current affairs flagship programme decided to elicit reaction to a speech variously described elsewhere as the speech of a 'bitter loser.'

Newsnight thus decided to interview two prominent Brexit-supporting Tories: lifelong Euro-sceptic Bill Cash and former party leader Michael Howard. These two Tory grandees had, once upon a time, been rumoured to have been involved in a coup against John Major, prime minister at the time. Major had infamously referred to this group of treacherous Tories as 'the bastards.' Now, the impartial BBC doesn't much care for Tories. And as for Brexit-supporting Tories . . .

Turning to Mr Howard first BBC interviewer Kirsty Wark introduced him as one of 'John Major's bastards,' to which Mr Howard in typical Tory fashion did not respond. Next up in the Newsnight studio it was the turn of Bill Cash MP. Wark opened her attack on him by similarly introducing him as 'one of the bastards . . .' Brexit supporting Tory MPs are 'bastards.' Job done. You could almost hear the sniggers issuing forth from the BBC studio and from The Ministry of Truth's many corridors.

'Unthinkingly accepted without question'

'Today's smear artists are sophisticated strategists . . . They must persuade people to form strong opinions,' writes Sharyl Attkisson'[1]. The objective of smearing is indeed to manipulate opinion, to ensure those opinions are as hostile as they can possibly be. Once smeared, once an individual is tarnished, it's a long if not impossible road back to restore standing:

> Reputation, reputation, reputation! Oh, I have lost my
> reputation! I have lost the immortal part of myself, and
> what remains is bestial. My reputation, Iago, my reputation![2]

When Michael Cassio laments the loss of reputation in Shakespeare's *Othello* it is an admission that the public forum – what that forum believes – matters, true or not. The aim of smearing continues Attkisson, is always to inflame public opinion, to rouse and channel the baser instincts of humanity against a specific target. This objective is achieved by brainwashing to the point where the message is uncritically accepted:

> The audience must get angry or become suspicious so they're
> motivated to take action. The message must be repeated so
> many times in so many venues, until it's unthinkingly accepted
> without question. It must take root and burrow deeply in the
> public consciousness.[3]

Nobody but nobody smears like the state broadcaster. It has an awful lot of 'venues' in which to repeat its innuendos. Smearing has played and continues to play a crucial role in its propaganda campaigns. Targets are selected with precision. Negative messages, just as Attkisson observes, are then replayed over and over again until BBC audiences truly believe that such-and-such is Hitler or such-and-such is a neo-Nazi intent on kick starting a reign of terror.

The reason is to protect the elite consensus which the broadcaster faithfully protects from closer scrutiny. 'Those who present a danger to the system by stepping outside the accepted limits of conformity,' remarks Arnold, 'have to be discredited and their influence destroyed.'[4]

The goal of smearing agrees Attkisson, 'is often to destroy ideas by ruining the people who are most effective in communicating them.'[5] Those who challenge BBC group-think present a very real threat to the system. Individuals who 'step outside' that system must therefore be discredited. By far the most effective way of doing this is to play the man not the ball.

The reason why organisations like the BBC use (indirect) smears so often is twofold: firstly, attacking the individual rather than the argument is the first response of the intellectually lazy. Easier to simply blow the dog whistle than spend time building a coherent, nuanced case. Secondly, as Cassio recognised, smears work. Perhaps this is because people are inclined to believe the worst. Whatever the reasons, in terms of sheer efficacy nothing compares to a smear, because even when proven to be false its fetid smell lingers on. Losing 'the immortal part' of oneself is not to be taken lightly.

Alinsky: play the man, not the ball

In Rules for Radicals, Saul Alinsky proudly cites the example of the Boston Massacre as an example of how smearing can work to override logic, facts and reality itself.[6]

History records that on the night of 5 March 1770, British soldiers opened fire on civilians killing and wounding several of their number. The incident was naturally seized upon by members of the American Independence movement as an example of British brutality. A deathbed confession by one of the Bostonians, Patrick Carr, painted a rather different picture. The townspeople had in fact attacked the soldiers first. The British army had merely been defending itself. For leading figures in the independence movement the confession severely diluted the very real propaganda value of the incident, if not obliterating it altogether. There was only one thing to do: delegitimise their colleague's deathbed testimony; play the man not the ball.

Soon, independence leaders spread rumours that the dead man had been an Irish papist whose loyalties actually lay with the Catholic church. Carr's character came under sustained attack. In short order his testimony fell out of favour. Job done. Boston became remembered as an act of British aggression.

'It (smearing) contributes to a climate of public ill will and distrust,' observes Kulp in an article entitled 'A Threat to Public Discourse,' 'that magnifies our differences, hardens opposition, and makes productive dialogue immeasurably more difficult.'[7] All of which is exactly what an unethical broadcaster might be hoping and expecting it might do. When the aim is to smear the last thing required is to make public dialogue easy. Smearing is geared precisely to close down debate down, not open it up.

Take the example of the individual known as Tommy Robinson. Smearing him as the 'ex-EDL leader' is clearly a tactic pre-conceived to take the heat out of Mr Robinson's activism as an anti-grooming gang campaigner. As a tactic it has worked to perfection: Robinson's sometimes combative attempts to unmask grooming gangs have often been mired in hysteria stemming from the BBC EDL smear. The impartial, broadcaster wished to make Robinson toxic. By continuously smearing him it has correctly calculated that his revelations about the activities of grooming gangs will be dismissed as the ravings of a 'far-right Islamophobe.' The debate is over before it has begun. Mission accomplished. Grooming gangs the length and breadth of the UK have consequently been able to act with impunity, officialdom terrified to act lest it too falls foul of the BBC smearing machine.

Following yet another high profile grooming gang trial in August 2017 a Labour MP claimed that fear of being branded 'racist' had indeed stopped officials from intervening in this and other cases.[8] Which state broadcaster do we know persistently smears individuals as 'racists?' As to the question of why a 'national' broadcaster – any broadcaster - would wish to discredit and silence individuals attempting to shine a light on this vile practice, we will leave for our readers to speculate. Bottom line: If you want the message to go unheard, first ensure the messenger is destroyed.

Plausible deniability

Smearing by proxy allows the BBC to besmirch individuals without facing any of the consequences that slander and libel ordinarily incur. Easier simply to get innocent members of the public to do your dirty work, and then ensure they receive maximum exposure. 'In Paris,' reported the BBC news website, 'protester Francoise Seme Wallon said

Mr Trump was "a nasty guy and he's dangerous for the whole world."[9] It's that old amplification trick once more, mainstream media bread and butter. The impartial, free and fair broadcaster can always be relied upon to pluck someone out of the crowd to duly broadcast its opinions, anonymous French citizens or anyone else for that matter. *We didn't call Trump names, a French girl did. This is what 'the world' thinks about Trump . . .*

When an ex-BBC (current NBC) activist writes on social media that she is 'well versed in the art of avoiding libel,' it is not just an idle boast. The broadcaster knows exactly how to foment discord without putting its own head on the block, usually by use of "quotation marks" or by reproducing social media posts, a particular favourite tactic down at Broadcasting House:

> **@McdonaldsCorp**
> @realDonaldTrump You are actually a disgusting
> excuse of a President and we would love to have
> @BarackObama back, also you have tiny hands.

Seen this way an unscrupulous broadcaster has limitless scope to amplify whatever lurid messages it chooses, hiding behind the mask of what is known as plausible deniability, a concept defined by Political Dictionary.com as, 'The ability to deny blame because evidence does not exist to confirm responsibility for an action. The lack of evidence makes the denial credible, or plausible.' As with Newsnight's 'bastard' comments and its Jacob Rees-Mogg smears plausible deniability allows the BBC to hurl insults at wrong thinkers while innocently claiming to be merely quoting the words of others.

Let's take a few examples which managed to end up splashed all over the impartial broadcaster's enormous media platform:

> **We didn't say Trump was a bum, a basketball player did:**
> Donald Trump: LeBron James calls president a 'bum'
> after Steph Curry comments
> bbc.co.uk

We didn't say Trump was a lunatic, N Korea did:
N Korea: 'Lunatic' Trump exploiting Otto
Warmbier's death
bbc.co.uk

We didn't say Trump was racist, this guy did:
Ben Rhodes: Trump opposition to Obama
was 'racist'
bbc.co.uk

'Bum,' 'lunatic,' 'racist,' – you get the picture. In the all above examples the broadcaster can claim to be merely reporting what people are saying and is therefore not responsible for whatever sentiments it publishes, however unpleasant.

So where are the positive Trump headlines? Although a typical BBC audience might find the idea of a positive Trump headline fantastical, the US president has plenty of supporters - it's just the BBC chooses to supress this support or, as in the case of Kanye West, attempt to undermine it. While an unscrupulous, ideological driven broadcaster would ensure its audience encountered only negative stories, an impartial operator would 'strive for journalism that is accurate, impartial, independent and fair.'

In 'Rules for Radicals' comrade Alinsky cautions to never, under any circumstances, acknowledge anything positive about the opposition. To do so instantly weakens the cultural Marxist cause. When Mr Trump donates $1 million towards hurricane relief and the BBC instantly try to undermine this gesture, the broadcaster is merely following the political agitator's advice to the letter: NEVER give the opponent a moment's respite. Attack every day, every night, every week and never stop attacking.

'A thoroughly modern bigot'
We've already noted that according to BBC 'comedy' Conservative MP Jacob-Rees Mogg holds 'horrifying reactionary values.' The urge to call him nasty names must therefore be simply overwhelming. Alas. Thanks to that pesky royal charter the 'national' broadcaster must refrain. Not a problem – just pay a 'comedian' a wedge of cash, allocate him or her a

slot on a primetime TV show and let him or her smear away on your behalf. Smearing by proxy. The introduction to Newsnight on 7 Sept 2017 was devoted to the BBC's dear friend Mr Rees-Mogg. Presenter Kirsty Wark kicked off the programme in the following way:

> 'A thoroughly modern bigot,' that was just one epithet used today to describe Tory backbencher Jacob-Rees-Mogg after he told GMB yesterday he was opposed to abortion in all circumstances . . .

From whom had this epithet come? BBC Newsnight weren't saying . . . This charming slur had in fact come from an anti-Tory, left-wing *Guardian* columnist. In its wisdom however the BBC decided not to give the lady in question one of its famous health-checks. Newsnight appeared to be amplifying views that perfectly coincided with BBC right-think.

Wark delivered her 'thoroughly modern bigot' smear with some relish. Get on the wrong side of Auntie and the neutral broadcaster will catch up with you, one way or another. Life would be so much easier for Mr Rees-Mogg if only he'd adopt BBC right-think. Nor was the broadcaster quite finished with the Tory Brexiteer. BBC Trending might not have picked up on that infamous re-tweet advocating for the silencing of victims of sexual grooming, or the 50,000-strong online campaign to have the MP who re-tweeted it disciplined, but it *did manage* to pick up on social media criticism aimed at Rees-Mogg, a straight, white, Brexit-supporting Catholic who, in a television interview with Piers Morgan, had expressed his opposition to gay marriage and abortion.

Some social media users also objected to Rees-Mogg's position. BBC Trending gleefully reported how an 'actor and writer' had started off a trend whereby users were encouraged to flood a popular Rees-Mogg Twitter hashtag with 'homoerotic images:'[10] Sure enough the #moggmentum hashtag was duly swamped with a barrage of homo-erotic images and plenty of distasteful language. All of which BBC Trending appeared to think was great fun. If you hadn't heard about this lark – swamping the #moggmentum hashtag with 'homoerotic' images, thanks to BBC Trending you had now . . .

In publishing third-party smears and insults the BBC could, as usual, pretend to be disinterested observers: *We didn't call Rees-Mogg homophobic . . . We didn't call him a thoroughly modern bigot . . .*

Unable to get away itself with labelling a member of the British Parliament as 'homophobic' the 'British' Broadcasting Corporation instead simply allocated a platform for a third-party to do its dirty work. 'Just adding a photo of my husband and me on our wedding day to homophobe Jacob Rees-Mogg's hashtag,' so went another tweet from a same sex couple and helpfully reproduced by BBC Trending. Whether it's Conservative MPs or Republican presidents, create a smear and there's more than a fair chance the BBC will soon have it up on one of its news pages. Create a similar 'tongue-in-cheek' meme about a Hilary Clinton or Diane Abbot however and its chances of seeing the light of day become negligible.

Predictably, BBC Trending duly failed to mention the huge amount of support the MP received. 'Why the fuss over Rees-Mogg's unremarkable views on abortion?' asked Fraser Nelson in *The Telegraph*.[11] Many others congratulated the politician for standing by his principles. With the help of a little bit of reverse astro-turfing (nobody supports Rees-Mogg) and a little amplification across the BBC media platform, the impartial broadcaster was able to promote its Rees-Mogg is homophobic smear with impunity.

'Welcomed by David Duke'

Encouraging individuals to smear on your behalf is only half the story. While the BBC is forbidden to directly smear, it manages to circumvent this requirement by resorting to implication.

One of the corporation's favourite (implied) smears involves attempting to link Donald Trump with the white nationalist group, the Ku Klux Klan, and in particularly to an individual named David Duke. BBC endeavours to link Mr Trump's name with that of Mr Duke know no bounds. So who is David Duke and why do the BBC take such great pains to manufacture a link between the two men? In the 1970s Duke was a member and then senior member of the Ku Klux Klan. Linking the 45th US president with Mr Duke any which way it can has thus become somewhat of a Holy Grail for the impartial broadcaster. As smears come they don't get any bigger than this one: Trump and the KKK!

Indeed, during Mr Trump's successful 2016 presidential campaign the BBC never tired of reminding its audience that Mr Trump had the support of 'Ex-KKK leader David Duke.' Whatever Mr Trump said or did, the neutral broadcaster made sure they obtained the thoughts of David Duke on the matter in hand. Mr Trump wants to cut taxes. What does David Duke think about that? Trump wants to build a wall. What does David Duke think? Trump likes mint choc ice cream. Does David Duke like mint choc ice cream? The BBC could have sought the opinions of hundreds of other political commentators, but didn't. There was only one individual it was interested in: ex-KKK Grand Wizard, David Duke. Whatever the Trump story, no matter how tenuous the link, the broadcaster was sure to drop in a David Duke reference somewhere.

In a BBC article about President Trump scrapping White House business councils we duly find:

> Mr Trump's remarks were **welcomed by David Duke**, a former leader of the Ku Klux Klan.[12]

A BBC article about the Charlottesville riots we find:

> Mr Trump's remarks were **welcomed by David Duke**, a former leader of the Ku Klux Klan[13]

A BBC article featuring George Bush Jnr and Snr we find:

> Mr Trump's remarks were **welcomed by David Duke**, a former leader of the Ku Klux Klan[14]

A BBC article attempting to undermine Melania Trump's campaign against online bullying we find:

> David Duke, who is running to become a senator in Louisiana, recently backed Donald Trump and the Ku Klux Klan newspaper has also endorsed him.[15]

Nor are associates of Mr Trump's immune from this most ubiquitous of BBC implied smears:

And the news that Steve Bannon . . . was the new White
House strategist was **welcomed by** former Ku Klux Klan
leader **David Duke.**[16]

In the run-up to the US presidential election the BBC was particularly
eager to imply that Mr Trump had David Duke's endorsement, which he
did not. 'Duke said during his radio show that he's not formally
endorsing Trump,' reported *The Daily Mail.*[17] And even if he had, a
former Republican politician backing the Republican candidate for the
US presidency rather than the Democrat candidate would not exactly be
earth shattering news. Republican backs Republican! Hold the front
page!

All of which mattered not a jot to the impartial, free and fair
broadcaster, who in its eagerness to smear Mr Trump developed an
inexplicable deaf and blind spot to any facts that contradicted its pre-
conceived smear. The mission was as cynical as it gets: persuade the
public (especially US voters) that there was some kind of affinity
between Mr Trump and David Duke in the hope of smearing the
billionaire as a racist. There was just one problem: lack of evidence.
Inconvenient as this fact was, it did not prevent the broadcaster from
trying so very hard to link the men together. BBC activists tried their
hardest to cement a relationship between the billionaire businessman
and the former KKK member.

Unfortunately for the broadcaster, on those occasions he has
been questioned about David Duke, Mr Trump's comments remain on
record:

1991 Interview with Larry King (L K)

L K: Did the David Duke thing bother you? Fifty-five
         percent of the whites in Louisiana voted for him

D T: I hate seeing what it represents, but I guess it just
         shows there's a lot of hostility in this country.
         There's a tremendous amount of hostility in the
         United States.

2000 Interview with Matt Lauer (M L)

ML: When you say the [Reform] party is self-destructing, what do you see as the biggest problem with the Reform Party right now?

D T: Well, you've got David Duke just joined — a bigot, racist, a problem. I mean, this is not exactly the people you want in your party. Reform Party now includes a Klansman, Mr. Duke, a neo-Nazi, Mr. Buchanan, and a communist, Ms. Fulani. This is not company I wish to keep.

2015 Interview with John Heilemann (J H)

J H: How do you feel about the David Duke quasi endorsement?

D T: I don't need his endorsement; I certainly wouldn't want his endorsement.

Twenty-five years of steadfastly rejecting the politics of David Duke. How then to explain the following social media post by the BBC's Nick Bryant, who styles himself a British 'rarity' who 'understands' America so well:

@NickBryantNY
Worth recalling today how Trump refused to disavow David Duke during the campaign

Either Bryant knew all about Mr Trump's consistent and oft-stated position viz-a-viz David Duke and chose to ignore it, or perhaps he just didn't think such trivialities were 'worth recalling . . .'

'55 disavowals on 15 public occasions'

As the BBC is only too aware Mr Trump has consistently expressed nothing but disdain for David Duke over the years, but to acknowledge as much would do irreparable harm to its anti-Trump narrative. 'From 1991 until election day in November 2016,' notes Alberto Martinez, 'Donald Trump repudiated and disavowed David Duke or the KKK no less than 55 times on 15 public occasions.'[18] All of which would have come as news to Nick Bryant that genuine British 'rarity' with his deep knowledge of all things American.

The truly shocking thing here is not that the mainstream media and the BBC did not know about these instances, but that they *did know*. They just chose not to say. When Bryant tells us it's 'worth recalling' that Trump did not disavow David Duke he is merely putting the finishing touches on a well-rehearsed trap used throughout the 2016 US presidential campaign by the legacy media.

As transparent as its David Duke/KKK trap was, the BBC and friends realised its massive smear potential and used it accordingly. As Martinez shows, the Republican candidate was consistently harassed by the mainstream media in the run up to the 2016 US elections. Mainstream hacks were waiting for a single instance when Mr Trump did not jump to their demands to 'disavow' David Duke for the zillionth time. When Trump decided to stop playing this ridiculous game, Bryant and friends duly went hysterical. 'Trump does not disavow David Duke!' Here's how they did it:

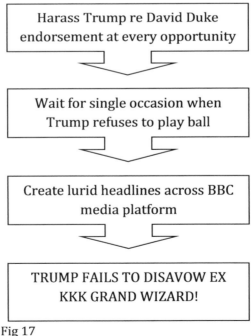

Fig 17

Martinez also reminds his readers about the President's past deeds, before that is the BBC attempted to paint him as David Duke's best buddy:

> Trump cultivated friendships with many prominent African Americans. He welcomed Jews and African Americans in his social club. He sued Palm Beach for excluding African Americans and Jews in other social clubs. He supported Jesse Jackson's Rainbow/PUSH Coalition to pressure corporations to promote blacks and minorities. He praised minorities in his construction projects. He made campaign contributions to several political candidates who are African Americans and minorities.

The broadcaster has honed its smearing by implication tactic to perfection. Its determination to link Republicans (and conservatives) with extreme nationalist ideologies is a defining feature of its 'journalism' amply illustrated in its portrayal of Sarah Huckabee-Sanders, to whom we turn next.

'Sanders left without answering'
Words, as the BBC is fond of reminding us, can have consequences. Words precede actions:

> Karen Pollock from the Holocaust Educational Trust said: "The Holocaust did not start with the gas chambers, it started with words; with hate-filled rhetoric.[19]

> bbc.co.uk

In her role as White House Press Secretary, Sarah Huckabee Sanders faces an avalanche of questions from a pool of largely hostile reporters on a weekly basis. Attended by several hundred journalists all jockeying for position, White House daily briefings have always been hectic, noisy affairs.

The tweet sent out from a BBC White House activist on 31 October 2017 referred to one such briefing:

233

@Tara_Mckelvey
Today journalist April Ryan asked Sarah Sanders: "Does
this administration believe slavery was wrong?" Sanders left
without answering.

It doesn't take a genius to work out what McKelvey is implying here:
Sarah Sanders could not or would not answer the question; she must
therefore support slavery, ergo the Trump administration also supports
slavery. As crude and as transparent as this attempt to smear is, it's not
the whole story - not by a long, long way.

First, let's take a look at some of the replies to McKelvey's tweet
which managed to obtain 2,500 re-tweets and over 3,500 likes.

Replying to @ Tara_Mckelvey

➢ Sarah Sanders is a heinous monster

➢ SHS is disgusting.

➢ Silence speaks volumes. Again, I have no words for this
  entity that is housed in a human shell

➢ This administration would bring back slavery

➢ This entire administration is filled with White Supremacists!

➢ They don't believe it's wrong because they want ethnic cleansing.

➢ She's a racist from a racist family who works for a racist.

➢ Ask her again tomorrow April, every day. I want to hear it
  from her evil mouth

➢ Sanders is a witch on all counts

➢ OMG!!!! She's just an evil Huckabee daughter of an evil father.

If something looks like incitement and sounds like incitement, then chances are what you have is incitement:

The Free Dictionary:
Incitement: an act of urging on or spurring on or rousing to action or instigating.

Metropolitan Police:
The offence of incitement to hatred occurs when someone acts in a way that is threatening and intended to stir up hatred. That could be in words, pictures, videos, music, and includes information posted on websites.

In the aftermath of McKelvey's tweet a shocking amount of anger was directed towards Sarah Huckabee Sanders and the Republican Party. Amongst other things, the White House Press Secretary is variously labelled 'disgusting,' 'a heinous monster,' 'a witch,' 'a racist,' and a woman who has an 'evil mouth.' The Trump administration is also labelled 'racist,' 'evil' and one that 'wants ethnic cleansing' and 'would bring back slavery.'

Disturbing as these reactions are, as far as the BBC was concerned its activist had done a sterling job. She had smeared Ms Huckabee Sanders and the Trump administration in one foul swoop. Job done.

For those interested in the truth it will not come as any surprise to learn that McKelvey's tweet had only the flimsiest of relationships with what had actually happened.

Smelling a rat: A CNN contributor
Let's look at what actually happened and then compare with the BBC correspondent's tweet. Reaching the end of the briefing Ms Huckabee Sanders finishes a point about the alleged Russian e-mail hacks. Signalling that the event is over and preparing to leave, the Press Secretary continues:

Thanks so much guys . . . Hope you have a happy and safe Halloween . . .

As she is closing the briefing down several voices can be heard attempting to grab the Press Secretary's attention. The assembled journalists have begun talking amongst themselves, heckling or getting up to leave. Huckabee Sanders has already turned around and is leaving the podium a few seconds later when a voice shouts: 'Does this administration believe that slavery is wrong?' By the time this question is fired out of nowhere the Press Secretary has all but left the podium. A total of 8 seconds elapse from Huckabee Smith's final remark about Russia, her Halloween comment and her leaving the lectern.

The question is posed by a certain journalist named April Ryan. As to whether it is appropriate to scream such a random question out loud when the official press conference is clearly over, and what the motivations behind such an outburst could possibly be, we leave for the reader to judge. Suffice to say Ms Ryan chose a particularly apt moment to 'ask' her question – and what a question! Ryan had saved her 'question' for the end, the very, very end.

White House media conference protocol is actually pretty well established: The Press Secretary - who is familiar with most if not all of the assembled reporters in the White House press corps – simply nominates a reporter by name who then asks his/her question. When the conference is over the Press Secretary leaves the room. In haranguing Ms. Huckabee Sanders after the conference had finished Ryan was breaking the etiquette observed and adhered to by the presidential team and journalists alike.

In her tweet Mckelvey tells us that Ms Huckabee Sanders 'left without answering,' which is of course technically correct. Notice how in order to mislead her audience the BBC reporter purposely misrepresents the situation: Somebody asked a question about slavery – Huckabee Sanders left without answering. Reading this tweet out of context one might well assume that the White House Press Secretary left the room *because* of the question, that she was desperate to *avoid* the question – exactly what McKelvey wishes her followers to think. Is it any surprise then that the tweet garnered such vitriol towards Ms. Huckabee Sanders?

In its report of the press conference, *The Washington Examiner* sheds some light on the context. We are already starting to build a quite different picture of events compared to the BBC's version:

Does this administration think that slavery is wrong? Ryan asked as Sanders left the podium. Sanders did not respond to that or other questions called out to her from reporters in the room as she was leaving.[20]

Notice that Sanders did not respond to 'that or other questions . . . as she was leaving the room.' These are facts that the BBC reporter very much does not want her followers to know about. Put very simply, Ms Huckabee Sanders was assailed by a volley of questions from all over the floor as she left the room, as is quite usual at these times. In other words, this was a fairly typical end to a White House briefing with noisy journalists shouting out questions over one another. The slavery question – random and entirely out of context as it had been - had thus just been one of many questions shouted at the end of the briefing.

Thus, what McKelvey leaves out of her tweet i.e. the context, is just as important – more so - as to what she decides to tweet. The BBC White House activist fails to mention that::

- The press conference had officially ended

- Ms Huckabee Sanders was in the process of leaving the stage when Ryan 'asked' her question

- The rest of the assembled journalists were also shouting questions

- Ryan is a CNN contributor and highly antagonistic to both Ms Huckabee Sanders and the Trump administration

Perhaps most telling of all, McKelvey does not for one moment consider the appropriateness of such an outburst and the reasons why a Trump-hating journalist might have decided to act in such a provocative way.

'Just what are you insinuating?'

While McKelvey's artful tweet triggered plenty of adverse reaction to the Trump administration, Huckabee Sanders and Republicans in general just as it was calculated to do, others were not as quick to swallow the bait. As ever, it was left to social media users to fill in the large and gaping gaps left by the BBC activist:

Replying to @Tara_Mckelvey

> This is misleading. April's question came after @PressSec had already ended the briefing.

> She left because the daily briefing was over. Just what are you insinuating? The room was full of shouted questions at the time.

> I can't stand Sanders but she had already left the podium when asked the question. Let's not become like the right and skew the facts.

'Forcing someone to dispute a preposterously untrue allegation is just as much slander as making the accusation,' observes Ryan Holliday.[21] Imagine the following scenario: Mayor of London Sadiq Khan is holding a press conference. As Mr Khan thanks the press for their attendance and leaves the stage a voice suddenly screams: 'Do you agree that homosexuality should be outlawed?' It's a journalist from *The Sun* newspaper. Now the majority of us would probably agree that there is a time and place for everything. We might also agree therefore that attempting to hijack a press briefing (which has already ended) with an inflammatory 'question' such as this – one clearly designed to catch the London Mayor on the wrong foot - probably does not require the dignity of a response. So, let's imagine how Ms Mckelvey might have responded had this incident occurred:

Sadiq Khan harassed by Islamophobic r-wing journalist while leaving briefing. Very aggressive. Mayor taken by surprise.

The BBC activist having selected just those details which fitted her anti-Republican narrative, it was left as ever to social media users to fill in the gaping holes:

> Let me guess, she's going to report back with "The WH did not reply when asked if they thought slavery was wrong". Whatever it takes to keep pushing their failed and ridiculous narratives.

> She asked that absurd question at the end on purpose, so it would look like Sarah was avoiding the question.

'Six broken ribs and lacerations to the lung'

Three days after Mckelvey's tweet, Republican Senator Rand Paul was happily mowing his lawn on 3 November 2017 when he was subject to a vicious attack by a neighbour which left him with six broken ribs and lacerations to his lung. His attacker Rene Boucher, a registered Democrat, had a history of posting anti-Trump memes on social media. Research revealed that the 59-year old anaesthetist was a firm #NeverTrump fan. Moves by the mainstream media to paint the incident as a trivial dispute over gardening issues were quickly quashed by neighbours of Mr Paul and Mr Boucher in the Rivergreen gated community where both men lived.[22]

'This was not a "scuffle," a "fight" or an "altercation," as many in the media falsely describe it,' said Paul's wife Kelley. 'It was a deliberate, blindside attack. The impact left Rand with six broken ribs, three displaced, pleural effusion and now pneumonia. This has been a terrible experience; made worse by the media's gleeful attempts to blame Rand for it, ridiculing him for everything from mowing his own lawn to composting.'[23] As for the BBC, it elected to run with the gardening incident line . . .

Among Boucher's litany of anti-Trump Facebook posts (since removed) were many references to the supposed Trump-Russia collusion pushed by BBC and their mainstream media friends. Although Boucher had not directly targeted Senator Paul in his social media posts, he had posted scathing and critical comments towards the Republican party and its policies.

Stacking the deck

Amongst its vast armoury of tricks employed to influence opinion one tactic in particularly has become a perennial favourite among BBC producers. Whether it's the 6'o Clock News, The One Show, Newsnight or the Victoria Derbyshire Show, the tactic is one and the same: ensure the dice is always loaded against your opponent. As with any casino the neutral broadcaster always ensures the odds are heavily stacked in its favour.

The easiest and most effective way to load the dice in television land is simply to ensure the enemy is outnumbered. It is no accident that should they appear on a BBC discussion programme, a member of any of the despised tribes – UKIP, DUP, Brexiteers etc. - will inevitably find themselves outnumbered by at least two to one (three to one if the BBC presenter is factored in). Whether it is Ian Paisley, Nigel Farage, Boris Johnson or whoever the BBC happens to disapprove of, he or she will always be up against many more opposing voices and as a result will always appear to be articulating a minority opinion.

> **@Anon**
> #BBCQT So the majority of the panel support Remaining
> in the EU and apparently the majority of the audience in
> Leave voting Dover support remaining in the EU.

Never more is this orchestration apparent than in Question Time, the BBC's topical panel show. The five person panel is supposed to be representative of the broad spectrum of UK political opinion: Left (Labour) Right (Conservative) and Centre-left (Liberal) are represented each week. The remaining guests are made up of minor party politicians (Green, SNP, UKIP, Plaid Cymru) and various individuals from the world of journalism, business and entertainment. In reality, the composition of the panel is often heavily tilted in favour of BBC right-thinkers.

For example, an appearance by say Iain Duncan-Smith (Right) will invariably be 'balanced' by political opponents representing Labour (Left) Green (Left) Liberal (Centre-Left) and a comedian/actor who in keeping with the entertainment profession will naturally be of a left-wing persuasion. Add in the Liberal-left bias of the show's presenter and the ex-Conservative leader could typically expect to find himself outnumbered five-to-one. The result is of course that the voice deemed by the BBC to hold the 'wrong' opinions (Duncan-Smith) will be constantly on the defensive, under fire from an artillery attack of unified voices. It's a simple but effective tactic. As far as losing an argument is concerned nothing works better than this isolation tactic. Throw in an audience largely hostile to Duncan-Smith and the house odds increase further.

Let's analyse the composition of Question Time's panels in the aftermath of the 2016 EU referendum. Given that the UK voted by 52-48% to leave the EU one would expect that this split would be reflected in the makeup of the programme's panel i.e. a more or less equal spilt between panellists who supported Remain or Leave, the balance perhaps tipped in favour of Leave. No such luck. Figure 18 breaks down the number of supporters for each side in 37 editions of the programme in the twelve month period following the vote to leave the European Union.

The only occasion the panel tipped in favour of Leave in the 37 editions under examination - Leave (3) Remain (2) - just so happened to be in Boston, a constituency that voted 75% to Leave the EU. Given that BBC QT panels are selected randomly this Boston anomaly must have been purely coincidental . . .

BBC bias towards the Remain side of the EU debate is perfectly in keeping with the broadcaster's strident views regarding membership of the European Union. According to research undertaken by NewsWatch, between 2005 and 2015 of 4,275 guests appearing on BBC Radio 4's Today programme, only 3% supported Britain's withdrawal from the EU. The majority – nearly 100% - supported continued membership. The writers also note the scarcity of Eurosceptic left-wing voices on BBC output. They hypothesise this is due to the BBC deliberately trying to frame the EU question as one of Right v Left. Between 2002 and 2017, the writers found only 14 left-wing guests (0.2%) in favour of EU withdrawal.[1]

A former BBC executive hints at the corporation's pro-EU sympathies when recalling its Europhile governors. Promoting the EU was, 'The one cause where I spotted encouragement from governors for the BBC to take a particular line. I believed that BBC news did underplay Eurosceptic arguments.'[2] 'Encouragement,' - coming from a fiercely loyal ex-BBC executive, the choice of language is particularly interesting.

	Remain	Leave
30/06 Preston	3	2
07/07 Brighton	4	1
15/09 Salisbury	4	1
22/09 Sutton Coldfield	3	2
29/09 Boston	2	3
06/10 Neath	4	1
13/10 London	4	1
20/10 Hartlepool*3	3	1
27/10 Gloucester	4	1
03/11 Watford	3	2
10/11 Southend*	3	1
17/11 Stirling	3	2
24/11 London	4	1
01/12 Wakefield	3	2
08/12 Maidenhead	3	2
12/01 Solihull	3	2
19/01 Peterborough*	3	1
26/01 London	3	2
02/02 Wallasey	4	1
09/02 Torquay	3	2
16/02 Glasgow	4	1
23/02 Stoke	3	2
02/03 Bedford	4	1
09/03 Sunderland	4	1
16/03 Bognor	3	2
23/03 Bangor	4	1
30/03 Carlisle	3	2
06/04 Gillingham	3	3
27/04 Oxford	4	1
04/05 Wigan	3	2
11/05 Edinburgh	4	1
18/05 Norwich	3	2
25/05 Salford *	3	0
01/06 Barnet	3	2
08/06 London	3	2
15/06 Coventry	4	1
22/06 Plymouth	4	1
	125 (69%)	56 (31%)

Fig. 18

What then of the BBC response to all this evidence of pro-EU bias? To discredit and deny. For example, NewsWatch's decades' long analysis was dismissed as 'flawed.' Unfortunately, the broadcaster does not provide either explanation or evidence of any flaws.

It's not just BBC panels that are tipped in favour of right-think, its audiences also have a happy habit of reflecting the broadcaster's stringent opinions. Composition of BBC panels and audiences do not happen by accident.

'There's a lot of Remainers here tonight'

The number of times an ordinary member of a BBC audience turns out to be a political activist just goes to show the extent of how coincidence rules our lives. When a member of the Hereford (18 January 2018) Question Time audience was allowed to go on an elongated anti-NHS harangue BBC weather-watchers had a distinct feeling of déjà vu. The rant coincided perfectly with the BBC view of the NHS: *Tories are evil. They're killing the NHS* etc. If this didn't happen to be a political programme produced by such a fair broadcaster, one might have been forgiven for thinking there was more to this 'random' scenario than met the eye.

Just who was this individual with the strident anti-Tory views? Twitter turned detective. It soon transpired that the 'random' audience member who had been allowed an unusual amount of time to criticise the NHS and Tories was none other than a left-wing political activist and Labour candidate for Hampstead. Social media wasn't having any of that. 'They bus in lefties from far and wide,' remarked one social media user, 'When #bbcqt came to my home town none of the audience had a local accent.'

> **@Anon**
> I was once in the Labour party office in Slough when QT
> called and asked how many tickets they wanted

Some 62% of the population of Scarborough voted to leave the European Union in the 2016 referendum. So when Question Time rolled up in the Yorkshire town in December 2017 panel and audience might have been reasonably expected to reflect this overwhelming Euroscepticism. Not a jot. It's not only QT panels that are tipped in favour of Remain, the audiences too are invariably made up largely of Remain supporters.

On the night in question in this Eurosceptic town the panel duly consisted of 4 Remain supporters and just one Leaver - par for the BBC course. It was the composition of the audience however that raised more than a few eyebrows. Throughout the broadcast it appeared that the audience consisted mainly of Remain supporters: 'I wish we'd never had the flaming referendum,' said one audience member. It was a pro-EU view that seemed to be shared by much of the studio. Were the good folk of Scarborough, in line with a favourite BBC narrative, now expressing their regret for having voted to leave the bloc? 'There's a lot of Remainers in here tonight!' exclaimed programme host David Dimbelby at one point. It certainly appeared that the North Yorkshire town had finally come to its senses in line with BBC-think.

Referees, crooked and straight

One way to think of the BBC and the position it occupies in the national debate is to compare it to a sports referee. Now it goes without saying the officials in any sporting event must be above reproach. Tennis or cricket umpire, rugby or football referee, the job of any official is to uphold parity, to ensure both sides play by the rules and are treated fairly.

The same is true of a BBC representative. He or she is bound to remain at all times impartial. In much the same way as a boxing referee is compelled to behave, so the BBC activist is obliged not to promote the interests of one fighter at the expense of his opponent. Imagine a scenario though in which the boxing ref *did* carry his prejudices into the ring, favouring one fighter. There are any number of ways a bent referee could tip the balance to the advantage of his preferred fighter. For example, when it comes to low blows he could choose to do one of two things: ignore or penalise, depending on which boxer is committing the violation. In fact there are a multitude of ways the experienced referee can assist his favoured fighter.

Similarly, the BBC presenter, interviewer or producer has at his/her disposal an abundance of tricks which allows them to influence the outcome of their own contests. For example, when it comes to interviews here are just some of the tactics the impartial BBC referee employs dependent upon compliance with BBC right-think. Liberals, Europhiles, pro-Palestinians, Democrats etc. can expect much gentler treatment than their conservative or Euro-sceptic counterparts:

Right-thinkers e.g. Liberal-Europhiles	Wrong-thinkers e.g. Cons-Euro-sceptics
Tone	
Friendly, polite	Aggressive, rude
Complimentary, deferential	Scathing, cynical
Conduct	
Amicable, chatty	Confrontational, formal
Encouraging: flatters	Hectoring: baits
Allows speaker to finish	Interrupts regularly
Allows to speak at length	Frequently talks-over
Accepts most/all arguments	Challenges most/all arguments
Reiterates, validates points	Misrepresents points
Speaks quietly, evenly	Raises voice, abrupt
Body language	
Nods, smiles, laughs etc.	Shakes head, frowns, snorts etc.

Fig. 19

When consistently applied to one's friends (right-thinkers) and one's enemies (wrong-thinkers) these behaviours act in a supervisory capacity – a ubiquitous BBC approval-disapproval mechanism. The BBC referee is tipping the balance towards its favoured fighter. Next time you watch say Newsnight's Emily Maitlis or Kirsty Wark interview Europhiles and Eurosceptics notice the very different treatment meted out to each side.[4]

As useful as our boxing analogy is it does however have its limits. For a start, partisan boxing referees are in fact the exception rather than the rule. Regrettably, the same cannot be said of the average BBC activist. Moreover, in the boxing ring there can only be a single opponent, while the BBC will ensure the presence of at least two if not three opponents whenever and wherever possible.

PART FOUR
CASE STUDIES

Imagine if the BBC were honest[1]

Craig Murray
Former British ambassador to Uzbekistan

① Sopel says: Deconstructing a BBC activist

② Harlow: 'A Brexit hate crime'

③ Violence on both sides: Charlottesville

④ 'Sticking up for Antifa'

⑤ 'Quiet and safe in Malmö'

⑥ 'Hilarious,' the assassination of Katie Hopkins

Sopel Says: Deconstructing a BBC activist

Throughout this book, we have deliberately referred to BBC employees as activists rather than journalists. The reason for this choice is straightforward enough, and is best articulated by a journalist writing for *Al-Jazeera* who makes the following, crucial distinction between journalists and activists:

> Activists interpret facts to suit his or her agenda. The journalist's job is to interpret, contextualise, and convey the nuances of a particular issue. He or she must not editorialise, which can lead to manipulation.[2]

In other words while a journalist approaches a story with an open mind, the mind of an activist is already made up. The journalist reaches a conclusion at the end of his/her investigations; the activist on the other hand starts with a conclusion and works backwards. For example, imagine a scenario – an admittedly grim one - in which the US presidential aeroplane, Air Force One crashes. The president himself manages to pull 5 of the 8 crew out of the burning wreckage to safety. Three crew members perish. In line with its pre-written narratives, how the BBC reports this incident will depend wholly on the identity of the president. For Obama the headline might read:

> Obama rescues five crew members from burning wreckage

If the event occurred during the Trump presidency however, the BBC headline would likely read something along the lines of:

> Trump leaves three crew members to perish in burning wreckage

In both these renditions the objective broadcaster could claim to have reported the facts. As ever, it's not what facts are reported rather *how* they are reported that makes a crucial difference as to how the story is perceived. This particular tactic, as we have already seen, is one of focus. By the way it chooses to report from choice of headline downwards – the broadcaster can greatly influence how its audience will respond. The focus, tone and presentation is based not on an objective analysis of the facts, but entirely on the broadcaster's prejudices. This approach is not journalism. It is political activism. In our hypothetical example Obama is portrayed as a hero, Trump as a villain. It all depends on those BBC narratives: *Obama is very, very good; Trump is very, very bad.* The Al-Jazeera article continues:

> By nature, an activist would be selective in his or her sources, materials and facts. This will present a distorted and partial snapshot of the issue.

> An activist tries to influence the debate whereas a journalist helps create an informed debate.

In the light of these comments let's consider another hypothetical situation. Imagine that Mr Trump makes the following comments in an interview regarding immigrants to the United States:

> Of course I don't like immigrants who disrespect our nation and our flag. But I do like are immigrants who respect our country and its values.

First and foremost a real journalist would consider such a speech in its entirety. In fact an impartial journalist might think the president's comments so self-evidently true for further comment to be unnecessary. Not so a political activist. An activist would carefully edit the speech to fit his/her pre-written narrative: *Trump is very, very bad* (master); *Trump hates immigrants* (sub-narrative).

Fake news would have a field day. Thus, headlines likely to appear all over CNN/BBC/Guardian/New York Times media platforms would read something along the following lines:

> Trump: I don't like immigrants

> Trump criticises immigrants

> Immigrants: Trump stokes up nationalist rhetoric

> Trump thinks immigrants "disrespect" American values

Trump: Immigrants "disrespect our nation and our flag"

Immigrants: Trump's comments welcomed by David Duke

By simply selecting those parts the speech which fit its narrative and by omitting those that do not Britain's impartial, free and fair broadcaster has a headline it can milk. Any corrections and retractions can of course be done quietly, at a later date, after the headlines has had its full impact. With few users likely to click through to the main story – the majority content to browse its headlines – and with fewer still bothering to locate and check the source and context of the original quotation, it's a win-win for fake news.

But that's not all. The crafty broadcaster has another trick up its sleeve. More often than not the BBC will attribute such headlines to CNN, *The New York Times* or other members of the United States' rabidly anti-Trump mainstream media. The reason is simple. Should the story be exposed for its fakery – a common enough occurrence - the BBC can shrug its shoulders and lay the blame squarely on CNN and friends: *We were only quoting what CNN said* . . . A double whammy: the broadcaster gets its smear, but without taking any of the responsibility.

'A message that has to be conveyed'

In contrast to journalists, propagandists have no intention of reporting facts. While a journalist starts the day with an open mind, the propagandist has already written the story. The difference between journalism that strives to be fair, objective and open-minded and political activism masquerading as journalism is set out in the example below (fig. 20) using one of the broadcaster's most cherished narratives: *the British police force is institutionally racist.*

Just like its view of the British working classes, the BBC is utterly convinced that the dark forces of racism are at work within the British constabulary. Lack of empirical evidence is not enough to deter the broadcaster's opinion either. The working class is racist. The British police force is also racist. In BBC land there the matter rests. It is then simply a case of finding whatever 'evidence' it can, no matter how scant. Extrapolation, whereby an outlier is identified, is the broadcaster's usual method of 'proving' its thesis to itself.

BBC activism	V	Objective journalism
The police are institutionally racist	**START POINT**	Are the police institutionally racist?
Amplification & suppression Misrepresentation Health-checks Smearing etc.	**PROCESS**	Investigative journalism Fidelity Balance Integrity etc.
The police are institutionally racist	**CONCLUSION**	The police may/may not be institutionally racist

Fig. 20

The comments which follow were made by Tim Hayward in response to a BBC Panorama documentary entitled 'Saving Syria's Children' which he maintains had 'manipulated' key facts. Having analysed BBC Panorama's methods, The Professor of Environmental Political Theory at Edinburgh University makes the following crucial distinction between the conduct of real journalists and those who could more appropriately be labelled political activists or propagandists:

> A journalist starts the day with a blank notepad and goes out to investigate what has been going on; she comes back with a report that she could not have anticipated producing at daybreak. A propagandist, by contrast, starts the day with a message that has to be conveyed and his task is to produce a report that most persuasively conveys that message.[3]

As we go through the following case studies it will be worth bearing in mind the very profound difference between journalists whose aim is to inform the debate, and those whose aim is purely to influence it.

'The obvious ones'

Among the BBC's favourite anti-Trump smears (of which there is an inexhaustible supply) for their sheer disingenuity and vindictiveness, two in particular stand out: *Trump mocked a disabled man and Trump said Mexicans are rapists and thieves.* You probably heard these memes repeated throughout the entire BBC media platform during 2016-2017 and beyond. There was just one small problem: Both smears were demonstrably false, the epitome of fake news. Nonetheless, the BBC never tired of repeating accusations that were as malicious as they were false.

In an article written for the BBC website in November 2016 ('US election: The Disunited States of America - whoever wins') North America editor Jon Sopel repeated just these very claims (and more) in a single paragraph. 'Where to start?' asked Sopel when discussing the 2016 US presidential campaign citing incidents he claimed, 'just boggle, confuse and occasionally fry the brain.'

> Well there are the obvious ones - Donald Trump describing Mexicans as thieves and rapists, him mocking a disabled person, disparaging POWs, wanting to ban all Muslims.[4]

Let's assess each of Mr Sopel's claims one by one. This will allow us to do several things: analyse Mr Trump's words and actions without the assistance of 'neutral' activists like Mr Sopel, and, just as importantly, to consider the context in which such words occurred – an endeavour Mr Sopel and his 20,000 plus colleagues, pressed for time as they are invariably are, never quite seem able to do: mention the context in which these remarks occurred. Those claims once more:

- Mr Trump mocked a disabled person
- Mr Trump described Mexicans as thieves and rapists
- Mr Trump wants to ban all Muslims
- Mr Trump disparages POWs

Claim #1 Mr Trump 'mocked a disabled person'

In a television interview of 2015 prospective US presidential candidate Donald Trump was quizzed over remarks he had made at a recent rally regarding reactions to the Twin Towers attacks of 2001, the worst terrorist atrocity ever carried out on American soil. In the interview, Mr Trump reiterated those comments to ABC's George Stephanopolous:

> There were people that were cheering on the other side of New Jersey, where you have large Arab populations. They were cheering as the World Trade Center came down. I know it might be not politically correct for you to talk about it, but there were people cheering, as those buildings came down . . .

The political landscape having undergone a seismic change since that horrific September afternoon, allied with a mainstream media intent on silencing any criticism of the Islamic faith and its followers as well as being dedicated to ending Mr Trump's run for presidential office, *The Washington Post* and friends seized on the billionaire's comments. No sooner had Mr Trump made his comments, and having apparently 'fact-checked' those same remarks, the Post *et al* predictably declared that no such events had ever happened. *Trump is lying, there were no celebrations in New Jersey after 9/11. American-Arabs had not celebrated the fall of the Twin Towers. Period.*

So when a contemporaneous news article surfaced which seemed to support Mr Trump's assertion, the mainstream media was not best pleased. In fact it was furious. And when it emerged that the article in question had appeared in the very same *Washington Post* now leading the anti-Trump charge of liar, liar pants on fire, not for the first time the newspaper had serious egg on its face. So much for the Post and its 'fact-checkers,' who had somehow failed to notice a crucial article written by one of its own journalists![5]

The article in question had been written by a certain Serge Kovaleski who, on September 18th 2001, just one week after the atrocity, reported that:

> In Jersey City, within hours of two jetliners' plowing into the World Trade Center, law enforcement authorities detained and questioned a number of people who were allegedly seen celebrating the attacks and holding tailgate-style parties on

rooftops while they watched the devastation on the other side of the river.[6]

In a subsequent article, Kovaleski confirmed the information he had used to write this article had been supplied to him by the Jersey City Police Department.

'No media reports'

Can you possibly guess what the BBC verdict on this one might possibly be? In an article impartially entitled, 'Donald Trump: 24 things the next president believes,' the broadcaster declared that:

> Donald Trump repeatedly claimed that on 11 September 2001, there were thousands of Arab-Americans celebrating in New Jersey after two planes flew into the Twin Towers. He says such public demonstrations "tell you something" about Muslims living in the US. However, there are **no media reports** to back up the claim.[7]

Two words immediately stand out in this BBC assertion: 'repeatedly' and 'thousands.' As far as we can ascertain (See for example the 2015 ABC interview just quoted) Mr Trump mentioned 'hundreds' and 'thousands' on just a single occasion, a rally at Alabama on 21 November 2015. Meanwhile the US president referenced the alleged celebrations on several other occasions without mentioning hundreds or indeed thousands. To claim therefore that Mr Trump 'repeatedly' made this claim is false. Notice also how the BBC choose to highlight 'thousands' rather than 'hundreds' in the above paragraph. We'll leave our readers to work out the impartial reason why that might be . . .

According to the BBC there were 'no media reports' (in bold no less!) No media reports apart that is from the by now infamous *Washington Post* media report of September 18, one of the most widely read newspapers in the world. A little bit of digging by independent journalists such as Mark Steyn revealed yet more contemporaneous media reports: New York radio stations WABC and WPLJ had carried reports.[8] Days after the attack, both *The San Francisco Chronicle* and *The New York Times* had carried reports detailing celebrations and the effect on community relations. CBS reporter Pablo Guzman told viewers that the FBI were investigating an apartment building that had been 'swarming with suspects' who had apparently cheered as the planes crashed into the Trade Centre.[9]

Three days after the attack in a column entitled 'The Issue is Radical Islam,' *The New York Post's* Fred Siegel observed that,:

> Here in New York, it was easy to get angry listening to
> Egyptians, Palestinians and the Arabs of nearby Paterson, N.J.,
> celebrate as they received word of the murderous attacks in
> New York and Washington.[10]

Interviewed on the David Letterman show on 17 September, Dan Rather had this to say about the celebrations which never took place:

> There are several reliable reports of one of these cells – a cell
> – across the Hudson River . . . and I don't know whether this is
> a fact – but there are several eye witnesses who say this
> happened – they got on the roof of the building to look across -
> they knew what was going to happen, they were waiting for it
> to happen, and when it happened they celebrated – they jumped
> for joy

'We did have some [reports of] celebrations,' observed former Mayor of New York, Rudy Giulliani, 'there were pockets of celebration, some in Queens, some in Brooklyn.'[11]

Semantics: the liberal backstop

Their anti-Trump narrative seriously wobbling, the liberal media started to play semantics. Hadn't the original *Washington Post* report stated that the celebrations were only 'alleged' and weren't there only 'a number of people' questioned?

For reasons not at all clear, the Post *et al* seemed to think these quibbles clinched their argument, irrefutable proof that Mr Trump *had not seen* reports about individuals celebrating the disaster.[12] Noting how the liberal media had deviously shifted its attack, Steyn succinctly observed:

So now we're no longer arguing about whether there were even any reports of any New Jersey residents celebrating 9/11, but merely the number that were doing so.[13]

Steyn had called it right. From initially denying any celebrations had ever occurred, the Post was now quibbling about *how many* people had allegedly celebrated the tragedy. The paper simply could not bear to admit that Mr Trump had been right.

Like many fellow New Yorkers Mr Trump recalled media reports that had implied that certain elements within New Jersey's American-Arab community might have indeed celebrated the tragedy.[14] By 2015 however telling the truth was no longer politically expedient. Despite the existence of his article, Kovaleski soon started to distance himself from it. There were bigger fish to fry. For the mainstream media, embarrassing Donald Trump was a far, far higher priority than objective and truthful reportage. Rabidly anti-Trump television networks checked their archives for 9/11 only to find . . . nothing.

Moreover, the writer now working for the anti-Trump *New York Times*, now made a claim that would play a crucial role in the mainstream media hysteria to follow. Kovaleski vaguely claimed to have met Mr Trump in person some time 'in the late 80s or early 90s.' Having met hundreds if not thousands of reporters and media people in the ensuing quarter of a century, it was a claim that the billionaire businessman, perhaps not unsurprisingly, would neither be able to confirm or deny.

At a South Carolina rally soon after Kovaleski and co had started what Mr Trump felt was a cynical ploy to undermine his integrity, in typical Trump style the tycoon hit back. When telling the crowd of Kovaleski's recent repudiation of his own journalism and with one eye firmly fixed on satire, Mr Trump launched into what looked like a generic impression of a back-tracking individual, in this case Mr Kovaleski. Arms flapping wildly while apologising incoherently, Mr Trump's act might not have been the most refined impression ever seen on an American stage, but the South Carolina crowd seemed to understand and enjoy the moment well enough. Unbeknownst to Mr Trump, the liberal-left media sharks were already circling. They smelt blood.

The MSM sting

Indeed, it didn't take anti-Trump entities long to concoct a sting that surpassed even their own low standards of morality. *Washington Post*, *New York Times*, CNN, BBC, a race to the bottom began in earnest.

Noting that Mr Kovaleski had a disability called arthrogryposis, a condition which locks the wrist into place rendering it immovable, and with a sinister seed already germinating in their minds, mainstream media hacks reviewed the footage of the Trump rally. Could they possibly frame the Republican candidate? Maybe. The hacks were looking for a specific moment – just one - a moment within Mr Trump's impression when the position of his right hand might *just* have resembled the disability of the man he was lampooning up there on the South Carolina podium. It was worth a try. Just imagine the propaganda value. After what must have been a painstaking frame by frame analysis of Mr Trump's performance, the media hacks got what they were looking for: a millisecond of footage in which Mr Trump's hand momentarily rested in a position similar to how Mr Kovaleski's disabled hand habitually rests. Bingo!

According to Kovaleski recall, he and Trump had met long, long ago in the mists of time. It was a claim not lost on the media. Mr Trump therefore must have known all about the disability, must have remembered the precise nature of how Mr Kovaleski's disability manifests itself in the wrist of his right arm – if nothing else a quite stupendous feat of memory, that is assuming Mr Trump and Mr Kovaleski had indeed met all those years ago. Then, the presidential candidate had seemingly decided to perform a tasteless skit of a disabled man in front of not only a worldwide television audience, but in front of a censorious public and a psychotic anti-Trump media, presumably some form of latent suicidal tendency. It made complete sense, at least in the morally bankrupt minds of mainstream media hacks. Activists from the liberal-left media – from CNN to the BBC – were beside themselves with anticipation.

The sting was on. Could it possibly get any more cynical? In their zeal to smear the property mogul, the liberal hacks were only too happy to exploit Mr Kovaleski's disability. No matter, they had their smear. As Saul Alinsky always maintained, and as Communists have proven time after time, the end always justifies the means.

And what a smear! Donald Trump mocking a disabled man! Everywhere you looked . . . CNN, NBC, BBC, *Guardian, Washington Post, New York Times,* the newly created image of Mr Trump and Mr Kovaleski juxtaposed next to one another appeared. Hilary Clinton wasted no time denouncing Mr Trump. Neither did Hollywood. In fact the pious and the sanctimonious from Madonna to former actor Robert de Niro were lining up to take shots. As smears get, they didn't get any more destructive. Why, it was almost too good to be true . . .

'An attack so exaggerated and perverse that a child should have seen through it, and yet just plausible enough to fill one with an alarmed feeling that other people, less level-headed than oneself, might be taken in by it.'[15]

The BBC Claim

Naturally, the BBC could hardly wait to spread this most cynical piece of fake news throughout its entire network. A selection of BBC News headlines which followed:

Donald Trump criticised for mocking reporter with disability

Donald Trump denies mocking disabled reporter

257

Donald Trump under fire for mocking disabled reporter

If the sheer number of BBC headlines did not convince you of Mr Trump's basic lack of humanity, the message that invariably followed such proclamations surely would. Notice how Mr Trump's guilt in the following generic paragraph that appeared on many of its reports is taken for granted by the impartial, free and fair 'national' broadcaster:

> Mr Trump performed an impression of Serge Kovaleski, who suffers from a congenital joint condition, at a rally in South Carolina.

There was however just one small detail: it was NOT an impression of Mr Kovaleski; it was actually an impression of nobody in particular and as such one performed many times by Mr Trump over the years. Had it taken the trouble to carry out appropriate checks, the BBC nor any other impartial observer could possibly have reached the conclusion that Donald Trump mocked a reporter's disability. In short, had the BBC just simply performed the role of journalists rather than political activists it would have concluded that Mr Trump was mocking an individual based on his ungallant behaviour *not* his disability.

But the BBC was not going to let this outrageous slur disappear without first extracting maximum smear value from it. Eighteen months after the alleged impression occurred (and almost as long after it had been thoroughly debunked) the BBC was still regurgitating one of its favourite smears when covering the 2017 Oscars, where it made a special point of noting how Meryl Streep 'referred to Trump's mocking of a disabled reporter . . .'[16]

We didn't say Trump mocked a disabled reporter, Meryl Streep did. We're just reminding you, in case you had forgotten . . .

'All his impressions look the same'
Debunking this BBC smear is child's play. The US-based political commentator Anne Coulter it was who drew attention to some research by a group called Catholics 4 Trump. The group noticed that Mr Trump had performed the exact mime – arms flailing wildly, incoherent mumbling – later in the same South Carolina speech when imitating a US

General of whom he was also directing criticism. Thus, the routine was clearly not a Serge Kovaleski impression as the BBC claimed.

Further research by the group revealed Mr Trump performing exactly the same mannerisms at an earlier rally when the billionaire had imitated Republican rival, Senator Ted Cruz. He had also performed the gestures at subsequent events.[17] Juvenile as some may find such mannerisms it soon transpired that Mr Trump's gestures are regularly deployed when the US president is referencing individuals of whom he disapproves, part of a satirical routine let's call them. For the record, neither the US General nor Ted Cruz have disabilities.

In her article, 'Media invented lie about Trump mocking disabled reporter,' Coulter notes that:

> If a jury ever saw these videos, it would acquit Trump immediately. Trump's impression of a groveling reporter is just like his imitation of a groveling general and just like his imitation of a groveling U.S. senator. He's like Rich Little that way: All his impressions look the same.[18]

Coulter continues:

> The media knew damn well that Trump does the arm-waving routine whenever he's pretending to be a flustered person. But they never allowed the public to see the clip of Trump doing the same imitation of a general. That is proof that the media knew they were lying.

Ms. Coulter went on to note how the media purposely hid Mr Kovaleski from view once the row erupted. Usually the likes of CNN and the rest of their anti-Trump colleagues cannot wait to parade the latest Trump 'victim' on national television, however slight the accusation might be. Only not this time.

There was a very simple explanation for this reticence: The liberal-left media knew that the moment the public saw Mr Kovaleski in real life, the moment it saw the actual extent of his disability, its little ruse would fall flat on its dishonest face – even without viewing the raft of video evidence of previous performances. While Mr Trump's routine always involves waving his arms around Mr Kovaleski's wrist is fully locked into one position. It never moves. Mr Trump's 'impression' and his alleged target's disability are, in fact, worlds apart but the dishonest liberal media already knew this. Hence, it ensured that the only image the public got to see of Mr Kovaleski was the one it had deliberately concocted – the still of him juxtaposed next to President Trump.

Crude, yes, but as a means of inflaming the social justice mob, as far as Jon Sopel and the BBC were – *are still* - concerned, a most effective tactic nonetheless. How then to explain Mr Sopel and the rest of his BBC colleague's behaviour? There are two possible explanations: Either they knew all along that Mr Trump had not mocked a reporter's disability, but ever-eager to report the very worst about the US president went ahead and reported fake news anyway; or they had simply not done enough 'fact-checking' in the first place – a prime example of lazy, sloppy reporting.

We know from Quentin Sommerville's reply to *The Sun* that unlike some media organisations the BBC doesn't do sloppy or 'lazy' journalism. So that only leaves the first option. Sopel and the rest of his BBC colleagues deliberately and knowingly reported what they knew to be fake news. An ethical journalist meanwhile might have reported events thus: *A picture circulating around social media purports to show Donald Trump performing a skit of a disabled reporter at a recent rally. However, Mr Trump performed the same routine later in the same rally to mock an American general. He has also performed the same gestures to mock Senator Ted Cruz. It would seem therefore that Mr Trump is not mocking the man's disability.* Jon Sopel's version? 'Trump mocked a disabled man.'

Claim #2 'Mr Trump described Mexicans as thieves and rapists'

Cars reflect national characteristics... a Mexican car's just going to be a lazy, feckless, flatulent oaf with a moustache, leaning against a fence asleep, looking at a cactus with a blanket with a hole in the middle on as a coat.

BBC Top Gear, Series 16

'Offensive, xenophobic, humiliating remarks'

As offensive as these remarks had been Britain's 'national' broadcaster had not quite finished its stereotyping of Mexicans. Later in the same programme another Top Gear host claimed that Mexican food resembled 'refried sick' and 'sick with cheese on it.'

These comments so incensed Eduardo Medina Mora, Mexico's Ambassador to the UK, he wrote to the BBC demanding an apology accusing the presenters of stirring 'bigoted feelings against the Mexican people.' The joke had not gone down particularly well with its targets. 'These offensive, xenophobic and humiliating remarks,' continued Mora, 'only serve to reinforce negative stereotypes and perpetuate prejudice against Mexico and its people.'[19]

Mr Sopel's second claim is just as easy to debunk as his first, if not more so. Did Donald Trump really say that Mexicans are thieves and rapists? With a population of around 125 million that's an awful lot of potential rapists and thieves. *Brainwashing Britain* got to work doing that thing the BBC most fears (and would dearly love to impair) independent research.

At this juncture we'll start by making the observation that Mexicans is the plural form of the noun (Mexican + s). Such plural forms are used in English to represent generic categories e.g. 'cats like milk' when 'cats' represents the entire class of animal. In this instance we are thinking of cats generically. It's a distinction worth bearing in mind over the pages that follow.

'Cross border criminal activity'

To media behemoths such as CNN and BBC context can only ever dilute the carefully selected memes used to represent a story. As with the Kovaleski smear, the BBC and friends would very much prefer for you not to delve too deep into its proclamations – with good reason. Even a cursory check of the context surrounding this ubiquitous BBC meme reveals several key facts the broadcaster consistently failed to mention in its multitude of anti-Trump Mexican propaganda pieces.

Its own Mexican stereotyping notwithstanding ('lazy, feckless and flatulent oafs') the irony-free broadcaster never tired of repeating Mr Sopel's claim. Let's have a look then at the comments that so enraged the BBC from a speech made by Mr Trump on 26 June 2015:

When Mexico sends its people, they're not sending their best. They're sending people that have lots of problems, and they're bringing those problems with us. They're bringing drugs. They're bringing crime. They're rapists. And some, I assume, are good people.

There. Mr Trump's original words, and thanks to the Internet summoned up in just a matter of seconds. Is it any wonder that the BBC is at the forefront of leading the charge to censor the free flow of information on the World Wide Web?

Take a look at those words again: 'They're not sending us their best.' What could Mr Trump have possibly meant? The distinction is clear enough: the president is not referring to those Mexican citizens who enter the US legally, but rather those who enter the country's southern border *illegally*.[20] Along with its impartial counterparts such as CNN, the BBC omitted to inform its audiences that these comments were made by Mr Trump during a speech the focus of which was illegal migration from Mexico into the United States. Nonetheless, it suited the broadcaster's purposes to detach these comments from their context. Mr Sopel's claim is thus already unravelling. His implication that the president was describing Mexicans generically – all Mexicans (Mexican + s) – as criminals is, even under cursory scrutiny, patently false.

Who then was Mr Trump referring to? The president was in fact specifically talking about the tens of thousands of illegal aliens who flout US immigration law and who are, by definition, committing a criminal act. Note that Mr Trump clearly differentiates this group who bring with them problems from 'the best' – those Mexican (and other) nationals who enter the US via the appropriate legal protocols. Within the former group – illegals - Mr Trump concedes that there are also 'good' people. Thus, we already have at least four distinct categories of (Mexican) people, at least according to the US president:

- Mexicans who do not emigrate to the United States, legally or illegally – i.e. the vast majority of Mexico's 123,000,000 citizens
- Illegal Mexican immigrants (not Mexico's 'best') Approximately 192,000 illegal crossings in 2016[21]

- Illegal Mexican immigrants ('some good people') from the same 192,000 figure.
- Legal Mexican immigrants who enter the US via proper immigration protocols ('best people') 150,000 in 2016[22]

Thus Mr Trump's comments were specifically made in reference to the 192,000 immigrants illegally entering the US in 2016, a tiny fraction of Mexico's overall population.

Having made the sort of distinctions that Mr Sopel and friends in the legacy media were determined to ignore at any cost, next we turn to the United States Department for Home Security (DHS) the agency charged with among other duties immigration control and management. Just ten months into Mr Trump's tenure as US president the DHS reported that Homeland Security Investigations had:

> Conducted 32,958 total criminal arrests and seized $524 million in illicit currency and assets over the course of investigations into human smuggling and trafficking
> , cybercrime, transnational gang activity, narcotics enforcement
> , human smuggling and other types of cross-border criminal activity.[23]

The extent of 'cross-border criminal activity' is truly staggering. Those Mexicans involved in these activities are not Mexico's 'best' people according to Mr Trump. But Jon Sopel and his colleagues already knew this – or if they did not would have heard plenty of anecdotal evidence regarding the very real issues of drug and gang-related crime in and around the United States' southern border.

Was Mr Trump right then in assuming that a significant number of those entering the US illegally are or have been involved in criminal activity? Yes, according to ICE (U.S. Immigration and Customs Enforcement) who reported that: 92 percent (101,722) of aliens ICE arrested between January 20, 2017 and the end of FY2017, were:

> Removable aliens who had a criminal conviction or a pending criminal charge, were an ICE fugitive, or were an illegal re-entrant.

The same individuals who Mr Trump had declared were 'bringing problems' to the US. Had Mr Sopel and his colleagues engaged in some rudimentary journalistic research they too might have discovered these facts for themselves. President Trump was certainly making good on his promise to protect US citizens - much to BBC fury. Everybody was a winner, apart from the criminals of course. The DHS statement ended on the topic of employee satisfaction:

> In addition to these improved numbers, the Federal Employee
> Viewpoint Survey (FEVS) results for CBP and ICE personnel
> significantly improved this year, reflecting that the
> Administration is allowing them to faithfully execute their
> duties and fully enforce the law.

In other words, thanks to the Trump administration, for the first time in a long time US immigration personnel were achieving results, and more importantly, as a result of their efforts America was becoming a safer place.

'The widespread mischaracterisation of his words is stunning'

So, did Donald Trump say 'Mexicans are rapists and thieves?' No, he never said (or even implied) that (all) Mexicans are rapists or thieves. By purposely reporting Mr Trump's statement out of its original context the BBC activist could nonetheless imply that the businessman was talking about *all* Mexicans. That a proportion of immigrants are forced to cross the US-Mexico border illegally is because a significant number have been involved in previous criminal activity: drugs, guns, prostitution and even murder (not the 'best' people).

There were however only a few lone voices of integrity in what became a mainstream media feeding frenzy, real journalists guided not by anti-Trump narratives but by journalistic principles of integrity and fairness:

> About this time, Trump is beginning to get pounded mercilessly
> in the media for saying 'all Mexicans are rapists.' Except he never
> said that. The widespread mischaracterisation of his words is
> stunning from my viewpoint as a traditional journalist.[24]

Stunning is indeed the word. This is because mainstream media activists from CNN to the BBC deliberately chose to misinterpret Trump's very precise words. Truth did not matter. What mattered was the chance to smear, to inflame and manipulate. 'The media needs to stop telling this lie about Donald Trump,' said University of Texas at Austin History professor Alberto Martinez, 'I'm a Sanders supporter and value honesty. Trump's words on Mexicans have been misconstrued by all sides. This liberal, Puerto Rican professor says enough.'[25] On claims that Mr Trump had called Mexicans 'thieves and rapists,' Martinez said, 'That's not what he said. That's not what he meant. It was just a remark about some of the criminals crossing the border.'

Nonetheless, Mr Sopel and his colleagues persisted in spreading this damaging piece of fake news at every opportunity much to the consternation of real journalists. 'Professor Martinez and I are lone voices in the wilderness,' wrote Sharryl Attkisson. 'The media would largely continue misconstruing Trump's words and position on this issue throughout the campaign and beyond.'[26]

What Jon Sopel should have reported were words to the effect that: *Mr Trump claims a high percentage of Mexicans illegally crossing the border could be involved in criminal activity*. But he couldn't. He couldn't do this because such a statement would have been factually correct and would have thus had no propaganda value for the BBC: Trump said Mexicans are thieves and rapists . . .

Claim #3 Mr Trump 'wants to ban all Muslims'

For this claim, we start with a selection of BBC news website headlines:

An unjust and discriminatory Muslim ban, US group says

Trump Muslim ban plan erased from website

The World Tonight: Outcry over Trump's 'Muslim ban'

The Newsroom: UK MP Condemns US Muslim Ban

bbc.co.uk

BBC hysteria reached fever pitch when in January of 2017 the Trump administration announced a temporary travel ban (90 days) applicable to nationals of seven 'countries of concern' as identified by previous US administrations. Iran, Iraq, Libya, Somalia, Sudan, Syria and Yemen had been identified by counter-terrorism agencies as countries involved in harbouring suspected terrorist groups.

Typically, the BBC immediately dubbed the measure a 'Muslim ban.' Inflammatory, disingenuous and just plain wrong this one had all the hallmarks of a classic BBC smear.

'Trump wants to ban all Muslims'
Did Donald Trump's administration want to 'ban all Muslims?' Not according to the facts:

Largest Muslim countries	Population	Subject to Trump's 'Muslim ban'
Indonesia	209,000,000	X
Pakistan	176,000,000	X
India	167,000,000	X
Bangladesh	134,000,000	X
Nigeria	77,000,000	X
Egypt	77,000,000	X
Iran	74,000,000	✓
Turkey	71,000,000	X
Algeria	35,000,000	X
Morocco	32,000,000	X

Fig. 21 Source: World Atlas

From the perspective of the world's most populous Muslim countries, Mr Trump's 'Muslim ban' applied to just 74,000,000 people from a combined population of over one billion (1,052,000,000) or just 7% of the total.

In terms of the public, the temporary travel ban had widespread support. A Politico/Morning Consult poll of May 2017 revealed that 60%

of respondents supported the ban pertaining to seven countries considered to be incubators of terrorist groups.27 Back in BBC land, eager for the US president to use the words 'Muslim ban' but thus far disappointed, the impartial broadcaster simply decided to put these very words into the president's mouth:

@BBC News (World)
'Orlando justifies my Muslim ban 'says Donald Trump.

This particular headline appeared on the BBC news website after a gunman – Omar Mateen – had opened fire on a gay nightclub in Orlando, Florida killing 49 people and injuring 53 others. In the aftermath of the incident the US president renewed calls for a temporary restriction on travel to the US from known terrorist incubating countries – a move, as we have already noted, that had widespread support in the United States at least among the American public 57% of whom supported the proposed measure in the latest polls ('Most Support Temporary Ban on Newcomers from Terrorist Havens').28

Addressing an audience in Manchester, New Hampshire on June 13, the day after the attack Mr Trump had made an impassioned speech about the state of US immigration in which he affirmed his determination to tighten US immigration policy and procedures. The BBC's Anthony Zurcher responded directly to the speech with a typically measured and objective anti-Trump hit-piece bizarrely entitled, 'Orlando justifies my Muslim ban.'29

But where precisely had that highly inflammatory attention-grabbing quotation come from? When had Mr Trump said such words? As far as can be ascertained, President Trump (nor any member of his administration) has ever referred to the temporary travel ban placed upon seven terrorist-incubating countries, as a 'Muslim ban' or indeed 'my' or 'our Muslim ban.' Could this headline then be an archetypal example of fake news? Look at that headline again and note how it is presented by the BBC as a direct quotation from the American president:

'Orlando justifies my Muslim ban' says Trump

So exactly where and when did Mr Trump allegedly say, 'Orlando justifies my Muslim ban?'

We at *Brainwashing Britain* have watched Mr Trump's New Hampshire speech over and over again, but as yet have not heard him utter the words attributed to him by Mr Zurcher and the BBC. Had the BBC been listening properly? Not once in the 32-minute speech does Mr Trump mention a 'Muslim ban' belonging to either him or anyone else in his administration. What the Republican presidential candidate does say however is:

> I will suspend immigration from areas of the world where there is a proven history of terrorism against the United States, Europe or our allies . . .

'Orlando justifies my Muslim ban?' It would appear that Mr Trump said no such words. As we have seen, the impartial broadcaster sometimes mishears certain statements.. The fact that it just so happens to mishear words – key words – when the American president speaks ('War will follow') or, as on this occasion, invents entirely new phrases which it attributes to him - is presumably a common enough mistake in any busy, politically neutral news room.

While not once mentioning 'my Muslim ban' – the quote attributed to him by the BBC, Mr Trump does speak about 'Muslim communities,' 'Muslim allies' and 'Muslim countries.' The BBC however did not seem too interested in this part of the president's speech. Wrong narrative perhaps? As the BBC activist did not reply to our request for clarification we can only assume the broadcaster had somehow inadvertently mixed up its quotes. It happens.

Things you don't see on the BBC
So where did the seven countries on Mr Trump's so-called 'Muslim ban' originate? They had in fact been identified as potential threats to US (and world) safety before Donald Trump ever arrived in The White House. The nations in question had been drawn from the Terrorist Prevention Act of 2015 compiled by . . . the Obama administration. The 2015 'Visa Waiver Program Improvement and Terrorist Travel Prevention Act of 2015' named Sudan, Iran, Syria and Iraq while Libya. Somalia and Yemen were added to the list in 2016.

Where	When	What	Who
Syria	1979	'State sponsor of terrorism'	Carter (Democrat)
Iran	1984	'State sponsor of terrorism'	Reagan (Republican)
Sudan	1993	'State sponsor of terrorism'	Clinton (Democrat)
Iraq	2015	'Country of concern'	Obama (Democrat)
Libya Somalia Yemen	2016	'Country of concern'	Obama (Democrat)

Fig. 22

Indeed, six out of the seven countries had been designated as 'state sponsors of terrorism' or 'countries of concern' not by Donald Trump and the Republican Party, but rather by previous Democrat administrations. For reasons best known to himself, Mr Sopel (and the BBC) had not so much as even blinked when Obama's Democrats had first identified the potential terror threats from these countries.

Sopel's claim – that 'Mr Trump wants to ban all Muslims' - was unravelling, and fast. Moreover, the temporary travel suspension was not absolute. There were in fact several exceptions. The Departments of State and Homeland Security could also grant exceptions on a 'case-by-case basis,' and 'when in the national interest, issue visas or other immigration benefits to nationals of countries for which visas and benefits are otherwise blocked.'[30] Indeed, the word 'Muslim' is not mentioned once in the entire Executive Order.

Claim #4 'Mr Trump disparages POWs'

Mr Sopel's fourth assertion has more substance than his other three claims, though based on what we have seen thus far that would not be very difficult.

When discussing veteran Republican senator John McCain during a television interview, the conversation turned to the octogenarian's disputed war record with Mr Trump remarking: '[John McCain] is a hero because he was captured. I like people who weren't captured.'

Mr Trump's comment here certainly suggests a critical attitude towards those military personnel unfortunate enough to be captured and held by the enemy as prisoners of war ('I like people who weren't captured.') Based on that comment we find ourselves in partial agreement with Mr Sopel with regards to this particular claim. Partial because by selecting 'disparages' (present simple tense) rather than 'disparaged' (past simple tense) Mr Sopel is hoping to plant in his reader's minds the suggestion that Mr Trump criticises POWs *habitually* which he does not. The McCain comment was, as far as we can tell, a one-off. Thus, the correct terminology should have read: Mr Trump 'disparaged' POWs i.e. on a single occasion.

If Brainwashing Britain were the BBC . . .

But in true BBC fashion might we not now try to mitigate the evidence in some way as the corporation invariably does for the Clintons, Obamas and Democrats of this world or anyone else it supports? Let's go into damage limitation mode. Taking our cue from the BBC, in an attempt to deflect attention away from our inconvenient conclusion we could conceivably have started this, our analysis of Mr Sopel's fourth claim, with evidence suggesting there is strong support for Mr Trump in the US military and within its veteran community. Taking out another leaf from the BBC playbook we could then have sneaked our admission in a single, solitary paragraph towards the end of the text.

Let's imagine for a moment then that having found a Sopel-claim we had to agree with, however irksome we found it, we at the 'impartial, free and fair' Brainwashing Britain simply decided to adopt our default position: bury that which does not agree with our narrative, or failing that try every trick we know in an effort to discredit it. If we had wished to mislead our readers, this is how we might have opened our fourth point a la BBC:

> Research by Yougov.com shows Mr Trump enjoys strong
> support among US military veterans: 'Donald Trump's support
> remains high following John McCain controversy.'[31]

How about that for a positive spin? By starting on such an upbeat note we are already half-way to mitigating Mr Sopel's claim. If military veterans support Mr Trump, what's the problem here? We could have then gone on to make a meal out of some of the data from this poll, ensuring that the data we selected cast Mr Trump in as positive a light as possible.

We could certainly have ensured that our readers came across the following point made by YouGov when discussing the difference in popularity between Mr Trump and Mr McCain in the eyes of US military veterans, some of whom might well have been POWs themselves or known colleagues who had been:

> Even more striking, veterans and those currently in the military are more likely to have favourable views of Trump than to have favourable views of McCain. 41% say they have favourable views of McCain, while more than half are favourable to Trump

So far so good. Do you see what we are doing here? We're softening the admission that must surely come – sooner or later – that Mr Sopel has called one of his four claims correctly, painful and as gloomy as that makes us feel.

But why hurry? We don't need to make that admission just yet. There's plenty of time. Maybe people will get bored, not bother reading the whole article – and even if they do we'll have exposed them to so much positive spin the impact will hardly be that great.

Next, we could have turned to research carried out by *Military Times*, a specialist publication aimed as the name implies at US armed forces personnel and which informs its readers that:

> President Donald Trump enjoys far stronger support among members of the military than the American public at large, according to the latest scientific Military Times poll.[32]

Following on from this we could have obtained some plaudits about the US Commander in Chief from some pro-Trump groups such as Veterans for Trump, who could have told us all about their respect and admiration for the 45th US president and how he would never knowingly disparage POWs – he loves the military far too much for that etc. And then, finally, right at the end of our glowing article, we could have sneaked in the comment about John McCain. We could have gone even further: we could, in our summary, have cast doubt as to whether Mr Trump actually even *said* the words in the first place – pure BBC trickery. And of course there would be no need to trouble ourselves with actually repeating those original words – no need at all – people might get the wrong idea ('I like people who weren't captured'). We'd very much prefer our readers were not reminded of those particular words.

To undermine Mr Sopel's case further we could have used some choice language and grammar to describe Mr McCain (e.g. 'enemy' 'harsh critic') in the hope that such a tactic would further undermine the case against Mr Trump. From here we could even have slipped in some sly nudges about Mr McCain's disputed war record.

Thus in next to no time we could easily soon have arrived at a paragraph modelled on the BBC school of 'journalism:'

> Mr Sopel was referring to comments said to have been made
> by Mr Trump about his Republican enemy and harsh critic,
> Senator John McCain. McCain, whose war record has been
> criticised . . .

Do you see what we did there? Just by our choice of language, focus and presentation of the piece we've turned a potentially damaging claim by Mr Sopel into something far less harmful. 'Comments said to have been made?' Did Mr Trump say these words or not? We're really not that sure. We can't corroborate Mr Sopel's claims one way or the other, just like the BBC couldn't corroborate whether Mr Trump had spoken to the disabled child J K Rowling swore he had ignored.

Easy when you know how.

In just a couple of sentences we've practically neutralised Sopel's sting. Had we been propagandists this is what we could have so easily done. We could have done all these things and more, but no; although we appreciate the BBC's chicanery and ruses as much as the next hacktivist, we at *Brainwashing Britain* do not wish to tread a similar path. Thus we can conclude:

Sopel says	Reality check
Trump mocked a disabled man	False
Trump wants to ban all Muslims	False
Trump says Mexicans are rapists and thieves	False
Trump disparages POWs	True and false

Fig. 23

US commentator Laura Ingraham it was who summarised how, in their desire to misrepresent Mr Trump, the mask was slipping from so-called journalists:

> **@IngrahamAngle**
> The activists masquerading as "objective" journos have never been truly exposed before by a politician bef @realDonaldTrump came along

As the case of the BBC's, North America Editor goes to show, Ms Ingram had called it correctly. Another beauty.

Harlow: A Brexit 'hate crime'

We are open in acknowledging mistakes when they are made
and encourage a culture of willingness to learn from them.[1]

bbc.co.uk

I t was just another Saturday night in Harlow, an unremarkable town situated about 30 miles north east of London. At 11.30pm people were still milling around the town's shopping precinct – the first of its kind in the UK to be pedestrianised. Some were heading home from the pub or going on to clubs. Others were stopping off for takeaways. Picked up by CCTV groups of teenagers hung around chatting, messing around on bicycles, showing off the way teenagers do. It was, in every respect, a typical August evening. And then something dreadful occurred.

The group of teenagers became involved in a dispute with Arkadiusz Jozwik, a 39-year old Polish national. A punch was thrown. Mr Jozwik fell to the ground, hitting his head on the concrete whereupon he was immediately rushed to hospital. Two days later the unfortunate man died of his injuries. As bland and scant as they might have seemed, those were the facts. There was nothing to do but to treat Mr Jozwik's death with the dignity it deserved while allowing the authorities to go about their business of piecing together the events of this tragic evening. Until, that is the BBC rocked up into town.

What is Fake News?
Stories that may have some truth to them, but the facts aren't
clear or checked properly, or the writer has exaggerated some of
it to mean what they want it to.

bbc.co.uk

'The fear is that this was a frenzied racist attack triggered by the Brexit referendum,' announced the BBC 6 'o clock news on 31 August. 'A Polish man beaten to death in Essex,' declared BBC's Newsnight programme later that same evening, 'could it be the latest example of hate crime post-Brexit?' Leaving aside the deliberate exaggeration (Is it even possible to be 'beaten to death' with a single punch?) the attempt to link the incident to Brexit was pure speculation and thus little more than a deliberate attempt to mislead. 'Harlow 'hate crime' murder: Arek Jozwik's family devastated,' so read the headline on the BBC news website.'[2] The dust might not have yet settled on this tragic event and police were investigating several leads, but the BBC were already amplifying the lead – one of several lines of investigation - which most suited their own post-Brexit 'hate crime' agenda, which read: Brexit has unleashed a wave of 'hate' crimes throughout the UK. *Brexit is very, very bad...*

Coming just weeks after the UK's vote to leave the European Union, the ever-respectful BBC had seized upon this tragic story with what can only be described as relish. Mr Jozwik's death received the kind of attention reserved for the demise of royalty. After months of searching, did the BBC finally have a 'hate' crime it could blame upon Brexit?

Ever since the June 23 vote to leave the EU the broadcaster had been pushing a narrative calculated to stoke the fires of fear and division: *Brexit is very, very bad* (master narrative) *People who voted for Brexit are racist and xenophobic* (sub-narrative). Just days after the vote and the BBC had already started to amplify this narrative wherever possible. 'Polish media in UK shocked by post-Brexit hate crimes' announced the BBC website on June 28th:

> Britain's Polish community has been left shocked by incidents
> of hate crime reported since the British referendum to leave
> the EU.[3]

The article went on to catalogue a host of anecdotal reports of 'abuse' that had 'appeared widely on social media in the UK.' The BBC then duly amplified a *Guardian* article claiming UK Poles were 'absolutely terrified' to be in post-Brexit Britain. And yet while all this BBC hysteria was going on the police investigation had not even reached preliminary conclusions regarding what had actually led to this senseless tragedy.

So when the BBC's John Sweeney arrived in Harlow in the aftermath of the tragedy, the Newsnight reporter did so with the objective of pushing the post-Brexit 'hate' crime angle for all it was worth. His mission was simple: to link the tragedy somehow – anyhow –

to Brexit. Though police had stressed hate crime motivation was just one of several possible lines of enquiry, Sweeney's report, which aired on the September 1st edition of Newsnight, had eyes (and ears) for only one possible explanation. 'It's concerning that the widespread media are reporting this as a hate crime,' said Detective Chief Inspector Martin Pasmore of Essex Police, 'when in fact that is no more than one line of inquiry in a number of inquiries, which we are delving into to try and establish the truth.'[4]

The BBC activist however wasted no time in introducing his thesis. In the opening of his report he declared that the tragedy had 'implications' for the 'politics of identity in Britain today.' Talk about jumping the gun. Was Sweeney privy to information not available to the police? How else could he make such a sweeping and unproven generalisation? Anyone unfortunate enough to encounter a group of youths looking for trouble late at night will testify that 'identity' has little or nothing to do with their motivations. Often sparked by excessive alcohol consumption, violent flashpoints have long been an unwanted feature of town centres up and down the country - never more so than on week-ends. Mr Jozwik's death might have borne all the hallmarks of anti-social behaviour of the very worst kind, but such facts were not going to stop the BBC from prosecuting its own preferred anti-Brexit narrative.

Fake news was simmering. It was about to be stirred by Britain's 'national' broadcaster.

The BBC's hate crime 'epidemic'

But what about the 'surge' in incidents of 'hate' crimes? Did not that prove the EU vote had unleashed visceral feelings only held in check by virtue of Britain's membership of the bloc? Weren't certain sections of British society just waiting for a green light to enable them to let loose these bottled up, hateful feelings kept in check only thanks to EU membership? The BBC seemed to think so.

However, in its haste to prove a hate-crime explosion there were a few crucial aspects in terms of context the broadcaster had not examined. While the BBC grimly reported on hate-crime 'surges' and 'epidemics' many people had reservations. Writing in *The Spectator*, Brendan O'Neil suggested that the post-Brexit 'spike' in hate crime incidents was, 'likely down to the fact that various officials actively trawled for evidence of hate post-Brexit, imploring people to phone police hotlines . . .'5 O'Neil was referring not to an increase in actual crimes, but rather to a 'spike' in the ways and means of reporting such crimes with a plethora of organisations in their eagerness to report incidents, looking and sounding ever more like ambulance chasers. 'What the BBC calls an 'epidemic,' continued O'Neil, 'is a product of the authorities redefining racism and prejudice to such an extent that almost any unpleasant encounter between people of different backgrounds can now be recorded as 'hatred.'

With various bodies touting for hate-crime business in the wake of the referendum, reporting of such crimes had indeed never been easier: no evidence required, no questions, no doubts – just a matter of completing (anonymously if desired) an online questionnaire provided by organisations like True Vision. Worryingly, these self-reporting systems contain no safeguards or checks to prevent against the inclusion of false or erroneous reports. Nor are the problems of subjectivity addressed. After all, one person's hate crime can be another's misunderstanding. The rubric of the police's 'Hate Crimes Operational Guidance' admits as much:

> The perception of the victim, or any other person, is the defining factor... the victim does not have to justify or provide evidence of their belief, and police officers or staff should not directly challenge this perception.

The key word is of course *perception*. That no evidence is required would surely trouble anyone of even mildly libertarian disposition. And so in a climate where people were being positively encouraged to report 'perceptions' a spike in hate crimes duly appeared. For example, three days after the June 23 referendum, the BBC duly reported a much-cited incident of 'post-Brexit hate crime.'6 Racist graffiti had allegedly been scrawled on the walls of the Polish Social and Cultural Association in Hammersmith, West London. Subsequently, the graffiti had been washed off the centre's walls. What then had the graffiti said: Go Home Poles? Poles not welcome? Strangely, BBC reports never mentioned the actual content of the message. The reason for this omission may or may not have had something to do with the rather obscure nature of a message which read: "F**k you OMP." So who or what is OMP? The OMP is in fact a centre-right Polish think-tank that supported Britain's decision to leave the EU. That this supposed hate-crime had in all likelihood therefore been committed by Polish nationals living in the UK was not, of course, part of any BBC narrative. It was yet another 'post-Brexit hate crime.' Britain's impartial, free and fair broadcaster didn't fancy digging too deep either, not when it came to its beloved hate crimes.

BBC 'epidemic' or self-fulfilling prophecy?

Far from witnessing the 'ugly' post-Brexit June 23rd landscape insisted on by Sweeney and the BBC, the vast majority of communities seemed to be getting on with their lives much as they had done on June 22nd. No, the BBC was adamant, the UK was in the midst of what it termed a 'hate-crime epidemic.' Had the UK really become the nasty, intolerable place overnight that the 'national' broadcaster insisted it was, or was this merely wish fulfilment of an overwhelmingly pro-EU media with the BBC at its helm?

As observed by Civitas and others, perceptions not actual crimes had increased.[7] In an atmosphere made febrile by a media determined to facilitate a hate crime 'epidemic,' people had indeed started to report perceptions. The mainstream media's hate-crime epidemic, ceaselessly propagated by the BBC, bore all the hallmarks of a phenomenon well known to psychologists:

> The self-fulfilling prophecy is, in the beginning, a false definition of the situation evoking a new behaviour which make the original false conception come true. This specious validity of the self-fulfilling prophecy perpetuates a reign of error. For the prophet will cite the actual course of events as proof that he was right from the very beginning.[8]

This type of behaviour was witnessed most infamously during the Salem witch trials. After one witch had supposedly been identified, numerous other testimonies followed in quick succession with the result that a hitherto small unassuming village suddenly became overnight, witchcraft central. A very vicious circle had been set in motion. It was one in which any accusation, however ridiculous, could now be given credence. Revealingly, this exceedingly common phenomenon – the self-fulfilling prophecy – was never considered by the BBC *et al* as a possible explanation for its sudden 'epidemic' for a single moment; to have done so would have rather spoilt this, its most cherished anti-Brexit narrative.

Indeed, in the weeks that followed the broadcaster pushed its hate crime narrative for all it was worth despite the tentative nature of police enquiries. Stories linking 'Harlow' with 'hate crime' came thick and fast. A BBC report of 11 September reporting a community meeting in the town is a fairly typical example. 'European nationals' the BBC gravely announced were 'considering leaving' Harlow. If you took the BBC at its word, the unremarkable Essex town had undergone a profound and cataclysmic identity change since the EU referendum, a transformation which had traumatised the town's non-British population.[9]

The BBC's insistence on a UK hostile to foreigners was in sharp contrast to most people's realities. 'None of us had ever suffered any racism,' Mr Jozwik's brother Radek told the media. 'I never thought his death was race-related. I think he was in the wrong place at the wrong time. English people have always been friendly and welcoming.'[10] Statements such as this however were absolutely not part of any BBC narrative which preferred instead to stoke up yet more fear, more division:

> Harlow murder: Arek Jozwik's brother installs CCTV over attack fears
>
> bbc.co.uk

'Mention names'

A man on a mission, Sweeney was absolutely determined to link the tragedy to 'hate' and by extension to Brexit. 'Arek answered his phone in Polish,' states a breathless Sweeney at one point during his report, 'and that, people say, is the trigger for what happens next.' People? Which people precisely? The Newsnight report does not of course offer any evidence or witnesses for this assertion.

A little while later Sweeney interviews a young Polish man, Eric, who we are told was known to the victim and who, right on cue, delivers an almost pitch perfect speech: 'Since the Brexit all the British people think they've got the green light to do what they want, they feel very secure to be racist . . .' Had this been any other organisation apart from the impartial, free and fair BBC, it might have looked suspiciously as if the 'evidence' was being made to fit a narrative that had already been written. The Newsnight report ends with Mr Jozwik's associate, Eric once more:

Eric:	I don't know if I can mention names . . ?
Sweeney:	Mention names
Eric:	I mean Nigel Farage, thank you for that cos you are part of this death and you have blood on your hands thanks to you, thanks for all your decisions, wherever you are . . . yeah it's your call
Sweeney:	Nigel Farage has always denied this allegation. As the search for clues and answers continues, the fear is that two poisons have come together to a lethal result
	Report ends

'To have blood on one's hands'[11]

When Newsnight's star witness uttered those immortal words, 'Nigel Farage has blood on his hands,' Brainwashing Britain's linguistic alarm bells started to ring. How interesting, thought we, a non-native English speaker happily and comfortably using complex idiomatic language not only correctly, but in front of the television cameras. Hmm . . . It didn't sound quite right. What was wrong with 'I blame Nigel Farage?' It was almost as if Eric had received a little bit of private coaching in the art and use of English idioms . . .

'Nigel Farage has blood on his hands.' We have to admit as second language skills go it's a particularly impressive turn of phrase, one you would hardly use every day. It's also very catchy, very dramatic, but above all else very memorable. In fact, it's just perfect for BBC news headlines. First things first: So what exactly is an idiom? According to

Dictionary.com an idiom is, 'An expression whose meaning is not predictable from the usual meanings of its constituent elements.' For example, if I accuse you of 'taking me for a ride' I am not literally talking about journeys, rather I am accusing you of deceiving me, of lying. For second language learners idioms can be especially difficult to master: when and where should such language devices be used? Faced with these difficulties English learners often choose simpler language to express themselves (e.g. 'I blame Farage') a strategy known as avoidance. The English language having several thousand such expressions - each with a highly specific meaning – idioms can prove exceptionally difficult to master:

> Second language teachers would probably agree that even their most advanced students tend to avoid using idioms.[12]

> Since idioms are figurative expressions that do not mean what they literally state and since they are so frequently encountered in both oral and written discourse, comprehending and producing idioms present language learners with a special vocabulary learning problem.[13]

> We find these expressions mostly in native speakers' language . . . idioms are more neglected word expressions in language use and learning. [14]

Was somebody taking Newsnight viewers for a ride so the broadcaster could continue with some of its favourite narratives? Had Eric received some 'coaching' for the camera in the art of the English idiom – a very tricky area for language learners. *Nigel Farage is very, very bad* (sub-narrative: *Nigel Farage is an accessory to murder!*)

'Rigorously tested'

'Blood on his hands . . .' For reasons best known to himself, the BBC activist fails to challenge this outrageous claim. And precisely what allegation had Mr Farage 'always denied?' That he had been indirectly responsible for the possible manslaughter of a Polish citizen in Harlow? The further this BBC report went on the more tenuous it became. And what did Sweeney mean when declaring that Mr Farage had 'always denied this allegation?' For how long had he been in denial? Presumably, Sweeney meant in the 48 hours since the incident had occurred, making the use of 'always' a somewhat odd choice of term.

What is clear, is that by allowing this extraordinary allegation to go unchallenged, demanding it even ('Mention names'), some might infer that Sweeney was tacitly lending his support to the charge, a conclusion flagrantly in breach of the organisation's commitment to impartiality and fairness, an ethos re-iterated in the BBC's own editorial guidelines:

> Contributors expressing contentious views, either through an interview or other means, must be rigorously tested while being given a fair chance to set out their full response to questions.[15]

Had Eric's allegation been 'rigorously tested' and if so how? (assuming they *were* his own words.) With the police investigation barely a few days old what did John Sweeney and the BBC know that the police did not?

The correct course of action – the fair course of action - would surely have been to have edited out Eric's 'blood on the hands claim' or better still, not to have cajoled him in the first place. Newsnight's editors had, however, decided to include the accusation in the final cut in what was obviously a deliberate editorial decision. Did the BBC not consider such an allegation to be contentious – an accusation that a British politician had been somehow complicit in possible manslaughter? It is difficult not to reach the conclusion that the BBC agreed with this incredible assertion - that the ex-UKIP leader did indeed 'have blood on his hands,' a quite extraordinary supposition to make under any circumstances, more so given the tentative stage of the police enquiries.

Furthermore, according to its own editorial guidelines, when airing contentious opinions such as the 'blood on hands' accusation, the BBC has an obligation to, 'provide an opportunity to respond when appropriate.'[16] Yet Nigel Farage nor anyone else who could have rebutted this incendiary and provocative claim were allowed to do this. The accusation was left hanging in the air. The BBC for its part, simply continued flogging its 'post-Brexit hate crime' angle for all it was worth. The broadcaster was on a roll. Provided they tallied with its 'ugly' post-

Brexit mood, it was more than happy to print the speculative opinions of individuals such as the Police and Crime Commissioner for Essex who said, 'I think there's certainly a swell of opinion... that wasn't there a few months ago. It seems to coincide with the Brexit vote.'[17]

Meanwhile those on the ground – namely the Essex police - rightly refused to be drawn into the BBC's narrative. This was by no means the first time a gang of teenage thugs had set upon a member of the public with disastrous consequences.[18] As events would prove soon enough police circumspection was entirely the right course of action.

Sweeney's allusion to 'two poisons' in the conclusion to his piece left little doubt as to the impartial view of both he and his employers - one of those 'poisons' presumably being his 'ugly' post-Brexit mood. However, what evidence there was pointed, if anything, to a clear case of anti-social behaviour by a gang of known thugs and troublemakers – not the kind of narrative the BBC wanted to hear nor the reason for John Sweeney's Essex odyssey.

A little under a year later the full facts which lead to Mr Jozwik's death finally came to light. Suffice to say, what actually happened on that awful night in Harlow had nothing whatsoever to do with the BBC's version of events.

'Light years away'

On July 31, almost a year after the tragic events, Chelmsford Crown court reached a verdict: A 16-year old was charged with manslaughter. Mr Jozwik had died as a result of a fracas, the kind of drunken confrontation that takes places every week-end up and down the UK. A subsequent court hearing in September 2017 heard the full story. It was in fact Mr Jozwik who had initiated the confrontation on that fateful evening: 'It is accepted by the crown that the deceased and his friend were affected by alcohol and approaching the youths at all was seen as unnecessary,' said Patrick Upward QC. 'They made racist remarks to the youths and invited violence from those youngsters and they were considerably bigger and stronger than the young people. It was after the deceased pushed one of the youngsters that this defendant did what he did.'[19]

This tragic event never did have anything to do with Brexit. Nor did it have anything to do with the 'ugly' post-Brexit world conjured up by John Sweeney and Newsnight. Having smeared Nigel Farage and insisted that Brexit had unleashed a wave of violent racism that had ended in tragedy, the BBC Newsnight activist must have been a picture of contrition upon hearing the verdict. Not quite. An ardent tweeter, on the day of the verdict Sweeney's twitter feed was conspicuously lacking in any form of acknowledgment let alone apology. Nigel Farage certainly did not receive an apology. Brexit voters did not receive an apology. July 31 saw Sweeney busily tweeting alright, but not about Harlow. The BBC activist was tweeting – furiously so – images of Victorian oil paintings. As this terrible story reached its sad climax at Chelmsford County Court such was his absorption in all things pre-Raphaelite, John Sweeney seemed to have forgotten all about the unfortunate Mr. Jozwik.

'A mass of imbecile enthusiasms'

'Parsons was Winston's fellow employee at the Ministry of Truth. He was a fattish but active man of paralysing stupidity, a mass of imbecile enthusiasms – one of those completely unquestioning, devoted drudges on whom the stability of the Party depended. At the Ministry he was employed in some subordinate post for which intelligence was not required . . .'[20]

In September 2017 the 16-year old perpetrator was sentenced to three years' detention in a youth offenders' centre. Writing for *Conservative Woman,* David Keighley noted the huge gulf between the narrative pushed by the BBC and what had actually occurred:

> With Friday's sentencing at Chelmsford Crown Court of the youth responsible for Mr Jozwik's death, we know the full story. And it was light years away from what can now be seen as the BBC's deliberate anti-Brexit editorial drive.'[21]

Having originally plastered the Harlow 'hate' crime all over its many platforms together with headlines that would have frankly shamed the tabloid press, in electing to report the court's sentencing verdict on the Essex page of its news website the BBC had buried the final (and most crucial) part of this story far, far away from the gaze of the casual reader.

There were no headlines on the BBC 6 'o clock news; no mention on BBC Newsnight. As far as the BBC was concerned, Mr Jozwik might never have existed. Compassion, or something like it.

Despite the court's acceptance that it had in fact been Mr Jozwik who had initiated the violence, the BBC had still not given up on promoting its own fictitious version quite yet: 'Mr Jozwik,' reported BBC Essex, 'had just bought a pizza when he was set upon shortly after 23:30 BST.'[22] Not *quite* the judgement of Chelmsford Crown Court which had found that Mr Jozwik had initiated the violence.

'280 words on their BBC Essex website'

As sentencing was announced on September 11, Mr Sweeney was once again busily re-tweeting images of impressionist paintings on Twitter as well as re-tweeting CNN and J K Rowling. The BBC activist was having a pretty busy time of it. There was however one topic missing yet again from his Twitter feed on this particular day . . .

'Since the judgement and despite the fact that many have written in to the BBC demanding that something is done, all they have done is put up 280 words on their BBC Essex website,' Nigel Farage told listeners to his LBC radio show. 'Frankly I am disgusted with this . . . I demand an apology from the journalist (Sweeney) who cooked up this story, who egged on the witness (Eric) in the way he did.'

> **@IainDale**
> I wonder if any pundits will now apologise for linking the
> death in Harlow of Polish man Arkadiusz Jozwik to Brexit.

'They won't. They do their damage and move on regardless of truth or accuracy,' replied one social media user. 'If the theme collapses of its own burden of fabrication,' note Chomsky and Herman in their analysis of media propaganda, 'the mass media will quietly fold their tents and move on to another topic.'[23] The academics were right. BBC Newsnight had indeed quietly folded away its tent after its narrative had collapsed.

Mr Farage went on to describe how the BBC's attempt to link him to the tragedy had effected not only his life, but the lives of his family: 'At the time I couldn't even go out to buy a newspaper without abuse being hurled at me,' wrote Mr Farage in an article entitled *The BBC's slur has caused my family misery.* 'All of us lived in fear of reprisal,' noted Mr Farage.[24] Regardless, no apologies were forthcoming from Broadcasting House.

Sweeney's silence following what for him turned out to be a very inconvenient judgement, should surprise nobody. Mud sticks. And on those rare occasions when it might not, on those occasions when the dirt starts to resemble fake news you can always engage in an orgy of inconsequential tweeting to pass the time, impressionist or post-impressionist. By aggressively pushing Harlow as a hate-crime from the off, the senior Newsnight reporter's smears had already succeeded.

'Often a decision to lie simply suggests that your number one concern is the immediate result,' observes Sweeney's Newsnight colleague, Evan Davis, 'with little weight put on the long-term impact of the lie's detection.'[25] Burying the verdict on the regional pages of its news website was simply the final act of a well-rehearsed BBC procedure: smear big, apologise small (or preferably not at all). As far as BBC Newsnight was concerned Arkadiusz Jozwik's death no longer fitted its anti-Brexit master narrative.

Journalist Brendan O'Neil wasted no time criticising a left-wing media that had indeed forgotten all about the victim once his death had no longer become politically useful: 'Mr Jozwik's tragedy is no longer interesting to them,' observed O'Neil, 'It's an embarrassment, in fact, since it stands as grim proof of how far they lost the moral and political plot last August in the wake of the Brexit vote. So shush his death. Hide it. Forget it.' One BBC activist in particular achieved these ends by tweeting the work of Monet, Renoir *et al.* O'Neil's conclusion is particularly succinct: 'As firmly as they turned this tragic man into a political symbol, they now bury his life and death to save their own blushes.'[26]

As to concerns regarding how the BBC attempted to portray events in Harlow as a post-Brexit 'hate' crime, a racist attack committed by individuals acting under the influence of Nigel Farage, following a complaint by News Watch, the BBC launched an internal investigation. 'We don't always get it right, and should quickly and openly admit it when we don't,'[27] notes Nick Robinson, which brings us rather neatly to the result of that BBC 'enquiry.' Not guilty. BBC Complaints fully vindicated BBC News, BBC Newsnight and the behaviour of its senior reporter John Sweeney.

Charlottesville: 'Violence on both sides'

When it comes to ensuring their narratives – and only their narratives – come to occupy the public forum remaining there unchallenged, mainstream media organisations led by the BBC have an enviable track record. This pre-eminence does not however happen by accident. As Chomsky and Herman note, the legacy media's modus operandi is well-established:

> If the articles are written in an assured and convincing style, are subject to no criticisms or alternative interpretations in the mass media, and command support by authority figures, the propaganda themes quickly become established as true even without real evidence. This tends to close out dissenting views even more comprehensively, as they would now conflict with an already established popular belief.[1]

Thus the goal is to quickly monopolise the debate while marginalising 'dissenting views.' BBC, ITV, Channel 4, CNN, MSNBC, *New York Times, Washington Post, The Guardian, The Independent* etc. - Safety in numbers, 'authority figures' all singing from exactly the same elite consensus hymn sheet.

With its enormous television, radio and social media presence, the BBC is easily able to establish the first of these goals, monopolisation. As for marginalising dissent, its unceasing smear campaigns (and of course those ubiquitous BBC health-checks) especially against 'conservative' or 'right-wing' media (and commentators) such as Breitbart, RT or Fox News is usually enough to 'close out' if not completely nullify opposing points of view. Domination, naturally leads to audacity. 'This in turn opens up further opportunities for still more inflated claims,' observe Chomsky and Herman, 'as these can be made without fear of serious repercussions. 'Similar wild assertions made in contradiction of official views would elicit powerful flak...'[2]

Emboldened by membership of an all-powerful media legacy network, and therefore safe in the knowledge its narratives will not be challenged, the BBC and organisations like it can go on to produce ever more 'wild assertions,' ever more 'inflated claims.' And anyone daring to challenge this consensus can expect 'powerful flak' in return. Bear in

287

mind these observations as we turn our attentions to Charlottesville, our next case study and one whereby, as we shall see, thanks to its pre-eminent position within the mainstream media axis, Britain's 'national' broadcaster helped propagate a narrative so powerful opposing voices were not just closed down in the manner described by Chomsky and Herman, but rather completely obliterated. As ever, it achieved this aim largely by passive-aggressive intimidation: those daring to dissent could so easily find themselves subjects of smear campaigns, tarred and feathered by snarling Twitter mobs who just so happened to have read a few BBC headlines . . . When it comes to psychological intimidation, Britain's 'national' broadcaster has few rivals.

A BBC narrative
BBC coverage of the Charlottesville riot of August 2017 was a master study of outrage and indignation. It had everything: Neo-Nazis, white supremacists, KKK, David Duke and Donald Trump all wrapped up with a good dose of right-wing inspired violence and even death! What's not to like? The 'national' broadcaster had a field day. The BBC narrative went something like this:

> Vicious 'white supremacists' decided to descend upon
> Charlottesville, Virginia, for a march entitled, 'Unite the right.'
> Local people gallantly defended their town, preventing the
> white nationalists from wreaking havoc

> A peaceful protestor was killed by a white supremacist
> Donald Trump said there had been violence on both sides,
> which was a lie: the violence had come only from 'white
> supremacists'

> President Trump even praised the 'white supremacists' saying
> there were 'many fine people' amongst their ranks. This proved
> that Donald Trump was also a 'white supremacist.'

Would it surprise anyone to know this is a less than truthful account of events that weekend in Charlottesville? Britain's impartial, free and fair broadcaster had once again simply extrapolated those aspects which fitted its pre-written narratives, chopped, shaped and twisted, before using its rendition to inflame public opinion. Along with its allies in the legacy media, the broadcaster had soon concocted an official version of events that, as ever, told only half a story - if that.

Let's begin with the 'C' word so dreaded by the BBC – context. As ever with the BBC what it chose *not* to report was just as important as that which it *did* report. And in Charlottesville there was plenty that it chose not to report.

'One man with a swastika'

In response to the Charlottesville council's plans to remove a statue of General Robert E. Lee from the town's Emancipation Park, several groups decided to organise protests. According to the BBC, the march - dubbed 'Unite the Right' – consisted of three disparate groups who were united by their ideology: the KKK, 'neo-Nazis' and 'white supremacists/nationalists.' However, there were in fact representatives of plenty of other groups in Virginia that afternoon prosecuting their right to peacefully protest - groups that did not fit the BBC's 'white supremacist, neo-Nazi' narrative.

With over 57,000 Facebook followers, The Virginia Flaggers is a collection of Virginians from all over the state who stand against 'those that would desecrate our Confederate Monuments and memorials.' Engaged in a legal battle to preserve southern heritage, the Flaggers' fight to preserve their heritage has been a long, arduous journey. It's message is not one that would not necessarily fit any BBC 'neo-Nazi' or 'white supremacist' narrative:

> The VA Flaggers reject any person or group whose actions
> tarnish or bring dishonour upon the Confederate soldier or his
> reason for fighting, including those groups and persons using
> our cherished flag as a symbol for their own dishonourable
> purposes.'

The VA Flaggers were joined by several other heritage groups anxious to preserve historical landmarks. One such groups, the 'Save the Robert E. Lee statue Facebook Group,' has over 18,000 Facebook followers. Days before the rally the group had made the following announcement:

> As many of you are aware, there are planned demonstrations in and around Lee Park this weekend. Our focus steadily remains on the preservation of this historically & artistically significant monument of Virginian Robert E. Lee.

Not quite then the frothing, raging white nationalists of BBC activism. Unable to make them complicit in its 'white supremacist' narrative, the broadcaster simply whitewashed groups like this and the VA Flaggers from its many Charlottesville reports. BBC audiences would have no doubt been completely ignorant about the Monument Fund set up by the Robert E Lee Facebook group to fight plans to remove statues of Generals Lee and 'Stonewall' Jackson from Virginia's parks and gardens. Employing the services of a team of lawyers, the fund filed a lawsuit in March 2017 to prevent the local council from 'moving or defacing war memorials (that) would violate Virginia law.'

No white nationalists here much to BBC dismay, just a group of citizens attempting to raise funds to stop the local council erasing historic monuments. While the BBC somehow failed to mention law-abiding heritage groups who had come to Charlottesville to make their feelings known, the impartial, free and fair broadcaster did however have plenty of time for those propagating any of its own pre-written narratives: 'One picture tweeted by author J K Rowling,' reported the BBC, 'showed a man on the street carrying a swastika flag. . .'[3]

'I hate seeing white people in Orangeburg'

The BBC's 'white supremacist' narrative was in fact much more nuanced than the broadcaster cared to admit. At best, it was in fact only half the story. Whilst there were white nationalist groups present in Charlottesville, heritage and preservation groups were also present exercising their right to protest what they saw as a politically motivated attack on their history. Both groups had applied for and been granted permits to conduct their protests over the proposed removal of confederate statues – another fact the BBC was not too keen on discussing.

For the Virginia Flaggers and the Robert E Lee Facebook groups it was the latest stage of an ongoing battle with Virginian authorities, not that readers and listeners to any BBC platform would have known about any such context. BBC audiences heard but one story: White supremacists! White supremacists! White supremacists! The background to these protests would not have fitted any BBC narrative. In a typically impartial article entitled, 'A reckoning in Charlottesville,' while heritage groups are barely mentioned, the writer can hardly hide his admiration for a certain Wes Bellamy who is described in the following glowing terms:

> Mr Bellamy is the first black deputy mayor of the city. A sharply-dressed, outgoing character, emphatic in his desire to see the statue removed.

The article continues in the same reverential tones:

> Mr Bellamy stopped in the park to speak to residents, who congratulated him on passing his doctorate that day, and to local police officers, some of whom he knew by name. Then he headed off, under strict instructions from police, as the white nationalists came into town, to keep his whereabouts on Saturday a secret.

Mr Bellamy's sanctity is well established. He's loved by everyone. A victim of his own popularity, he is forced to flee before the 'white nationalists' arrive holding their candles and lights to begin a vigil. What the article does not mention is that in his 'emphatic desire' to see this statue (and others) removed from Virginia, heritage groups suspected the Deputy Mayor of carrying out a policy deliberately calculated to inflame, and one which they considered highly disrespectful to their history and traditions.

For an organisation that likes nothing more than to dig into the past of (certain) individuals, in the case of Charlottesville's Deputy Mayor, it was time for a BBC free pass. Yet Bellamy's recent history of inflammatory remarks had been well-documented. Indeed, even a cursory perusal of his past social media activity sheds an entirely different light on this 'sharply-dressed, outgoing character.'[4] And here, just for the record, a flavour of some of Bellamy's past tweets that led some to label him as an anti-white racist, charges that Mr Bellamy denied via a Facebook post in which he declared, 'I am not a black supremacist, a racist or misogynist.'

> I don't like white people, so I don't like white snow!!!!!!!

> I really #hate how almost 80% of the black people here talk white.

> I hate seeing white people in Orangeburg

For the sake of decency we have omitted a series of sexually explicit tweets sent from the same account. Following criticism of his tweeting, in December 2016 Mr Bellamy resigned from his teaching job and stepped down from his seat on the Virginia Board of Education. According to his critics, Bellamy's 'emphatic desires' stemmed not from a sense of overriding civic duty, but rather from his anti-white ideology expressed so eloquently via social media. So, not quite the hero portrayed by the BBC, 'sharp' suits notwithstanding.

'Entirely white and male'
Already it is clear that the there is a lot more to the BBC's carefully constructed Charlottesville narrative than first meets the eye. The broadcaster was selecting that which fitted its narrative, while rejecting that which did not. In BBC Land this was all about 'white supremacists' (and Nazis, of course) intent on causing havoc and intimidating folk like the sharply-dressed Mr Bellamy.

There were a few other details that in its urgency to keep up with events in Charlottesville, the scrupulously fair broadcaster 'forgot' to mention. For example, it forgot to add that some of what it insisted calling 'peaceful' protestors had arrived in town armed with mace spray, baseball bats, rocks, guns and even flame throwers.

On the night before the march, 'Unite the Right' organised a candlelight vigil. According to the BBC's 'man on the ground,' marchers chanted anti-Semitic slogans ('Jews will not replace us') during this vigil, which if true would give them plenty of common ideological ground with those Al Quds marchers habitually ignored by the same broadcaster when they march in central London.

The next day, against a backdrop of a heavy police presence, the 'Unite the Right' march set off for Emancipation Park. Attempting to enter the park the nationalist and conservationist groups were accosted by 'anti-fascists' who had somehow gained access to a part of town reserved solely for the safe passage of the marchers. Confrontations ensued. The right-wing and heritage groups were determined to enter the park. Left-wing groups were just as determined to block their progress, legal permit notwithstanding. The BBC take on all of this was a masterclass of objective testimony:

> In a column they surged into the park, using sticks and their fists to shove aside anti-fascist counter-protesters. Then they blocked off the entrance with shields. Inside, David Duke, the former grand wizard of the Ku Klux Klan, grinned and waved as the crowd, almost entirely white and male, cheered him on, chanting his name and putting their arms up in Nazi salutes.

Reading this one could be forgiven for thinking this is an excerpt not from an objective news report, but from a piece of prose fiction. Whether you believe this impartial account or not is immaterial to the facts: the marchers were attempting to gain access to the park as per their permit, and were obstructed from doing so. Not a BBC narrative, but merely the plain facts. At this point the BBC activist almost strays worryingly off narrative when describing the 'Unite the Right' marchers as 'a motley crew of militia, racists, and neo-Nazis, and some who said they simply wanted to defend their Southern history.' Here for the first (and last) time the BBC acknowledge, albeit briefly, that legitimate protest groups were present in Charlottesville. It was a mistake that would not be repeated.

'Peaceful' counter protestors

Without any discernible irony, the BBC activist then goes on to describe a moment when the 'peaceful' counter-protesters set upon and beat a lone individual. Notice, the matter of fact presentation here of what was a vicious and sustained attack. Notice the lack of outrage too. If one didn't know any better one might discern indifference verging on tacit approval lurking behind this description:

Daryl Vaughan, 24, who came from Newcastle, Virginia to join the white nationalists, got caught alone, surrounded by anti-fascist protesters who beat him, kicking him in the face and chest as he lay on the ground.

The 'anti-fascist' protesters referred to here are composed largely of two groups: Antifa and Black Lives Matter. Clad in their traditional uniform of black military clothing, faces masked by handkerchiefs and backpacks loaded with an array of missiles, such is the level of violence associated with this extreme left-wing group there have been calls in the United States for Antifa to be assigned as domestic terrorists. One week after it had been started on Change.org by a female in Spain, a petition in to declare the group a terrorist organisation had gained over 70,000 signatures.

As we shall see, a substantial section of the BBC's 'peaceful' protestors were anything but peaceful. Credit where credit is due – BBC focus was split for both sides: its focus on the nationalists and conservationists was entirely on the former (nationalists); focus on the peaceful and violent counter-protestors was also entirely on the former (peaceful protestors). Balance, BBC style.

'Waiting for violence to take place'
While the excitable BBC predictably attempted to link events in Charlottesville with Donald Trump, the story was taking an altogether more sinister turn. Eye witness accounts implied that far from segregating the two opposing groups in line with standard procedure, police had actually stood back thereby allowing right and left-wing protestors to come together - a dereliction of duty that might well have contributed to the tragic event that followed. During the ensuing melee a 32-year old woman was knocked down by a car driven by a young nationalist. Nineteen people were also injured in the incident.

But could the tragedy have been avoided? Fingers pointed at Charlottesville's Democratic Mayor and Virginia Governor Terry McAuliffe, friend to the Clintons and fierce Trump critic. It soon emerged that riot police had indeed been instructed to stand down, thereby allowing the opposing sides to meet head on. Rumours suggested the police had received their orders directly from the Mayor. The allegation that this had been a deliberate attempt to stoke confrontation refused to go away. Had Trump's enemies deliberately created chaos in order to smear the President's name? It certainly seemed that way. As riot police stood by, flashpoints were occurring. Law enforcement waited. Why were police not managing the situation as per well-established protocol? 'They should have set up a barrier separating the opposing groups like they usually do,' remarked one social media user. 'It's almost as though the politicians there WANTED violence to break out,' observed another, 'to bring attention to this group & try to tie them to Trump & voters.'

At the very least this seemed to be a clear case of police negligence, at worst collusion. If proved to have any substance, the implications could be profound. Were American law enforcement agencies acting as facilitators to civil disobedience, standing by as rioters clashed on the streets thereby putting lives in danger? Were the police actually soliciting violence? Whatever the reasons, law enforcement had failed to prosecute their duty, with fatal consequences.

These were profoundly serious charges. But not apparently serious enough to interest the BBC. There was a good reason for BBC reticence: to have covered this story might have taken the corporation to places it did not want to go – i.e. admission that Democrat officials may have attempted to set up the Trump administration, a ploy that had backfired with disastrous consequences. It was a turn of events not part of any anti-Donald Trump narrative and was thus completely ignored.

While the BBC studiously ignored a potentially massive story of Mayoral and police corruption – normally irresistible topics for the broadcaster - the alleged police stand down had been noted by plenty of neutral observers. 'White supremacist! White supremacists! White supremacists! The impartial broadcaster had its narrative, and it was sticking to it. A possible democratic set-up was not part of the elite consensus for Charlottesville, which had been composed well in advance of the actual rally. Meanwhile, real journalism was taking place. The American Civil Liberties Union of Virginia tweeted that:

> Law enforcement was standing passively by, seeming to be waiting for violence to take place, so that they would have grounds to declare an emergency, declare an 'unlawful assembly' and clear the area [5]

It seemed almost unreal, that American law enforcement had been instructed to not prosecute their duties as per the oath of honour in which officers swear to uphold the United States constitution, enforce all federal, state, and local laws. As unbelievable as it appeared, eye witness testimony insisted that the police had deliberately sought to bring the two groups together.

As this incredible story broke - a story that went right to the heart of American justice - what, might we ask was Britain's impartial, free and fair 'national' broadcaster doing? Answer: busily attempting to smear the US President's name.

The BBC meltdown

The mainstream media machine really got going after comments made by Donald Trump in which the president condemned the violence on both sides in Charlottesville, i.e. by nationalists and Antifa. Mr Trump had also correctly observed that there had been 'violence on many sides.' The BBC went wild. Violence on many/both sides! Nonsense! Crazy! Madness! How could Trump possibly condemn violence on many/both sides? Surely violence by Antifa – beating up bystanders, blinding people with mace spray, stamping on heads – surely that sort of violence, the right sort of violence, should be praised, not condemned? Was the President mad? Just as Chomsky and Herman predict, the President's comments elicited 'powerful flak.' Britain's 'national' broadcaster went into meltdown.

Soon enough a flurry of articles came flying out of Broadcasting House each and every one expressing incredulity that the President could condemn vicious and violent attacks by be-masked thugs armed with baseball bats, knives and flame throwers. Had Trump finally lost the plot? Left-wing violence was not violence at all. The point is that Antifa had come to confront people marching to preserve Confederate statues. The knives, bats, guns and flame throwers were clearly integral to that goal.

When Mr Trump mentioned there had been 'many good people' among the marchers, the BBC and its legacy media allies threatened to blow a blood vessel. As the activists knew only too well, the President was in fact referring to the conservation and heritage groups (the same groups studiously ignored by the BBC) and their fight to preserve historical landmarks, a struggle overwhelmingly supported by the US public. No matter. The BBC simply omitted to inform its audience about precisely whom the president had been referring to, in much the same way Mr Sopel had done with his 'Mexicans are thieves and rapists' device. This way, the media could inflame its followers by implying Mr Trump had actually called white nationalists good people: if Charlottesville was all about 'white supremacists' and 'Neo-Nazis' then ergo Mr Trump must have been talking about them, right? Wrong. It was a lie, a wilful, deceitful lie that Britain's 'national' broadcaster was more than happy to perpetuate.

'The president,' so went one BBC report, 'described the crowd as including some "very fine people" and implied a moral equivalence between white supremacists and anti-racist protesters.'[6] This interpretation only works of course provided you have taken considerable pains not to mention the many heritage groups and ordinary, concerned Virginians present in Charlottesville that day. In reality, the crowd did include some "very fine people." It's just that the BBC and friends had whitewashed them from their dishonest Charlottesville narrative.

Never had Chomsky's and Herman's analysis of the mass media rung truer than in Charlottesville. The BBC *et al* had long ago constructed their narrative. 'Dissenting views' had already been comprehensively closed out. By creating hysteria over Mr Trump's factually correct statements, the mass media had incorrectly assumed it could bully the president into accepting its extraordinary narrative, one that condemned nationalist violence but condoned that perpetuated by a domestic terrorist organisation. The 'national' broadcaster and its allies in the legacy media had over played their hand. Indeed, the more Mr Trump refused to be intimidated, the greater BBC hysteria became.

'No, Clive Myrie, Antifa thugs are NOTHING like the D-Day heroes'

Having gone out of its way to insist that there was no 'moral equivalence' between the right and left-wing inspired violence at Charlottesville, and expressing round-the-clock outrage when President Trump condemned violence and hate on 'both sides,' it was difficult not to conclude that the BBC's attitude to Antifa violence was something less than critical. Indeed, the corporation's North American Reporter expressed incredulity at the mere suggestion: 'When the president on Saturday said there were "many sides" to blame, he meant it.'[7] The activist seemingly disagreed with President Trump's assertion that violence, irrespective of from where it emerges, is to be universally condemned.

Perhaps therefore it should not have come as a surprise when just days after events in Charlottesville, BBC newsreader Clive Myrie shared a tweet showing an image of WWII soldiers disembarking on the beach for the D-Day landings accompanied with the caption: 'Some armed Antifa thugs heading to disrupt a peacefully-assembled white nationalist gathering.' Equating Antifa terrorists with WWII veterans was one form of moral equivalency that did not trouble the BBC at all – far from it. Many social media users did not seem to agree with the analogy. 'Comparing Antifa to WW2 vets,' wrote one social media user, 'isn't a compliment to Antifa, it's a disgusting insult to WW2 vets.'

@Anon
No, @CliveMyrieBBC, Antifa thugs are NOTHING like the D-Day heroes.

Did Mr Myrie agree with the analogy being made between violent left-wing thugs and World War II heroes? 'Retweeting,' lest we forget, 'suggested people were associated with the views expressed . . . ' Tacit support of Antifa by the mainstream media troubled many people:

@DineshDSouza
Antifa is MORE dangerous than the rag-tag Skinheads & KKK b/c Antifa has the backing of powerful leftists in politics & media

At times it certainly appeared the MSM was running cover for this violent mob, and in doing so ensuring that its campaign of terror continued unimpeded.

'What Trump said versus what I saw'
A short film produced by BBC activist Joel Gunter proved very popular on the BBC news website. Provocatively entitled, 'What Trump said versus what I saw'[8] – a less than subtle attempt to suggest that the US President is a liar – the film gives an 'eye witness' account of the

Charlottesville riot, or more accurately a BBC account of events in the Virginian town.

Gunter's video must be viewed with some caution. In keeping with the BBC's Charlottesville narrative, the video does not even attempt to hide its anti-Trump bias. At the same time, while foregrounding the behaviour of one side (white nationalists) it predictably downplays the antics of the other side (Antifa). For example, while the film readily shows what it calls 'armed militaristic white nationalists,' it conspicuously fails to show similarly armed left-wing groups such as Redneck Revolt who attended the rally armed with rifles.

Not that we needed reminding – the BBC made sure of that – but what Trump 'said' was that there had been 'violence on both/many sides.' Attended by conservationists, white nationalists, the KKK, Antifa, Black Lives Matter and members of other disparate left-wing groups like the aforementioned Redneck Revolt, there had indeed been 'many sides' present at the rally, all of whom had participated in the violence to some degree. What the President had 'said' had therefore been factually correct. Typically, when faced with facts that cruelly exposed its narrative, the impartial, free and fair broadcaster decided to add its own somewhat eccentric spin to events in West Virginia . . .

'Local' people

'Trump is right,' concedes Gunter in his video, 'there was violence on both sides. I saw counter protestors throw bottles, rocks and paint.' The BBC activist then goes on to make the following astonishing distinction: 'But here's the problem with this one – the majority of counter-protestors there on Saturday were locals . . .' Yes, you read that correctly - violence perpetuated by 'locals' was, in Gunter's estimation, less serious than that committed by the other side! Here's what one eye witness – a student – told the LA Times:

> I saw [a] man from the white supremacist crowd being
> chased and beaten. People were hitting him with their signs.
> A much older man, also with the alt-right group, got pushed
> to the ground in the commotion. Someone raised a stick over
> his head and beat the man with it, and that's when I screamed
> and ran over with several other strangers to help him to his feet.[9]

According to Gunter these acts of violence were somehow justified because they had been committed by what he claimed were 'locals.' But were the left-wing protesters really just an ordinary group of 'locals' out to gallantly defend their town as Gunter would have us believe? A political journalist on the scene reported that, 'Shortly before 10 a.m. we noticed protesters making way for a new group marching from the east. We ran over to discover that the new group was a battalion of Antifa members from all across the country. . .'[10]

New York City Antifa @NYCAntifa

Help Charlottesville, VA defend their community on Aug 12 from possibly the biggest neo-Nazi rally the US has seen in decades. #DefendCville

#DEFENDCVILLE
CALLING ALL ANTI-RACISTS!
WEEKEND OF ACTION CVL | 8/11 – 8/13

There were indeed many locals at the march, but these 'locals' did not interest Gunter one bit. Indeed, before being hijacked by extremists, the march was all about 'local' people objecting to the removal of a 'local' statue from a 'local' park. The following social media post is from a Charlottesville resident, M.K:

> I am a citizen of Charlottesville and yesterday was a horrible
> day for my city. This whole march was started by the city's vice
> mayor who is a racist black man who decided to try to make a
> name for himself by removing a historical statue of Robert E Lee.
> He wants to erase history. After the citizens of Charlottesville
> voiced their opinion that the statue should stay Wes Bellamy
> kept pushing the issue. These are the facts. This has nothing to
> do with Trump. Wes Bellamy and the city council brought this
> mess upon our city. Race relations here have been set back 60
> years.

Whatever opinions an individual holds, however disagreeable, does not and cannot justify beatings on public streets, whether administered by visitors or indeed Mr Gunter's 'locals.' Was there then violence on both/many sides? Short answer: yes. And despite Mr Gunter's equivocations, to those on the receiving end it was equally painful, equally horrendous and equally inhumane. The President condemned violence on 'many sides.' The BBC however wanted him to condemn the violence on one side only.

Things you won't see on the BBC . . .

Had you used the BBC as the sole source of information for this story you would have read a lurid story of violent Donald Trump-supporting 'white supremacists' who had arrived in town to wreak havoc, a motley gang of goose-stepping 'Neo-Nazis' met with brave resistance from one or two brave 'locals'. But this was at best a partial rendition. There was much more to Charlottesville than the BBC's white supremacist narrative.

Let's summarise all the relevant information the BBC did not include in its coverage of Charlottesville:

- The United States First Amendment guarantees citizens the right to free speech
- 'Unite The Right' had a permit to hold a protest rally. Left-wing group Antifa arrived to confront the marchers.
- Heritage and conservation groups had organised the march to protest against the removal of historical statues – the latest stage of a legal battle with Virginia authorities
- The Deputy Mayor of Charlottesville, who was driving the campaign to have the statues removed, had made anti-white racist and sexist remarks
- Some Antifa protestors were armed with pepper spray, clubs, missiles, firearms and flame throwers
- There are calls to classify Antifa as a 'domestic terrorist organisation' in the United States
- Charlottesville police had been ordered to 'stand down.' Numerous reports confirm that police had been explicitly ordered not to prosecute their duties on August 12th.

- According to the BBC, the KKK is Trump's 'base'.[11] As of 2016, The Southern Poverty Law centre estimated the Klan has between 5-8,000 members. In the 2016 US presidential race, 62,979,636 people voted for Donald Trump

Although the politically neutral BBC disagreed vehemently with the protester's right to march in faraway west Virginia, First Amendment notwithstanding, some 'hate' marches receive a free pass. When the annual anti-Semitic Al Quds march literally passes by its doorstep in central London, BBC outrage and hysteria are in very short supply. How odd:

@Anon
A small group of neo-Nazis walk the streets in Charlottesville and everyone immediately recognizes it as hateful and anti-Semitic. Huge Al Quds rallies every year, across the planet, ppl are gathered to scream about killing Jews and no one bats an eye.

Reality versus the BBC
Now let's place on record the factual account of Charlottesville, which can be compared with the BBC narrative at the beginning of this chapter:

Concerned by the efforts of Charlottesville's Deputy Mayor to remove a statue of General Robert E Lee from a park in the town, conservationist and heritage groups organised a protest to take place on 12 August 2017. The Deputy had expressed anti-white sentiments on social media leading some to believe his persistent efforts to remove the statues were based upon racial prejudice and a desire to inflame local Virginian residents. According to a poll for NPR/PBS NewsHour, a majority of US citizens say that Confederate statues should remain in situ:

DO YOU THINK STATUES HONORING LEADERS OF THE CONFEDERACY SHOULD

Remain as a historical symbol	62%
Be removed because they're offensive	27%
Unsure	11%

Meanwhile white nationalist groups also obtained a permit to protest. Whipped up by the mainstream media and armed with various missiles and weapons, Antifa members arrived from all over the United States. On the day of the rally the domestic terrorist group attempted to prevent the marchers from reaching their muster point. Virginian police allowed the opposing sides to clash resulting in the death of a 32-year old female, knocked over by a young nationalist. In the aftermath of the riot, President Trump condemned violence on many/both sides. The BBC and the mainstream media strongly believed Mr Trump should have not condemned violence committed by Antifa.

Shortly after events in Charlottesville, Gunter turned up in Boston to give his unique brand of commentary on another 'far right' rally.

'A few anti-police chants'

The Boston Free Speech Rally had been due to take place 19 August, just one week after events in Charlottesville. Overwhelmed by tens of thousands of protesters, participants at the rally ultimately had no choice but to disband the event. But now the BBC had a potentially bigger headache: Rally dispersed and its small number of attendees long since gone, who to blame for events that followed instigated by what it chose to call 'peaceful anti-racist protesters?'

Provoked to boiling point by the BBC and its mainstream media allies and now with no target to unleash their anger, protesters turned their attentions towards the Boston police. The mood started to get nasty. In downtown Boston the BBC's 'peaceful' protesters began to attack the police:

> **@realDonaldTrump**
> Looks like many anti-police agitators in Boston.
> Police are looking tough and smart! Thank you.

Amateur video footage showed several violent flashpoints as police were confronted by baying mobs. Indeed, the violence against police escalated to such an extent that the Boston Police Department soon felt compelled to take to social media to plead for calm. Here's how events unfolded as per Twitter's timeline:

7.32 pm
@bostonpolice
#BPD is asking individuals to refrain from throwing urine,
bottles and other harmful projectiles at our officers.

7.44 pm
@joelmgunter
Barely any "antipolice" agitators. A few anti-police chants.
1000s of peaceful protestors. Many thanked officers.

7.48 pm
@bostonpolice
#UPDATE #BPD confirming rocks being thrown at officers
on Tremont at West.

Wherever the BBC activist was hanging out 'on the ground', it was not on
the streets of Boston where police were being subjected to sustained and
vicious attacks. Social media responded to Gunter with a mixture of
sarcasm and anger:

Replying to @joelmgunter

➤ Throwing urine on the police is a strange way to thank them.
Is that really a custom among liberals?

➤ Really....then who's throwing piss and rocks at the cops...the
Nazis again???

➤ You going to apologize, pal? Or is fake news worth the
propaganda value?

➤ Just waiting to see if you have any ethics at all... since you
were obviously mocking what Trump said.

➤ Kind of looks like you are a knee-jerk fool with an agenda and
not a journalist, doesn't it Joel?

> ➤ They were throwing urine, faeces and object to police....
> don't lie

> ➤ Maybe you watch #FakeNews. The police commissioner
> says otherwise

'Heavy clashes'

When fake news is rife, so important to have journalists
debunking on the ground.

BBC World News reporter

Several hours after the violence had begun and both President Trump
and The Boston Police Department had appealed for calm, and with the
chances of misleading the audience diminishing by the minute, the BBC's
activist 'on the ground' was finally forced to admit the reality of the
situation. A long day of 'debunking' had finally come to an end:

9.15 pm
@joelmgunter
It's turned violent in Boston. Heavy clashes between counter
protestors and police.

9.33 pm
@joelmgunter
It seemed like everything was going to pass peacefully in Boston.
Violent clashes now downtown. Police using mace

'Sticking up for Antifa'

We have already chronicled mainstream media sympathy towards the group known as Antifa. Arguably, had this group not turned up in Charlottesville and Boston, these rallies would have passed off peacefully enough. Moreover, had the rallies not made media headlines some of the more unsavoury groups present would not have obtained the publicity they sought.

It isn't just Charlottesville and Boston that end in violence. Wherever there is a Donald Trump rally Antifa manage to appear, arriving in numbers from all over the United States. And wherever Antifa go, violence is never far away:

> They block roads, pelt his supporters with eggs, kick and beat them, tear at their hair, beat on their cars, rip up their signs, and call them names. Rarely, a Trump supporter gets violent with the demonstrators. Almost exclusively, the news media faults Trump for the violence wherever it occurs.[1]

Nonetheless, the mainstream media attitude to Antifa remains equivocal. As far as the BBC is concerned it can hardly be expected to chastise this hard-left group, not when it is doing so much to assist with the realisation of some of the corporation's key narratives. Perhaps this explains why, post-Charlottesville, the broadcaster was so determined to berate the president for condemning violence on both/many sides.

It was not exactly clear how, or indeed why, the BBC thought the US president should ignore a growing phenomenon in the US in which it had become normal to witness large gangs of masked thugs wielding baseball bats, attacking both the public at large and police officers with rocks and bags of human excrement. Burning cars, smashing up shops and generally causing civil disturbance wherever they happen to gather, ignoring the self-styled 'anti-fascists' of Antifa was not as easy as the BBC might have imagined. Ulf Poschardt, a journalist at Germany's *Die Welt* newspaper, was just one of many commentators watching the antics of this group with something approaching horror: 'Their black uniforms reveal that their aesthetic is inspired by Mussolini's black shirts,' observed Poschardt. 'They act like fascists. They create fear and insecurity.'[2] Poschardt was writing after the so-called 'anti-fascists' left

130 police officers injured and caused substantial damage to property in the German city of Hamburg in the run up to a G20 summit of 2017. While most observers were horrified at the antics of these self-styled 'anti-fascists' certain impartial state broadcasters could barely hide their admiration.

Antifa: the alt-left at large

By summer 2017 Antifa had firmly established itself as a menacing presence in both Europe and the US. In February 2017, clad in their black uniforms and masks, the group showed up at the University of California, Berkeley to protest an event where media pundit Milo Yiannopoulos was due to speak. Chaos ensued. Left-wing protestors attacked the police with fireworks, pepper sprayed bystanders, looted a Starbucks café and attacked individuals whom they suspected of being Trump supporters. The event, organised by Berkeley College Republicans, was cancelled. Here was an event where violence had most certainly not been on 'many sides' – it had been on one side only: Antifa and the alt-left.

'Frankly, the idea that initiating violence is the solution to politics is the preserve of bonkers ideologues or thugs out looking for a fight,' observed *The Telegraph*, 'and that's just as true on the left as on the right.'[3]

While conservatives and Trump supporters emerged relatively unscathed from the Yiannopoulos Berkeley event, such was not the case at a subsequent rally. Following the Patriots' Day demonstration held at Berkeley's Civic Centre Park on Saturday 15 April eleven people had been left injured, seven of whom required hospital treatment as Antifa wrought havoc upon the event. The list of items confiscated from the BBC's 'peaceful' counter-protestors included a stun gun, pepper spray, mace, axe handle, knives, wooden dowles, poles and concrete-filled cans.

In one notoriously violent attack a mask wearing thug attacked a Trump supporter with a metal bicycle lock, smashing the lock repeatedly onto the victim's head. The cowardly assault was caught on video and posted to YouTube. Following a campaign by Internet provocateurs 4chan the perpetrator was subsequently identified as 28-year old Eric Clanton, a Democrat-supporting former college professor.

It later emerged that Clanton had attacked a total of seven people with his metal u-lock, one so badly that he had sustained a head laceration requiring five staples. Clanton was charged with four counts of assault with a deadly weapon with the special allegation of causing great bodily injury. Upon his arrest police had found 'anti-fascist' material – flags, pamphlets etc. – together with face coverings and a u—lock at his West Oakland home. The offender also sported an 'anti-fascist' tattoo on his left bicep. While his actions were roundly condemned by the majority of media commentators and politicians, in alt-left circles Clanton was hailed a hero.

With a catalogue of intimidation and violence behind them as witnessed at Berkeley and elsewhere, it seemed curious therefore that the BBC desired president Trump to ignore the actions of Antifa in Charlottesville. On the contrary, the broadcaster continued to demand a free pass for the group. 'Eric Clanton' returns a total of '0' results on the BBC's comprehensive news website.

'Someone pinch us!'

In August 2017 a curious article appeared on the Trending section of the BBC news website with the headline: 'Far-right smear campaign against Antifa exposed by Bellingcat.' Yes, you read that headline correctly. But surely there was some mistake here – it seemed too ludicrous for words - was the 'national' broadcaster really engaged in an Antifa public relations exercise? Organisations such as Ayrshire Against Fascism (AAF) could barely contain their excitement nor disbelief:

> **@AyrshireAF**
> This is the BBC. Actively exposing fake Antifa accounts.
> The BBC sticking up for Antifa... Someone pinch us!

As bizarre as it seemed, the publicly-funded broadcaster really did appear to be sticking up for this vicious, left-wing organisation. Hardly surprising then that 'anti-fascist' accounts such as this one were so shocked.

And as far as Belllingcat is concerned, the entity quoted in the BBC article as exposing this dastardly plot against the be-masked thugs of Antifa - 'Even casual conversation with him reveals,' remark *Off Guardian,* 'the embarrassing truth that his "research," so lauded in the popular media, consists of entry-level computer skills and an awful lot of smoke-blowing.'[4] As for Bellingcat's cosy relationship with the mainstream media the amateur sleuth appears to be somewhat of a useful idiot. 'A disposable shill for dodgy claims and ludicrous propaganda,' conclude *Off Guardian*, 'that the real players do not want permanently attached to themselves or their legacies.'

'Appears to aim to discredit Antifa groups'

Back to that extraordinary BBC article: 'Far-right smear campaign against Antifa exposed by Bellingcat.' Firstly, aside from the fact that BBC Trending spends an inordinate amount of time obsessing over what it terms the 'alt/far-right', it is not entirely clear why the smear 'campaign' such as it was (a single meme) is classified as 'far-right.' We are unable to find any evidence that the meme in question was produced by a member or group affiliated to the 'far-right.' Furthermore, it is also not entirely clear how a single, one-off meme constitutes a 'campaign.'

Assuming it is actually possible to smear a violent, anarchic organisation in the first place, what exactly had incensed the BBC so much? BBC Trending certainly appears to have a thing about the 'alt-right.' They even write impartial books about it.[5] Was that the trigger: the 'alt-right' daring to smear the alt-left?

The 'smear' referred to in the BBC article is an image portraying the face of a battered and bruised young woman. In the top corner of the image is the red and black flag associated with Antifa. At the top of the image are the following words: '53% of white women voted for Trump.' Towards the bottom of the image are the words: '53% of white women should look like this' i.e. battered and bruised. The image appears to be a call for violence, specifically against white, female Trump supporters.

What seems to have rattled the BBC was the alleged attempt to pass the image off as the creation of Antifa, this despite its ignoble history of randomly attacking Trump supporters of both sexes. The following paragraph is fairly typical of a BBC article that appears genuinely free of irony:

> The campaign appears to aim to discredit Antifa groups at a time of heightened tension in the United States . . . [6]

The idea of 'discrediting' Antifa left some social media users bemused as well as incredulous:

@FarLeftWatchOrg
The @BBC is upset people are smearing a group that stabs horses, burns cars, and violently attacks Trump supporters.

The irony didn't end there. Referring to what it described as 'prominent far-right individuals', the article went on to explain the modus operandi of these scurrilous 'far right' operatives who haunt Internet message boards, sullying the name of Antifa:

> Accounts appearing to belong to anti-fascist groups tweeted the memes, calling on activists to physically attack women who voted for Trump.

> Prominent far-right individuals such as Joseph Paul Watson also retweeted the memes.

Extensive research fails to reveal a 'prominent far-right' individual named 'Joseph Paul Watson.' The BBC article *might* be referring to Paul Joseph Watson, a journalist and social media commentator who alternately describes himself as conservative or libertarian, but not 'far right.' BBC identification of 'Joseph Paul Watson' left some social media users perplexed:

@Anon
How is it possible to 'smear' Antifa? And who is Joseph Paul Watson?

The mystery of 'Joseph Paul Watson' deepened: just exactly who was this 'prominent far right' individual? Perhaps BBC Trending had simply confused two entirely separate individuals. After all, an article raging against smears would surely not do that which it purported to find so objectionable: smear an individual. It wouldn't, would it ..?

Having smeared the mysterious 'Joseph Paul Watson' BBC Trending then goes on to credit none other than Bellingcat with exposing this dastardly plot via what it termed his 'online investigation.' Bellingcat had another scalp. In actual fact, the smear 'campaign' was viewable to anybody who happened to drop by the popular 4chan image-boards upon which the memes had originally been posted. Not quite an expose; in fact not even close to an expose. The hoaxers at 4chan had in fact been waiting and hoping for the mainstream media to drop by: 'This wasn't designed to be a false flag . . . it was literally designed to be media bait so they'd spread it for us,' wrote one 4chan anonymous user.

Social media users familiar with 4chan's notoriously provocative ruses responded to the BBC Trending article with a mixture of mockery and scorn:

> **@Anon**
> BREAKING: 4chan made memes to troll people. Truly ground-breaking journalism

Never ones to let an opportunity to smear Mr Trump pass and running out of steam not to mention credibility, using that old BBC pivot trick, the BBC Trending article bizarrely ended up at . . . the Charlottesville march of two weeks' earlier:

> Following the march, US President Donald Trump accused left-wing groups of being as equally to blame as far-right protestors for the violence, drawing widespread condemnation for equating the two.

The BBC was sticking grimly to its guns: violence committed by Antifa - by the likes of Eric Clanton - could be excused, pardoned and perhaps even tacitly encouraged, certainly admired. Without fully or even partially explaining why, BBC Trending appeared to believe that left-wing groups were not 'equally to blame' for violence such as occurred at Charlottesville and Berkeley where Antifa had viciously attacked police and bystanders while rampaging through the streets.

> **@Anon**
> #Antifa breaks nose of a Trump supporter who happens to be Latino. News you won't hear on #BBC

As revulsion towards Antifa's viciousness increased, so too did support for Trump's condemnation. Indeed, after yet another Antifa rout at Berkeley in late August 2017 during an anti-Marxist rally, even *The Washington Post* ran with a headline that supported Trump's observations: 'Black-clad Antifa members attack peaceful right-wing demonstrators in Berkeley.'[7] When an Antifa activist implored rowdy fans of the Philadelphia Eagles football team to 'burn a police station for me,' revulsion only increased further. The 'anti-fascists'' hatred towards law enforcement was not calculated to win friends. It did however appear to attract the admiration of certain publicly-funded mainstream media broadcasters.

President Trump's condemnation of left-wing violence in the aftermath of Charlottesville *et al* was starting to look ever more correct, ever more judicious. 'I think we should classify them (Antifa) as a gang,' Mayor of Berkeley Jesse Arreguin told CBS San Francisco. 'They come dressed in uniforms. They have weapons, almost like a militia and I think we need to think about that in terms of our law enforcement approach.'[8] That bastion of American liberalism *Time* magazine also appeared to disagree with the BBC when arguing that, 'Neither Left nor Right has a monopoly on virtue or violence.'

'The BBC gets it'
Growing evidence of Antifa violence captured on film, the mainstream media had little choice but to eventually condemn the left-wing anarchists, albeit reluctantly. All of which made BBC Trending's spirited defence of the anarchists even more unfathomable. The broadcaster's sympathetic stance towards the domestic terrorist organisation certainly pleased some people though:

> **@Anon**
> The BBC gets it #antifa

However, it soon transpired that not only had there been violence on 'both sides' but according to intelligence reports, this violence was usually started by . . . Antifa – the very same entity BBC Trending was gallantly defending from those 'far-right smears' circulated by the apocryphal Joseph Paul Watson and others.

Even left-wing media organisation Politico admitted the culpability of Antifa when noting, 'that by April 2016, authorities believed that "anarchist extremists" were the primary instigators of violence at public rallies against a range of targets.[9] The same article also confirms the joint responsibility for blame on both sides – Left and Right – regarding subsequent violence, while confirming the role played by Antifa in initiating confrontations:

> Even before Charlottesville, dozens and, in some cases, hundreds of people on both sides showed up at events in Texas, California, Oregon and elsewhere, carrying weapons and looking for a fight. In the Texas capital of Austin, armed Antifa protesters attacked Trump supporters and white groups at several recent rallies, and then swarmed police in a successful effort to stop them from making arrests.

The Politico article also reveals how in 2016, the US Department of Homeland Security formally classified Antifa's activities as 'domestic terrorist violence.' All of which cut little ice with the neutral BBC who continued to express their amazement that Trump could actually condemn 'both sides.' By September 2017 the neutral broadcaster was doubling down – continuing to obsess about Trump's 'violence on both sides' comments. An article entitled 'Charlottesville: Trump repeats 'both sides' rhetoric' once again ignored left-wing violence as perpetrated by Antifa, and for the umpteenth time repeated the phrase 'both sides' in what had become an obsessive BBC meme:

> US President Donald Trump has repeated the controversial argument that "both sides" were at fault in white supremacist violence last month.[10]

The Violence in Charlottesville, note, had been of the 'white supremacist' variety only. Not a single mention of Antifa. According to the BBC article, with his remarks, Mr Trump had 'revived controversy.' However the 'controversy' such as it was emitted solely from organisations tacitly (or overtly) supporting Antifa's agenda, organisations such as CNN and the BBC. For those opposing the vicious tactics of this extreme left-wing group there was no controversy and never had been: violence is violence irrespective of what type of hood the perpetrator happens to be wearing.

Recalling Clive Myrie's Antifa = WWII heroes re-tweet, John Nolte deftly summarised the left-wing media's defence of the terrorist group thus:

> To encourage Antifa's wave of violent suppression, our media either ignores and downplays their crimes, promotes their cause as righteous, blames their violence on Trump and his supporters, compares them to heroic World War II soldiers, or in the case of NBC's Chuck Todd attempts to legitimize this violence against the political right.[11]

Sticking up for Antifa? The BBC certainly 'got it.'

Far Right v Far Left: Violence on both sides?

Take a look at the following tweet from the UK editor of the BBC's 'respected' Buzzfeed website:

@Buzzfeed UK editor
All I want for Christmas is full Communism now

Remember that one? Probably not because the eagle-eyed BBC - the same BBC which spends hours trawling 4chan and other Internet messaging sites for the slightest mention of the word 'Nazi' - somehow managed to miss this extraordinary tweet.

Now imagine for a moment that a Breitbart London editor had tweeted, 'All I want for Xmas is full Fascism now.' Allow yourself a moment to imagine the scale of BBC outrage. This is one tweet that its 20,000 + activists would *not* have missed. Might this outlook help to explain why the BBC demanded President Trump condemn right-wing violence at Charlottesville while demanding that he also remained silent about the exploits of Antifa? Might it also explain those copious amounts of BBC news articles invoking 'Nazis' and 'Neo-Nazis' while barely ever mentioning the threat posed by the anarchy of Communists and Marxists?

	Far-right	Far Left
No of victims	25,000,000	94,000,000+[12]
Political system	Totalitarian	Totalitarian
Aka	Nazism	Communism
	Fascism	Marxism
Charlottesville	White nationalists	Antifa anarchists

Fig. 24

So, would Britain's impartial, free and fair broadcaster at least admit there has been violence on 'both sides' throughout history? Why not have a perusal of its news website and see with whom you think the 'right-wing' broadcaster's sympathies lie . . .

'Quiet and safe in Malmö'

Should Donald Trump happen to say that the sea was blue, the BBC would do everything in its power to prove it is any colour *but* blue. It would turn to one of its 'independent' experts who would duly tell the unbiased broadcaster that the sea is actually grey, occasionally black, often green and even red and orange, but never, never ever is it blue. The headlines would soon come pouring forth: 'Eminent scientist: "Trump is lying . . ."'

A comment made by Donald Trump in February of 2017 indeed sent the liberal-left media into something verging on meltdown. In a speech made in Florida, the US President made reference to an incident that had apparently happened in Sweden 'last night.' On first sight it appeared Mr Trump might have been mistaken inasmuch as there had not been a major incident reported in Sweden on the night alluded to, at least not of the terrorist related variety. The country had however long been suffering under an epidemic of gang related crime extending to rapes, murders, arson and violent attacks. Here's the remarks that were to trigger the BBC so badly:

> We've got to keep our country safe. You look at what's happening in Germany, you look at what's happening last night in Sweden. Sweden, who would believe this? Sweden. They took in large numbers. They're having problems like they never thought possible.

The BBC scoffed, oh how it scoffed. What was this ridiculous buffoon talking about now? 'Sweden,' wrote the BBC news website – sweeping generalisation notwithstanding - was 'baffled' by his comments. 'His implication was that something terrible had occurred in their country, in fact, it had been a normal February weekend.'[1] What the impartial broadcaster considers as 'normal' is, however, not entirely clear as we shall see.

Fancy suggesting that Sweden was not a multicultural haven of peace and tranquillity. How dare he! The BBC's army of activists simply couldn't wait to mock, scorn and ridicule the US president. Sure enough a deluge of anti-Trump articles, interviews and reports came pouring out of Broadcasting House in the days that followed. In an article entitled 'Trump tries to explain remark about Sweden amid confusion,'[2] the neutral broadcaster went into overdrive:

> Former Swedish Prime Minister Carl Bildt was among those who Mr Trump's comment, suggesting that he had "been smoking."

> Social media users ridiculed the American leader, joking about imaginary situations involving Swedish institutions like the pop group Abba and furniture store Ikea.

> The mocking hashtag #lastnightinSweden was soon trending on Twitter.

Nor did the tone of the BBC article improve as it progressed. Cult members including £2milion-per-year BBC football presenter Gary Lineker quickly took to Twitter to dutifully follow the lead:

@GaryLineker
Thoughts are with everyone in Sweden at this difficult time

BBC glee continued apace. 'Last night in Sweden' – what about it? shrieked BBC activists besides themselves with excitement. As there had been no serious terrorist-related incidents recorded in the Nordic country 'last night,' the BBC could now imply that Mr Trump had deliberately set out to deceive his audience in Florida. In order to achieve this end it simply constructed a straw man argument: Trump had said – *implied* – that something 'terrible' had happened in Sweden last night. It hadn't. Ergo Trump is a liar.

> 'Trump's wrong, it's 'quiet and safe' in Malmö'
> bbc.co.uk

But was the US President really suggesting there had been a major terrorist incident in Sweden as the BBC was claiming? We can find no evidence of suggestion of terrorist attacks - terrible or not - anywhere in these words, can you? What Mr Trump was actually referring to – as the

BBC and the rest of the Liberal media knew only too well – was the epidemic of largely gang-related crime experienced by western European countries extending to rape, murder, arson and violent attacks. As far as Sweden's descent into a state of affairs where serious crime has become an increasingly common phenomenon, Mr Trump had in fact been closer to the truth than the BBC would care to admit.

'The BBC did not see any visible signs of trouble'

Ever eager to undermine Mr Trump the BBC immediately set off for Malmö, Sweden's third largest city and where two of its activists, 'asked people if Donald Trump was right about Sweden's immigration policy.' So, was Mr Trump right? Was the Nordic country experiencing significantly increased levels of criminal activity? You can probably guess the impartial answer to that question . . .

In the film that follows, the BBC crew interview various residents of Rosengård, a district of Malmö home to a large immigrant population. Of those people expressing views, only one person has anything negative to say about the situation in the city ('If I had children, I wouldn't let them go out after dark') Typically, this single voice of dissent is countered by many more voices expressing a positive attitude towards the city; stacking the deck - that most ubiquitous of BBC tricks. Indeed, the overwhelming impression from the BBC report is one of a harmonious, peaceful city:

> During two days of filming the BBC did not see any visible signs of trouble . . .'

The BBC thus chose to headline its report, 'Trump's wrong, it's 'quiet and safe' in Malmö.'[3]

Yet had the BBC activists cared to peruse local media they would have learnt of some very disturbing incidents in Malmö since (and before) the beginning of the year. The BBC had not however arrived in Malmö to report the truth. Their mission in the city was simple: to discredit the US president. The activists had not arrived with a blank notepad. On the contrary, their notebooks were already full: *Trump is very, very bad* (master narrative) *Trump is a liar* (sub-narrative). *(Mass) migration is very, very good; Sweden (Malmö) is very peaceful* etc.

'There are shootings, car fires and so much s*** going on in Malmö'
Had the BBC activists cared to look, they would have found a whole
catalogue of highly disturbing incidents happening in the once peaceful
city. A quick check of local media would have turned up plentiful stories
describing the effect of the city's crime wave upon local residents.
Swedish media is jam-packed full of victims' stories. In fact, they are
impossible to miss . . .

Take the story of local resident Leija Heco who in January 2017
watched in horror as flames consumed her newly acquired Chevrolet,
leaving it a burnt out shell. The 28-year old had just said goodbye to her
father after visiting him in the Fosie district of Malmö.

'It's horrible,' a traumatised Ms. Heco told Expressen.se, 'I lived in
New York for six years but crime in Malmö is actually worse.'[4] Ms. Heco
lives in the Malmö district of Lönngården where car fires have become
'commonplace.'[5] Reflecting on the differences in crime between her
home city and New York, she observed that, 'There (New York) you see
police on every street corner, not here. No, Malmö has become a worst
city. I feel it's a societal problem, there are shootings, car fires and a lot of
s*** happening in Malmö.'

Arguably the most worrying 'societal' problem occurring in
Swedish cities is the increased threat of sexual violence towards women.
After another suspected rape in late December 2017 in the Högaholm
area of Malmö, one local resident, 50-year old Lena Blom, spoke for
many women when she told the media, 'I do not go out in the evenings
anymore.' Winter 2017-18 and the women of Malmö had every reason to
be fearful.

Earlier that month a 17-year old girl had been gang-raped in a
children's playground in Hasselgatan. Two other similar attacks had
occurred in November. Little wonder as 2018 arrived the atmosphere in
and around the city was febrile. With tensions high and a potential
epidemic on its hands, the Malmö police department issued a statement
advising women not to go out after dark, or to go around in pairs if
necessary. Under political pressure the police later withdrew this advice.
While statements could be withdrawn, the reality facing Malmö law
enforcement services could not so easily be ignored. Not only did local
police have a serious of suspected gang-rapes to investigate, resources
were also required to handle a worrying number of attempted child

abductions in the city. 'If you feel that someone in any way has unwanted contacts with children please contact us immediately,' said police chief Nils Norling addressing himself to city parents beside themselves with anxiety.[6] The report by 24Malmö.se into yet another disturbing phenomenon to plague the city had opened on a particularly sobering note:

> In recent weeks, 24Malmö.se has repeatedly written about events around the city where men are suspected of having chased children but also trying to attract children in food stores. In addition, a man is suspected of shooting five little girls at a school in Malmö.

Fearing for the safety of his young family, one young father decided to leave Malmö for good. 'It is mainly because I and my partner do not want our children to grow up in an insecure environment,' he explained adding, 'In the area where we lived, the drug traffickers and addicts were relatively open. It's not an environment I want my daughter to grow up in.'

Nor are the types of concerns articulated here unique. On a visit back to Malmö, the Los Angeles-based Swedish model and singer Jennifer Åkerman echoed these sentiments. In the past, the 28-year old had reputedly expressed her own reservations regarding the Swedish city. 24Malmö.se wanted to know why the celebrity was not fond of Malmö. 'I really do not know,' replied the model with admirable diplomacy, 'I'm not so fond of Stockholm either. It has more to do with Sweden. I get anxious easily when I'm in Sweden for a long time.'[7]

'Malmö is a lost city'

In its eagerness to prosecute its set narrative, the BBC team somehow missed a whole raft of similar reports swirling around both national and local Swedish media, and which revealed a city experiencing a quite unprecedented plague of criminal activity together with heaps of civic concern. 'Is it time to leave Malmö?' pondered a Dagens Nyheter journalist in an article entitled, 'Unresolved murders spread horror in Malmö,'[8] 'Malmö as a city is fucked up,' wrote one resident on social media.

Incidents reported around the time of the BBC visit to Malmö included arson attempts, a wave of street robberies including a recent armed robbery in the city centre, as well as several assassination attempts and other gun related crimes. Just weeks before Mr Trump's comments, shocking images had circulated of migrant gangs rioting on New Year's Eve in the city's Mollevang square. 'Malmö is a lost city,' declared photographer Freddy Mardell after witnessing the mob aiming rockets at local police who declined to leave the safety of their patrol cars.[9] 'Swedish teenagers gathered in a large group to avoid being robbed,' he also revealed.

Had they bothered to do some rudimentary research, the BBC visitors would also have heard how, on the 18th of February – just days before they arrived in the city - a man armed with an axe had attacked local police. A little more research would have undoubtedly lead them to the terrible story of three Malmö teenagers who had been shot just weeks' earlier, caught up in the city's raging gang wars. And who knows just how the activists would have reacted if they had bothered to check a report into public perception of crime, the result of which were released in ... February 2017.

The Annual Security Survey conducted by the Malmö police department found that a whopping 77% of the city's residents felt insecure in their home city – worried they too might become victims of the spiralling crime wave.[10] Had they cared to look still further, BBC activists would also have encountered a tragic story still fresh in the minds of the people of Malmö. On the evening of the 13th of February, a 20-year old man had been shot dead in cold blood outside a restaurant at the central Möllevångstorget square - a murder which prompted Sweden's Justice Minister Anders Ygeman to organise an emergency visit to Malmö in order to discuss the increasing level of violence occurring on its streets.[11]

'I and the government take developments in Malmö very seriously'
As reported by Malmö.com, the city had indeed been reeling under a glut of similar violent incidents, all of which had seemingly passed the BBC activists by:

The 20-year-old man who was killed outside a restaurant on Sunday is only the latest in a string of shootings that have taken place in the city since the New Year.

On January 3, a 22-year old man was shot dead in the Fosie area of Malmö, and a week later a 16-year-old boy was shot dead at a bus stop in Rosengård. Last week, a caretaker in Malmö was shot when he was out spreading salt on the pavement in a housing area, to prevent them from being slippery. He is still in hospital, being treated for life threatening injuries.[12]

'I and the government take the developments in Malmö very seriously,' Minister Ygeman told the media during his visit to the beleaguered city just days before the BBC rocked up. 'Organized crime and gangs have grown too strong. We have to take action.'[13] The headline chosen by Dagans Nyheter, one of Sweden's most widely read newspapers, spoke of 'Significant concern in Malmö.'

Nor could the BBC activists claim ignorance. High profile visits such as those of Mr Ygeman were making headline news. National and local media were also tracking the catalogue of shootings and murders that had afflicted the city: 'Fifteen murders in eleven months. Nine of them lethal shootings,' reported Sydsvenskan on February 4th in an extended article delving into the whys and wherefores driving Malmö's spate of murders.[14]

Violence was not just contained to Malmö's streets. Just a fortnight before the BBC arrived, Radio Sverige revealed that the city's main hospital had been forced to close its doors to members of the public between the hours of 21.00 and 05.00 – a measure deemed necessary for the safety and protection of medical personnel.[15] 'Staff have been exposed to threats during their working hours,' revealed a hospital spokesman. As a further measure, hospital management also decided to post security guards at the hospital entrance who would admit patients and relatives visiting the hospital's emergency unit. Arriving in February, just days after Sweden's own Justice Minister had spoken of his 'significant concern for Malmö,' BBC activists could not have picked a better time to witness first-hand the volatility in this once tranquil city.

'An upward violent spiral'

The horrific murder of a 16-year old Iraqi boy in the Rosengård district of Malmö on January 14th occurred just weeks before the BBC declared the city to be 'quiet and safe.' VLT.se was yet another media outlet to note how the police could no longer cope with the sheer volume of crime: 'Another murder attempt in Malmö - Police: "We need more resources"[16]

Although by no means unusual for a city by now accustomed to violent crime, this particular murder prompted Stefan Sinteus to write an open letter to the city in which Malmö's chief of police begged not only for the public's patience but also its help. Sinteus spelled out the city's problems bluntly enough:

> We have in Malmö an upward violent spiral of great measure. Malmöpolis is currently investigating eleven murders and eighty-eight murder attempts. Add further violent crime, abuse, assaults, robbery and fraud.'[17]

The latest victim of Malmö's street violence had simply been waiting for a bus home from school when he had been murdered. Police investigators soon hit a brick wall. Fearing reprisals, the young victim's friends and classmates were reluctant to speak about the murder with the consequence that the police investigation stalled. 'They are scared. They are terrified and are wondering who's going to be shot next,' said the school's headmaster.[18] Witnesses had good reason to keep quiet. A 23-year old man, reputedly an eye witness, was shot dead in Rosengård just weeks later.[19]

Faced with a wall of silence, Sinteus' letter soon went viral. 'It goes without saying,' wrote Sinteus, 'that the police in Malmö are in an extremely strained position.' The veteran police chief's letter hinted at the scale of the task facing his officers:

> Several employees from the Police National Operations Department (NOA) arrived in Malmö last week, and additional employees are expected this week. There is a great understanding that we in Malmö need reinforcement in the position which we are in.

'The situation,' continued Sinteus, 'is serious and the situation is by no means optimistic.' He was not the only police officer to break ranks. A social media post by retired police officer Peter Springare went viral after it had been posted on Facebook in February 2017, just days before the BBC arrived in the country:

> I'm so fucking tired. What I will write here below is not politically correct. But I don't give a shit. What I will tell all you taxpayers is forbidden for us state employees to peddle, even though it's true.
>
> Here we go; this week I have dealt with: rape, aggravated rape, sexual assault, extortion, abuse of justice, illegal threats, violence against the police, drug offences, serious drugs crime, attempted murder, rape again, extortion again and assault. Countries that represent the week's crimes: Iraq, Iraq, Turkey, Syria, Afghanistan, Somalia, Somalia, Syria again, Somalia, unknown country, unknown country, Sweden. Half the suspects, we can't know for sure because they don't have any valid papers, which in itself usually means that they lie about nationality and identity.

Springare worked the beat in Örebro, a city of about 120,000 inhabitants 200 kilometres west of Stockholm. By shining a light on the city's burgeoning criminal element and moreover the ethnicity of offenders, he earned the wrath of a Swedish establishment going to extraordinary lengths to conceal such sensitive information. Multi-cultural Sweden had to succeed at any cost – there were far too many agencies and individuals whose reputations hung on its success. Springare didn't care though. He'd seen enough. The time had come to speak out.

In an interview later that year he revealed why he had chosen to speak out: 'I am deeply concerned with developments,' he told *Katerina Magazine*:

> I'm wondering how far it must go before people in decision-making positions and politicians wake up and see where we are heading. You continue to bury your head in the sand - you go out and say you have full control. It's the other way around, we've lost control.[20]

'100s of victims'

By summer 2017, and with the situation in Malmö threatening to spiral out of control, the city's authorities turned to the United States for help. The city's Crime Prevention Council sent a delegation to New Haven, a city situated to the north of New York and one credited with having reduced worryingly high homicide rates thanks to the introduction of innovative policing methods.[21]

Desperate as such measures may seem, Malmö was sending out a cry for help. New-fangled methods of crime control notwithstanding, with autumn approaching, the city's police chief Stefan Sintéus turned to the military for help. In September, 160 troops arrived in the city to bolster his under siege police force.[22] Despite the arrival of the military, Malmö (population 320,000) remained a city struggling to cope with soaring levels of crime which were now compounded by a wave of car thefts targeting prestigious vehicles such as BMW and Mercedes as reported on local media:

Large theft wave continues in Malmö - 100s of victims[23]

Over the course of a single October weekend, more than a dozen such vehicles were stolen in what the police believed to have been orchestrated raids. The situation was threatening to spiral out of control.

Perhaps it should therefore have come as no surprise when Sydsvenskan reported in November that the city's prison population was now twice as high of those of Stockholm (pop: 900,000) and Gothenburg (pop: 580,000).[24] Indeed, as long ago as 2012 the Local.se had drawn attention to the disproportionate number of gun related crimes occurring in Malmö in comparison to the country's two largest cities ('Gun violence 'most common' in Malmö').[25] At times it seemed nobody was safe in this once peaceful city, certainly not the police and not even its most innocuous public servants as revealed when 24Malmö.se reported on what they called 'a new phenomenon' that autumn:

In connection with funerals in Malmö, it has been shown funeral guests often carry weapons, sometimes openly. All 230 employees at Malmö Cemeteries Administration will now be trained how to handle weapons.[26]

If the city's graveyards could not be relied upon to be 'quiet and safe' spaces, where could? Not, apparently, Malmö's schools. Growing violence within the city's secondary school system had been yet another new phenomenon noted in recent years. Back In 2015 the Local.se had shocked its readers when reporting goings on at a Rosengård secondary school daily subjected to 'violence, threats and visits from criminal gangs,' all of which had ultimately led to the school's closure. 'The City of Malmö,' noted the Local 'will now hire a security firm in order to make the school environment safer.'[27]

Two years down the line the situation in Malmö's schools had seemingly not improved. In November 2017 a brawl at the city's Einar Hansengymnasiet high school was serious enough for police to attend.[28]

'Sweden's Chicago'

One particularly invidious development of the 'New Sweden' is the prevalence of crimes involving hand grenades, a phenomenon virtually unknown prior to mass migration. Such was the concern caused by the use of these devices in a wide variety of crimes, in December 2017 The Week newspaper reported that the Swedish government had proposed a three-month hand grenade amnesty to come into effect between October 2018 and January 2019. Yes, you read that correctly - a hand grenade amnesty! ('Sweden plans grenade amnesty as attacks soar')

For many people Sweden's grenade problem first came to light in 2016 when an 8-year old British boy was killed in a grenade attack on a Gothenburg apartment. It was not however an uncommon occurrence in the 'New Sweden.' Even before the Gothenburg attack after visiting a 'port city' Reuters had already drawn attention to a growing trend that had 'shocked a Nordic country that prides itself on safety' and 'led to worries criminality is out of control.'[29] The 'port city' referred to by Reuters? Malmö . . .

In their 2015 report, the news agency had interviewed Goran Mansson head of Malmö's bomb squad: 'As bomb squad chief in the western port city of Malmö, Mansson has been busy with a dozen grenade attacks in the last few months.' Indeed, the prevalence of firearms and grenades in Malmö had led the media to dub the city 'Sweden's Chicago.' It wasn't just Malmö that at times resembled the very worst crime-ridden cities the United States could offer. Speaking to

Sverige Radio in December 2017, Swedish Chief Prosecutor Lise Tamm compared the Stockholm suburb of Rinkeby to a 'war zone.'[30] Research presented by Sverige Radio compared the level of gun crime in Sweden's largest cities with that of cities in neighbouring countries, the station noting that, 'Neither police, nor experts, have managed to explain the reason behind the escalating violence . . .'

Number of people injured in shootings in major Nordic cities 2010-15[31]	
Stockholm (Sweden)	189
Gothenburg (Sweden)	109
Malmö (Sweden)	63
Copenhagen (Denmark)	30
Oslo (Norway)	30
Helsinki (Finland)	10

Fig. 25

Ongoing research conducted by Malmö University, Karolinska Hospital and Stockholm University painted a similarly bleak picture of Sweden's social problems when stating that the country experiences, 'four to five times more fatal shootings per capita than Norway and Germany.' 'Sweden's gun violence on par with Mexico, researchers say,' so went a headline on Malmö.com in autumn of 2017.[32]

Writing for *The Spectator* magazine in an article entitled 'How Sweden became an example of how not to handle immigration,' political commentator and member of Sweden's Moderate Party, Tove Lifvendahl observed that, 'A parallel society is emerging where the state's monopoly on law and order is being challenged.'[33] Lifvendahl went on to quote Amur Rostani, an academic specialising in crime based at Stockholm University: 'Today, the gang environment is – well I don't want to exactly call it the Wild West, but something in that direction.' In June 2017 Swedish police announced they had added eight new areas in the country to its list of areas considered to be 'especially vulnerable' – three of them in Malmö (Nydala, Hermodsdal and Lindängen).

Let's summarise just some of the key events the BBC's activists had somehow contrived to 'miss' which were happening in and around their 'quiet and safe' February 2017 visit to Malmö:

- Malmö police chief Stefan Sinteus' 'open' letter of 27 January begging the public to help his beleaguered police force
- Media reports describing Malmö's growing list of unsolved murders, most recently occurring on January 3, 12 and February 12
- Retired police officer Peter Springare's viral Facebook post of 3 February lamenting Sweden's descent into a country riddled with crime
- The emergency visit to Malmö by Sweden's Justice Minister on 13 February
- The 16 February release of Malmö police's Annual Security Survey which revealed 77% of people feared they would become victims of crime

The strange and inexplicable case of Malmö's 48-hour crime respite
With so much happening in Malmö in and around January and February 2017 - theft, murder, arson, robbery, muggings, assaults and attempted assassinations to name but a few, it is only by a sheer miracle that the BBC activists completely missed this nightly carnival unfolding on the streets beyond their hotel. Just how they had managed to miss hi-profile ministerial visits, statistical crime reports, 'open' letters from police chiefs, not to mention the daily catalogue of crime as reported by local media is anyone's guess.

Being the fair minded folk we are at Brainwashing Britain, we refused to believe that the impartial broadcaster had arrived in Malmö with not even the slightest intention of reporting fairly and objectively. If we could only establish the dates the BBC stayed in Malmö, perhaps we could explain why they returned home to tell their believers so unequivocally that, 'Trump is wrong: it's quiet and safe in Malmö.' Perhaps there had been a 48-hour amnesty. Perhaps the BBC had arrived at the very moment the city's criminal fraternity had decided to take a well-deserved winter break. Had the BBC even been to Malmö? Perhaps they had taken a wrong turn, ended up in one of the migrant-free visegrad nations, Poland, Czech Republic or Hungary where life could more truthfully be described as 'quiet and safe.'

With this noble aim in mind, we decided to ask the BBC to divulge the exact date its activists had rocked up in the Swedish city. We knew they claimed to have arrived in the city sometime towards the end of February 2017, presumably before the 24th of the month when its 'quiet and safe' article appeared on the BBC website. Time to solve the mysterious lull in Malmö's crime wave once and for all.

'Malmö most dangerous city in the Nordic region'[34]

Whatever the BBC activists had been doing during their 48-hour sojourn to the city, it appears that research might not have been particularly high on the agenda. The Swedish murder rate during the 1970s, for the record, remained stable at just under 1 per 100,000.[35]

Murder Index 2016	Murders per 100,000
Malmö Pop: 330,000	3.4
Paris Pop: 2,200,000	1.8
London Pop: 8,800,000	1.3
Copenhagen Pop: 1,300,000	1.1
Berlin Pop: 3,600,000	1.0

Fig. 26
Sources: Sydsvenskan, Brå,
Statista, World Atlas and HD.

'The BBC makes a huge range of information available'

On which two February nights in 2017 did the BBC stay in Malmö? A simple enough question to answer. Filing a Freedom of Information (FOI) request with the transparent broadcaster would be a piece of cake – well wouldn't it?[36] A little while later the reply duly arrived. It was time to end this mystery once and for all:

> The information you have requested is excluded from the Act because it is held for the purposes of 'journalism, art or literature.' The BBC is therefore not obliged to provide this information to you and will not be doing so on this occasion.

If that sounded convincing, the icing on the cake was yet to come:

> That said, the BBC makes a huge range of information available about our programmes and content on bbc.co.uk . .

'What life is really like in Sweden'[37]

Later in the year the BBC decided to double down on its 'Sweden is fluffy' narrative. It might have been six months since Mr Trump's 'last night in Sweden' remarks, but the BBC was *still* looking to discredit the US president. The article that appeared on its news website allocated generous coverage to a collection of photographs purporting to present what the BBC declared was representative of 'What everyday life is really like in Sweden.'

> When US President Donald Trump launched this criticism of European refugee policy during a rally in Florida, Sweden was baffled. His implication was that something terrible had occurred in their country, in fact, it had been a normal February weekend.

As a form of cultural rebuttal,' continued the BBC article 'a group of leading Swedish photographers have collaborated on a project to show what life is really like for a typical Swede.'

As to what constitute 'a normal February weekend' the broadcaster does not clarify. Moreover, what a 'normal' weekend in Malmö might look and sound like is not expanded upon. What with so many firearm offences in the city, not to mention hand grenade attacks, the quietness in Malmö can only be imagined. Here's a list of shootings and murders carried out with firearms over a 12-month period in this 'quiet and safe' Nordic haven of peace and tranquillity:

Murders and attempted Murders using firearms in Malmö 2017	
3 Jan	18 year old woman shot at Västra Kattarpsvägen
	Man died after shooting at Docentgatan
	Shooting at private house in Påskliljegatan
4 Jan	Bus shot at Lindängen Center
6 Jan	One seriously injured after shooting at Persborg
9 Jan	Attempted murder in Fosie
12 Jan	16-year-old Ahmed Obaid murdered in Rosengård
22 Jan	18-year old shot at Lindängen, seriously injured
25 Jan	Man shot in leg at Nydala
1 Feb	16-year old shot in leg in Malmö
4 Feb	Group of young men shot at in Eriksfältsgatan
8 Feb	Caretaker shot dead at Pildammsparken
12 Feb	23-year old murdered at Möllevångstorget
2 Mar	60-year old shot at Fosie
4 Mar	Two men shot at Kronetorpsgatan, one dies
6 Mar	Apartment shot at Kroksbäck
11 Mar	Man injured in shooting at Fosie
13 Mar	Man shot outside restaurant in Ystadvägen
29 Mar	Man shot at Lindeborg
30 Mar	Shots fired at Folksångsgatan townhouse
	23-year old man shot dead in Rosengård
16 Apr	Shots fired in Påskliljegatan area, cartridges found
28 Apr	Kidnapper shot at Holma
11 May	20-year old man shot at Fosievägen
12 May	Two shootings at Sörbäcksgatan
28 May	45-year old murdered at Möllevångstorget
10 Jun	Man shot and killed at Lantmannagatan
23 Jun	House shot at in Rosengård
27 Jun	Apartment shot at in Rosengård
2 July	Three people shot at Hyacintgatan
7 July	Man shot in centre of Rosengård

11 July	Shooting at Bergsgatan
14 July	Murder attempt at Bennets väg
	Man shot at Holma torg
	Shots fired in Rosengård
16 July	Man injured in armed robbery at Persborgstorget
18 July	Shots fired at family home in Almvik
4 Aug	Two men shot at Bragegatan
13 Aug	Three shot in Ystadgatan club
30 Aug	Man shot at Lönngatan
1 Sep	20-year old man shot at Rosengård
4 Sep	Car shot up at Katrinelund
16 Sep	Man shot in Rosengård
19 Sep	Man injured at Västra Skrävlingevägen
27 Sep	Two men shot in Rosengård
17 Oct	Shooting reported at Eriksfältsgatan
3 Nov	Apartment shot at in Ramels väg
30 Nov	Shooting at Eriksfältsgatan: one dead, one injured
1 Dec	Shots fired at car in Thomsons väg, Rosengård
4 Dec	Man seriously injured in Hyllie shooting
28 Dec	30-year old shot dead at Nydalaskolan

Fig 27. Source: Expressen.se

The BBC's rosy pictures of Malmö and Sweden in general were however sharply at odds with the results of The National Security Survey (NTU), published by Brå, the country's Crime Prevention Council in November 2017 which found, 'The proportion (of respondents) who state that they are subjected to what is known as a crime against an individual is at the highest level since the measurements began in 2006.'[38] The report made for sobering reading. Increases in a wide range of categories including threats, harassment, fraud, sexual offences and muggings were recorded. The report's authors go on to caution that:

> Young women aged 16-24 are the most vulnerable to sexual offences, 14 percent reported they had been subjected to at least one such crime in 2016. Among men in the same age group, 1.2 percent reported that they had been exposed.

Percentage of the population exposed to different types of crime against individual person[39]	Increase (%) 2005-16
Fraud/deception	43
Vulnerability to sexual offence	200
Harassment	34
Threats	22
Muggings	40

Fig. 28

Of even more concern was the possibility that the statistics in each of Brå's categories were likely being seriously under-reported: 'The majority of crimes in the NTU have not been reported to police,' warned the report, going on to add, 'of those exposed to sexual offenses in 2016, only 11 percent stated that they reported the incident to the police.' Why then were victims failing to report crimes? According to Brå, 'The most common reason for not reporting the crime is that the victim does not believe the police can do anything.'

In November of 2017 Swedish media reported on a survey by Demoskop of 2,029 women which found half of those questioned felt restricted in their everyday movements for fear of abuse.[40] It also found that almost half of the women surveyed avoided secluded environments. Such concerns for personal safety have led to increased calls for 'feminist urban planning' – localities specifically planned to provide maximum security and safety for lone females, further testament to 'what everyday life is really like in Sweden.'

A research project published in July 2018 entitled 'What Worries the World' asked the citizens of 26 countries for their views on topics such as crime and violence, immigration, poverty and education. In the category of Crime and Violence, Sweden ranked the fifth most concerned country behind the likes of Mexico and South Africa. While 50% of Swedes said they were worried about crime, the average world figure was 32%. By way of contrast, the number of US citizens worried about crime stood at 29%. Sweden occupied first position regarding worries about the rise of extremism with a figure of 27% - three times higher than the world average. In terms of where their country was heading, a massive 73% of Swedes thought their country was headed in the wrong direction, or what we could usefully call the BBC direction.[41]

'Thoughts are with everyone in Sweden at this difficult time'
Although Mr Trump's suggestion that everything was not quite as rosy in the Swedish garden as some would have it was met with flippancy by sneering multi-million pound BBC presenters, those actually living the reality of multi-cultural Sweden might have found more than a grain of truth in the president's comments.

For example, in December 2017 a gang of twenty-one masked men threw Molotov cocktails at a synagogue in central Gothenburg while children huddled together inside. One terrified youngster sent her mother a desperate SMS text: 'Mum, I'm starting to get scared', and that '20 masked men were throwing burning objects.'[42] Three men were later arrested.

> **@Anon**
> So tonight a group of people throw firebombs at the synagogue in Gothenburg, Sweden, while Jewish teenagers were having a party inside. Let me be perfectly clear: The Swedish government have failed us Jews. We are not safe here. Shame on you. Shame on you.

The elderly in particularly have reason to fear for their safety in the 'New Sweden.' In February, local media reported on a 90-year old woman who had been robbed in Malmö – what the BBC would presumably consider to be a 'normal February' type of incident. A few months later media reports described the mugging of an 80-year old female in the Limhamn district of the same city. In December that year, Malmöpolis awoke to reports of how an 86-year old woman had been robbed at knifepoint. In that they had not suffered physical injury, such elderly victims had escaped relatively lightly. 'What everyday life is like in Sweden . . .' Others were not so lucky.

The case of Helgar Stenmark was a case in point.[43] Having just returned from a visit to local shops, the frail 89-year old discovered an unknown man hanging around the back of her property in Norsjö, a small town in northern Sweden. The man – recently arrived from Afghanistan – attacked and killed the unfortunate Ms. Stenmark. It was just the latest in a long line of crimes against the most vulnerable in society.

'Swedish woman takes porridge title'

Life in the 'New Sweden' has its challenges. Mass migration brought diversity to the country, but also a raft of social challenges. 'In its rush to portray itself as a beacon of tolerance to the world,' a native of Malmö tells Brainwashing Britain, 'Sweden has abjectly failed to integrate such huge numbers of immigrants into society, with the result that major towns and cities are becoming something like ghettos. The Swedish political and media establishment simply refuse to acknowledge this reality. And so the situation becomes ever graver.'

However, had you been solely watching, reading or listening to the BBC's coverage of Swedish news in 2017, you could have been forgiven for thinking Sweden is a progressive haven of peace and tranquillity. That is not to say the corporation threw a blanket over Swedish news in 2017, on the contrary. From news about Ferdinand the lost moose to tales of meatball mountains - when something important happened in the country of Abba, the BBC were right there. Here's a selection of our favourite BBC Sweden headlines from 2017:

Looking for Ferdinand the white moose

Meatball mountain shuts Swedish road

Swedish woman takes porridge title

Meet Boaty McBoatface's Swedish cousin

No time to change sanitary products

Sweden to hold 'man-free' music festival

Why Swedish workplaces aren't as equal as you think

'Quiet and safe in Malmö . . .'

To get an idea of just how 'quiet and safe' it really is in the Swedish city, we present a selection of headlines reported by local media over a typical seven day period in November 2017 during the first drafting of *BBC: Brainwashing Britain?*

30 Nov
- A person is reported to be dead after shooting
- Two men suspected of raping man at Fosieanstalt.
- Women were violated and persecuted several times
- 22-year-old suspected of murder attempt and robbery
- Four arrested for two different killings in Malmö
- More and more seek care for HIV in Skåne
- Amnesty will remove hand grenades from the street
- Arrested for murder and assassination attempt at Eriksfältsgatan

29 Nov
- Suspected assassination attempt - injured man entered restaurant
- Several suspects for rape in prison
- Woman threatened and robbed by unknown persons
- 90-year-old woman exposed to crime
- Drug smuggler sentenced in district court to five years
- After shooting: "It has become an insecure house"
- The police warn: "Make sure empty cars are locked"
- A 28-year-old man was arrested for robbery
- Older gentleman found a sawn off shotgun in a bin
- Laser attack against the Coast Guard aeroplane
- Attempted fire attack in Malmö

28 Nov
- Building burned: "More or less total damage"
- Grocery store robbery: personnel injured
- Tens of thousands of crowns stolen from older dementia patients
- Women deprived of freedom and abused
- Car fire in Malmö tonight

27 Nov	Burglary and gross theft - one is prosecuted
	Young woman beaten and robbed by two men
	Two men beat a person at a school in Malmö
	Skåne: driver convicted of sexually abusing young girl in school taxi
	Burglary in store in central Malmö
	Patient broke jaw and nose of employee
	School robbery in Malmö: "They've taken everything"
	90-year-old woman robbed in her home at Malmö

27 Nov
Burglary and gross theft - one is prosecuted
Young woman beaten and robbed by two men
Two men beat a person at a school in Malmö
Skåne: driver convicted of sexually abusing young girl in school taxi
Burglary in store in central Malmö
Patient broke jaw and nose of employee
School robbery in Malmö: "They've taken everything"
90-year-old woman robbed in her home at Malmö

26 Nov
Night watchman attacked at Adelgatan
Man attacked at Tenorgatan Malmö
Knife attack: student attacked during class
Two cars torched at the Battlehouse in Malmö.
Man beaten up at Posthusplatsen

25 Nov
31-year-old man threatened a nurse at SUS in Malmö
Man attacked at Claesgatan
Gun found in apartment

24 Nov
Security guards chased thieves - attacked by bangers
Marijuana driver caught with lots of jewellery
Police patrol attacked with darts
Police attend knife brawl in Docentgatan, Malmö
Car has started burning on church road, Lockarp
80-year-old woman robbed of purse in Limhamn
55-year-old detained for two assassination attempts
Sentenced for robbery of 84-year-old man at Rosengård
In Malmö another two suspected rapes have occurred

'Hilarious'-The Assassination of Katie Hopkins

O ut of thousands of theatre shows produced in the UK very year, one in particular seemed to fascinate the 'national' broadcaster throughout 2016 and 2017. Indeed, the BBC's promotion of this particular play was as tireless as it was admirable:

> From Aidan Turner and Vanessa Kirby in starring roles to two heavyweight productions of Macbeth and a new musical about the assassination of Katie Hopkins - there's much theatre to look forward to around the UK in 2018.[1]
> bbc.co.uk

> The Assassination of Katie Hopkins considers the boundaries of liberal tolerance and the pervasive power of social media
> Programmes | BBC Two

> Playwright Chris Bush on her new musical, The Assassination of Katie Hopkins...
> Programmes | BBC Radio Wales

> A composer from Oxford has been working on music for a controversial production called The Assassination of Katie Hopkins.
> News | Oxford

And so it went on. And on, and on prompting Ms Hopkins to tweet:

> **@KThopkins**
> The state broadcaster promoting my assassination.
> Curious times

'The BBC is in no sense promoting anyone's "assassination"

Beyond the relatively small audience who are interested in and attend live theatre, there can't have been too many people who would have known that Theatre Clwyd was set to produce a play provocatively entitled 'The Assassination of Katie Hopkins' as part of its 2018 season.

Not, that is, until the BBC decided to give the play a series of major plugs. The broadcaster even turned up on the streets of Mold, the small Welsh town home to Theatre Clwyd! The play's producers suddenly had publicity beyond their wildest dreams. As to whether the 'national' broadcaster should be promoting a play that appears to be inciting murder, that's a matter for the BBC and others to ponder. Should they ever consider this question, you can probably have a wild guess at what impartial conclusion might be reached . . .

Ms Hopkins herself was not impressed. As a vocal critic of just the sort of narratives cherished by the BBC – mass migration, feminism, transgenderism, and the cult of victimhood in general, the former Mail Online columnist has undeniably made many enemies in the left-wing media. But promoting murder? Curious times indeed. Matters of taste and decency aside, the BBC film crew duly rocked up in Mold to conduct a series of 'spontaneous' interviews with members of the public or vox pops as they are known in the industry. News of the play's imminent production had caused 'strong feelings amongst shoppers in Mold this afternoon,' announced the BBC reporter:

Vox pop 1:	I think it's hilarious. Er, I think it's a great thing for them to do . . .
Vox pop 2:	I really, really think it's hilarious . . . I'm actually looking forwards to seeing it . . .
Vox pop 3:	I'd see it. I'd see it. I like musicals and I dislike Katie Hopkins . . .

Strong feelings indeed: three 'random' members of the public all in favour of the production and, surprise, surprise, none against it. Good old BBC editing . . . However, this age old BBC trick did not fool some people: 'interview ONLY those saying they LOVE the idea & would go to see it,' remarked one social media user, one of many such comments.

The BBC was quick to defend its enthusiastic promotion of the play: 'I regret very much that you have been the subject of death threats,' so responded David Jordan, the BBC's Director of Editorial Policy and

Standards to Ms Hopkins, before bizarrely adding, 'As you will know some BBC correspondents have also been subject to threats.' Precisely why Jordan chose to include this last piece of information is not entirely clear, unless of course it was some sort of weird quid pro quo: *We (BBC) get threats, so why shouldn't we produce content which encourages (death) threats towards you?* Notice how in this odd piece of whataboutery, the BBC executive is careful to state that correspondents have been subjected to 'threats' without specifying what sort. Presumably not death threats. 'The BBC is in no sense promoting anyone's "assassination," concluded Jordan.

While the BBC claimed to see no link between promoting a play inciting murder with events in the real world, many others did: 'So, by pushing an idea into the public consciousness, they (the BBC) bear absolutely no responsibility should some nutter decide to act on it. Hmm,' wrote one social media user clearly not impressed by Jordan's response. 'Pretty sure there is a legal case for incitement to violence here,' wrote another.

'Her empathy and her self-sacrifice has been endless'

It wasn't just BBC news that appeared to be promoting violence towards Katie Hopkins. The plot of an episode of an online BBC Three series also centred around a story involving extreme violence towards her. Under normal circumstance the broadcaster takes a very stern view towards violence against females. But not on this occasion. This was different. This was Katie Hopkins, wrong-thinker.

Set in the fictitious offices of the Pak Nation, a TV production company, 'Coconut' features a cast of almost exclusively Asian characters. Episode 2 of the series centres around Ms Hopkins winning the award of 'National Treasure of 2017.' The columnist is then immortalised in the form of a bust which is later unveiled as the programme's main character, Ahmed Armstrong delivers a speech:

> Today we are at Ealing cricket club and we are about to unveil Katie. Rumours are circulating that Katie herself will be coming down. From naming her daughter after the poverty stricken nation of India to gaining four stone, her empathy and her self-sacrifice has been endless . . .

As the end credits roll, a member of the Pak TV production team – Tommy Khan comes forward and proceeds to viciously smash the bust to smithereens using a cricket bat while a crowd of onlookers cheer him on. As Armstrong addresses the audience, Khan carries on his disturbing assault with what can only be termed vigour and pure hatred.

End sequence BBC Three Coconut 'National Treasure' (Fig. 30)

Wielding a bat, Tommy Khan prepares to attack a bust of Katie Hopkins

Egged on by the onlookers, Khan strikes the bust

The crowd cheer wildly as Khan smashes the bust to pieces

The vicious attack continues as the onlookers continue to cheer

TV violence and real life

The possible influence of television violence upon impressionable minds has long been a subject of interest among researchers. One of the most shocking cases linking media to real-life violence occurred on 29 November, 2009 in Indiana when a 17-year old strangled his 10-year old brother to death. The teenager revealed how he was inspired by a character in Dexter, a popular television series in which a police forensic expert moonlights as a serial killer. The teenager – subsequently dubbed 'The Dexter Killer' – told investigators how he identified with the television character.

In their research into the social impact of television upon young adults, Hoffner and Buchanan (2005) discuss 'wishful identification' which they define as 'the desire to be like or act like the (television) character.'[2] A 2017 study by Iowa State University found that the influence of television violence upon young adults is consistent across cultures. Participants in this study had an average age of 21 and were of European, Asian, American and Australasian heritage.

Psychologists also have a keen interest in the effects of media violence upon children and adults: 'In both childhood and adulthood, certain cues in the media may trigger the activation of aggressive scripts acquired in any manner and thus stimulate aggressive behaviour.'[3] In a major study conducted by Mount Sinai Hospital in New York, researchers concluded that media violence can indeed influence individuals with 'abrasive' personalities.[4]

In their summary of the academic research into the effects of television violence, Comstock and Paik (1987, 1991) conclude that certain factors in the portrayal of media violence may heighten the likelihood of influence. [5] In other words, the manner in which violence is presented can ultimately effect whether or not an individual decides to carry out similar acts in the real world, so called 'copy-cat' crimes. The academics conclude that influence is increased when:

	Coconut
Portrayal of violence is justified	Yes
Portrayal of the perpetrator is similar to the viewer	Yes
Portrayal of violence is not subject to critical commentary	Yes
Portrayal of violent acts please the viewer	Yes
Reward or lack of punishment for perpetrator of violence	Yes

In the episode of 'Coconut' in question, the perpetrator of the violence towards Ms Hopkins, Tommy Khan, is an uber cool Asian television presenter, just the type of character therefore whose actions might influence an impressionable audience pre-disposed to dislike Ms Hopkins.

Though watched by a crowd of onlookers, it is interesting to note that not a finger is lifted to halt Khan's frenzied attack on the effigy of Ms Hopkins. This raises the uncomfortable question of socially acceptable violence, that certain kinds of violence may be approved and even tacitly encouraged depending on the victim's identity - what Chomsky and Herman label 'unworthy victims.' Indeed, as Khan smashes the effigy to pieces there is no commentary – critical or otherwise. There is however overwhelming approval, manifest in cheers and whoops from the crowd. Onlookers are not at all horrified to witness this gratuitous act of violence – just the opposite in fact.

Judged by the obvious pleasure this spectacle provokes in the onlookers, it would seem entirely possible that, having watched this violent scene, some viewers of BBC Three's 'Coconut' might be left with the impression that attacking Katie Hopkins would naturally incur the admiration of their peers. What kind of overall message then does this horrific sequence transmit to its audience? That violence against Katie Hopkins is ok, socially acceptable? Cool?

'Hilarious,' even?

In their analysis of the mass media, Pratkanis and Aronson explain why media models are so persuasive: 'They serve as a cue to indicate that a certain behaviour is legitimate and appropriate. After watching a prizefight it seems OK to 'punch someone's lights out.'[6] After watching a super cool DJ smash Katie Hopkins' head in with a bat, could this BBC 'comedy' have been implying that such behaviour was not only legitimate but appropriate too? In her study into brainwashing, Kathleen Taylor would appear to think so:

> There is in fact considerable evidence that mass media models of the world we live in have a significant impact on us. These portrayals of 'real' life . . . can shape our behaviour in ways we may not recognise.[7]

'Would fuckin love to bat you'

The following social media exchange occurred not long after episode 2 of 'Coconut' had originally been broadcast in August of 2017. Ms Hopkins' original tweet referred to here had accompanied an attached image of two scantily clad women posing on a magazine front cover. Her implication that blaming men for ogling female models who are only too happy to pose provocatively did not go down well with some users:

> **@KTHopkins**
> How dare men objectify women, see them as sexual beings
> or touch their chuffing knee. God damn men. Perverts the lot.
>
> **@Anon**
> Would fuckin love to bat you
>
> **@KTHopkins**
> You play cricket? Such fun. I'm in.
>
> **@Anon**
> Give me a time and place. I'll be there.

A troll who would love to "bat" Katie Hopkins. But from where could he/she have possibly got such a very specific as well as horrifying idea? 'Would happy smash your head in,' wrote another user to Ms Hopkins. There's a pattern developing here: social media users announcing they would like to smash Katie Hopkins' head in with a cricket bat, which by an uncanny coincidence is precisely what happens to the effigy of Ms Hopkins' head at the end of . . . BBC Three's 'Coconut,' not that the BBC is 'promoting anyone's assassination' of course. Heaven forfend!

'I fantasise about Katie Hopkins' head'

Though the BBC's Director of Editorial Policy and Standards did not specify the precise nature of the 'threats' to BBC correspondents he claimed had occurred, they could not have been any worse than a case reported by *The Times* in which 21-year old Madihah Taheer fantasised about beheading the very same Katie Hopkins, the imagined assassination of whom the BBC were treating so lightly, so gaily. ('It's hilarious')[8]

'I fantasise about Katie Hopkins' head. She's the biggest kuthi [bitch] of them all,' Taheer is alleged to have said during a conversation on WhatsApp recorded in 2015. Just a week after the BBC had rocked up in Mold to so generously plug 'The Assassination of Katie Hopkins' at Theatre Clwyd, Taheer was found guilty of preparing to commit terror attacks along with her husband. As a young Asian female Taheer was within the exact demographic at whom BBC Three's online 'comedy' had clearly been aimed:

> **The Independent:**
> Madihah Taheer: Woman who fantasised about beheading
> Katie Hopkins convicted over terror plot
>
> **ITV.com News:**
> Woman whose dream was to behead Katie Hopkins convicted
> over UK terror plot

Oddly, while the rest of the media focused on Taheer's violent fantasies towards Ms Hopkins, this was one of those rare occasions when the columnist did not interest the BBC at all. 'Couple jailed for plotting Birmingham terror attack,' went the BBC headline with no mention of Ms Hopkins or indeed Taheer's lurid fantasy in either headline or text. On the contrary, in another article the broadcaster attempted to paint Taheer as the victim of 'obsessive love,' the naïve accomplice of a deranged husband. It begins:

> At the top of 21-year-old Madihah Taheer's Facebook profile is
> a painting depicting what appears to be a Muslim warrior from
> antiquity, galloping away from battle with a maiden clinging
> tightly to him. She gazes lovingly into his eyes. She is in the arms
> of her conquering hero.
>
> It was a secret love. She said she wanted to escape her family and
> charismatic Mirza said he was going places.[9]

After publicising a play about the columnist's imagined assassination and following it up with a scene in which an effigy of Ms Hopkins' head is violently smashed to smithereens with a cricket bat, it would appear that the BBC was understandably keen to downplay – erase – headlines linking Ms Hopkins to violent fantasies. Because the BBC were in 'no sense promoting anyone's 'assassination.' Nor was the broadcaster promoting smashing Hopkin's brains in with a cricket bat – 'in no sense.' That was a mere coincidence. It is, after all, BBC 'comedy' where battery against a (wrong-thinking) hi-profile female is considered 'hilarious.'

'State television smear pieces'

When an individual breached security at Russian Radio station Echo of Moscow In October 2017, he had just one thing in mind: to find and inflict maximum harm upon journalist Tatiana Felgenhauer, Deputy Editor in Chief as well as a presenter at the popular station. The deranged man eventually located Ms Felgenhauer in the station's offices. What followed was a shocking example of how media smears can act as a catalyst to real-life violence.

'The stabbing of Tatiana Felgenhauer,' reported *The Telegraph*, 'follows state television smear pieces against the radio station and a series of attacks that forced another Echo of Moscow host to flee the country.'[10]

The assailant calmly stabbed Ms Felgenhauer in the neck, who was then rushed to hospital where she was said to be in a stable condition. It was later revealed that the attacker, a 48-year old dual Russian and Israeli citizen, had never actually met the presenter.

'I have never met her in reality but I have seen and felt her,' he allegedly told authorities. 'She was very obtrusive, she was in my head.' The attack bore similarities to a scene from a Russian television drama serial Sleeping in which a female journalist is stabbed in her office.

'Like bombarding St Paul's with a pea shooter'

Horrified at what he had witnessed on this BBC 'comedy,' one viewer decided to make a complaint: 'They [The BBC] basically gave me the runaround. It was a total farce.' The viewer continues: 'They ducked and dived and pulled every trick in the book – anything to avoid giving me a straight answer to a simple question: how could they justify this level of violence toward a hi-profile female? They told me it was just "fiction," but Kate Hopkins is not fictional. In the end I just gave up. Their twisting and turning sucks the life out of you . . .'

The BBC complaints process

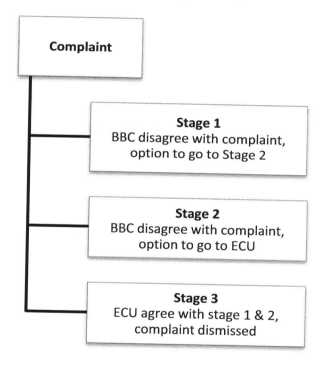

Fig 31

Although the BBC is inundated with complaints every day, few if any get any further than the starting blocks. *The Referee* Magazine summed up this pointless exercise when joking that making a complaint to the corporation was, 'like bombarding St Paul's with a pea shooter.'[11]

To no one's surprise, the army has exonerated itself of pretty much all blame. But its findings lack credibility, both because the inquiry was solely carried out by the very institution accused of committing the abuses . . .[12]

bbc.co.uk

From 214,864 complaints received in 2016/2017 only 36 were upheld in their entirety.[13] The golden rule is that the more innocuous the complaint the more likely the BBC will make an admission, eventually.

While it will never admit to inciting hatred towards Nigel Farage, promoting violence towards Katie Hopkins or attempting to undermine democratic votes such as Brexit, there's a much greater chance the broadcaster will admit to something entirely frivolous - that Henry VIII's codpiece was not of Tudor but rather Stuart design, that Gardener's World was cancelled because of Snooker. This way, the broadcaster can demonstrate just how jolly seriously it takes the opinions of the people who fund it, in which case it might bury a tiny apology deep in on its website far from prying eyes, but don't count on it.

CONCLUSION
'A publicly-funded rogue broadcaster'

When the broadcaster is part of a totalitarian system
it may require a revolution to eject
broadcaster and government together.[1]

Sir Hugh Greene
BBC Director General 1960-69

Having got this far, and having sampled just a tiny fraction of the BBC's many subterfuges, tricks and ruses, who could not but surmise that something is rotten deep within the state broadcaster. *Something* is going on down at Broadcasting House and has been for some time:

> **@Anon**
> When I was growing up the BBC represented my country. Now it has morphed into some sort of globalist, cultural-relativist monstrosity, obsessed with Trump, race, trannies and 'diversity' while ignoring its impact. The BBC has played a central role in the decline of UK society.

Propaganda recall has a single, overarching aim: to persuade the masses to accept that which their instincts tell them to reject – manipulation of the many by the few. War is a prime example. Since its inception in the 1920s, The Ministry of Truth has perfected the art of propaganda to such an extent it can claim to not only be the biggest propaganda machine in the world, but arguably its finest ever exponent. Reflect upon some of the examples we have presented within the pages of this book. Recall how, with a single tweet, a BBC activist incited hatred against the White House press secretary, Sarah Huckabee-Sanders in what was a deliberate, wilful act of dishonesty. Think back to how the BBC gleefully promoted the imagined assassination of media commentator Katie Hopkins ('it's hilarious'). Nor are these isolated examples. Britain's state broadcaster churns out stories like these every hour of every day.

In *Brainwashing Britain* we have highlighted just a few examples of how the BBC attempts to whip up antipathy towards conservative MP Jacob Rees-Mogg ('He's an absolute rotter, isn't he?'). As for what can only be described as the broadcaster's hate campaign against the 45th president of The United States of America and his family, no more needs to be said. Donald Trump and Jacob Rees-Mogg might be democratically elected politicians, but in the BBC's eyes, first and foremost they are wrong-thinkers. They do not share the BBC's 'progressive' (Marxist) worldview. Furthermore both are white, Christian heterosexual males! In BBC land this is a demographic of the past, 'old Europe' ('a dying breed') and if the broadcaster can do its bit to speed up the process, so much the better.

As crazy and as wacky as it sounds, like its ideological cousins at CNN, the BBC however insists it is impartial. Yet even a cursory glance at its content reveals this assertion to be wholly false, a prime example of the kind of 'big lie' favoured by the expert propagandist. Faced with a government that is not the solution but rather a very large part of the problem, what can the ordinary citizen do in the face of such audacity and dishonesty? You could switch off the television or better still ditch the TV licence altogether. What about Strictly? Match of the Day? Catch 22. A prison from which there appears to be no escape . . .

Undaunted, the broadcaster simply marches on. Parents and families marching in unison to protest the (lack of) official response to the Manchester Arena terror attack are smeared as 'far right,' when in fact they are ordinary citizens – mums, dads, brothers, sisters and grandparents. The Swedish city of Malmö is described as 'quiet and safe' when in fact it is experiencing an unprecedented rise in serious crime. One hundred thousand recipients of Universal Credit are told they will lose their benefits at Xmas, when the number is nothing like that. BBC audiences are informed that Donald Trump threatens war with Iran ('War will follow') when in fact the president said 'more (sanctions) will follow.' What is happening at The Ministry of Truth is more than just mere incompetence. Whereas bad practice can always be rectified, there is no quick fix for institutional malfeasance on the scale it appears to be occurring down at Broadcasting House. We can only assume this culture to be commensurate with a wider agenda. Has Britain's 'national' broadcaster truly evolved into 'a globalist, cultural-relativist monstrosity,' one furthermore that has played (and continues to play) 'a central role in the decline of the UK?'

According to some commentators there is a struggle going on right now between two powerful forces, a stealthy confrontation between two implacably opposed entities: populism (of the people) and globalism (of the elite). In this life or death dialectic, there can be but one victor. Far from remaining a detached observer of this epic encounter, and in direct contravention of its royal charter obligations, Britain's 'national' broadcaster long ago decided to throw its considerable weight into the ring. As of 2018, the BBC has effectively morphed into a globalist propaganda machine - one that also just happens to produce a ballroom dancing programme and screens Saturday night football highlights.

The tendency towards politicisation is not a recent phenomenon. It is worth highlighting again the revealing observations of ex-BBC producer Antony Jay: 'Almost anything that made the world a freer, safer and more prosperous place, you name it, we [BBC activists] were anti it.' Meanwhile a social media user applauds what he feels is the BBC's uncanny knack of being, 'Wrong on society. Wrong on politics. Wrong on culture. WRONG ON EVERYTHING.'

> When we had all that migration from eastern Europe, people
> like me focused too much on the economic benefits in terms of
> the rate we were growing and not enough on the experience
> of communities. At the time I was at the BBC and let's be
> clear, the BBC got this completely wrong - we did not listen to
> millions of our viewers at the time.[2]

These are the thoughts of former BBC Economics Editor Robert Peston summing up the corporation's unerring ability to be 'wrong on everything' when pondering upon the BBC's policy on mass migration.

When reflecting on his own BBC career, Robin Aitken appears to agree: 'Looking back it is extraordinary how wrong-headed were the conclusions we reached.'[3] Another social media user puts the case somewhat more bluntly:

> I am certain that the very first step that must be taken in order to save the country from becoming initially a socialist basket case followed shortly by an Islamic hell hole, is to get rid of the BBC and its 24/7 fog horn propaganda.

Who or what then then is going to stop this out-of-control, tax-payer funded behemoth, because one thing is for certain: the British government never will. As Hugh Greene observes, when government and broadcaster are both part of the same totalitarian system, 'revolution' may be required to 'eject' these globalist entities simultaneously. Two world views pulling in opposite directions, fractures seem probable, inevitable. Yet BBC resolve never wavers for a single moment. If anything its globalist sympathies become ever more entrenched, its antipathy towards populists ever more resolute. The 'British' Broadcasting Corporation starts to feel . . . well, more global, less British.

While the broadcaster obsesses over 'Nazis' and the 'far right' ordinary people go about their daily lives. BBC rhetoric meanwhile escalates. Its attacks on populist figures and anyone else intent on preventing the eradication of the nation state continue. Britain's state broadcaster can always be relied upon to target any entity deemed a threat to the vested interests of the global elite. For example, populist Jair Bolsanoro's landslide victory in the 2018 Brazilian elections brought forth a typical BBC reaction:

@Anon
The BBC branded the new President as soon as his election was announced. 'Far Right, racist, misogynist, homophobe' This was repeated at each 'news' bulletin. No explanations, just a stream of vile insults & invective. Shame on the BBC

At this juncture it is worth reminding ourselves what Populism actually means. According to Britannica.com, Populism is a:

Political program or movement that champions the common person, usually by favourable contrast with an elite. Populism usually combines elements of the left and the right, opposing large business and financial interests but also frequently being hostile to established socialist and labour parties.

'Champions the common person . . .' 'Hostile to established socialist and labour parties . . .' Perhaps this explains BBC hostility towards a movement that continues to gain traction across Europe and even South America. Could it be that BBC wrong-thinkers are simply those individuals who oppose its globalist mantras aka the elite consensus?

But isn't the BBC supposed to be impartial? Is it not compelled to remain detached, objective? Despite its very vociferous protestations, the broadcaster is in fact a ferociously political animal. From fracking through abortion and Scottish independence, the BBC has a dog in every fight, a narrative for every occasion. Like its 'respected' friends at Buzzfeed and CNN, the behaviours and actions of Britain's 'national' broadcaster seem at times to be more commensurate with those of hardcore political campaign groups than impartial media professionals, royal charter notwithstanding. Britain's impartial, free and fair broadcaster truly loathes certain political parties and demographics (the 'despised tribes'), and what is more is dedicated to doing everything in its power to bring about political, social and cultural change that reflects its own prejudices - more precisely those of the vested, global interests.

Herein arguably lays the reason for much of the dissatisfaction with dear, old Auntie: The objectives of the elite can't help but violently clash with those of ordinary people - always have and always will. Suffice to say, the objectives of an elite band of Marxist-inspired technocrats are hardly those of hard-working families whose concerns lay less with grandiose ideological projects and more with the trivialities of everyday life - mortgages and such like. While the thought of resetting (western) society might thrill the hardcore BBC activist, it is more likely to leave ordinary people cold. Put simply, the broadcaster's 'obsession with 'Trump, race, trannies and diversity,' might not be shared by the majority of the audience it is supposed to serve:

Do you trust BBC News to give unbiased political coverage?[4]

Yes	9%
No	85%
Undecided	6%

39,341 votes – Final result

'The BBC,' notes Civitas, 'pays lip service to impartiality but acts more like a political party with a policy manifesto.'[5] What the BBC thinks – what it wants – is certainly not taken lightly in Whitehall. BBC wishes have a habit of steering government policy. In his seminal work on the topic of propaganda, Edward Bernays notes that,

> Those who manipulate the unseen mechanisms of society constitute an invisible government which is the true ruling power of our country.[6]

Power behind the throne . . .

During his premiership, the spectre of BBC censure undoubtedly haunted former prime conservative minister David Cameron. Should he have dared disagree with the broadcaster's line on matters of same-sex marriage, mass immigration, feminism, diversity and the full range of left-wing social justice narratives, Mr Cameron was terrified that he might be fatally smeared by the BBC as . . . a conservative! Or worse still, right-wing. His transformation into social liberal was assured. Government policy followed suit. In order to appease the BBC yet more, Mr Cameron went even further when suggesting that Parliament was 'too white,' that it was crying out for more 'diversity.'[7] David Cameron had earned himself a BBC reprieve. He was 'one of us' – a BBC right-thinker.

Upsetting a smear machine is not for the feint-hearted, especially those who wish to pursue long and fruitful careers in the public domain. And so the tail continues to wag the dog. What then might be the end game of this globalist alliance of state broadcaster and western liberal political establishment? Throughout this book it has been suggested that while the 'British' Broadcasting Corporation has many strings to its impartial bow, above all else it has a single, over-arching purpose: to ensure maximum exposure is allocated to the views of the elite consensus until its minority worldview becomes accepted as 'what everyone thinks' - or at least what everybody *appears* to think (BBC right-think). It achieves this end largely through deception.

Similarly, we've remarked how the broadcaster attempts to portray majority opinion as eccentric, and wherever possible extremist ('what nobody thinks') 'There must be someone who agrees with Trump's 'Muslim ban' right?' Remember that BBC trope? Turned out that 55% of Europeans and a whopping 62% of Americans agreed with the US president, a fact that Britain's impartial, free and fair broadcaster somehow managed to omit from its scrupulously fair coverage.[8] It did however manage to include the outrage of the political and media establishment, an assortment of right-thinking 'crats' - Democrats, bureaucrats, technocrats, the progressive elite – people like us.

The objective is always the same: to control what is considered acceptable or unacceptable within the public forum, to narrow its scope until all alternatives to the elite consensus become viewed as extreme. Notice for example how the broadcaster strives to make toxic any political party standing outside the UK's liberal mainstream consensus (i.e. Tory, Labour, Lib-Dem). The BBC it is who defines those boundaries, tacitly of course, by offering free passes to those who conform like David Cameron, while ensuring maximum (negative) exposure for those who do not e.g. Jacob Rees-Mogg. Put so much as a toe outside those confines defined by the BBC and life can and will become a living hell, a daily gauntlet of scorn, abuse and even death threats. The broadcaster has more than enough power to effect the democratic process.

'We are approaching a stage where,' observes Spectator editor Damien Thompson, 'in its arch and disingenuous way - a publicly funded rogue broadcaster may be able to nudge a British government out of office.'[9] The 'national' broadcaster calls the political tune. Politicians who care about their legacy and reputation dance to this tune. Imposing its minority worldview on the British populace does not come without a certain amount of collateral damage, however. The BBC works non-stop to undermine, discredit, mock and satirise opponents of its 'progressive' globalist agenda, but at what cost? It seems that the corporation is slowly but surely alienating ever greater swathes of the British population. Dissatisfaction levels appear to be at record highs. Despite what Ipsos MORI claim, increasing numbers of people appear not to want its services, paid or even free for that matter:

Television licence fee cancellations 2008-2017 (millions)[10]

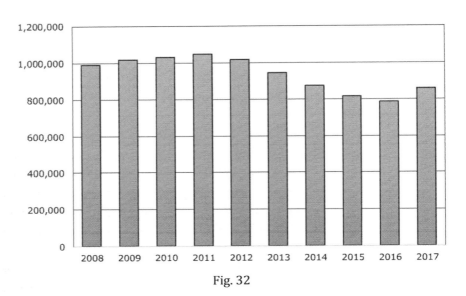

Fig. 32

Nearly 10 million television licences were cancelled in the UK between 2007 and 2017, suggesting a profound malaise deep within the state broadcaster. It's not all doom and gloom though. 'Only' 860,000 people cancelled their television licences in 2017 . . . [11] Crisis? What crisis? As far as the BBC is concerned all is as it should be in its garden.

However, when it comes to the health of BBC plc, whatever optic we choose tells the same sorry story: sustained losses in terms of audience retention and TV licence cancellations. Take for example the nightly BBC 6 'o and 10 o clock news. Compared to the early 2000s, as of 2017 both the corporation's main evening news bulletins had suffered substantial audience losses (millions):

6 'o clock news				10 'o clock news		
	2000	2017	%		2002	2017	%
Mon	6.32	4.87	-23	Mon	5.38	4.07	-24
Tue	6.43	4.67	-27	Tue	5.15	4.13	-20
Weds	6.18	4.76	-23	Wed	5.38	4.08	-24
Thur	6.17	4.57	-26	Thur	5.21	4.14	-21
Fri	5.95	4.52	-24	Fri	5.31	3.89	-27

Fig. 33 Source: barb

Meanwhile, in BBC-land, the broadcaster asserts that:

> More people than ever before are turning to the BBC for reliable, impartial information they can trust.[12]
> bbc.co.uk

Between 2012 and 2018 The BBC News Channel - the corporation's 24 hour rolling news service - lost a whopping 36% of its audience.[13] In the age of 'fake news' surely, *more* not less viewers should be tuning in to Britain's 'most trusted' news source in the expectation of receiving impartial news about say, 'Trump, race, trannies and diversity?' Not happening.

It's not just BBC news programmes that are haemorrhaging viewers either. The following table presents average viewing figures (millions) between 2001-02 and 2017 for some of the BBC's most enduring shows:

	2000-01	2017	%
Casualty	9.91	5.24	-47
EastEnders (Tues)	12.07	6.57	-46
Holby City	8.15	4.40	-46
Antiques Roadshow	8.95	5.54	-38

Fig 34 Source: Barb

Can this catastrophic loss be solely attributable to the arrival of digital and Freeview television services? It can't be down to cost. For as the broadcaster is fond of reminding people, a television licence works out at just £2.89 per week – the price of a pint of beer. And yet the exodus continues. It makes no sense: with brilliant staff producing brilliant content for just a few pounds a week, the BBC continues to lose substantial numbers of viewers as well as licence fee payers. Perhaps the reasons run a little deeper. Could this crisis be related to the BBC's radical agenda? Perhaps 24/7 globalist propaganda is just a big turn off – who knows? The BBC appears not to.

'Can we have an episode of Dr Who that isn't stuffed to the rafters with left wing politics?' asks a social media user. 'It's an entertainment show, not a party political broadcast.' A few BBC shows have however been bucking the trend, which suggests that the audience is still out there. Strictly Come Dancing is that rare phenomenon of the modern BBC: a programme that has increased its audience share.

It's not just television where the BBC is experiencing substantial losses. Radio listenership has also been falling steadily away. For example, in just six years between 2011 and 2017, Radio 1 lost a massive 20% of its audience.[14]

The BBC response to this crisis? There hasn't been one. Instead, it is far more common to encounter boasts about the BBC's increasing *global* reach ('A quarter of a billion people tuning in') in which the corporation basks in what it claims to be an upturn in BBC engagement - largely through visits to its news website and expansion of its World Service: 'Two of the other big factors in our audience increases have been the growth of our BBC Arabic and BBC Persian services.' In its End of Charter Review the BBC Trust makes the following comment:

> Internationally the BBC's audiences continue to grow and in November the BBC announced 11 new language services in the biggest World Service expansion since the 1940s.[15]

The key word here is of course 'internationally . . .' There is however, a fly in the ointment of this staggering success story. Although the folk of Iran, Afghanistan and Tajikistan now receive the BBC World Service and can surf to their hearts' content on the BBC news website, those lucky people are not actually *paying* for any of these services. Not a single penny. It's free propaganda![16] The BBC has managed to increase its reach by giving away free stuff, a nothing if not eccentric business model. Bottom line: The corporation's paying customers are jumping ship at alarming rates; growth meanwhile is solely due to an increase in non-paying customers; only in BBC land could such a paradox exist.

'The cracks are beginning to show,' admitted the BBC Director General when raising the thorny issue of BBC finances, adding that the organisation's spending was 'unsustainable,' He also went on to say that BBC needed, 'to find more money.'[17] One direction the corporation is however determined not to travel is a model of voluntary subscription. If they happened to wake one fine morning to find themselves compelled to pay for its services like UK customers, the corporation's international fan club might be a little less enthusiastically disposed towards Britain's impartial state broadcaster. They would not be the only ones:

@Anon
The BBC needs to find its own way of funding itself. The public are sick of your left leaning, social engineering propaganda. You are no longer relevant to our lives #ScrapTheTVTax

In the age of Amazon and Netflix, Britain's 'national' broadcaster stubbornly refuses to move with the times, immersed, or so it seems, in a funding model conceived in the 1920s. Instead of resisting change, has not the time come to embrace the modern world of digital subscription media, and by doing so back up its claims that Auntie is just as popular in the 21st century as she was back in her 1950s heyday? 'If the BBC is as popular as it says,' comments a social media user, 'then it would have no problem moving to a subscription model.'

If the BBC became an opt-in, subscription-only service, would you pay £12.25 a month to subscribe to its contents?

Yes	19%
No	81%

6,714 votes – Final result

Quite simply, if the BBC was to switch to a subscription model it would implode. Take-up of its services would be risible. Just how much longer it can continue in its present form however is anybody's guess, but the day must surely come when government is forced to step in. For an organisation that delights in smearing the RT (Russia Today) television channel as Russian propaganda 'funded by the Kremlin,' the irony of a BBC directly 'funded by 10 Downing Street' will surely not be lost. Kiss goodbye to the independence mask forever. Broadcaster and government would (officially) be as one.

If the BBC television licence was abolished, how likely would you be to voluntary subscribe to BBC services?[18]				
Very likely	Likely	Neutral	Unlikely	Very unlikely
4%	11%	17%	18%	49%

For now, the corporation stumbles on. The more money it spends, the fewer (paying) customers watch and listen to its programmes. Not to worry. In BBC land there's a ruse for everything. Plummeting ratings and millions of customers dumping the TV licence can always be explained away or if not, simply ignored, as future Director General Greg Dyke observed when boss of rival broadcaster TV-am:

> We consistently beat the BBC, which then did what the BBC always did. When they were wining they crowed about ratings, when they were losing they decided ratings didn't matter and we were too downmarket.[19]

And besides, as that old 'subversive' himself Hugh Greene once intimated, would it be such a terrible thing after all if the BBC was solely made and consumed by people like us, smart, cultivated people – people of the Inner and Outer Party:

> Are we not doing more for democracy if we sometimes,
> even quite often, give great pleasure to a few people even
> at the cost of provoking many into switching off?[20]

As of 2018 the broadcaster has certainly succeeded in 'provoking many into switching-off.' The BBC's grip on the nation loosens by the day: 'The BBC no longer controls the national conversation,' lamented Gabriel Gatehouse when reporting from Sweden for BBC Newsnight in summer 2018.[21] 'The BBC no longer has the magisterial presence it once had,' confessed veteran broadcaster Sir David Attenborough.[22]

From the BBC perspective however all is well. In fact it couldn't be going any better. The air of what former BBC executive Will Wyatt calls 'an economy of self-congratulation' infuses the air of Broadcasting House in 2018 much as it always has done. It might be alienating (paying) audiences on an unprecedented scale, but Britain's 'national' broadcaster is, as ever, pretty sure it's got things just about right. 'We won't stop,' declares the BBC's 'Head of Diversity, Inclusion and Succession,' when outlining the way forward for the corporation. 'We're going further and achieving more than ever.'

Thus it's going to get a whole lot worse, before it gets any better. Expect the broadcaster to double and triple down, to push its 'progressive' agenda harder than ever, and in doing so drift ever further away from the behaviour and actions associated with an impartial news organisation. Expect therefore the corporation to become ever more belligerent in its attacks on the Internet and especially on independent sources of information, its calls for censorship to get ever louder. In 2018 the BBC Director General was among the signatories of a letter to *The Sunday Telegraph* claiming there was an "urgent" need for independent oversight of social media . . .[23] Like all animals facing extinction, the corporation will lash out at those whom it perceives to be a threat to its privilege and globalist agenda. Expect therefore its rhetoric to become ever more inflammatory, ever more unhinged, its 'far/alt-right' tag used to smear ever growing numbers of ordinary people. When the BBC says it 'won't stop,' this is one boast you really can believe in:

@BBC News:
Should women be spelt womxn?

The Telegraph:
BBC will have more gay characters in its shows to combat 'heteronormative culture'[24]

@bbcthesocial:
Tasting condoms because . . . why not?

The Sunday Times:
BBC staff told to use non-binary pronouns[25]

Nothing is going to stop the broadcaster's agenda, not tanking audience numbers, escalating complaints, burgeoning TV licence cancellations nor the deafening roar of online mockery and incredulity. We are sorely tempted to speculate about the BBC endgame, the precise nature of its final destination. By campaigning against movements as well as individuals who resist its globalist agenda, Britain's state broadcaster ensures the march through the institutions continues apace. The Marxist utopia ruled by technocrats – people like us – creeps ever closer. As it does, liberty, freedom of thought and speech get further and further away, remnants of a distant past inhabited by 'Little Englanders' and 'sunburnt meatheads' who, once upon a time, believed all that they saw and heard on the 'British' Broadcasting Corporation aka Britain's dear old, reliable Auntie.

A BBC future should be a thing to behold. In an article entitled 'Poor? Stupid? Racist? Then don't listen to a pampered white liberal like me,' the BBC's chief political editor Andrew Marr fantasises a future where 'state power' resides in the hands of right-thinkers like himself and his colleagues. In the meantime wonders Marr, what can smart civilised people do when working class proles ignore your inherent moral and intellectual superiority? Marr thinks he knows:

> And the final answer, frankly, is the vigorous use of state power to coerce and repress . . . I firmly believe that repression can be a great, civilising instrument for good. Stamp hard on certain 'natural' beliefs for long enough and you can almost kill them off.[26]

By 'natural beliefs' this BBC right-thinker means all sorts of weird superstitions held by the 'poor, stupid and racist,' e.g. that there are only two genders; that the best candidate for a job should be judged on ability, not affiliation to any particular BBC-approved minority group; that encouraging six-year olds to transgender is a little early in life etc.

If this 'final answer' sounds rather like the modus operandi deployed by the Party of Orwell's dystopian nightmare, that's because it is. The 'progressive' mask must one day slip, revealing when it does the authoritarian lurking behind it and the tax-payer funded boots that will one day 'stamp' some sense into the proletariat. 'Progress in our world will be towards more pain,' explains Party zealot O'Brien as *1984* draws to a close. 'In our world there will be no emotions except fear, rage, triumph and self-abasement.'[27] 'Mad gleam' in his eye, O'Brien continues:

> If you want a picture of the future, imagine a boot stamping on a human face – for ever . . . The face will always be there to be stamped upon. The heretic, the enemy of society, will always be there, so that he can be defeated and humiliated.[28]

Whether it's stamping on Marr's 'natural beliefs' such as $2 + 2 = 4$, or whether it's stamping on a human face for perpetuity, as far as the cultural Marxist/Party right-thinker is concerned, the end always justifies the means.

It is ex-Ministry of Truth member George Orwell to whom we turn for our final thought. Much ground has been covered in this book, but we have only scratched the surface of the 'British' Broadcasting Corporation. There is so much more to say.

We haven't mentioned for example, the indoctrination technique known as Common Purpose training so beloved by the British establishment, the BBC included. Nor have we mentioned ex-BBC stalwarts such as Jimmy Savile. We haven't had time to delve into the treatment of people like Sir Cliff Richard and Lord McAlpine. Much to our chagrin we have barely scratched the surface of TV Licencing, the BBC's attack hounds who ensure that the aged, infirm and unemployed cough up their television licence fees via all sorts of ingenuous methods - the most notorious of which are its infamous threatening letters devised to terrify the vulnerable through the use of legalese. We could have said a whole lot more about Britain's impartial, free and fair 'national' broadcaster . . . Alas, space dictated otherwise.

But we do have space for one final thought.

Though we have written a book, we could in truth have simply drawn the reader's attention to a single sentence from *1984* to make our point. The final word then goes to Orwell, the writer who tried so hard to warn us what happens when media propaganda machine and authoritative government work together to enslave the citizenry. When watching, reading or listening to the BBC, we urge you never to forget the words which follow. For here is a sentence that summarises the modern BBC aka The Ministry of Truth more succinctly and elegantly than we could ever hope to:

> The essential act of the Party is to use conscious deception
> while retaining the firmness of purpose that goes with
> complete honesty. [29]

Bibliography

Alinsky, S. (1989) Rules for Radicals 2nd ed, Vintage

Aitken, R (2007) Can We Trust the BBC? Continuum

Arnold, G. (1992) Brainwash: The Cover-up Society, Virgin Books

Attkisson, S. (2018) The Smear: How Shady Political Operatives and Fake News Control What You See, What You Think, and How You Vote, Harper Collins

Benn, T. (1988) Office Without Power: Diaries Vol.2, 1968-1972, Hutchinson

Bernays, E. (2005) Propaganda, Ig Publishing

Briggs, A. (1985) The BBC: The First 50 years, Oxford University Press; 1st edition

Burns, T. (1977) The BBC: Public Institution and Private World. Macmillan

Carey, J. (1992) The Intellectuals and the Masses, Faber and Faber

Chomsky, N. & Herman, E. (1995) Manufacturing Consent: The Political Economy of the Mass Media, Vintage

Cromwell, D. (2012) Why Are We The Good Guys? Zero books

Culbert, D., Cull, N., & Welch, D. (2003) Propaganda and Mass Persuasion: A Historical Encyclopaedia, 1500 to the Present,' ABC-CLIO

Dyke, G (2004) Greg Dyke: Inside Story, Harper Collins

Epstein, E. (1975) News from Nowhere: Television and the News, Random House

Greene, H. (1969) The Third Floor Front: A View of Broadcasting in the Sixties, The Bodley Head Ltd.

Hitler, A. (1925) Mein Kampf, Boston: trans. Ralph Manheim, Houghton Mifflin

Holliday, R. (2018) Trust Me I'm Lying: Confessions of a Media Manipulator, Profile Books

Iowa State University: 'Cross-cultural study strengthens link between media violence, aggressive behaviour,' ScienceDaily, 11 April 2017.

Jay, A. (2007) Confessions of a Reformed BBC Producer, Centre for Policy Studies

Jowett, G. & O'Donnell, V. (1992) Propaganda and Persuasion, 2nd edn. Newbury Park, CA: Sage Publications

Jubb, A. & Keighley, D. (2018) The Brussels Broadcasting Corporation? How pro-Brexit views have been marginalised in the BBC's news coverage, Civitas

Jubb, A. & Keighley, D. (2014) Impartiality at the BBC? An investigation into the background and claims of Stuart Prebble's 'Independent Assessment for the BBC Trust, Civitas

Le Bon, G. (1896) The Crowd: Study of the Popular Mind, Batoche Books

Lochner, L. P. (ed.) (1948) The Goebbels' Diaries, Hamish Hamilton

McElwee, M. & Gaskarth, G. (2003) The Guardian of the Airwaves? Bias and the BBC, Cchange

Merton, Robert K. (1948), "The Self Fulfilling Prophecy", Antioch Review, Vol. 8, No.2 (Summer) pp. 193-210

Mosey, R. (2015) Getting Out Alive: News, Sport and Politics at the BBC, Biteback

Orwell, G. (1948) 1984, Penguin

Pratkanis, A. & Aronson, E. (1991) Age of Propaganda: The Everyday Use and Abuse of Persuasion, W. H. Freeman & Co Ltd

Scruton, R. (2016) Fools, Frauds and Firebrands: Thinkers of the New Left, Bloomsbury Continuum

Seaton, J. (2015) Pinkoes and Traitors: The BBC and the Nation 1974-1987, Profile Books

Sissons, P. (2011) When One Door Closes, Biteback

Stewart, C. (ed) (1975) The Reith Diaries, Collins

Stourton, E. (2009) It's a PC World: What it means to live in a land gone politically correct: What It Means to Live in a World Gone Politically Correct, Hodder

Welch, D. (2002) The Third Reich: Politics and Propaganda (2nd ed.) Routledge

Werth, N; Panné, J-L; Paczkowski, A; Bartosek, K; Margolin, J-L (1999), Courtois, Stéphane, ed., The Black Book of Communism: Crimes, Terror, Repression, Harvard University Press

Whitehouse, M. (1977) Whatever Happened to Sex? Wayland

Wyatt, W. (2003) The Fun Factory: A Life in the BBC, Aurum Press

Notes

Introduction

1 'We're not biased – the BBC hasn't changed,' Radio Times, 1 Sep. 2018
2 Greg Dyke: Inside Story, p. 10
3 When One Door Closes, p. 266
4 'Heavy losses feared as The Guardian forecasts it will burn £90m in cash this year,' The Telegraph, 1 Feb. 2017
5 The Fun Factory: A Life in the BBC, p. 138
6 'Why the licence fee is the best way to fund the BBC,' bbc.co.uk, 14 Jul 2014
7 BBC Trust: End of Charter Report, March 2017, p. 21
8 BBC Media Centre: BBC Annual Report, July 19th 2017
9 'Learn how the BBC is working to strengthen trust and transparency in online news,' bbc.co.uk, Dec. 8th 2017
10 'The best way to tackle BBC bias is make it plain for all to see,' The Guardian, April 5th 2017
11 Manufacturing Consent, p. 2
12 Brainwash: The Cover-up Society, p. 20
13 Office Without Power, pp. 109-10
14 Nicholas Johnson, member of the Federal Communications Commission, quoted in, News from Nowhere: Television and the News, p.6
15 When One Door Closes, p. 247
16 Can We Trust the BBC? p. 206
17 Amusing Ourselves to Death, p. 160

CONTEXT

The BBC and The Marxists

1 Confessions of a Reformed BBC producer, p. 9
2 'The BBC's cultural Marxism will trigger an American-style backlash,' The Guardian, Jan. 24th 2007
3 Formed in October 1922, the British Broadcasting Company as it was then known, was formed just a matter of months before the birth of the Frankfurt School.
4 The Intellectuals and the Masses, p.43
5 Rules for Radicals p. xix
6 'The BBC's cultural Marxism will trigger an American-style backlash,' The Guardian, Jan. 24th 2007
7 Rules for Radicals, p. xix

8 'Left uses college for "indoctrination," CBS News, Jan. 25th 2012

9 Rules for Radicals, p. xiii

10 'To survive as a Tory teacher, you have to keep quiet,' The Spectator, Feb. 6th 2016

11 1984, p. 301

12 'How the BBC fell for a Marxist plot to destroy civilisation from within,' Mail Online, Sept. 27th 2011

13 The Third Floor Front, p.133

14 Whatever Happened to Sex? P.17

15 Confessions of a Reformed BBC Producer, p. 4

16 Ibid, p. 6

17 Ibid, p. 1

18 Can We Trust the BBC? p.179

19 1984, p.235

20 Fools, Frauds and Firebrands: Thinkers of the New Left, p. 12

21 'Five Minutes with Colin Crouch,' lse.ac.uk, Feb. 9th 2013

22 Who will guard the guards themselves? A Latin phrase found in the work of the Roman poet Juvenal from his Satires.

The cult of the BBC

1 John Pilger on 'Going Underground,' Russia Today, Dec. 9th 2017

2 1984, p. 16

3 BBC Editorial Guidelines 15.4.5

4 'Social Networking and Other Third Party Websites ,' Editorial Guidelines, bbc.co.uk

5 Brainwashing: The Science of Thought Control, p. 51

6 Age of Propaganda, p. 138

7 'We Owe Arabs nothing,' Sunday Express, Jan. 4th 2004

8 'David Bellamy tells of moment he was "frozen out" of BBC,' The Telegraph, Jan. 22nd 2013

9 Confessions of a Reformed BBC Producer, p.12

10 English Socialism - the dominant ideology of The Party in 1984.

11 1984, p. 63

12 When One Door Closes, p. 322

13 See for example, '2,000 men 'sexually assaulted 1,200 women' at Cologne New Year's Eve party,' The Independent, July 11th 2016

14 Can We Trust the BBC? p. 144

15 Brainwashing: The Science of Thought Control, p. 50

16 Ibid. p.51

17 1984, p. 16

18 Terror, Love and Brainwashing, p. 142

19 When One Door Closes, p. 322

20 1984 p. 240
21 Quoted in: The BBC: Myth of a Public Service, p. 31
22 Manufacturing Consent: The Political Economy of the Mass Media, p.2
23 Ibid, p.394
24 Ibid, p.302
25 The Rise of the Outsiders: How Mainstream Politics Lost its Way, p. 139
26 1984, p. 61
27 Quoted in 'The BBC: Myth of a Public Service,' p.31
28 Manufacturing Consent: The Political Economy of the Mass Media, p. 394
29 When One Door Closes, p. 266
30 'Confessions of a Reformed BBC Producer,' p. 9
31 Interview with Patricia Hodgson in Pinkoes and Traitors, p.305
32 Greg Dyke: Inside Story, p. 208
33 Brainwashing: The Science of Thought Control, p. 59
34 Age of Propaganda, p.305
35 The New Believers, p. 23
36 Terror, Love and Brainwashing, p.14

The BBC Type

1 Quoted in, The BBC: The First 50 years, p.151
2 Portland Place: Secret diary of a BBC secretary, p. 258
3 Can We Trust the BBC?, p. 3
4 BBC Radio 4 Today, Dec. 1st 2017
5 'HERE IS THE SNOOZE BBC News Channel's staff accused of wasting taxpayers' cash as workers photographed sleeping on the job and 'even bring DUVETS to work' The Sun, Nov. 17th 2017
6 Portland Place: Secret diary of a BBC secretary, p. 58
7 The Fun Factory: A Life in the BBC, pp. 30-31
8 Confessions of a Reformed BBC Producer, p. 9
9 Can We Trust the BBC? pp. 25-26
10 The Fun Factory: A Life in the BBC, p. 43
11 1984, p. 246
12 The Intellectuals and the Masses, p. 21
13 Orwell, Notes on Nationalism
14 'Self-hatred at the BBC,' Prospect, Nov. 19th 2006
15 The Third Floor Front, p.138
16 'Self-hatred at the BBC: The broadcaster is feeling guilty about its liberal guilt. Can it fix it?' Prospect Magazine, Nov. 2006
17 See for example, 'The Anti British Broadcasting Collective ' Going-Postal.com, Sep. 3rd 2016

18 Getting out Alive: News, Sport and Politics at the BBC, p.165
19 The Third Floor Front, p.137
20 It's a PC World, p.75
21 'Out-of-step BBC urged to rethink 'PC police,' The Guardian,
Oct. 26th 2006
22 Confessions of a Reformed BBC Producer, p. 6
23 Millennium People, p. 155

Licence to Print Money
1 Greg Dyke: The Inside Story, p. 165
2 'Severance and wider benefits for senior BBC managers,' National
Audit Office, July 1st 2013, p. 5
3 'BBC's TV licence bullies are exposed: How ruthless bosses order staff
to catch 28 people a week for bonuses of £15,000 a year,' Mail Online,
Feb. 26th 2017
4 'Nearly three-quarters of convicted TV Licence non-payers are
women,' The Register, July 17th 2017
5 'Why the licence fee is the best way to fund the BBC,' bbc.co.uk,
July 14th 2014
6 'BBC struggling to make case for licence fee as support stalls ,' The
Times, Dec. 26th 2014
7 'Public want BBC licence fee scrapped,' The Telegraph, July 6th 2014
8 'Fury over 25% wage rise for 500 BBC staff as nurses and cops face pay
cuts,' The Sun, Apr. 5th 2018
9 'Severance and wider benefits for senior BBC managers,' National
Audit Office, July 1st 2013
10 According to research carried out by Hargreaves Lansdown, Byford
topped a list of just five BBC executives looking forward to sharing a £26
million pension pot. See: 'Top BBC executives will enjoy pensions
'costing £26m,' The Telegraph, July 6th 2009
11 'BBC under fire after giving almost 1,800 staff a pay raise above ten
per cent last year — costing you £13.9million,' The Sun, Aug. 23rd 2017
12 'BBC flouting salary cap rules to inflate wages for top earners,' The
Times, Apr. 6th 2018
13 Source: Annex to the BBC Annual Reports and Accounts 2016/17
14 Evans announced his retirement from his Radio 2 show in autumn
2018 to join Virgin Radio. There was no suggestion from any party that
he had been 'poached.'
15 'BBC stars endure grim day of self-flagellation after pay details made
public,' The Guardian, July 19th 2017
16 'BBC offers to protect stars from abuse as it gears up to publish
£150k-plus salaries,' The Telegraph, July 16th 2017

17 BBC Presenters, Actors, Reporters Survey,' Ipsos MORI, July 19th 2017

18 'The Great BBC Survey,' Survey Monkey

19 'Christopher Hitchens on Polling,' on medium.com, Nov. 17th 2016

20 'BBC Annual Report 2016/17,' bbc.co.uk, July 19th 2017

21 'BBC pay report: Chris Evans and Gary Lineker top list amid glaring gender gap,' The Telegraph, July 19th 2017

A 'Right-wing' broadcaster

1 Can We Trust the BBC? p.39

2 Ibid. p.206

3 Pinkoes and Traitors: The BBC and the nation 1974-1987, p. 312

4 Confessions of a Reformed BBC Producer, p. 14

5 The BBC: The First 50 years: Asa Briggs p.118

6 Brainwash: The Cover-Up Society, p. 147

7 'What is the loneliest job in Britain: being a Tory at the BBC,' Mail Online, Feb. 17th 2017

8 Can We Trust the BBC? p. 25

9 'Self-hatred at the BBC,' Prospect, Nov. 2006

10 'There was massive left-wing bias at the BBC,' The New Statesman, Sept. 20th 2010

11 The Guardian of the Airwaves? Bias and the BBC,' pp. 45-50

12 'Which politician is on Question Time the most? It's not Nigel Farage,' The Guardian, Mar. 19th 2015

13 'We are biased, admit the stars of BBC news,' Evening Standard, Oct. 21st 2006

BBC and CNN: Soulmates in impartiality

1 'Protesters flood streets of Hamburg as G20 wraps up,' CNN, July 8th 2017

2 'G20 protesters bringing 'criminal violence' to Hamburg put locals offside,' ABC News, July 9th 2017

3 The Rise of the Outsiders: How Mainstream Politics Lost its Way, p. 174

4 'How much does CNN hate Trump? 93% of coverage is negative,' Washington Times, May 23rd 2017

5 'News Coverage of Donald Trump's First 100 Days,' Harvard Kennedy School

6 'CNN obsessed: 92 percent of airtime on Trump, 96 critics to 7 supporters,' Washington Examiner, May 16th 2017

7 'How much does CNN hate Trump?' 93% of coverage is negative. The Washington Times, 23 May 2017

8 For an analysis of the bias inherent in US political polling methodology see for example, 'Media Polling, M & A Polling and President Trump's Ratings, McLaughlinonline.com, Apr. 27th 2017

9 'REPORT: President Trump's Approval Is Higher Than Media Claims,' Conservativeinstitute.org, Sep. 4th 2017

10 'Donald Trump might be more popular than you think,' Politico.com, Mar. 2nd 2017

11 Confessions of a Reformed BBC Producer, p.8

12 'Obama warns against irresponsible social media use,' bbc.co.uk, Dec. 27th 2017

13 Crossing Divides: The benefits of having friends who aren't 'just like us,' bbc.co.uk, Apr. 22nd 2018

14 'Hard Evidence: How biased is the BBC?' New Statesman, Aug. 23rd 2013

15 'Hard Evidence: How biased is the BBC?' The Conversation, Aug. 23rd 2013

NARRATIVE

Right and Wrong-think

1 1984, p. 85

2 'Sunburnt meatheads' – this casually racist remark refers to white people who have had too much sun and is closely related to the anti-white term 'gammon.'

3 Upon being informed of BBC policy regarding employee use of social media, the individual in question deleted 'BBC Script Editor' from his Twitter bio in or around June 2018.

4 Brainwashing: The Science of Thought Control, p.49

5 Post-Truth, p.280

6 BBC Newsnight, 22nd August 2017

7 Can We Trust the BBC? p.19

8 'There are too many women on Radio 4 and they're always moaning,' The Spectator, June 9th 2018

9 'BBC launches ambitious new diversity and inclusion strategy,' bbc.co.uk, Apr. 28th 2016

10 'The Great BBC Survey,' Survey Monkey

11 1984, p. 241

Caucasians are very, very bad

1 The JVS Show, BBC Three Counties Radio, Oct. 4th 2017

2 'BBC sacked me for being a white man,' Mail Online, Oct. 6th 2016

3 'Stop white men explaining stuff, says BBC boss,' The Times, Aug. 24th 2018
4 'No Brexit bounce for the name Nigel,' bbc.co.uk, Sep. 20th 2017
5 'Could this Willenhall baby be the last Nigel?' bbc.co.uk, Sep. 28th 2017
6 'C4 survey and documentary reveals What British Muslims Really Think,' Channel4.com, Apr. 11th 2016
7 'BBC chief to be quizzed as MPs voice fears that harassment victims are being silenced,' The Independent, Jan. 26th 2018

Donald Trump is very, very bad
1 BBC 1, Monday, Jan. 8th 2018
2 This Week, Jan. 11th 2018
3 'Has Melania Trump 'liked' a tweet mocking her marriage?' bbc.co.uk, May 3rd 2017
4 'Learn how the BBC is working to strengthen trust and transparency in online news,' bbc.co.uk, Dec. 8th 2017
5 These comments were made before the activist added the following to his Twitter profile in summer 2018: 'Views expressed ≠ BBC's'
6 Trust Me I'm Lying, p. 202
7 'Obama spied on Trump's campaign. Where's the outrage?' Washington Times, May 17th 2018

Brexit is very, very bad
1 The best way to tackle BBC bias is make it plain for all to see,' The Guardian, Apr. 5th 2017
2 The Archers, BBC Radio 4, Aug. 8th 2017 Omnibus
3 See for example 'The Brussels Broadcasting Corporation? How pro-Brexit views have been marginalised in the BBC's news coverage,' published by Civitas.
4 'Steven Moffat: Brexit voters delayed female Doctor,' bbc.co.uk, Dec. 4th 2017
5 'PROMS HIJCKED BBC accused of turning the Proms into a platform for anti-Brexit fanatics ,' The Sun, July 19th 2017
6 'Barenboim's Brexit speech was out of order,' SlippedDisc.com, July 17th 2017

The BBC and fake news
1 BBC News at One, 22 January 2018. Thanks to Is the BBC biased blogspot for bringing this example to our attention.
2 'We were fed lies about the violence at Orgreave. Now we need the truth,' The Guardian, July 22nd 2015
3 See, The BBC: The Myth of a Public Service, p.175

4 'Orgreave campaigners call for BBC strike coverage apology,' bbc.co.uk,
June 18th 2014
5 The Reith Diaries, entry for May 11th 1926, p. 15
6 Getting out Alive: News, Sport and Politics at the BBC, p.163
7 'The Great BBC Survey,' Survey Monkey
8 Intercept, Dec. 8th 2016
9 'Learn how the BBC is working to strengthen trust and transparency in
online news.' bbc.co.uk, Dec. 8th 2017
10 'Who Can We Trust? - Creditplus Consumer Survey,' Creditplus.co.uk
11 The Smear, p. 8
12 'Teaching fact from fiction,' bbc.co.uk, Dec. 5th 2017
13 Post-Truth, p. 119
14 'Universal credit: 'Thousands' without Christmas payments,'
bbc.co.uk, Nov. 26th 2017
15 'The Rise of the Outsiders: How Mainstream Politics Lost
its Way, p.266
16 Newsnight, BBC2, July 6th 2017
17 'Arrests made as Manchester protest by UK Against Hate 'turns nasty,'
bbc.co.uk, June 12th 2017
18 'Germany leads fightback against fake news.' bbc.co.uk,
Feb. 16th 2017
19 Quoted in Brainwash: The Cover-up Society, p. 8

PROPAGANDA

Ministry of Truth
1 Going Underground, RT, Dec. 4th 2017
2 1984, p. 244
3 Mein Kampf, pp 180-181
4 The Goebbels' Diaries, p. 22
5 Age of Propaganda, p. 126
6 'Israeli policewoman stabbed to death in Jerusalem,' bbc.co.uk,
June 16th 2017
7 Interview with Mike Sergeant, Feb. 10th 2018. For more examples of
Bowen's 'latitude,' see 'Jeremy Bowen is biased,' Is the BBC biasedblog?
8 Manufacturing Consent, p. 298
9 'Doctor Who: Role was offered to black actor, says Steven Moffat,'
bbc.co.uk, June 3rd 2016
10 The BBC: The First 50 years, p. vi
11 1984, p.6
12 Ibid p. 49

13 Manufacturing Consent, p.1
14 Brainwash: The Cover-up Society, p. 42
15 Ibid. p.11
16 'Learn how the BBC is working to strengthen trust and transparency in online news,' bbc.co.uk, Dec. 8th 2017
17 Age of Propaganda, p.132
18 'Propaganda and Mass Persuasion: A Historical Encyclopaedia, 1500 to the Present,' p. XX

Make 'em laugh: BBC 'comedy'
1 Rules for Radicals, p.75
2 1984, p.17
3 'Crowd Psychology,' psychology.wikia.com
4 'Spotted: a right-wing comedian on the BBC,' The Spectator, Jan. 6th 2018
5 The Mash Report, BBC 2, Feb. 16th 2018

Make 'em cry: The fear factor
1 1984, p. 16
2 The Third Reich: Politics and Propaganda, p. 26
3 Can We Trust the BBC? p. 181
4 Age of Propaganda: The Everyday Use and Abuse of Persuasion, p.217
5 Ibid, p. 311
6 'Nazi hunts' are a sign of our hyperventilating times,' Unherd, Aug. 10th 2018

Focus
1 'Four charged with hate crime for Chicago Facebook Live attack,' bbc.co.uk, Jan. 5th 2017
2 'Texas governor says Houston recovery a 'multi-year project,'' bbc.co.uk, Sep. 1st 2017
3 'Kate Steinle: Trump outrage over murder case acquittal,' bbc.co.uk, Dec. 1st 2017

Health Checks
1 BBC Question Time, Oct. 19th 2018
2 'Piers Morgan's axing prompts transatlantic schadenfreude,' bbc.co.uk, Feb. 24th 2014
3 Post-Truth, p. 279
4 'Racist', 'fascist', 'utterly repellent': What the world said about Donald Trump,' bbc.co.uk, Dec. 9th 2015
5 'Confessions of a Reformed BBC Producer,' p.1

6 'Most Europeans want immigration ban from Muslim-majority countries, poll reveals,' The Independent, Feb. 7th 2017
7 Ibid.
8 'Most Support Temporary Ban on Newcomers from Terrorist Havens,' Rasmussen Reports, Jan. 30th 2017
9 'First Muslim Ban Poll Finds Americans Support Trump Order by 7-Point Margin,' Slate, Jan. 31st 2017
10 'Nearly Half of Australians Favor a Ban on Muslim Immigration, a New Poll Finds, Time, Sep. 21st 2016
11 'Racist', 'fascist', 'utterly repellent': What the world said about Donald Trump,' bbc.co.uk, Dec. 9th 2015
12 'Pew: Liberals Trust CNN, Conservatives Trust Fox News, and No One Trusts BuzzFeed,' New York Mag, Oct. 21st 2014
13 Buzzfeed.com, Dec. 27th 2017
14 'Buzzfeed's Trump report takes 'fake news' to a new level,' New York Post, Jan. 10th 2017

Bias by omission
1 Martin Dillon and bias at the BBC,' Judecollins.com, Dec. 3rd 2017
2 'Goldman Sachs chief on Brexit: 'I would have thought there would have been a worse outcome by now,' Evening Standard, Apr. 22nd 2018
3 'Iraqi man threatened to "kill all the English" after bursting into church service in Barnard Castle,' The Northern Echo, July 22nd 2017
4 'The time when America stopped being great,' bbc.co.uk, Nov. 3rd 2017
5 The Poliak Lecture given at Columbia University, America - Holding on to Objectivity, Richard Sambrook, Director, BBC World Service and Global News Division
6 'Elizabeth Warren agrees Democratic race 'rigged' for Clinton,' bbc.co.uk, Nov. 3rd 2017
7 'JK Rowling apologises over Trump disabled boy tweets,' bbc.co.uk, Aug. 1st 2017
8 'Fake news: how to cut through the crap in a post-truth world,' Marie Claire, Mar. 1st 2017
9 Quoted in: Why Are We The Good Guys? p.86
10 'More than 100 cross-party politicians demand action over 'Muslim Problem' article in Sun newspaper,' The Independent, Aug. 15th 2017
11 'Rotherham paedo gang victim claims 'authorities made me feel like a racist when I reported attacks 14 YEARS ago'' The Sun, May 15th 2017
12 'Max Clifford, king of fake news,' bbc.co.uk, Dec. 11th 2017
13 The Smear, p. 52
14 'Trump tweets cartoon of train hitting CNN reporter,' bbc.co.uk, Aug 15 2017

15 Melania Trump mocked for 'positive social media' speech,' bbc.co.uk, Feb. 27th 2018
16 'Solihull councillor in anti-Muslim tweet probe' bbc.co.uk, Sep. 26th 2017

Misrepresentation
1 'LABOUR LEFTIE LEWIS' BIAS Labour frontbencher Clive Lewis admits broadcasting biased news reports while working as BBC journalist ,' The Sun, Jan. 28th 2018
2 Statement to the Catholic Herald, Oct. 1th 2003
3 'Chris Matthews: Trump-Russia collusion theory 'came apart' with Comey testimony,' The Washington Examiner, June 8th 2017
4 'Comey accuses Trump administration of 'lies,' The Hill, Aug. 6th 2017
5 For an analysis of Comey's competence see, 'James Comey: Not Just Incompetent But He Placed American Lives at Risk,' Spectator.org, May 12th 2017
6 'Remarks by President Trump to the 73rd session of the United Nations general Assembly | New York, NY, whitehouse.gov, Sep. 25th 2018

Amplification and Suppression
1 'Why Are We The Good Guys?' p. 53
2 'Fake news: Universities offer tips on how to spot it,' bbc.co.uk, Nov. 9th 2017
3 'Astroturfing: what is it and why does it matter?' The Guardian, Feb. 8th 2012
4 'Former Tory aide renews call for anti-Brexit party,' bbc.co.uk, Aug. 11th 2017
5 'This Huge New Study Reveals What The British Public Really Wants From Brexit,' Buzzfeed, Aug. 11th 2017
6 'Donald Trump, 'Flaccid dumplings' and the short-fingered feud,' bbc.co.uk, Dec. 16th 2016
7 'Post Truth,' p.171
8 Accessed December 2016

The BBC smear machine
1 'The Smear,' p. 68
2 Othello, Act 2 sc. 3
3 'The Smear,' p.68
4 'Brainwash: The Cover-Up Society,' p.32
5 'The Smear,' p.3
6 See Rules for Radicals p. 30

7 Issues in Ethics - V. 7, N. 3 Fall 1996.

8 'Fear of being called racist stops people reporting child sexual exploitation concerns, Labour frontbencher claims,' The Telegraph, Aug. 10th 2017,

9 'Donald Trump protests attract millions across US and world,' bbc.co.uk, Jan. 21st 2017

10 'Homoerotic images flood 'Moggmentum' tag,' bbc.co.uk, Sep. 7th 2017

11 'A new bigotry in the name of tolerance? Jacob Rees-Mogg shows it's time to stand up against liberal orthodoxy,' The Telegraph, Sep. 7th 2017

12 'Business councils disband over Trump remarks,' bbc.co.uk, Aug. 16th 2017

13 'Trump again blames Charlottesville violence on both sides,' bbc.co.uk, Aug. 16th 2017

14 'Bush presidents wade into Trump furore over Charlottesville,' bbc.co.uk, Aug. 16th 2017

15 'US election daily dig: Melania Trump's anti-bullying crusade,' bbc.co.uk, Nov. 4th 2016

16 'Trump says US to quit TPP on first day in office,' bbc.co.uk, Nov. 22th 2016

17 'Just the endorsement you don't want: KKK's notorious David Duke says 'voting against Donald Trump...is really treason to your heritage,' Mail Online, Feb. 25th 2016

18 'The Myth of Trump and the KKK,' New Standard Press, Dec. 19th 2016

19 'Charlottesville: What made Trump remarks so offensive?' bbc.co.uk, Aug. 16th 2017

20 'Reporter April Ryan asks White House if slavery was 'wrong'' The Washington Examiner, Oct. 31st 2017

21 'Trust Me I'm Lying,' p. 173

22 'Rand Paul's neighbors rip media 'landscaping dispute' reports,' Washington Examiner, Nov. 8th 2017

23 'Rand Paul's Wife Breaks Silence on Husband's Attack: 'This Was Not A Scuffle,' The Western Journal, Nov. 22nd 2017

Stacking the deck

1 For the full report see: The Brussels Broadcasting Corporation? by David Keighley and Andrew Jubb.

2 'The Fun factory,' p. 236

3 *Denotes an edition whereby it is not possible to ascribe Remain or Leave sympathies to one or more members of the panel.

4 See for example the Sep. 4th 2018 Newsnight interview of pro-Remain MP Sarah Wollaston (uninterrupted) and Pro-Leave EU MP Jacob Rees-Mogg (consistently interrupted)

CASE STUDIES

Sopel says: Deconstructing a BBC activist

1 'Imagine if the BBC were honest,' craigmurray.org.uk

2 'The case against: Can journalists be activists?,' Al-Jazeera, Apr. 10th 2017

3 'BBC Panorama As Propaganda? Controversy over Saving Syria's Children,' Tim Hayward blog, Mar. 9th 2017

4 'US election: The Disunited States of America - whoever wins,' bbc.co.uk, Nov. 7th 2016

5 The reason is of course quite clear: afraid of what it might find, the liberal mainstream media had no appetite at all for anything resembling thorough checks of its archives.

6 'Northern New Jersey Draws Probers' Eyes,' The Washington Post, Sep. 16th 2001

7 'Donald Trump: 24 things the next president believes,' bbc.co.uk, Nov. 9th 2016

8 'Jersey Sure' at https://www.steynonline.com/7313/jersey-sure

9 'Jersey City 9/11 Celebration Report CBS,'

10 'The Issue is Radical Islam,' The New York Post, Sep. 14th 2001.

11 'People did cheer 9/11, says ex-NYC mayor Rudy Giuliani,' bbc.co.uk, Dec. 1st 2015

12 Whether the individuals concerned had or had not actually been celebrating the attacks is, of course, beside the point – a mainstream media ruse to deflect away from the issue in question: Had there been media reports of alleged post 9/11 celebrations which Mr Trump could have seen and heard? The answer to that question is clearly, yes.

13 'Jersey Sure,' Steynonline.com

14 For further reports of possible 9/11 celebrations see: 'Some Jersey City Muslims did celebrate 9/11, cop and residents say,' NJ.com, Dec. 22nd 2015

15 1984, p. 16

16 'Golden Globes 2017: La La Land sweeps awards,' bbc.co.uk, Jan. 9th 2017

17 The True Story: Donald Trump Did Not Mock a Reporter's Disability,' Catholics4Trump.com, July 27th 2017

18 'Media invented lie about Trump mocking disabled reporter,'
AnnCoulter.com, Aug. 31st 2016
19 'Mexico wants apology after "Top Gear" tirade,' Reuters,
Feb. 3nd 2011
20 As to why people choose to enter the US illegally, this is largely due to
the country's strict immigration rules, a protracted process that involves
paperwork, checks and culminates with a US embassy interview.
21 'What we know about illegal immigration from Mexico,' Pew Research
Centre, Mar. 2nd 2017
22 'Frequently Requested Statistics on Immigrants and Immigration in
the United States,' Migration Policy Institute
23 Dhs announces progress enforcing immigration laws protecting
Americans. 'Full statement available at: www.dhs.gov
24 The Smear, p. 187
25 'The media needs to stop telling this lie about Donald Trump. I'm a
Sanders supporter — and value honesty,' Salon, Dec. 31st 2015
26 The Smear, p. 188
27 'Poll: Majority of voters back Trump travel ban' Politico, July 5th 2017
28 'Most Support Temporary Ban on Newcomers from Terrorist Havens,'
Rasmussen Reports, Jan. 30th 2017
29 'Orlando justifies my Muslim ban' says Trump,' bbc.co.uk,
June 14th 2016
30 'Executive Order Protecting the Nation from Foreign Terrorist Entry
into the United States,' whitehouse.gov, Jan. 27th 2017
31 'Donald Trump's support remains high following John McCain
controversy,' YouGov.com, July 24th 2015
32 'Military Times Poll: What you really think about Trump,' Military
Times, Oct. 23rd 2017

Harlow: A Brexit 'hate crime'
1 'Learn how the BBC is working to strengthen trust and transparency in
online news,' bbc.co.uk, Dec. 8th 2017
2 'Harlow 'hate crime' murder: Arek Jozwik's family devastated,'
bbc.co.uk, Aug. 31st 2016
3 'Polish media in UK shocked by post-Brexit hate crimes,' bbc.co.uk,
June 28th 2016
4 'The great hate-crime lie: The Essex street brawl death of a Pole after
the referendum was seized on by liberals, the BBC and Remainers as
proof Brexit provoked racist attacks. Only one problem: his death had
NOTHING to do with race,' Mail Online, Sep. 22nd 2017
5 'The truth behind the Brexit hate crime 'spike,' The Spectator,
Feb. 15th 2017

6 'Racist' graffiti on Polish cultural centre in Hammersmith,' bbc.co.uk, June 26th 2016

7 'Hate crime: the facts behind the headlines,' Civitas: Briefing note: October 2016 p. 7

8 Merton, Robert K. (1948), "The Self Fulfilling Prophecy", Antioch Review, Vol. 8, No.2 (Summer) pp. 193-210

9 'Harlow murder inquiry: Concerns remain over alleged 'hate crime,' bbc.co.uk, Sep. 11th 2016

10 'WE'RE GOING TO STAY' Brother of Polish immigrant Arek Jozwik killed by a single punch from a British teen reveals family is committed to living in UK despite tragic murder,' The Sun, Sep. 9th 2017

11 'To have blood on one's hands' appears to be a favourite BBC phrase. In a BBC Hardtalk interview of September 2018, the presenter accused Italian politician Matteo Salvini of 'having blood on his hands,'

12 'Steering Clear: Avoidance in the Production of Idioms, Suzanne Irujo, International Review of Applied Linguistics in Language Teaching, Vol. 31, Issue 3

13 Teaching Idioms, Thomas C Cooper, Foreign Language Annals, Volume 31, Issue 2, May 1998, Pages 255–266

14 'Idioms and Importance of Teaching Idioms to ESL Students: A Study on Teacher Beliefs,' Sridhar Maisa, and Dr. T. Karunakaran, Asian Journal of Humanities and Social Sciences, Volume 1 – Issue 1, May 2013

15 BBC Editorial Guidelines: Impartiality; Contentious Views and Possible Offence: 4.4.18

16 BBC Editorial Guidelines: Impartiality; Personal View Content: 4.4.30

17 'Harlow murder: Polish officers patrol streets where Arek Jozwik was killed,' bbc.co.uk, Sep. 15th 2016

18 See for example the murder of Gary Newlove in Warrington 2007, which has many similarities with the Jozwik case. In another case, a gang of teenagers viciously attacked 44-year old Simon Clarke in January 2016 in West Yorkshire, an attack that was captured by CCTV.

19 'Arkadiusz Jozwik manslaughter in Harlow: The full sentencing remarks' EssexLive.news, Sep. 8th 2017

20 1984, p.26

21 'BBC bias turns street scuffle into anti-Brexit cause celebre,' The Conservative Woman, Sep. 11th 2017

22 'Arkadiusz Jozwik death: Teen sentenced for manslaughter,' bbc.co.uk, Sep. 8th 2017

23 Manufacturing Consent,' p.34

24 'The BBC's slur has caused my family misery,' The Telegraph, Sep, 19th 2017

25 Post-Truth, p.165

26 'A killing in Harlow: the shame of Remainers,' Spiked Online, Sep. 15th 2017
27 'Is 'guerrilla war' being waged on news broadcasters?' bbc.co.uk, Sep. 28th 2017

Charlottesville: 'violence on both sides'
1 'Manufacturing Consent,' p.34
2 Ibid.
3 'Charlottesville: One killed in violence over US far-right rally,' bbc.co.uk, Aug. 13th 2017
4 'A reckoning in Charlottesville,' bbc.co.uk, Aug. 13th 2017
5 'ACLU Virginia response to governor's allegations that ACLU is responsible for violence in Charlottesville,' acluva.org, Aug. 14th 2017
6 'The time when America stopped being great,' bbc.co.uk, Nov. rd 2017
7 'Trump again blames Charlottesville violence on both sides,' bbc.co.uk, Aug. 16th 2017
8 'What Trump said versus what I saw,' bbc.co.uk, Aug. 16th 2017
9 'Who was responsible for the violence in Charlottesville? Here's what witnesses say ,' LA Times, Aug. 15th 2017
10 'An Exclusive Look At How Virginia Police Emptied Emancipation Park,' The Daily Caller, Aug. 16th 2017.
11 "Does he (Trump) not want to offend his base?" asked the presenter of BBC2's Newsnight programme on 16 August when puzzling why Trump had not 'explicitly' condemned the KKK.

Sticking up for Antifa
1 The Smear, p. 200
2 'The new fascist violence of the left - and their friends,' Die Welt, July 7th 2017
3 'Like or loathe him, the Berkeley riots prove Milo Yiannopoulos is right on free speech,' The Telegraph, Feb. 7th 2017
4 'The tragi-comedy that is "Brown Moses" OffGuardian.org, Aug. 18th 2015
5 For an analysis of BBC Trending's alt-right obsession see: 'I've Been Wendling My Way Back To You Mike,' at Is The BBC Biased blogspot
6 'Far-right smear campaign against Antifa exposed by Bellingcat,' bbc.co.uk, Aug. 24th 2017
7 'Black-clad Antifa members attack peaceful right-wing demonstrators in Berkeley' The Washington Post, Aug. 28th 2017
8 'Berkeley Mayor: We Should Classify Antifa 'As A Gang,' San Francisco CBS Local, Aug. 28th 2017

9 'FBI, Homeland Security warn of more 'antifa' attacks,' Politico.com, Sep. 1st 2017

10 'Charlottesville: Trump repeats 'both sides' rhetoric,' bbc.co.uk, Sep. 15th 2017

11 'As Its Influence Wanes, Increasingly Militant MSM Promotes Violence and Censorship,' Breitbart.com, Sep. 1st 2017

12 The Black Book of Communism: Crimes, pp. 92–97; 116–21.

'Quiet and safe in Malmö'

1 'What everyday life is really like in Sweden,' bbc.co.uk, Sep. 12th 2017

2 'Trump tries to explain remark about Sweden amid confusion,' bbc.co.uk, Feb. 20th 2017

3 As far as we can ascertain, the US president had not mentioned Malmö in his Florida speech, nor had he specifically mentioned the city in any subsequent speeches.

4 'Leila's car was set on fire by vandals,' expressen.se, Jan. 9th 2017

5 For a report into how extensive this problem is in Malmö see for example, 'Malmö police deploy drone to catch fire-starters,' The Local.se, Aug. 18th 2016. For a report into potentially co-ordinated attacks on cars in Malmö see: '16 cars torched overnight in Malmö, Swedish police puzzled for motive,' rt.com, Aug. 12th 2016. For a report into the extent of the problem throughout Sweden see: 'Wave of car burning crimes in Sweden moves to poor Stockholm suburb.' Reuters.com, Aug. 16th 2016

6 'Here is the police's important message for Malmö citizens,' 24Malmö.se, Nov. 14th 2017

7 'Hollywood wife: "I'm not so fond of Malmö," 24Malmö.se, Sep. 10th 2017

8 'Unresolved murders spread horror in Malmö,' Dagens Nyheter, May 20th 2017

9 "Jihad! Jihad!" - Arab mob attacks in Malmö,' Fria Tider

10 'Fewer victims - but more Malmö residents are worried,' 24Malmö .se, Feb. 16th 2017

11 Sydsvenska's in depth report into Malmö 's spate of murders was published in February 2017 and coincided with the arrival of the BBC in the city: 'Several murders in Malmö still unresolved,' Sydsvenska.se, Feb. 25th 2017

12 'New fatal shooting in Malmö,' Malmö.com, Feb. 13th 2017

13 'Ygeman till Malmöborna god inte brottsligheten,'Malmö.se, Feb. 13th 2017

14 'The violence in Malmö has stepped up,' Sydsvenskan, Feb. 4th 2017

15 'Acute services lock doors at certain times,' Sverigesradio, Feb. 7th 2017

16 'Another murder attempt in Malmö - Police: "We need more resources" Vlt.se, Jan. 15th 2017

17 'We depend on you to be able to solve these violent crimes. Therefore, I am appealing to you now. Help us," Sydsvenskan, Jan. 27th 2017

18 'Police in Swedish city appeal for public help amid 'upward spiral of violence,' rt.com, Jan. 28th 2017

19 'Witness to the murder of the 16-year old murdered in Malmö,' Helahalsingland.se, Mar. 31st 2017

20 'Many people have no idea how serious the situation in Sweden is"' Katerina Magasin, Oct. 20th 2017

21 'Malmö police chiefs want to introduce US methods to reduce murder,' Sydsvenskan, June 25th 2017

22 'Police chief in Malmö interested in calling in military to relieve the police,' NyheterDag, Sep. 29th 2017

23 'Large theft waves continue in Malmö - 100s of victims,' 24 Malmö.se, Oct. 9th 2017

24 'Chief prosecutor in Malmö strikes alarm: "All time high" on prisoners forcing police to put other serious crimes on hold,' Sydsvenskan, Nov. 25th 2017

25 'Gun violence 'most common' in Malmö,' thelocal.se, Feb. 2nd 2012

26 'New phenomenon in Malmö - armed funerals,' 24Malmö.se, Oct. 8th 2017

27 'Malmö school 'too dangerous' for students,' thelocal.se, Mar. 1st 2015

28 'Witnessing violence in the world of school: "It happens constantly", 24Malmö.se, Nov. 16th 2017

29 'In a port city, grenade attacks shatter Swedish sense of safety,' Reuters, Aug. 9th 2015

30 'Rinkeby is almost like a war zone,' Sverigesradio.se, Dec. 5th 2017

31 'Fatal shootings on the rise in Sweden,' Sverigesradio.se, Nov. 2nd 2015

32 'Sweden's gun violence on par with Mexico, researchers say,' Malmö.com, Sep. 5th 2017

33 'How Sweden became an example of how not to handle immigration,' The Spectator, Sep. 3rd 2016

34 'Malmö most dangerous in the Nordic region - but not "Sweden's Chicago," Sydsvenskan.se, Feb. 20th 2017

35 See: Sven Granath 'Homicide in Sweden' in 'Handbook of European Homicide Research' pp 405-419

36 Freedom of Information reference: RFI20171680

37 'What everyday life is really like in Sweden,' bbc.co.uk, Sep. 12th 2017

38 'More private individuals are subject to crimes,' Bra.se, Nov. 15th 2017

39 Adapted from: Percentage of the population exposed to different types of crime against individual person 2005-2016, Source: NTU.

40 'Every fifth woman worries about being subjected to abuse,' samhallsnytt.se, Nov. 17th 2017

41 'What Worries the World,' Ipsos.com, July 2017

42 'Three arrested for Molotov cocktail attack on synagogue in Sweden,' The Independent, Dec. 11th 2017

43 'Prosecutor: The murdered woman in Norsjö was almost 90 years old,' nyheteridag.se, Oct. 19th 2017

'Hilarious' – The assassination of Katie Hopkins

1 'The theatre shows you won't want to miss in 2018,' bbc.co.uk, Dec. 28th 2017

2 Cynthia Hoffner & Martha Buchanan: 'Young Adults' Wishful Identification With Television Characters: The Role of Perceived Similarity and Character Attributes.' Media Psychology , Volume 7, 2005 - Issue 4, Pp. 325-351

3 L. Rowell Huesmann, 'Psychological Processes Promoting the Relation Between Exposure to Media Violence and Aggressive Behavior by the Viewer.' Social Issues, Volume 42, Issue 3, Fall 1986 , Pp 125–139

4 'Watching violent films does make people more aggressive, study shows,' The Telegraph, 10 Sept 2014

5 Summarised by Smith, Marilyn E: 'Television Violence and Behavior: A Research Summary,' ERICDIGESTS.org

6 Age of Propaganda, p. 151

7 Brainwashing: The Science of Thought Control, p.80

8 'Woman in terror case dreamt of beheading Katie Hopkins,' The Times, Oct. 14th 2017

9 'The Birmingham couple who put IS at heart of marriage,' bbc.co.uk, Oct. 26th 2017

10 'Kremlin critic journalist stabbed at offices of Moscow news radio station,' The Telegraph, Oct. 23rd 2017

11 'The BBC: The First 50 years,' p. 90

12 'Rohingya abuses: Myanmar army report clears itself of blame,' bbc.co.uk, Nov. 14th 2017

13 BBC Reference CAS-4666901-QNSJTF

CONCLUSION

1 The Third Floor Front, p. 73
2 'BBC got it wrong on migration' Daily Express, Oct. 7th 2018
3 Can We Trust the BBC, p. 9
4 Who to trust: A social media poll with 39,000 respondents or a 1,000-strong Ipsos MORI poll bought and paid for by the BBC and conducted in leafy Twickenham? We'll leave the reader to decide which, if any poll, to trust.
5 'The Brussels Broadcasting Corporation?' p. xiii
6 Propaganda, p. 37
7 'MPs are too white, says David Cameron.' The Telegraph, June 29th 2014
8 'Growing support for Muslim ban,' Yougov.com, Mar. 28th 2016
9 'The BBC's love-in with Jeremy Corbyn has major implications for Britain and needs to stop,' The Sun, June 27th 2017
10 Source: FOI Reference: RFI20171662, RFI20171664 and RFI20141946. Note this does not include automatic cancellations for over 75s.
11 Television licence cancellations show no signs of slowing down. According to an FOI request (RFI20180165) there were almost 74,000 cancellations in January 2018 alone.
12 'BBC's global audience rises to 372m,' bbc.co.uk, May 25th 2017
13 'Quarterly reach of BBC News in the United Kingdom (UK) from 1st quarter2012 to 2nd quarter 2018 (in 1,000 viewers)' Statista.com.
14 BBC Trust: End of Charter Report, March 2017. As substantial as this loss is, it is small beer compared to losses sustained by Today – Radio 4's flagship news programme. See: 'BBC Radio's Today show loses 800,000 listeners in just a year, ' Belfast Telegraph, Aug. 3rd 2018
15 BBC Trust: End of Charter Report, March 2017, p 4
16 The next stage of BBC World Service expansion will be funded by the British government to the tune of £289 million: BBC Trust: End of Charter Review, March 2017, p. 21
17 'BBC boss Tony Hall admits 'we need to find more money,' ITV.com, Sep. 18th 2018
18 'The Great BBC Survey,' Survey Monkey
19 Greg Dyke: Inside Story, p. 86
20 The Third Floor Front, p.74
21 BBC Newsnight, Aug. 1st 2018
22 BBC Newsnight, Oct. 3rd 2018
23 'Top broadcasters including BBC and Sky call for 'urgent' watchdog to police social media giants,' The Telegraph, Sept 2nd 2018

24 The Telegraph, Oct. 12th 2018
25 The Sunday Times, Oct. 13th 2018
26 'Poor? Stupid? Racist? Then don't listen to a pampered white liberal like me,' The Guardian, Feb. 28th 1999
27 1984, p. 303
28 Ibid, p. 307
29 1984, p. 244

Printed in Great
Britain
by Amazon